THE INSIDERS' ® GUIDE TO

Civil War Sites
in the Eastern Theater

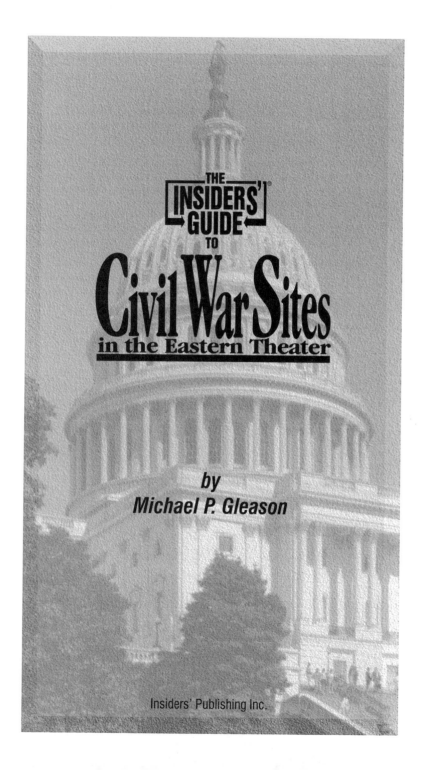

THE INSIDERS' GUIDE TO

Civil War Sites

in the Eastern Theater

by
Michael P. Gleason

Insiders' Publishing Inc.

Published and distributed by:
Insiders' Publishing Inc.
105 Budleigh St.
P.O. Box 2057
Manteo, NC 27954
(919) 473-6100

•

2nd EDITION
1st printing

•

Copyright ©1997
by Insiders' Publishing Inc.

•

Printed in the United States
of America

•

Publications from The Insiders' Guide®
series are available at special discounts
for bulk purchases for sales promotions,
premiums or fundraisings. Special
editions, including personalized covers,
can be created in large quantities for
special needs. For more information,
please write to Insiders' Publishing Inc.,
P.O. Box 2057, Manteo, NC 27954 or
call (919) 473-6100 x 233.

ISBN 1-57380-019-8

Insiders' Publishing Inc.

Publisher/Editor-in-Chief
Beth P. Storie

President/General Manager
Michael McOwen

Affiliate Sales and Training Director
Rosanne Cheeseman

Partner Services Director
Giles MacMillan

Sales and Marketing Director
Jennifer Risko

Creative Services Director
Mike Lay

Online Services Director
David Haynes

Managing Editor
Theresa Shea Chavez

Fulfillment Director
Gina Twiford

Project Editor
Dave McCarter

Project Artist
Mike Lay

Editorial Assistant
Amy Baynard

Special thanks to
Dale Gallon, courtesy of
Dale Gallon Historical Art,
P.O. Box 4343,
9 Steinwehr Ave.
Gettysburg, PA 17325.
Phone (717) 334-0430
for providing unique and
dramatic historic paintings.

Dedication & Acknowledgments

This project inspired me to learn more about my great-grandfather, Robert James Morris, who fought for the Confederacy. I always knew my family boasted a Civil War veteran, but it wasn't until 1993, while researching the first edition of this book, that I dug deeper into old records to investigate my great-grandfather's experiences.

Born in February 1838 in Louisa County, Virginia, he married his wife, Amanda, in October 1860. In late July 1861 — at age 23 and with Amanda four months pregnant — Robert enlisted in Company H of the 57th Virginia Volunteers (Rivanna Guard) in Charlottesville. His daughter, Sarah, was born in early December; Amanda died less than three weeks later during the Christmas holiday, due to birth-related complications. Unaware of his daughter's birth and his wife's death, Robert took a four-day holiday furlough, returned to Fluvanna County and encountered his wife's funeral procession on the road leading home.

Robert fought at Malvern Hill near Richmond in July 1862; at Manassas, Virginia, in late August; in the Confederate raid on Harper's Ferry and at Antietam, Maryland, in September; and at Fredericksburg, Virginia, in December. Back home that year, his daughter died before she was a year old. In April 1863, Robert fought at Suffolk, Virginia, and he was one of the survivors of "Pickett's Charge" at Gettysburg in July.

In May 1864, he fought at Chester Station, Virginia. He was injured at Drewry's Bluff, south of Richmond, and treated for facial injuries at Chimborazo Hospital in Richmond. A year later, in March 1865, Robert was back on the field at Five Forks, south of Petersburg, Virginia, and the following month his company joined Gen. Robert E. Lee's main army at Rice's Station and Sayler's Creek. He was at Appomattox when Lee surrendered on April 9, 1865.

Like so many veterans, Robert returned home after the war to resume a life of quasi-normalcy. He took up farming and carpentry, married a second time (to my great-grandmother, Ella Caroline) and had nine children including my grandmother, Blanche, born in 1890. In 1900, living near Keswick, Virginia, he applied for a $15 annual state pension based on his Civil War service. He was 82 when he died in November 1920 at his daughter's home in Richmond.

In 1993, during a visit to the Gettysburg National Military Park, I saw a photograph of my great-grandfather on the wall of veterans in the visitor center. The picture shows a young private in uniform with dark hair, olive complexion, gray eyes and a neatly trimmed beard.

My grandmother, Blanche, died in 1986. I regret not knowing enough about her father to ask for any details from her. But my mother, who is 80 and still lives in Charlottesville, was just 4 when her grandfather died. She remembers him as "a kind, gentle old man, with a white beard and goatee — like Colonel Sanders." I dedicate this effort to the memory of my great-grandfather, Confederate Private Robert James Morris.

This book — the original and the second edition — would not have been possible without the help and support of my wife, Kendall. She endured much more than she (or I) expected with this project, which included endless road trips, late-night research impulses and weekend rewrites. Through it all, with amazing patience, she scurried "one more time" to the library, photocopied hundreds of pages of books and read over my drafts — "Isn't this the 12th version of that personality profile?"

During the first edition, she went along on most all of the 10,000-plus miles needed to research this book, and she joined me on 3,000 miles of travel for this edition. We both thank the hundreds of helpful folks we met at battlefields, attractions, visitors centers, motels, inns, bed and breakfasts, restaurants, stores and shops.

How To Use This Book

A number of years ago, I was invited to a rural Virginia elementary school to speak with a class about the Civil War. The teacher was introducing local history to her young students, and the war seemed a likely topic to inspire and excite the class. My talk came at the end of a week-long project in which the youngsters read books and narrated excerpts from family diaries for their classmates. They reviewed collections of Matthew Brady photographs.

The class was prepared. I wasn't. In the question period following my talk, I was stunned when a young girl threw me a seemingly innocent curve. "When," she asked, "did the world go to color?"

It took a few moments before the question fully registered. Of course, I finally realized this youngster was a child of color television and videocassette recorders. Having just reviewed the black-and-white Brady photographs associated with the Civil War, her question was quite natural: When did the grass become green, the sky blue, the blood red? I don't remember my answer. But I know Civil War history never again seemed the same to me. In one brief question, a youngster taught me that the history of that war — indeed, history in general — is a matter of perspective. I learned that each of us absorb and appreciate history quite differently. It set me on a quest to "humanize" history and make it more appealing and interesting.

A number of educators and historians have turned from "academic" history to "popular" history in an attempt to make the subject more "real" and inspiring. Scholarly history, of course, is invaluable. Educators help us understand who we are. But the academic approach often is tedious and technical, particularly in our fast-paced, hectic lives. In our communications, transportation and even our food, "fast" has become the norm. Advances in computers and other technology have spawned new, faster ways to collect, process and disseminate information. We're just too busy with work and other responsibilities to absorb lengthy, detailed history and identify with our ancestors' lifestyles.

Popular history — or "public" history — takes a more personal approach to the subject, and it helps us understand the past through concise, human, identifiable stories. It puts history into perspective, and it recognizes that the experiences of common men and women are as important and as interesting as the exploits of heroes. In this way, it expands history's support base, makes the subject more inclusive and invites persons of all ages and ethnic backgrounds to go exploring. If the people we study were indeed mortal, with human strengths and frailties, why not use these stories to teach history?

There have been, by some estimates, no fewer than 50,000 Civil War-related publications in the past 25 years. They are as diverse as they are voluminous. There are academic texts and historical fiction novels, broad overviews of the political and social implications of the conflict and detailed chronicles on military battles, tactics and weapons. There are unique collections of war-related letters, diaries and poems. Still, 50,000 publications represent, on average, one book produced every single day since Appomattox in 1865.

So, why this *Insiders' Guide*®? This book

is for a Mid-Atlantic traveler who is interested in the history of the Civil War's Eastern Theater. The theater covered a vast expanse of land — east of the Appalachian Mountains from near Harrisburg, Pennsylvania, and south to the Virginia-North Carolina border. Whether you're a serious history student or a Civil War novice; whether you're making a specific trip or just passing through, you'll likely enjoy and appreciate the material we include.

Our tour information covers four states in 21 individual chapters. The region includes southern Pennsylvania, central and western Maryland, the eastern panhandle of West Virginia and all but the extreme southwestern part of Virginia. There are five separate tours (chapters) along the Appalachian highlands and Great Valley from Carlisle, Pennsylvania, to Lexington, Virginia; six in the Piedmont area from Gettysburg, Pennsylvania, to Lynchburg, Virginia; seven along the "fall zone" from Baltimore, Maryland, and Washington, D.C., to Petersburg, Virginia; and separate routes for Virginia's Upper Peninsula, Lower Peninsula and Appomattox.

Generally speaking, an individual tour begins in a historically significant community, runs north to south, covers about a day's worth of travel and details a varied selection of attractions and sites with addresses, telephone numbers and very specific directions and mileage figures to help you find your way. Directions are printed in a bold italic typeface to set them apart, and they are always preceded by a distinguishing symbol:

Each chapter begins with an overview of that tour's history and geography, and we include brief directions for getting to the starting point of the route. Most tours are natural continuations of the ones that precede them. Keep in mind that some tour routes include busy interstate highways, while others follow state routes and back-country roads. Anticipate heavy, congested traffic on many of the major highways, particularly in urban areas such as Baltimore, Washington or Richmond. Likewise, on less-traveled roads, like those in the western parts of the Mid-Atlantic, expect the unexpected — anything from school buses to slow-moving tractors.

For weather and road conditions, you usually will find a selection of stations on your car radio. For emergencies, remember that state and local police monitor citizen's band radios, usually on Channel 9 or 19. Except in a few remote areas (which are noted), all tour routes have adequate cellular telephone signals. In most chapters, we include the address and phone number for at least one local visitors center. Travel counselors at these locations can provide local maps and help you plan details.

At the end of each chapter we list additional information that might make your visit to the area more interesting — a rundown of annual events, arts and entertainment offerings, historic attractions that are not related to the Civil War and places to shop. These suggestions, of course, vary wildly among the tours. Some places, like Sharpsburg, Maryland, and nearby Shepherdstown, West Virginia, are especially scenic but have little traditional nightlife. On the other hand, Washington, D.C., and Williamsburg, Virginia, to name just two bustling sites, have a considerable number of motels, restaurants, places to shop and things to do when the driving day is done.

Each tour also include numerous photographs from the past and present. If you're a serious Civil War buff, we've added a number of "side trips" in each tour. These side trips are for military enthusiasts and anyone else interested in traveling a few extra miles to see a little-known site or simple highway marker. If you're interested in the war's humanizing stories as much as the battlefield details, we include a number of "personality" sketches — those personal stories that go behind the scenes of the serious action. We think these pieces help make our guide particularly special.

We dedicate Chapter 22 to our lodging suggestions, and these are usually only a sampling of what's available throughout the region. The same goes with our dining recommendations, incorporated in Chapter 23. For both accommodations and restaurants, we include a price code (explained in those chapters) to help simplify things.

Note that much of the area covered in this guide is detailed more thoroughly in several of our sister publications. You might find it helpful, depending on your region of concentration, to pick up a copy of *The Insiders' Guide® to Virginia's Blue Ridge, The Insiders' Guide® to Metro Washington, D.C., The Insiders' Guide® to Richmond, The Insiders' Guide® to Williamsburg* or *The Insiders' Guide® to Chesapeake Bay.*

The tour routes, of course, are a general guide. You can tailor your visit to fit specific interests. If you have plenty of leisure time, you may want to stop at each individual attraction listed or stay a day or two longer at places of particular interest. If you're pressed for time or working on a specific route or schedule, you can pick and choose among the various attractions detailed in each tour. For that matter, you can mix and match the individual tours — they need not be followed sequentially. Try jumping from Tour 7 (which ends in Leesburg, Virginia) to Tour 13 (nearby Washington), for example. The overview map will help you plot your course. Remember, it's a good idea to review the entire tour, including lodging, dining and shopping recommendations, before striking out. Reservations are a must, particularly during the summer tourist season.

So have fun. This is a traveler's guide — not a scholarly or technical treatise. We want to lead you through a historic, scenic region with a variety of informative material and individual, personal stories. Perhaps this will lead to more serious Civil War studies. As Thomas Jefferson once wrote, "History, by apprizing [students] of the past will enable them to judge of the future." Perhaps he studied Cicero, who wrote, "To know nothing of what happened before you were born is to remain forever a child." It is our hope that *The Insiders' Guide® to the Civil War in the Eastern Theater* will help you embrace some of yesterday's fellow-citizens and enjoy doing it.

— Michael P. Gleason
May 1997

Photo: Tourguide, Ltd.

Former worshipers at St. Thomas Church, Orange include CSA President
Davis and CSA Gen. Lee.

Table of Contents

Directory of Maps

Eastern Theater Overview

A light morning mist fell on Washington, D.C., on Monday, March 4, 1861. It was just enough rain to settle the dust along Pennsylvania Avenue, the inaugural parade route for the nation's 16th president, Abraham Lincoln.

Just before noon, Lincoln and his wife, Mary, left the Willard Hotel and rode with outgoing President James Buchanan in an open, horse-drawn carriage to the U.S. Capitol. There, on the East Portico, the new president took his oath of office. All around, on every visible rooftop, soldiers with fixed bayonets watched and guarded. The Capitol dome, sheathed in scaffolding, rose behind the ceremonial dais: A project to enlarge and resurface the dome was part of an overall effort to expand the Capitol. The work, Lincoln later said, symbolized the nation's union. Indeed, the union was very much on the mind of Lincoln, his audience and the entire nation. The new president, in his inaugural address, spoke of national survival.

"We are not enemies, but friends," he said. "Though passion may have strained, it must not break the bonds of affection. The mystic chords of memory stretching from every battlefield and patriot grave, to every living heart and hearthstone, all over this broad land, will yet swell the chorus of union."

Cradle of the Conflict

Lincoln's "broad land" was rather small compared with today's country. There were just over 31 million Americans — about an eighth of today's population — in 34 states. Most Americans — six in 10 — lived on farms. Communities were small; linked by simple dirt roads. The railroad was a relatively recent phenomenon.

Washington, the capitol city, was just 72 years old in 1861. The District of Columbia, straddling the Potomac River, was the centerpiece of the Mid-Atlantic, which became the scene of the Civil War's Eastern Theater. One of two principal theaters of operation during the conflict, the Eastern Theater was fought from the Atlantic coast to the Appalachians, from southern Pennsylvania, through Maryland and the present-day West Virginia panhandle, into nearly every part of Virginia.

The Civil War began in the Eastern Theater. John Brown raided Harpers Ferry in the Eastern Theater. Opposing armies tangled in the first major battle — on a small creek called Bull Run — in the Eastern Theater. The war ended at a rural Virginia courthouse named Appomattox in the Eastern Theater.

In between, for four weary years, the conflict raged in this area as fiercely as anywhere: in the mountains from Antietam, Maryland, to Winchester and New Market, Virginia; in the foothills from Gettysburg, Pennsylvania, to Brandy Station and Sayler's Creek in Virginia; on the edge of the Coastal Plain from Fredericksburg to Richmond to Virginia's Lower Peninsula. But looking at the Mid-Atlantic today, imagining the war's extensive death and destruction simply challenges the imagination. Spend any time at all in the area and two distinct points become obvious. First, the region is among the nation's most scenic. Second, it is steeped in an incredible abundance of early American history.

The region's natural beauty is surpassed only by its diversity. There are lavender mountains and lush, green valleys. There are rolling fields and farms of rich, fertile loam. Crystal clear streams feed mighty rivers that roll east to the sandy flatlands with their marshes and swamps. Not one of these picturesque locales escaped the ravages of the war.

America was born in the Mid-Atlantic, at small English settlements in the Tidewater region. The Virginia, Maryland and Pennsylvania colonies were instrumental in America's early stages of development and in the ultimate fight for independence. The nation's roots run deep in this soil — at Williamsburg and Annapolis, at Valley Forge and Philadelphia, at Yorktown and Richmond. None of these was spared during the war.

There are ironies to these stories. It's ironic that this land of natural beauty was subjected to so much of the Civil War's ugliness. And it's ironic that the conflict tore so roughly at the nation's fabric — a fabric created and strengthened in the Mid-Atlantic during the preceding 250 years. History, it seems, is simply a matter of time and place.

To appreciate the Civil War in the Eastern Theater, then, is to understand this region's origins from two inextricably linked viewpoints: time and place. History's natural timeline, from a perspective of "place," moves from west to east, from the mountains to the ocean. In terms of "time" — of European settlements and pioneers — it runs east to west, from coastal colonies to the upcountry. These histories are not static. Rather, they move back and forth, as if some large, mystical loom was at work, weaving the stories of characters and events into a tapestry of remarkable history. Erase the imaginary state and community boundary lines, remove the rather recent paths of modern roadways, and it's easier to visualize the three distinct areas of this region: the mountains, the Piedmont and Coastal Plain.

The Mountains

Four years — the time frame of the Civil War. As long as that may seem, those years are a mere blip on the ageless timeline of Appalachian geology. Imagine, if you can, a half-billion — that's 500 million — years ago, when two of the earth's major land masses first met in a series of violent collisions. One continen-

tal plate slammed against today's North America. The massive impact folded and buckled the land into ripples of corrugated ridges stretching 1,000 miles long and climbing more than 2 miles high. This was the birth of the Appalachian Mountains.

Time, of course, changed the face of these mountains. Rain and other climatic conditions eroded and sculpted the peaks, wearing them down to barely half their original height and creating a fertile, loamy soil that would eventually accommodate a wide variety of plants and animals. One of the most distinguishing features in the Appalachians is a grand, open valley running southwest along the eastern slope. It's a natural funnel. To the northwest, it's the Cumberland Valley; farther south, it's the Shenandoah Valley; still farther south, through the watersheds of the James, Roanoke, and New rivers, it's simply the "Great Valley."

Native Americans were the first inhabitants of the mountains and this Great Valley corridor. Here, long before European settlers arrived, the Indians lived and hunted. Their paths crisscrossed the mountains, connecting villages of different tribes. It could be said these natives were the continent's first "environmentalists" — they lived with, not off, the land. They left a legacy in an abundance of place names throughout the Eastern Theater. "Appalachian" itself is among the first words adapted from Native American language. It dates to 16th-century Spanish explorers who stumbled on a small Indian village called "Apalchen." Other names survive today: Shenandoah, Allegheny, Catoctin and Massanutten.

European exploration began here in the mid-18th century, when a flood of German and Scotch-Irish settlers migrated overland from Philadelphia and south along the Great Valley. The landscape no doubt reminded them of their Old World homelands. Other pioneer paths crossed west from the lower, eastern foothills. Homesteads sprang up all along the valley corridor's path — the Great Wagon Road.

These fiercely independent settlers ("mountaineers") and their succeeding families took part in a number of significant 18th-century struggles, including both the French and Indian War and the American Revolution. Daniel Morgan, the Revolutionary War general who defeated the British at Cowpens, South Carolina, in 1861, called the area home. So did Virginia militia Gen. Andrew Lewis, who led a victorious engagement against Native Americans at the Battle of Point Pleasant in October 1774. So did the Patton, Preston and Breckenridge families, all Scotch-Irish, who settled in the mid-18th century in Augusta County, Virginia. The Breckinridges were like many others who eventually migrated west to Kentucky. Ironically, one of the family's descendants, John Cabell Breckenridge, returned a half-century later as the Confederate commander at the Battle of New Market, only 60 miles north of his ancestors' home settlement.

The Civil War was into its first year before major action struck these highlands. Here, in the spring of 1862, CSA Gen. Thomas J. "Stonewall" Jackson led his troops in the Shenandoah Valley Campaign. Later, in September of the same year, after the capture of Harpers Ferry, troops fought battles at South Mountain and Antietam, both in Maryland. The following year, both sides maneuvered north in this region during the Gettysburg Campaign. In 1864, CSA Gen. Jubal Anderson "Old Jube" Early's Confederates pushed Union troops out of the Shenandoah Valley, moved on Washington, were repelled and returned here to meet defeat at the hands of USA Gen. Philip Henry Sheridan.

Today, these mountains are one of the nation's great outdoor playgrounds. The vast parks are popular retreats, especially during the changing of fall colors, and the farmland maintains the area's status as one of the nation's major agricultural and poultry centers. U.S. Highway 11 and Interstate 81 run the length of the Great Valley, along the path of the Great Wagon Road, from Pennsylvania, through western Maryland and the West Virginia panhandle and along the entire length of Virginia from north to south.

Rivers and Water Gaps

The rivers of the Mid-Atlantic are about as old as the mountains. They've always been the area's lifeline — threads that connect one geographic region to another — from the Appalachians to the Atlantic. They've carried a mighty cargo of mountain sediment. Small streams and rivulets that originated in the mountains grew in size and volume through centuries of precipitation. The Susquehanna, for example, begins high in western Pennsylvania and flows to the Chesapeake Bay. The Potomac starts in West Virginia, counting the Shenandoah and Monocacy rivers among its tributaries. Further south are the headwaters of the James River — Virginia's longest — and the Roanoke.

These rivers, rushing from their highest elevations, carved great water gaps through the smallest, easternmost mountain ridges. The gaps were ideal for pioneer settlements — Harrisburg, Pennsylvania, on the Susquehanna; Harpers Ferry, Virginia (now West Virginia), on the Potomac. An imaginary line runs parallel to the mountains, and connects the various water gaps. This line is the boundary between two geographic regions: the mountains and the Piedmont.

The Piedmont

Piedmont, in Italian, means "foot of the mountain." The Piedmont portion of America's Mid-Atlantic traces its origin to the same continental collisions that formed the Appalachian Mountains. Following a series of violent punches, a continental land mass pulled away from North America, and the Piedmont was "stretched" into existence. This dynamic created rock outcroppings, while volcanic rock simultaneously erupted from the earth's molten core. Erosion and weather through the ages smoothed the irregular land, leaving a rich, earthen carpet suitable for both woodland growth and farming.

The name Piedmont is used throughout Pennsylvania, Maryland and most of Virginia. In lower Virginia, where the state stretches along much of its border with North Carolina, the Piedmont is referred to as "Southside." The soil is different in Southside and accommodates tobacco, a plant Native Americans introduced to the colony's earliest settlers. A number of Indian tribes, especially the Monocans of Central Virginia, lived on the Piedmont, but most left at about the time Anglo pioneers pushed west from Tidewater. They left behind place names scattered across the region — there's the Rappahannock River in central Piedmont and the Appomattox River in Southside, to name two.

The northern Piedmont was settled mainly by Quaker, Scotch-Irish and German pioneers, most of whom headed west out of Philadelphia. Settlers in the central Piedmont were mainly Anglo pioneers — descendants of early English families in Virginia's Tidewater. The Piedmont's "landed gentry" included Thomas, the Sixth Lord Fairfax, whose vast property stretched from the Chesapeake Bay to the Allegheny Mountains. Early Piedmont communities include Lancaster and Gettysburg in Pennsylvania, Frederick in Maryland and Leesburg and Warrenton in Virginia. Lynchburg and Danville became notable Southside settlements.

Some of the young nation's best-known leaders called the Piedmont home: James Madison, James Monroe, John Marshall and Thomas Jefferson were among them. "There is not a better country society in the United States," Jefferson once wrote about his Piedmont homeland. The gentle hills here are evidence of an ancient time, when volcanic lava rolled along the earth's surface.

Great armies rolled along this land as well during the Civil War. In the first summer of the war, the North and South clashed on the plains of Manassas, south of Washington, D.C.. Throughout 1862, both armies crossed the Piedmont, battling at places like Cedar Mountain, Brandy Station and Bull Run, all in Virginia. Gettysburg was fought in Pennsylvania during the summer of 1863. In the final year of the war, troops led by CSA Gen. Robert E. Lee and USA Gen. Ulysses S. Grant wove across Southside Virginia from Petersburg, meeting at last at Appomattox.

Today, U.S. Highway 15 and U.S. Highway 29 run the length of the Piedmont, from Harrisburg, Pennsylvania, to Danville, Virginia. U.S. Highway 360 and U.S. Highway 460 cross in Southside. The farms throughout this region — in southern Pennsylvania and central Maryland, and in central and Southside Virginia — remain as evidence of early European settlers. Throughout much of the northern Piedmont, the local gentry still practice their adopted English heritage as horse breeders,

fox hunters and steeplechase race enthusiasts. Little homage, conversely, is paid to the simple, less prominent settlers who made this the nation's first great farm country. Their trade was grain, ground and bagged at any number of mills on the Piedmont's ample streams.

Rivers and the Fall Zone

The streams of the Piedmont feed larger mountain rivers that increase in size and momentum in their quest for the ocean. Pushing across the hard crust of the foothills, the rivers encountered less resistant rock. This became a distinct geographical location — where waters tumble over falls created by great outcroppings of rock. This is the "fall zone" that runs parallel to the mountains and the coast, separating the Piedmont and the Coastal Plain.

The fall zone was an ideal location for Colonial settlements. Towns grew along the zone, safely upriver as far as water transportation could go. Goods and crops from the hinterlands, mainly tobacco and wheat, were hauled across the Piedmont and loaded on boats headed for ports downriver. In time, a string of communities developed along the line of the fall zone, from Philadelphia to Petersburg, Virginia. Hamlets in Virginia along the fall zone date to the mid-17th century; Philadelphia dates to the 1680s. Baltimore was established on the zone line in 1720, and Washington was situated on the Potomac River falls 70 years later.

Some of the Civil War's heaviest fighting took place along the fall zone, particularly along the 100-mile stretch between the opposing capitals: Washington and Richmond. Opposing armies tangled at the Battle of Fredericksburg in Virginia in late 1862, and continued just months later at Chancellorsville, Virginia. The battles of the Wilderness and Spotsylvania were fought in Virginia in May 1864, and the siege of Petersburg lasted through the end of that year.

Today, this area of the Mid-Atlantic is part of the nation's heavily populated "urban corridor," and U.S. Highway 1 and Interstate 95 follow almost the exact fall line. The rivers here continue east, straightening and broadening in a more gentle flow to the Atlantic.

The Coastal Plain

Until a few million years ago, the Coastal Plain was submerged under water. Originally, the ocean lapped instead at the fall zone, now 100 miles upriver. On the Coastal Plain, the rivers are estuaries, susceptible to the ebb and flow of the ocean's tides. Mountain sediment becomes the sand of the beaches of the Chesapeake Bay and the Atlantic. The rivers of the Coastal Plain, particularly in Maryland and Virginia, have carved the sandy landscape into webbed "fingers" of land called peninsulas. Many of the river names are of Native American origin — Patuxent, Chickahominy and Rappahannock.

The Rappahannock River splits two of Virginia's historic land fingers. There is the Northern Neck, which lies between the Potomac and Rappahannock rivers and includes historic Westmoreland, Northumberland and Lancaster counties. And there is the Middle Peninsula, which lies between the Rappahannock and York rivers and includes King William, King and Queen and Gloucester counties. The Lower Peninsula lies between the York and James rivers. The James River meets the Atlantic at a place called Hampton Roads, which lends its name to the entire region of Virginia that is south of the James. Jamestown, the first permanent English settlement on the continent, was established on Virginia's Lower Peninsula on the James River. Maryland became a colony in 1632; Pennsylvania in 1681. The Maryland and Virginia colonies were established in a region controlled mainly by Powhatan, a noted Algonquin chief who ruled an area encompassing more than 8,500 square miles of the Coastal Plain.

Chesapeake became the single most significant place name settlers inherited from Native Americans on the Coastal Plain; tobacco, the most significant inherited crop. For a time, colonists made fortunes selling tobacco in England. They built estates along deep tidal rivers. Beginning in 1619, they imported African Americans as a slave labor force for the money crop. But tobacco required the richest loam, and it quickly exhausted the sandy soil. Eventually, planters abandoned the fields. They saw their hope for future wealth in land — land that lay beyond the fall line.

The Colonial population of the Coastal Plain grew and pushed west, upriver. In 1694, Maryland's capital was moved to the Severn River. Five years later, Virginia's capital was relocated at Middle Plantation — Williamsburg — which, with Annapolis, Maryland, was an important government center during the American Revolution. The British surrender in 1781 took place on the Lower Peninsula, at a small community named Yorktown. A number of prominent Americans had roots in the Coastal Plain, not the least of which was George Washington, the commander of the Continental Army, who was born on the Northern Neck in 1732.

Seventy-five years later, a mere 15 miles down the Potomac, another famous Virginia general was born — Robert E. Lee. The Civil War arrived early on the Coastal Plain. In the spring of 1862, the Union Army attempted a Richmond invasion, shipping troops down the Potomac and the Chesapeake Bay, then advancing up the Lower Peninsula. This became known as the Peninsula Campaign. The two ironsides, the *Monitor* and *Merrimac*, fought their battle at Hampton Roads in 1862. War action also took place upriver, east of Richmond and Petersburg, just before Confederates evacuated the two cities in 1865.

Today, Interstate 64 and Va. Highway 5 run east from Richmond along the length of the Lower Peninsula. U.S. Highway 17 runs east out of Fredericksburg, across the Middle Peninsula to Hampton Roads. Water-related industries, including tourism and fishing, are big business in the Tidewater. Crabs are a special Maryland delicacy. Peanuts and ham are notable products of the Virginia Tidewater. And there's an array of historical and recreational attractions in the area.

There is also ethnic diversity in the rich African-American heritage evident throughout coastal Maryland and Virginia, in Tidewater and Southside. Virginia is still home for a number of Native Americans, though they are much fewer in number. Today's Chickahominy, Eastern Chickahominy, Mattaponi, Upper Mattaponi, Nansemond, Pamunkey and United Rappahannock peoples are descendants of the area's first inhabitants.

Railroads

Rivers, and eventually their canals, dominated transportation in the Mid-Atlantic for over two centuries. This changed in the 19th century with the advent of the railroad.

In many places, particularly the mountains, rail lines simply followed the natural course of rivers that meandered through the Appalachians. To the northwest, rail lines originated in Hancock, Maryland, and in Martinsburg and Winchester, Virginia, funneled through Harpers Ferry and crossed central Maryland to Baltimore. Two rail branches — one in the Shenandoah Valley and another running north through Virginia's central Piedmont — met at Manassas Junction and linked with Alexandria, Virginia. Richmond was a rail center, with trains arriving from every direction. Lines ran to and from Fredericksburg, Virginia, on the north, Gordonsville, Virginia, on the east, and Burkeville and Petersburg in Southside. Another line ran southeast from Petersburg to Suffolk, Virginia.

The railroad played a role in the boundary disputes created with West Virginia's 1863 separation from Virginia — the nation's only map change that resulted from the Civil War. West Virginia cut away from Virginia mainly along the Appalachian ridges that form the eastern continental divide. However, the new state took in some land east of the divide in the Great Valley, thus forming an eastern panhandle along the Potomac. The panhandle was vital: It enabled the Baltimore and Ohio Railroad, a Union Army lifeline, to run totally within Northern territory.

The Hostilities Begin

Two years earlier, in 1861, it was a special, secret train that transported Abraham Lincoln to Washington, D.C., for his inaugural. There were a number of threats on Lincoln's life, so he was under heavy guard when his train rolled into Washington 10 days before his swearing-in. Elizabeth Lindsay Lomax, the widow of an Army officer, lived in Washington and kept a private diary in the 1850s and 1860s. On Inauguration Day — March 4, 1861 — she wrote: "This dreaded day has at last arrived. Thank Heaven all is peaceful and quiet." The newspaper Mrs. Lomax would read was printed late that day in order to carry the new president's inaugural address. "We read it aloud," she wrote in her diary. "There was no doubt of its sanity and its excellence."

Lincoln spoke of a nation on the brink of division. "Physically speaking," he said, "we can not separate. We can not remove our respective sections from each other nor build an impassable wall between them." He added, "A husband and wife may be divorced and go out of the presence and beyond the reach of each other, but the different parts of our country can not do this."

But the different parts of the country did build an impassable wall of sorts. Just 10 weeks later, Confederate cannon fired off Charleston, South Carolina. The Civil War was under way.

The Officers

Officers of the United States Army (USA) and Confederate States of America (CSA)

Throughout the text of this guide, for the sake of brevity, most officers are listed by their last name, preceded by their command — USA or CSA. Here, for easy reference, we list officers with their full names.

Union Officers

Averell, Gen. William Woods
Banks, Gen. Nathaniel Prentiss
Buford, Gen. John Buford
Burnside, Gen. Ambrose Everett
Butler, Gen. Benjamin Franklin
Cadwalader, Gen. George
Crook, Gen. George
Custer, Gen. George Armstrong
Davis, Col. Benjamin Franklin
Davis, Col. Hasbrouck
Duffie, Gen. Alfred Nattie
Ellsworth, Col. Ephraim Elmer
Fremont, Gen. John Charles
French, Gen. William Henry
Grant, Gen. Ulysses Simpson
Halleck, Gen. Henry Wager
Hancock, Gen. Winfield Scott
Hartsuff, Gen. George Lucas
Hooker, Gen. Joseph "Fighting Joe"
Hunter, Gen. David
Kearny, Gen. Philip
Keyes, Gen. Erasmus
Kilpatrick, Gen. Hugh Judson
McClellan, Gen. George Brinton "Young Napoleon"
McPherson, Gen. James Birdseye
Meade, Gen. George Gordon
Meigs, Lt. John Rodgers
Meigs, Quartermaster Gen. Montgomery Cunningham
Miles, Col. Dixon S.
Milroy, Gen. Robert Huston
Pleasants, Lt. Col. Henry
Pope, Gen. John
Porter, Adm. David D.

Rathbone, Maj. Henry
Reno, Gen. Jesse Lee
Reynolds, Gen. Joshua F.
Scott, Gen. Winfield
Sedgwick, Gen. John
Shields, Gen. James
Sheridan, Gen. Philip Henry "Little Phil"
Sherman, Gen. William Tecumseh
Sigel, Gen. Franz
Stoneman, Gen. George
Stoughton, Gen. Edwin Henry
Strother, Gen. David Hunter
Thomas, Gen. George Henry
Torbert, Gen. Alfred Thomas Archimedes
Wallace, Gen. Lewis
Wool, Gen. John Ellis

Confederate Officers

Anderson, Gen. Robert Heron
Armistead, Gen. Lewis Addison
Ashby, Gen. Turner
Beauregard, Gen. Pierre Gustave Toutant "P.G.T."
Bee, Gen. Barnard E.
Breckinridge, Gen. John Cabell
Early, Gen. Jubal Anderson "Old Jube"
Ewell, Gen. Richard Stoddert
Hampton, Gen. Wade
Hill, Gen. Ambrose Powell "A.P."
Hotchkiss, Maj. Jedediah
Hunton, Gen. Eppa
Iverson, Gen. Alfred
Jackson, Gen. Thomas Jonathan "Stonewall"
Jenkins, Gen. Albert Gallatin
Johnson, Gen. Bradley
Johnston, Gen. Joseph Eggleston

Jones, Gen. William Edmonson
Lee, Gen. Fitzhugh "Fitz"
Lee, Gen. Robert Edward
Lomax, Gen. Lunsford Lindsay
Longstreet, Gen. James "Pete"
Magruder, Gen. John Bankhead
Marr, Lt. John Q.
McCausland, Gen. John
Mosby, Col. John Singleton

Paxton, Gen. Elisha Franklin
Pelham, Maj. John
Pettigrew, Gen. James Johnston
Pickett, Gen. George Edward
Rosser, Gen. Thomas Lafayette
Steuart, Gen. George Hume
Stuart, Gen. James Ewell Brown "Jeb"
Withers, Col. R.E.

Exploring the Past With Pets

Michael and Kendall Gleason drove more than 10,000 miles researching the first edition of *The Insiders' Guide® to the Civil War in the Eastern Theater,* then drove another 3,000 miles to write this update.

For the latest edition, the Gleasons frequently took along their dog, Jack, a year-old, 80-pound, Yellow Labrador-Chesapeake Bay Retriever mix. Obviously a large animal, Jack survived the outings in the family Saturn because he simply loves to ride in the car, and because the Gleasons took several short excursions — no extended trips — from their home in Virginia's Tidewater.

But what about taking a pet on a longer, multiple-day vacation or history tour? The Gleasons ran into mixed reactions at attractions and lodging facilities along the tour routes presented in this guide. Some attractions have special walking areas for pets, but few allow pets on indoor tours. There is no standardized motel policy: Only a few allow pets; often there's a size requirement.

If you still insist on taking your pet along for the tours, "know your pet" is the advice of our expert, Dr. Cynthia M. Rhodes, a principal in the Gloucester Veterinary Hospital in Gloucester, Virginia. Dr. Rhodes is Jack's personal veterinarian. Gleason — Mike, not Jack — interviewed "Dr. Cindy" to get some professional tips for a traveler with a pet.

Dr. Cindy Says . . .

Taking your pet along on a road trip means you must "use common sense," according to Dr. Cindy. Some pets just don't travel well, she says, and if yours is one of those, you should consider leaving Fido or Fluffy with a house sitter or at a boarding facility. Ask your vet to recommend a sitter or boarder.

The size of your pet, says Dr. Cindy, is a consideration in planning a successful outing. Some animals, even Jack's size, take travel stress better than others. A small pet does make it easier to find accommodations at a motel or lodge. Dr. Cindy advises travel planners to call ahead to see if pets are allowed. Some motels welcome pets within a certain size range — dogs, for example, no larger than 30 pounds. If possible, check ahead for a reliable veterinarian at your destination. Again, you can ask your vet at home for a recommendation.

When you start your trip, Dr. Cindy says to make sure you have everything your pet will need: a bowl for water, food, treats, special toys and/or a blanket. Don't forget a dog's leash or a cat's special hideaway — a sky kennel is ideal. Remember to take along your pet's medication record. The veterinarian also says it's important to give your pet some quiet time away from children or hectic activity. A cat, for example, can curl up in a sky kennel for a quiet break or to calm the nerves.

"It is so important to remember," says Dr. Cindy, "that pets can easily overheat. So keep your vehicle ventilated while you're traveling and especially when you're parked. We've all heard horror stories about careless travelers who leave a pet in a car without ventilation or water." If the ocean is your summer destination, Dr. Cindy says a pet can easily overheat or become dehydrated at the beach.

Feeding a pet on the road is always a challenge. While on the highway, Dr. Cindy advises that you feed your pet smaller amounts of food, but on a more frequent basis. This keeps your pet from overloading and becoming sick. Take along your pet's own food supply from home, and stop at a grocery store along your travel route to replenish your pet food supply when necessary. When all else fails, you may be forced to stop at a drive-through window to get your pet some fast food. According to Dr. Cindy, order something basic for your pet like grilled (not fried) chicken or a hamburger without the condiments.

Remember, too, that pets need water — lots of water. Some pets also can become sensitive to changes in the water they drink. If this is true with your pet, take along water from home. "A pet is an important part of the family," says Dr. Cindy. "Give your animal special care to ensure a healthy, safe trip." On the road, she says, be as considerate of your pet as you are at home. "Use common sense," she adds.

Cynthia M. Rhodes wanted to become a veterinarian when she was a grade-school student in her hometown of Lexington, Kentucky. After attending Duke University, she received a degree in veterinary medicine from Auburn University in Alabama. In 1984, she accepted an internship at Gloucester Veterinary Hospital in Gloucester, Virginia, not far from the historic Jamestown-Yorktown-Williamsburg triangle.

Dr. Rhodes is now one of the four principals at the hospital. She is married to Warner Rhodes, an official with the Virginia Marine Resources Commission. The couple resides in Gloucester with their three children, Rachel, Christopher and Benjamin.

The Eastern Theater

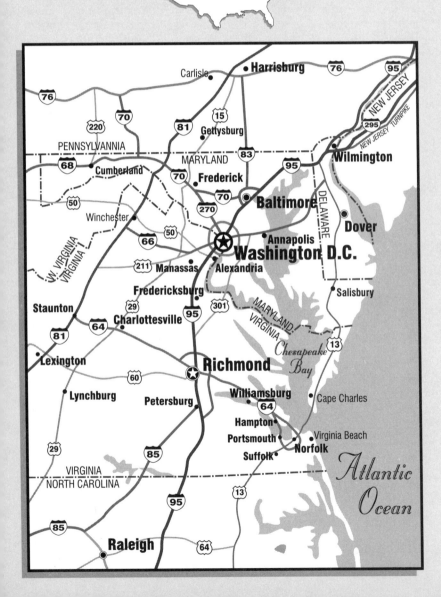

Prelude to War

The Civil War did not just spring up overnight. Nor was there one simple political or social issue involved. The seeds were sown earlier in our young nation's history — in a time frame that spans at least three decades, 1830 to 1860, with key events taking place in Washington and throughout the country.

This 30-year period was a time of rapid growth. It also was a time of erratic and ever-changing political leadership and allegiances. It was a time in which America was attempting to define its identity. The nation's population during these three decades increased from 12.8 million to nearly 31.5 million — an amazing 140 percent increase. The number of states grew from 24 to 34, reflecting the country's intense interest in settling beyond the Ohio and Mississippi river valleys. New states emerged in every region: Arkansas, Florida and Texas in the south; Iowa and Kansas in the nation's heartland; Michigan, Wisconsin and Minnesota in the "Old Northwest"; Oregon and California on the Pacific coast.

There were 10 presidents during the 30 years. Andrew Jackson, the first "modern" Democrat, was inaugurated as the nation's seventh president in 1829. Abraham Lincoln, the first "modern" Republican, was sworn in as the 16th chief executive in 1860. In between, there was not a single two-term president. The struggle for partisan leadership in the White House resembled a game of political badminton. Jackson and his fellow Democrats controlled presidential politics through the 1830s. A third party, the Whigs, was organized in the mid-1830s in an attempt to unite various coalitions opposed to what they considered Jackson's executive tyranny. They were re-markably successful during most of the 1840s, but party leaders never developed a strong, identifiable party program. Democrats reclaimed control of the White House in the 1850s. And Republican Lincoln was elected in 1860, on the eve of the Civil War.

Politicians, Places and Phrases: A Primer

During the three decades preceding 1860, there were a number of phrases, slogans, important laws and political names that became household words and benchmarks for a nation on a path toward an inevitable Civil War. Here is a rundown of some of the critical people and events that helped define antebellum America.

Slavery was a practice begun in the Virginia colony in 1609. It was peculiarly Southern, where economics centered on agriculture (tobacco and cotton) and African-American slave labor. In the North, an area with more advanced manufacturing and industrialization, the sentiment usually was **antislavery**.

As new states were admitted to the union, pro- and antislavery proponents became vocal. The **Missouri Compromise** was important federal legislation adopted in 1820. It allowed the admission of Missouri as a slave state, while Maine was cut from Massachusetts and admitted to balance the U.S. Senate with an equal number of representatives from slave and free states. This compromise outlawed slavery in the remainder of the Louisiana Territory, north of Missouri's southern boundary.

Even at that early date, the issues evoked concern. "We have a wolf by the ears," Thomas Jefferson said, "and we can neither safely hold him, nor safely let him go." **States' rights** was a term associated with South Carolina and its prominent political leader **John C. Calhoun**. This political position suggests a strict interpretation of the U.S. Constitution as it relates to federal powers and state autonomy. By the time Calhoun became President **Andrew Jackson**'s vice president, states' rights — **sectionalism** — were a source of heated debate in Washington and elsewhere in the country.

Nullification was another word attributed to Calhoun. He, along with fellow South Carolinians and other Southerners, said individual states existed prior to the formation of the United States. Therefore the states themselves, they argued, could interpret the U.S. Constitution and "nullify" anything they considered unauthorized or unconstitutional. South Carolina put its nullification philosophy into action in 1832, after Congress passed legislation that put protective duties — **tariffs** — on manufactured goods. Congressmen from the north and west supported the bill; Southerners, who had few manufacturing concerns, disliked it. South Carolina enacted an ordinance of nullification, which declared the national law unauthorized.

Secede — pronounced "sa-SEED" — means to withdraw from membership in an association. The act of seceding is known as **secession** — pronounced "sa-SESH-un." South Carolina, for example, considered its right to nullify a federal law an issue important enough to merit seceding from the union. After South Carolina enacted its ordinance of nullification, President Jackson charged Calhoun with treason and threatened to have him hanged. To the **Nullifiers**, the president said, "Secession, like any other revolutionary act, may be morally justified by the extremity of oppression; but to call it a constitutional right is confounding." Jackson added, "The laws of the United States must be executed. I have no discretionary power on the subject."

In 1833, as Jackson began his second term in the White House, his trusted friend, Martin Van Buren (not Calhoun), was the new vice president. That same year, Kentucky Senator **Henry Clay** helped the nation avoid a serious crisis over the tariff issue. Clay, a native Virginian and former secretary of state, had been an unsuccessful presidential candidate against Jackson the previous year. Clay devised a new tariff law designed to lower duties over a period of years. His plan gave South Carolina enough political elbow room to repeal its nullification ordinance, and in time, Clay became known as the **Great Compromiser**.

In 1840, the nation's population topped 17 million. Jackson's handpicked successor, Van Buren, faced a military hero, Whig William Henry Harrison, in his bid for re-election. Earlier in the year, Clay had challenged Harrison for the Whig nomination and lost. Clay, a presidential candidate in 1824, 1832 and later in 1844, commented, "I am the most unfortunate man in the history of parties; always run by my friends when sure to be defeated, and now betrayed when I, or anyone, would be sure of an election." An antislavery group called the **Liberty Party** also ran a candidate. Still, Harrison won. He was inaugurated the following March, but he became ill and lived just one month.

Vice President John Tyler, a man of more obscure political leanings, succeeded Harrison. Calhoun, meanwhile, became Tyler's secretary of state. In 1844, Clay ran for president again and lost to Democrat James Polk. Four years later, Whig **Zachary Taylor**, another war hero, became a presidential candidate. The frequently unsuccessful Liberty Party, with its antislavery platform, merged with the **Free Soil Party** and advocated that slavery be excluded in the territories and banned in new states. Taylor won the election. He, too, died in office and was succeeded by Vice President Millard Fillmore.

Massachusetts Senator **Daniel Webster** was a member of President Fillmore's cabinet. Webster gained national fame in 1830, when he spoke out against South Carolina's nullification principles. He served as secretary of state for both presidents Harrison and Tyler, and he was an unsuccessful Whig candidate for president in 1836. Webster was appointed secretary of state in July 1850, just four months after delivering his stirring speech in the U.S. Senate in support of the **Compromise of 1850**. This compromise was designed to prevent a national split over the issue of territorial slavery. In his famous **Seventh of March speech**, Webster said, "I wish to speak today, not as a Massachusetts man, nor as a Northern man, but as an American." He urged his fellow Northerners to accept a stronger fugitive slave law and Southerners to give up all thought of secession. "Peaceable secession!" Webster exclaimed. "Heaven forbid."

Illinois Senator **Stephen Douglas**, at 5-foot-4 and 90 pounds, was known as the **Little Giant**. He maneuvered the Clay-inspired Compromise of 1850 through Congress. The bill authorized the acquisition of the Southwest Territory after the Mexican War and again raised the issue of territorial slavery. California was admitted as a free state; the rest of the Southwest was divided into two sections, one with slavery and one without.

While adopting the 1850 compromise legislation, Congress passed another act to abolish slave trading in the District of Columbia and help slave owners recover runaways. Known as the **Fugitive Slave Act**, it was a new law for an old problem. It inflamed ill feelings between sectionalist leaders as well as proponents of both slavery and **abolitionism** — the act of abolishing or doing away with something. In this case, the term applied to abolishing slavery.

Uncle Tom's Cabin was written in 1852 by **Harriet Beecher Stowe** and heralded by abolitionists. It avoided self-righteous accusations and described slaves as victims of an evil, Southern system. It had a major impact on Northerner sympathizers. In England, Queen Victoria cried when she read it.

Senator Clay died in Washington in 1852; funeral services were held in the U.S. Senate chambers. Four months later, Secretary of State Webster died in Marshfield, Massachusetts. Senator Douglas, meanwhile, was an unsuccessful candidate for the Democratic presidential nomination. The nod went instead to Franklin Pierce, who defeated Winfield Scott, a hero of the Mexican War. Pierce was inaugurated in Washington in March 1853. Among Pierce's cabinet members was Secretary of War **Jefferson Davis**.

Senator Douglas returned to national prominence in 1854, when he introduced the Kansas-Nebraska Bill to establish a territorial government west of Missouri, divide the re-

gion into slave and free sections and repeal the law that banned slavery north of Missouri's southern border. The **Kansas-Nebraska Act**, the result of Senator Douglas' bill, prompted thousands of both pro- and antislavery supporters to pour into Kansas to try and take over the government. There were considerable outbreaks of death and destruction (thus the term **"Bleeding Kansas"**), including a raid at Pottawatomie led by abolitionist **John Brown**. Northerners, including Douglas' own supporters, were outraged by the Kansas act. The legislation destroyed the senator's presidential aspirations and led the nation farther down the road toward an inevitable national conflict.

"Free Soil, Free Speech, Fremont," was the slogan of the new Republican Party in the 1856 presidential campaign. The slogan was used by advocates who wanted to ban territorial slavery, end abolitionist literature and elect **John C. Fremont** as president. The Republicans skipped over Douglas to run Fremont against a Pennsylvania bachelor, James Buchanan, the ultimate victor.

Buchanan did little to stop the widening split between the North and South. In the **Panic of 1857**, a number of banks collapsed after American grain producers dropped grain prices in response to increased Russian grain exports. The South survived the 1857 panic, in large part, because of Europe's continued demand for cotton. Southerners, aware of the power of the cotton trade and convinced the North would avoid interfering with their states' rights philosophy, proclaimed **"Cotton is King."**

In its famous **Dred Scott Decision**, the U.S. Supreme Court ruled in 1857 that the Missouri Compromise was unconstitutional because it deprived slave owners the right to take their "property" where they wanted. In this case, Scott, a slave, was taken into the Wisconsin Territory, where slavery was banned.

A one-term Illinois congressman named **Abraham Lincoln** rose to prominence in 1858, challenging incumbent Senator Douglas. Lincoln, in his famous **"House Divided"** speech at the senatorial nominating convention, predicted "this government cannot endure permanently half slave and half free." Many, including conservative Northerners, took his speech as a call for abolishing slavery — a position Lincoln never supported prior to the Civil War. Throughout the campaign, particularly in a notable joint appearance in Freeport, Illinois, Lincoln pressed Douglas on two issues — the Senator's Kansas-Nebraska Bill and the Supreme Court's Scott decision. Of Douglas, it can be said he won the battle but lost the war: He defeated Lincoln in the Illinois senate race, but he lost to Lincoln in the presidential election two years later.

John Brown's Raid was a jolt that struck peaceful, prosperous **Harpers Ferry**, in the mountains of western Virginia, in 1859. Brown, the Kansas abolitionist, plotted for months before raiding the town because it was "the safest natural entrance to the Great Black Way." According to Brown, "Here, amid the mighty protection of overwhelming numbers, lay a path from slavery to freedom." Brown, a self-described "instrument of God sent to liberate all slaves," captured the federal arsenal and refused to surrender. He was captured two mornings later when federal troops stormed the arsenal. Brown was indicted and tried for treason in nearby Charles Town. To many, particularly in the North, he was a martyr.

"Dixie" was a song written in 1859 by a Ohio musician, Daniel Emmett. It begins, "I wish I was in the land of cotton." In time, it became the unofficial song of the Confederacy. The **Constitutional Union Party** was a third-party faction that adopted a platform in 1860 in support of the Union and the U.S. Constitution, without regard to sectional issues. While Lincoln and Douglas were the prime contenders for the presidency in 1860, the Constitutional Union Party ran Tennessean **John Bell**, a former U.S. Senator and secretary of war. Bell said Americans had a patriotic duty to "recognize no political principle other than the Constitution, the Union of the States, and the enforcement of the laws." He carried his home state plus Kentucky and Virginia, where sharply divided voters clearly realized that any possible bloodshed likely would erupt in their region.

Lincoln was elected president in 1860, and South Carolina seceded a month later. Then, in quick succession prior to the 1861 inaugural, the union lost six more states: Mississippi,

Florida, Alabama, Georgia, Louisiana and Texas. In time, four more states joined the new **Confederate States of America**: Virginia, Arkansas, Tennessee and North Carolina. Lincoln was inaugurated in March 1861. Douglas, the new president's old nemesis, held Lincoln's hat during the inaugural ceremony. Three months later, Senator Douglas died in Chicago, barely a month after the outbreak of the Civil War.

Kansas was admitted to the union just five weeks before Lincoln's inaugural. This new state aligned with 18 other Northern, non-slave states in the Northeast, north of the Ohio River and just beyond the Mississippi River. The **North** included the states of California, Connecticut, Illinois, Indiana, Iowa, Kansas, Maine, Massachusetts, Michigan, Minnesota, New Hampshire, New Jersey, New York, Ohio, Pennsylvania, Oregon, Rhode Island, Vermont and Wisconsin; and the territories of Colorado, Dakota Nebraska, Nevada and Washington. Separating the North and South were **border states** — Delaware, Maryland, Kentucky and Missouri, as well as the District of Columbia and the New Mexico Territory.

Jefferson Davis, a Kentucky native and longtime Mississippi resident, was a West Point graduate. His first wife, the daughter of military hero and president Zachary Taylor, died of malaria only a few months after they were married. Davis served in the Mexican War, as a U.S. senator and was Pierce's secretary of war. He was elected president of the Confederacy at a meeting of 37 delegates from five seceded states, who met in assembly in February 1861 in Montgomery, Alabama.

The first Confederate flag, or **"Stars and Bars,"** incorporated two horizontal red stripes separated by a white stripe. It included seven white stars in a blue field. This flag was adopted in March 1861 and raised over the Confederate Capitol, then in Montgomery, Alabama, by former President John Tyler's granddaughter. But this flag caused confusion at the Battle of 1st Bull Run in Virginia, because it looked very much like the Union's **"Stars and Stripes."**

Following the battle, CSA Gen. Pierre Gustave Toutant "P.G.T." Beauregard designed a battle flag for the Army of Northern Virginia. This flag, erroneously referred to today as the Confederate "Stars and Bars," was red with a blue St. Andrew's cross and 13 superimposed white stars. This is what many still call the Confederate flag. In May 1863, the Confederacy adopted a new national flag to replace the first Stars and Bars. It was white with the more familiar battle flag in the upper right corner. But this flag, when furled, showed only white, so a new design in 1865 added a red bar on the flag's white edge. Thus, the ANV's battle flag is what most identify with the Confederate flag.

Most of these phrases, slogans, important laws and political names eventually became household words throughout America. Combined, they help define the nation in the years that led up to the Civil War.

Tour 1
Sharpsburg

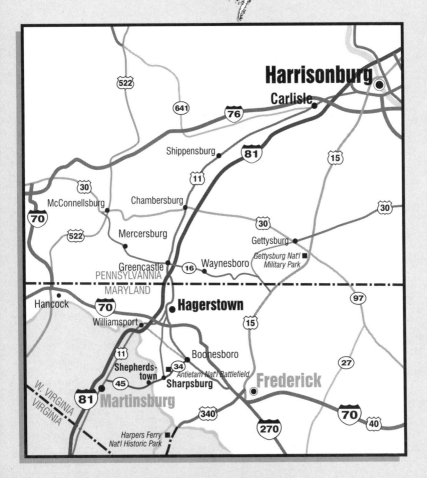

TOUR 1
Sharpsburg

About This Tour

The first tour covers the Cumberland Valley of Pennsylvania and Maryland, from Carlisle, Pennsylvania, to Shepherdstown, West Virginia. This route is the first of five in succession — T-1 through T-5 — that cover the long stretch of the Great Valley through Pennsylvania, Maryland, West Virginia and Virginia.

The Tuscarora and Kittatinny mountains, parts of the Appalachians, rise up to the west of the Cumberland Valley, the northern part of a vast trough that stretches into Maryland and Virginia to the southwest. The Catoctin Mountains form the valley's eastern boundary. The Susquehanna River, originating high in the Appalachians, cuts through the highlands at Pennsylvania's Blue Mountain. Harrisburg, the Pennsylvania capital, is on the fringe of the valley, at the Susquehanna River water gap. The Cumberland Valley stretches from Harrisburg south to the Potomac River, which forms much of the boundary between Maryland and West Virginia and Virginia.

The name "Cumberland" was first used in this region in 1754, with the construction of a fort that served as the headquarters for George Washington and British Gen. Edward Braddock during the French and Indian War. The fort was named for William Augustus, the Duke of Cumberland, son of England's King George II. Cumberland is also the name of the Pennsylvania county just across the Susquehanna from Harrisburg. The Cumberland Valley was once the home of various Native American tribes. The Great Wagon Road through the valley followed an old buffalo trail used by Native Americans to travel from the Southern highlands to the Great Lakes. German farmers began settling the region in the early 1700s, followed almost im-

mediately by Scotch-Irish pioneers. The fertile valley was a haven for German farmers, and their culture and lifestyle remain in evidence today.

This part of Pennsylvania and Maryland was a haven for runaway African-American slaves during the Civil War. Quakers ran the Underground Railroad in this area, just north of the Mason-Dixon line. Civil War action took place throughout the valley, beginning in 1862 and continuing through the next two years — before and after the Battle of Antietam in Maryland and the Battle of Gettysburg in Pennsylvania. CSA Gen. Jubal Anderson "Old Jube" Early was in this region in 1864 on an attempted invasion of Washington, D.C.

Travel Tips

Interstate 81 is a busy interstate highway, so watch for the numerous trucks. The various lane changes and narrow-lane construction sites create the potential for congestion and accidents. As a result, this tour — and the next two in the Great Valley — travel south mainly using U.S. Highway 11. That's just as well, as U.S. 11 is a more historic route, following the path of the Great Wagon Road. It leads through the heart of a number of quaint, attractive Cumberland Valley communities.

Generally, U.S. 11 is a divided, four-lane highway. Remember, though, that this is major farming country, so be alert to slow-moving farm vehicles. Several small local radio stations report weather conditions, but these only cover traffic in the most extreme circumstances. Citizens band radio users can find traffic on Channel 19. State police usually monitor Channel 9. Mobile telephone signals are sporadic in the Cumberland Valley vicinity. The tour ends in Shepherdstown, West Virginia, where we suggest you plan evening dining and lodging. Recommended accommodations are in Chapter 22. Dining suggestions are in Chapter 23. It is a good idea to review these recommendations before traveling through the region. In addition to our suggestions, there are the usual fast-food restaurants, gas stations, convenience stores and shops along U.S. 11.

Sharpsburg Tour Begins . . .

The first tour starts just south of Harrisburg, Pennsylvania, where I-81 and Interstate 76 (Pennsylvania Turnpike) intersect with U.S. 11.

Harrisburg, Pa.

Harrisburg is at the Susquehanna River water gap, where Englishman John Harris established a trading post in the early 18th century. By the mid-1700s, his son John Jr. operated a ferry across the Susquehanna — hence, Harris' Ferry. John Jr. laid out a town in 1785, and questions arose regarding what to name the village. The town is in the county of Dauphin, a French name, so state legislators thought it should be named Louisburg, for France's Louis XVI. But the community remembered its founder, and Harrisburg was the choice. John Harris Jr. died in 1791.

Harrisburg became the state capital in 1810, and it was incorporated as a city in 1860, just a year before the outbreak of the Civil War. Harrisburg escaped major war action, though there was a bit of action just across the Susquehanna at Lemoyne (see T-5: Gettysburg).

HARRISBURG TO CARLISLE, PA.
Exit south of Harrisburg on either U.S. 11, and continue south 18 miles to Middlesex, Pennsylvania, where U.S. 11 intersects with I-81 (exit 11). From this intersection, continue south on U.S. 11 for 3.2 miles to the entrance to the U.S. Army military post, Carlisle Barracks, north of Carlisle. Turn left into the post — a guard will direct you to parking just inside the guard house.

U.S. Army Military History Institute and Museum
Carlisle Barracks, Bldg. 22, Carlisle, Pa.
• (717) 245-3611

Carlisle Barracks, home of the U.S. Army's War College, has been the site of a military installation since the French and Indian War in the 1750s. Later, George Washington reviewed troops here during the Whiskey Rebellion, an uprising of backcountry farmers in Pennsylvania in July 1794. The farmers fought federal revenue officers who attempted to collect a

Harrisburg Personality: Governor Andrew G. Curtin

Pennsylvania Gov. Andrew Gregg Curtin served throughout the Civil War, and actively supported the Union cause. He was briefly considered as a vice presidential candidate in 1868, but he lost the bid and was instead named minister to Russia by President Ulysses S. Grant. Camp Curtin, a Union training (rendezvous) camp south of Harrisburg, was named in his honor.

Photo: Antietam National Battlefield

Gov. Andrew G. Curtin actively supported the Union cause.

liquor tax that had been enacted in 1791 to raise money for the national debt. Carlisle Indian School, the first non-reservation school for Native Americans, opened in 1879 at Carlisle Barracks, and Olympian Jim Thorpe was a student.

The U.S. Army Military History Institute, located on the military installation grounds, has a military library and a display of some Civil War artifacts. The library and display easily justify a visit to the grounds of this attractive, serene open military post. The institute has a vast collection of Civil War books, papers and photographs, and it possesses a voluminous record of Civil War regiments — both Union and Confederate. It is open free Monday through Friday from 8 AM to 4:30 PM, except federal holidays. It is handicapped accessible.

CARLISLE BARRACKS TO CARLISLE, PA.
Exit Carlisle Barracks and return to U.S. 11, turn left (south) and go 1 mile to the heart of Carlisle.

Carlisle, Pa.
Frenchman James Le Tort, who traded with the Native Americans, built a cabin in this region. By the mid-1750s, the settlement was called Carlisle — named for an English town. This was the home of two signers of the Declaration of Independence, James Wilson and George Ross. It was also the home of Mary Ludwig Hays, the Revolutionary War heroine also known as "Molly Pitcher." Dickinson College, one of Pennsylvania's oldest schools of higher education, was chartered in 1783, and one of its graduates was President James Buchanan, who was born just to the south near McConnellsburg. CSA Gen. Richard Stoddert Ewell's troops camped at Dickinson College in June 1863, just before Gettysburg.

CARLISLE TO SHIPPENSBURG, PA.
Exit Carlisle on U.S. 11 and continue south 11 miles to downtown Shippensburg.

Shippensburg, Pa.
Settled in the 1730s by Edward Shippen, Shippensburg is the second-oldest Pennsylvania town west of the Susquehanna River. One of Shippen's relatives, Peggy Shippen, married Benedict Arnold. The Cumberland-Franklin county line runs through Shippensburg. In June 1863, Union cavalry troops monitored CSA Gen. Robert E. Lee's movements in the Shippensburg vicinity.

SHIPPENSBURG TO CHAMBERSBURG, PA.
Exit Shippensburg on U.S. 11 and continue south 11 miles to downtown Chambersburg. U.S. 11 becomes Philadelphia Avenue and then Main Street through Chambersburg.

Between Shippensburg and Chambersburg is the boundary line for Franklin County, which suffered more Civil War activity than any comparable area north of the Mason-Dixon Line. Strategically located in the heart of the Cumberland Valley, this county was the target of three major Confederate cavalry raids, led by CSA Gen. James Ewell Brown "Jeb" Stuart in October 1862, Gen. Albert Gallatin Jenkins in 1863 and Gen. John McCausland in 1864.

Chambersburg, Pa.
Chambersburg is the Franklin County seat of government. Benjamin Chambers settled in the region in the 1730s, built a sawmill and a gristmill and laid out the town in 1764. Chambersburg was John Brown's base of operations prior to his raid on Harpers Ferry in 1859. Brown posed as a prospector while collecting arms; his headquarters was on E. King Street, which intersects U.S. 11 near the heart of downtown.

Following the 1862 Battle of Antietam, Chambersburg served as a supply and hospital center for the Union Army. More than 65,000 Confederate soldiers led by CSA Gen. Robert E. Lee camped in Chambersburg in June 1863, just before Gettysburg. More than 500 buildings, about two-thirds of the town, were destroyed by fire in July 1864 after CSA Gen. John McCausland demanded $100,000 in gold or $500,000 in U.S. greenbacks from the town as repayment for USA Gen. David Hunter's

Memorial Square Side Trip: Chambersburg Chamber of Commerce Information Center

From Market Square, go south on Main Street two blocks to Queen Street, turn left (east) and go two blocks to Second Street. The chamber of commerce center is at the corner of Queen and Second streets at 75 S. Second Street.

The chamber information center is in a building constructed of beautiful native blue limestone. Built to house a library, the building was purchased by the chamber for offices and an information center.

Ask travel counselors about their selection of history-oriented brochures, including one of a walking tour in downtown Chambersburg. A gift shop sells books on regional Civil War history. Open 9 AM to 5 PM daily, the center is handicapped-accessible. For more information, call (717) 264-7101.

Shenandoah Valley destruction. The Confederates made their demand at dawn — at 9 AM, despite objections from some Southern troops, the town was torched.

CHAMBERSBURG TO MEMORIAL SQUARE

Continue south on U.S. 11 (Main Street) to the downtown intersection where Main Street and U.S. Highway 30 (Lincoln Way) meet.

Memorial Square
Chambersburg, Pa.

Memorial Square, with its fountain, was known as "The Diamond" in the 19th century. On June 26, 1863, CSA Gens. Robert E. Lee and Ambrose Powell "A.P." Hill held council at The Diamond, and a star in the pavement near the fountain marks the place. The fountain was erected in 1878 to honor Franklin County soldiers.

MEMORIAL SQUARE TO FRANKLIN COUNTY COURTHOUSE

The Franklin County Courthouse is on the northeast corner of Memorial Square.

Franklin County Courthouse
Chambersburg, Pa.

The Franklin County Courthouse served as the 1863 headquarters of the provost marshal of CSA Gen. Richard Ewell's corps. As a result, a Confederate flag flew from the top of this building for a time.

Photo: Harpers Ferry National Historical Park

CSA Gen. A.P. Hill participated in many battles, including Antietam, Chancellorsville, Gettysburg and The Wilderness.

Chambersburg Side Trip: McConnellsburg, Pa.

McConnellsburg is on U.S. Highway 30, 21 miles west of Chambersburg. This is a bit of a hike, but Civil War buffs might want to visit McConnellsburg, if only for a drive through town along U.S. 30. McConnellsburg was incorporated in 1814 and laid out by Daniel and William McConnell. Two brief Civil War fights occurred in the town on June 24 and 29, 1863, just before Gettysburg. This is where CSA Gen. Bradley Johnson camped after his raid on Chambersburg in 1864. James Buchanan, the only Pennsylvanian to be elected president, was born near McConnellsburg in Cove Gap. The site is in the Buchanan Birthplace Historical State Park at Cove Mountain. Buchanan, elected president in 1857, tried to keep peace between the North and South. Still, he had no official reaction when South Carolina seceded in 1860.

CHAMBERSBURG TO GREENCASTLE, PA.
From Chambersburg, continue south on U.S. 11 for 11 miles to Greencastle.

Greencastle, Pa.

A Union cavalry unit marched into Greencastle in September 1862, after escaping from CSA Gen. Thomas Jonathan "Stonewall" Jackson's rout at Harpers Ferry (see T-2: Harpers Ferry). There were 20 Confederate casualties in Greencastle after a brief fight on June 20, 1863, just before Gettysburg. That day, USA Cpl. William Rihl, a member of the 1st New York Cavalry, was killed just north of Greencastle and became the first Union casualty north of the Mason-Dixon Line. Confederate soldiers controlled the town for nearly three weeks prior to the Battle of Gettysburg in June 1863.

Continue south on U.S. 11, which becomes Carlisle Street in Greencastle. The town square is at the intersection of Carlisle Street and Baltimore Street (Pa. Highway 16).

Town Square
Greencastle, Pa.

Union Hotel, a red brick structure on the southwest corner of Town Square, likely is the place where John Brown stayed during his visit to Greencastle in 1859. On the northeast corner of the square, across from the bank building, is a shoe store that was once Ziegler General Store, a busy place when Confederates marched through Greencastle in June 1863 just before Gettysburg. A week later, after Gettysburg, a 17-mile Confederate wagon train passed though town.

GREENCASTLE TO STATE LINE, PA.
Continue south on U.S. 11 for 5 miles south of Greencastle to State Line, Pa.

State Line, Pa.

The Mason-Dixon Line, the Pennsylvania-Maryland border, crosses at State Line. The boundary was surveyed by Charles Mason and Jeremiah Dixon in 1765 to align the border between the Pennsylvania and Maryland colonies. During the Civil War, the Mason-Dixon Line became an artificial boundary between the North and the South, although the Potomac River was the more realistic boundary between the two.

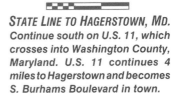

STATE LINE TO HAGERSTOWN, MD.
Continue south on U.S. 11, which crosses into Washington County, Maryland. U.S. 11 continues 4 miles to Hagerstown and becomes S. Burhams Boulevard in town.

Hagerstown, Md.

Jonathan Hager settled the village in the mid-18th century and named the new com-

Greencastle Side Trip: Waynesboro, Pa.

From Greencastle, take Pennsylvania Highway 16 east 8 miles to Waynesboro, Pennsylvania.

Waynesboro was settled in the mid-18th century and laid out in 1797. Founder James Wallace Jr, who served Gen. "Mad" Anthony Wayne in the American Revolution, named the town for his former commander. The Mason-Dixon Line's 105th milestone, a Crown-Stone marker that bears the crest of Lord Baltimore of Maryland and William Penn of Pennsylvania, is just south of town (see State Line, Pa., later in the tour). John Brown taught Sunday School in Waynesboro.

In July 1863, CSA Gen. Early raided Waynesboro and demanded the townspeople bake bread for his troops. North of Waynesboro, an Episcopal chapel — on the Mont Alto campus of Penn State University — was the final refuge for some of John Brown's men after Harpers Ferry (see more on John Brown's raid in T-2: Harpers Ferry).

Greencastle Side Trip: Mercersburg, Pa.

From Greencastle, take Pa. 16 west 10 miles to Mercersburg.

Mercersburg, named for a Virginia veteran of the Revolutionary War, Hugh Mercer, is the site of Mercersburg Academy. President James Buchanan's log cabin birthplace is at Mercersburg Academy. Harriet Lane, Buchanan's niece and his White House hostess, was born in Mercersburg. The community, 6 miles north of the Mason-Dixon line, was a haven for abolitionist activity during the two decades that preceded the war. Fugitive slave hunters claimed the ground here "swallowed up" their prey. They said "there must be an underground road somewhere." Thus, the origin of the Underground Railroad term.

munity Elizabeth Town, for his wife, Elizabeth Kershner Hager. But new settlers called it Hager's Town, which became a one-word name in 1814. Both U.S. 11 and I-81 cross the historic, east-west National Road at Hagerstown. The National Road, also known as the Cumberland Trail, was an extension of old U.S. Highway 40 across Maryland and was the nation's first federally funded highway. The National Road runs west to Cumberland, site of a western Maryland fort used by Col. George Washington as a headquarters during the French and Indian War. Later, it was the end of the line for the C&O Canal.

Because a number of roads converged on Hagerstown, the community was a busy place during the Civil War. Troops of both armies frequently passed through town, particularly before and after Antietam in 1862 and Gettysburg in 1863. More than 2,000 Confederates, victims of battles at South Mountain and Antietam, are buried at Rose Hill Cemetery in Hagerstown. In 1864, CSA Gen. Early's troops demanded $20,000 ransom from Hagerstown officials by threatening to burn the town.

Hagerstown Side Trip: Falling Waters, W.Va.

From Hagerstown, take U.S. 11 south 5 miles to Williamsport, Maryland, on the Potomac River. Continue south on U.S. 11 for 6 miles to Falling Waters, West Virginia.

CSA Gen. "Stonewall" Jackson was nearly killed while sitting under an oak tree at Falling Waters on July 2, 1861. A Union cannonball struck a tree limb, the falling limb narrowly missed Jackson and he escaped unharmed. In July 1863, CSA Gen. Lee, on a retreat from Gettysburg, was attacked by Union forces at the Battle of Falling Waters. The Confederates escaped south across the swollen Potomac River by building a bridge with lumber torn from all buildings in the vicinity.

HAGERSTOWN TO BOONSBORO, MD.

Continue southeast through Hagerstown on S. Burhams Boulevard, which becomes Wilson Boulevard, goes 1.5 miles and ends at Frederick Street (U.S. 40). Turn right on U.S. 40.

Along U.S. 40 is the site where CSA Gen. James "Pete" Longstreet entered Hagerstown in 1863 on his way to establish a base of operations in Pennsylvania. From this area, Confederate and Union forces went into battle at South Mountain and Antietam.

Continue south on U.S. 40 (Alt.) through Funkstown on Baltimore Street to the National Pike. Go 7 more miles to Boonsboro, where

U.S. 40 (Alt.) becomes Main Street.

Boonsboro, Md.

CSA Gen. "Stonewall" Jackson was nearly captured at Boonsboro in September 1862. Camped a mile east of town on the road from Turner's Gap, he walked his horse and barely avoided a group of Union cavalry. There was action in the streets of Boonsboro just before Antietam in September 1862, when CSA Gen. Fitzhugh "Fitz" Lee's cavalry fought Union soldiers. Churches and homes in Boonsboro were used as hospitals after Antietam, and opposing troops fought in the town the next year, in July 1863, after Gettysburg.

BOONSBORO TO SHARPSBURG, MD.

On Main Street in Boonsboro, at the traffic signal, turn right on Md. Highway 34 and go west 6.3 miles

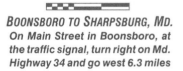

Hagerstown Personality: Oliver Wendall Holmes

In 1862, after the Battle of Antietam, two women — Mrs. Howard Kennedy and her daughter, Annie — found a wounded Union soldier lying in a Hagerstown road. The pair cared for the officer at their home, Mount Prospect. The injured captain was Oliver Wendall Holmes Jr. Oliver's father searched for his soldier son, and his travels inspired the poem, "My Search for the Captain." Oliver Jr. graduated from Harvard in 1861 at the age of 20. After the war, in 1866, he graduated from Harvard Law School and later became an Associate Justice of the U.S. Supreme Court. The Kennedy home, where he was nursed to health, is on W. Washington Street in Hagerstown.

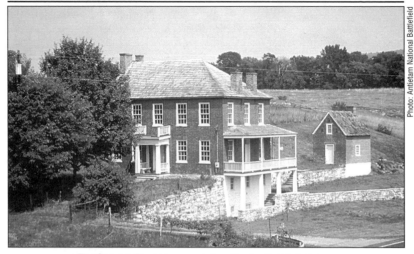

Photo: Antietam National Battlefield

The Sherrick Farm House was the site of action at Antietam.

to Sharpsburg. Md. 34 becomes
Main Street in Sharpsburg.

Sharpsburg, Md.

In 1763, following the French and Indian War, a real estate investor laid out a town where Antietam Creek flows into the Potomac River. The settlement was named for Horatio Sharpe, governor of Maryland at the time. Antietam is an Algonquian word that means "swift water."

SHARPSBURG TO ANTIETAM NATIONAL BATTLEFIELD VISITOR CENTER

Continue on Main Street, just beyond National Cemetery, to Md. Highway 65, turn right on Md. 65 (Church Street, Hagerstown Pike) and go 0.8 mile to the Antietam National Battlefield Visitor Center.

Antietam National Battlefield Visitor Center

Church St., Sharpsburg, Md.
• **(301) 432-5124**

Antietam — Sharpsburg — was fought September 17, 1862, and has been described as the bloodiest day of the Civil War. More soldiers were killed or wounded here than on

any other single day. The casualties exceeded 25,000, equally divided between the North and South. The battle climaxed the first of two attempts by CSA Gen. Robert E. Lee to take the war above the Potomac River, encourage antiwar sentiments in the North, gain Maryland support for the Confederate cause, solicit European interest in the Confederacy and draw Union troops from Virginia. A number of European nations, particularly England, observed the American Civil War with keen interest. In order to swing their allegiance to the Southern cause, however, these European countries wanted to see a demonstration of Confederate strength, and a successful invasion of the North would have been the leverage the South needed.

The stage for Antietam was set after Lee pushed north into Maryland following a victory in August 1862 at Manassas (Bull Run). Lee was followed by USA Gen. George Brinton McClellan (see T-14: Northern Virginia and T-19: Lower Peninsula). Lee sent CSA Gen. "Stonewall" Jackson to capture Harpers Ferry, while he stayed on the western side of Antietam Creek to delay Union troops crossing west into the valley through the gaps in South Mountain (see T-7: Monocacy). When Jackson returned from Harpers Ferry, the Southern troops consolidated for battle at Sharpsburg.

Antietam was fought in a 12-square-mile area, in three phases — morning, midday and afternoon. There were 40,000 Confederate troops facing a Union force more than twice that size. At dawn, USA Gen. Joseph "Fighting Joe" Hooker's artillery struck at Jackson's troops in a cornfield north of town. Hooker's men rushed the Confederates, who drove back the Union forces by 7 AM. An hour later, the Northerners counterattacked and regained some of Hooker's lost ground. Later, the opposing armies fought in an area now called the West Woods near the Dunkard Church. Forces under USA Gen. John Sedgwick suffered numerous casualties. USA Gen. William Henry French's men moved to support Sedgwick, and the four-hour, midday battle became known as Bloody Lane.

In mid-afternoon, USA Gen. Ambrose E. Burnside succeeded in crossing a stone bridge — it now is called Burnside Bridge — over Antietam Creek. Burnside advanced on the Confederates' right flank, just south of Sharpsburg. The Southerners were saved when CSA Gen. A.P. Hill's troops, on a forced march from Harpers Ferry, arrived in time to stop the advancing Federals. "War is a dreadful thing, " said Clara Barton, who treated the wounded during and after Antietam. "Oh, my God, can't this civil strife be brought to an end?"

The course of the war was greatly altered on that September day at Antietam. The battle was not a tactical victory for the Union Army, but it was just what President Lincoln needed to announce his Emancipation Proclamation. The proclamation shifted the war from a political issue to a struggle to free slaves.

The South was the world's leading source of "King Cotton," and it expected European governments, particularly in England and France, to intervene in the Civil War in its behalf. However, this international intervention became impossible when President Lincoln changed the course of the struggle into a crusade for human freedom and against slavery. President Lincoln used the battle at Antietam to issue a preliminary emancipation on September 22, 1862, saying he would free slaves in the South unless Confederates laid down their weapons. When the South refused to honor the presidential edict, the Emancipation Proclamation was issued on January 1, 1863.

The proclamation had another positive effect for the Federal effort in providing the Union with an opportunity to recruit African-American soldiers. Nearly 180,000 blacks donned the Yankee blue during the remaining two years of the war. In February 1865, Lincoln told a friend that the Emancipation Proclamation was "the central act of my administration, and the greatest event of the nineteenth century." An exponent of the proclamation was the 1865 ratification of the Thirteenth Amendment, which abolished slavery. (See more on the Emancipation Proclamation in T-13: Washington.)

The National Park Service operates the Antietam battlefield site. There is a fee — $4 per family; $2 for persons 17 and older. The facility includes a visitors center, which has an informative brochure on the Battle of Antietam. The brochure includes a motor tour route that covers all significant sights in the area. The center also features exhibits and audiovisual programs. It is open from 8:30 AM to 5 PM daily, with extended hours during summer. The center is closed Thanksgiving, Christmas and New Year's Day. There are extended hours during the summer months. It is handicapped-accessible.

The New York Monument at Antietam National Battlefield is included in a motor route tour.

SHARPSBURG TO SHEPHERDSTOWN, W.VA.

From the battlefield, return on Church Street (Md. 34) to Main Street in Sharpsburg, turn right (south) on Main Street and go 3.4 miles across the Potomac River to Shepherdstown, West Virginia.

Shepherdstown, W.Va.

The Potomac River forms the border between Maryland and West Virginia. This area of West Virginia was originally settled as part of the western region of Virginia. West Virginia then broke away from Virginia and obtained separate statehood in June 1863, just before Gettysburg.

In the panhandle, as in the rest of the Cumberland and Shenandoah valleys, loyalties were mixed during the Civil War. Shepherdstown was settled by Thomas Shepherd, who received a land grant in the early 1730s. During the French and Indian War in the early 1760s, the community was known as Mecklenburg. After the American Revolution, in 1787, James Rumsey demonstrated the first successful steamboat on the Potomac. A few years later, local residents honored their founder and changed the town name to Shepherdstown.

Imagine Shepherdstown — not Washington, D.C. — as the nation's capital. George Washington considered locating the nation's capital in Shepherdstown in 1790 but chose a place farther down the Potomac. Shepherdstown, considered West Virginia's oldest municipality, is in Jefferson County, named for Thomas Jefferson.

There was a skirmish at Blackford's Ford, downriver from Shepherdstown, on September 20, 1862. CSA Gens. "Stonewall" Jackson and A.P. Hill used the Potomac River ford near Shepherdstown on their way to the Battle of Antietam in 1862. CSA Gen. Lee, withdrawing from Antietam, was awakened just after midnight with news that Union forces captured his entire reserve artillery. The stories were exaggerated, but the Union did cross the Potomac and take four Confederate cannon. Union forces suffered heavy casualties when Hill mounted a vigorous counterattack.

Sharpsburg Tour Ends

Other Tour Points of Interest

Sharpsburg, Maryland, and Shepherdstown, West Virginia, offer little in the way of traditional nightlife. Forget about bustling shopping centers and movie theaters. This area is

Shepherdstown Personalities: West Virginians

West Virginia, it can be said, was a child of war. The Civil War pitted brother against brother and, in Virginia, county against county. Prior to the war, there already existed in Virginia a social difference between the eastern and western regions. These, in turn, led to political feuds. There were other differences: the distance between the two regions, the mountain barriers, the diverse physical settings, the separate commercial alliances and various misunderstandings and jealousies.

In early 1861, following President Lincoln's inaugural in Washington, crowds assembled in unorganized meetings throughout the western counties to debate the likelihood that Virginia might follow South Carolina's secession from the nation. The first organized meeting, a mass convention, was held at Clarksburg, Virginia — now in West Virginia — on April 22, 1861, a scant five days after Virginia approved an Ordinance of Secession. This group adopted a resolution that proposed a representative convention at Wheeling in May. Representatives of 24 Virginia counties sent delegates to the May 13 meeting that became known as the First Wheeling

— continued on next page

Photo: Antietam National Battlefield

Burnside Bridge is named for USA Gen. Ambrose E. Burnside

among the more rural locations listed in this book. As a result, the traveler has fewer choices for amenities and attractions, but the serenity is unequaled. Try to stay several days here — this area grows on you.

Arts

Shepherd College in Shepherdstown offers a number of cultural programs, including lecturers and guest speakers, throughout the school year. In particular, the **George Tyler Moore Center for the Study of the Civil War**, on German Street near the college campus, promotes the region's colorful Civil War history. The building that houses the center was purchased by the actress Mary Tyler Moore and given to Shepherd College as a tribute to her father, George Tyler Moore, a Civil War enthusiast. For more information, telephone Shepherd College at (304) 876-5000 during

Convention. Delegates at the three-day meeting decided to hold a more widely representative session in June.

The Second Wheeling Convention met in Wheeling on June 11. This time, 35 counties were represented. This second convention reorganized the state's western counties into a separate state government that it called the Restored Government of Virginia. It was this "restored government" in Virginia that made West Virginia's creation possible. The new legislature approved West Virginia's creation, and that technically satisfied a U.S. constitutional requirement that new states can be created only with the consent of the state whose territory is involved.

Francis H. Pierpoint, a forceful orator from Marion County, was elected governor of West Virginia. A convention met again in August 1861. It approved a state name — Kanawha — and passed an ordinance to select delegates to a constitutional convention. In November 1861, delegates approved a new name — West Virginia — and adopted a constitution that received voter approval in April 1862.

This first West Virginia constitution was silent on the question of slavery, however, and the U.S. Congress refused to admit the new state until it adopted an amendment

— continued on next page

— continued from previous page

providing for the emancipation of slaves. The bill for admitting West Virginia into the Union passed the U.S. Senate on July 14, 1862. It was approved by the U.S. House on December 30, and President Lincoln signed the legislation at midnight on December 31, 1862.

On April 20, 1863, after receiving word that West Virginians ratified their constitutional amendment, President Lincoln issued a proclamation that provided statehood for the territory 60 days later. Thus, West Virginia entered the Union as the 35th state on June 20, 1863. The northern and western boundaries of West Virginia, of course, were fixed because they were previously Virginia's borders with Maryland, Pennsylvania, Ohio and Kentucky.

The eastern boundary, along the Appalachian Mountains, bordered Virginia. This line holds a unique place in history: It is the only dual-state boundary created without a formal survey. The boundary was created with the county lines that existed at the time. It is clear the earliest conventions in Wheeling were uncertain which counties to include in the new state. There were numerous proposals on what territory to claim. One included Buchanan and Wise counties in southwest Virginia, which would have given West Virginia a panhandle on the south, similar to the panhandle along the Ohio River south of Pittsburgh. Another proposal would have placed the eastern boundary along the Blue Ridge Mountains, taking in all of the Great Valley region from Winchester, Virginia, to Abingdon, Virginia.

The matter was finally resolved when West Virginia decided to take in several counties east of the Appalachian Mountains — Berkeley, Greenbrier, Hamshire, Hardy, Jefferson, McDowell, Mercer, Monroe, Morgan, Pendleton and Pocahontas. Thus, in 1863, the number of Virginia counties dropped from an all-time high of 149 to 99 — a total of 50 counties were cut from Virginia to create West Virginia.

Berkeley and Jefferson counties were important additions to West Virginia. These eastern panhandle counties, east of the Allegheny Mountains, were purposefully tacked on so the Baltimore and Ohio Railroad, a Union lifeline, could be wholly within Northern territory. The new state sent 30,000 men to the Union army and another 10,000 to the South. More than a dozen Union generals, and nearly as many Southern generals, were from West Virginia.

After the Civil War, Jefferson and Berkeley county leaders changed their minds. They wanted to return to Virginia. Virginia ultimately sued West Virginia to recover the two counties, but lost the battle in the U.S. Supreme Court. Following West Virginia's admission into the Union, Governor Pierpoint's administration moved from Wheeling to Alexandria (see T-14: Northern Virginia) to govern the Virginia area under federal control. Pierpoint, known as the "Father of West Virginia," was named by President Lincoln as the provisional governor of Virginia after the Civil War. He moved to Richmond and served in that capacity until April 1868.

Another legal battle resulted after Virginia asked West Virginia to reunite after the Civil War's end. West Virginia refused. Virginia then asked West Virginia to pay part of the state debt at the time of separation. Legal battles continued over the debt issue until 1915, when the U.S. Supreme Court ruled that West Virginia owed Virginia $12,393,929.50. West Virginia made its final payment in 1939. Except for the secession of Southern states, West Virginia's creation became the only change in the nation's map as a result of the Civil War.

business hours, or telephone the center at (304) 876-5429.

Historic Sites

In Shepherdstown, Shepherd College was founded in 1871, just five years after the end of the Civil War. It is the namesake of Thomas Shepherd, founder of Shepherdstown. For more information, telephone Shepherd College at (304) 876-5000 during business hours. In Boonsboro, Maryland, the **Boonsborough Museum** is a small, quaint facility for avid history buffs. The museum has an erratic sched-ule, but when it is open — Sundays, from May through September, from 1 to 5 PM — it offers an extensive Civil War exhibit. The museum is at 113 N. Main Street in Boonsboro. For more information, telephone (301) 432-5151.

Shopping

Downtown Shepherdstown has a number of specialty shops, particularly those that cater to students at Shepherd College. Stroll along German, Princess and Washington streets.

Tour 2
Harpers Ferry

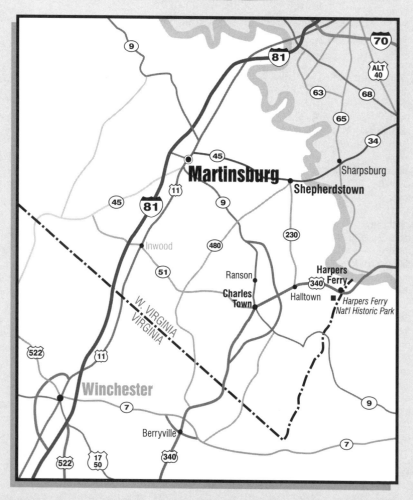

TOUR 2
Harpers Ferry

About This Tour

This tour route covers the lower portion of the Cumberland Valley, the West Virginia panhandle and the northern Shenandoah Valley. This tour is the second of five in succession — along with T-1: Sharpsburg, T-3: New Market, T-4: Staunton and T-5: Lexington — that cover the long stretch of the Great Valley that runs through Pennsylvania, Maryland, West Virginia and Virginia.

The tour begins by exiting Shepherdstown, West Virginia, at the end of T-1 and ends in Winchester, Virginia. Shepherdstown is about 24 miles west of Frederick, Maryland, and about 7 miles east of Martinsburg, West Virginia. This route, south of the Potomac River, follows the north-south trough through the mountains and takes the traveler from the Cumberland Valley to the Shenandoah Valley.

This area is part of the Great Valley that stretches along the eastern slope of the Appalachian Mountains. The Great Wagon Road through the Great Valley followed an old buffalo trail used by Native Americans — mainly the Tuscarora and Shawnee — to travel from the Southern highlands to the Great Lakes.

The Great Wagon Road was inundated by European pioneers, mainly German and Scotch-Irish settlers, who landed at Philadelphia in the early 18th century and settled this region's mountain highlands. Germans began settling in this region in the early 1700s, followed almost immediately by Scottish and Irish pioneers. The settlers found a fertile valley all along the Great Wagon Road, near the present-day cities of Morgantown, West Virginia, and Winchester, Virginia.

Civil War action took place throughout this region. In 1859, two years prior to the outbreak of war, John Brown staged a raid on Harpers Ferry. He was captured and later tried in Charles Town, West Virginia, where he was hanged. This area was included in CSA Gen. Thomas J. "Stonewall" Jackson's famous Shenandoah Valley Campaign of 1862, and there was significant action at Harpers Ferry, and at nearby Antietam and South Mountain, that year.

In 1863, CSA Gen. Robert E. Lee led his Confederate troops on a sweep through Winchester, Virginia, and Martinsburg, West Virginia, on the way north to the Battle of Gettysburg. In 1864, CSA Gen. Jubal Anderson "Old Jube" Early led his troops through the region, pushing north and east on an attempted invasion of Washington, D.C.

Travel Tips

The preceding tour — T-1: Sharpsburg — followed U.S. Highway 11, which runs parallel to Interstate 81. This tour utilizes more rural routes east of U.S. 11 before winding its way west to Martinsburg, West Virginia, and then Winchester, Virginia, two communities on U.S. 11 and I-81.

The rural roadways in the early part of this route, as well as U.S. 11 itself, weave through a number of quaint, attractive valley communities. Generally, U.S. Highway 340 and U.S. 11 are four-lane, divided highways. This is great farming country, so be alert to slow-moving farm vehicles. There are a series of small, local radio stations that report weather conditions — WINC 1400 AM, WNTW 610 AM and WBPP 104.9 FM are three — but these report on traffic conditions only in extreme circumstances. Citizens band radio users can find traffic information on Channel 19. State police usually monitor Channel 9. Mobile telephone signals are sporadic through this vicinity.

The tour ends in Winchester, where we

Photo: Harpers Ferry National Historical Park

These old Harpers Ferry buildings now house the John Brown Museum.

suggest you plan having dinner and spending the night. Recommended accommodations are listed in Chapter 22; our dining suggestions are in Chapter 23. It is a good idea to review these recommendations before traveling throughout this stretch of the Great Valley. In addition to our suggestions, there are the expected fast-food facilities, along with gas stations and shops, near Harpers Ferry, Charles Town and Martinsburg, all in West Virginia.

Harpers Ferry Tour Begins . . .

SHEPHERDSTOWN, W.VA. TO HALLTOWN, W.VA.

Exiting downtown Shepherdstown, follow signs for W.Va. Highway 230 south. Note that W.Va. 230 through downtown Shepherdstown changes street names — follow the route along German, Princess and Washington streets. Outside town, this two-lane country road runs through the rural countryside for 9

miles to Halltown. W.Va. 230 becomes Halltown Road in the village and ends at a junction with U.S. 340.

Halltown, W.Va.

Col. Lewis Washington, George Washington's great-grandnephew, lived at Beallair in the vicinity of Halltown. The colonel had a sword that Prussia's Frederick the Great gave George Washington. The sword was inscribed, "The oldest general in the world to the greatest."

John Brown, just before his raid on Harpers Ferry, captured Col. Washington in Halltown and held him hostage. Brown stole the famous sword and was wearing it when he was captured at Harpers Ferry.

HALLTOWN TO HARPERS FERRY, W.VA.
From the stop sign at Halltown Road, turn left on U.S. 340 and go 1.7 miles to Harpers Ferry.

Harpers Ferry, W.Va.

Harpers Ferry, originally called The Hole, is in the water gap of the Blue Ridge Mountains at the confluence of the Shenandoah and Potomac rivers. Robert Harper settled the village in the 1730s and operated a ferry across the Potomac. The town was incorporated in the mid-1800s, when there were about 3,000 residents.

In the late 1700s, President George Washington suggested Harpers Ferry as the site for a federal arsenal and armory. Work began on the armory in 1796, and it produced its first weapons in 1801. Meriwether Lewis, on his way to Pittsburgh, stopped in Harpers Ferry to pick up rifles from the armory for his famous Lewis and Clark Expedition. In 1803, Henry Dearborn, President Jefferson's secretary of war, issued a requisition for production of the Model 1803 rifle, and by 1810, more than 10,000 rifles were being produced a year.

The Harpers Ferry armory and arsenal helped the economy of the surrounding Virginia countryside. Small industries sprang up on adjacent Virginius Island. Business continued growing into the 19th century, with the arrival of the Chesapeake & Ohio Canal and the Baltimore & Ohio Railroad.

On October 16, 1859, this peaceful, prosperous town received a jolt. It was raided by John Brown. The abolitionist spent months plotting his attack on Harpers Ferry because it was "the safest natural entrance to the Great Black Way. . . . Here, amid the mighty protection of overwhelming numbers, lay a path from slavery to freedom."

A free African American, Heywood Shepherd, was the first casualty of the raid. He was shot after disobeying an order from Brown's men to halt. A self-described "instrument of God sent to liberate all slaves," Brown captured the federal arsenal and refused to surrender. He was captured two mornings later when federal troops stormed the arsenal's firehouse. Brown was indicted and tried for treason in nearby Charles Town (see separate listing).

Harpers Ferry was a strategic location during the Civil War, and troops of both armies occupied the town at various times. The arsenal and armory were destroyed in April 1861 by federal authorities, who set the buildings ablaze to keep the 17,000 stored muskets out of Confederate hands. In September 1862, just days before Antietam, CSA Gen. "Stonewall" Jackson captured a 12,500-man Union garrison at this river town. It was considered the largest surrender of Union troops during the war.

A Union cavalry group was able to avoid capture in an event known as the Davis and Davis Escape, engineered by USA Col. Benjamin Franklin Davis (from Mississippi, interestingly) and USA Lt. Col. Hasbrouck Davis of Illinois. The two Davises rode together at the head of the column of escapees. The Union soldiers reached the rear of their line at Greencastle, Pennsylvania, without losing a soldier. Along the way, the Federals captured nearly 100 Confederate ammunition wagons and their 600-man escort.

After the Confederate surrender at Appomattox, Harpers Ferry established a normal school for the education of freed African Americans. The school became Storer College — the lone bright hope for the post-war community. It closed down in 1955, and the college facilities are now used by the National Park Service for training exercises. The federal arsenal never reopened, and the town was hit by several Potomac floods. Later, the Potomac River bridge — where the tollgate keeper was a retired minister — became a favorite spot for eloping couples.

━━━━━━━━━

HARPERS FERRY TO HARPERS FERRY NATIONAL HISTORICAL PARK VISITOR CENTER

Entering Harpers Ferry on U.S. 340, the Harpers Ferry National Historical Park is on the east (right) side of the highway. Follow signs to the visitors center.

Harpers Ferry National Historical Park Visitor Center
U.S. Hwy. 340, Harpers Ferry, W.Va.
• (304) 535-6298

The visitors center provides a panoramic view of the national historical park's 2,500 acres in three states — Maryland, West Virginia and Virginia. The center has a brochure that outlines the extensive park sites in and around the lower section of Harpers Ferry. Various historic buildings in the park are highlighted on a map in the brochure. The sites are keyed to numbers marking important locations — more than two dozen in all — that include Bolivar Heights, Camp Hill, Virginius Island, Maryland Heights and Loudoun Heights, all rich in Civil War history.

Automobiles are restricted to only a few streets in Harpers Ferry, so it is best to use one of several buses that run every 10 to 15 minutes to transport visitors from the center to downtown and back. The buses are not handi-capped-accessible, but the National Park Service provides a special access van for handicapped visitors. Both the van and the buses are free. The visitors center is operated by the NPS and is open every day except Christmas from 8 AM to 5 PM. During summer, the center remains open until 6 PM. In winter, the NPS conducts weekend tours of Harpers Ferry, weather permitting. The center has restrooms, is handicapped-accessible and has a picnic area.

HARPERS FERRY TO
CHARLES TOWN, W.VA.
From the Harpers Ferry National Historical Park, return to U.S. 340, turn left (west) and go 4.7 miles to Charles Town city limits.

Charles Town, W.Va.

Charles Town is the county seat of Jefferson County, West Virginia. Its two-word name keeps it from being confused with Charleston, the West Virginia state capital. In the 1780s, George Washington's youngest brother, Charles, laid out this community. Today, the city bears his name, and many of its streets are named in honor of Washington family members. The Jefferson County Courthouse, for example, is at the corner of George and Washington streets.

Harpers Ferry Personality: John Brown

John Brown, a Connecticut native, was an abolitionist all his life. A religious fanatic, Brown moved to Kansas in 1855 to join in the fight to keep the state from being admitted to the Union as a slave state. He was accused of leading an anti-slavery siege of bloody murder in the Kansas Territory in 1856, and he began developing plans in 1857 for an invasion of the South to free African-American slaves.

Brown planned a stronghold for free African Americans in the western Virginia mountains. He considered Harpers Ferry a perfect location because of its proximity to the Mason-Dixon line that forms the Maryland-Pennsylvania border. Brown had an arsenal with thousands of arms to outfit his guerilla force.

Brown's "army of liberation" struck on the night of October 16. Barricaded in the armory's firehouse, Brown and his band of 21 fellow abolitionists were captured when federal troops stormed the building. The reserve Virginia militia, led by Brevet Col. Robert E Lee and Lt. James Ewell Brown "Jeb" Stuart — both later Confederate generals — included an aspiring 21-year-old actor named John Wilkes Booth. Brown was tried and convicted of murder, treason and conspiracy. He was hanged December 2, 1859 at Charles Town (see separate listing). A Northern martyr, Brown was immortalized in the marching song, "John Brown's Body."

Photo: Harpers Ferry National Historical Park

John Brown was indicted, tried for treason and hanged in Charles Town, WVa.

This overhead shot shows the Master Armor's House at Harpers Ferry.

James and Dolley Madison were married in 1794 near Charles Town at an estate, Harewood, where Dolley's sister, Lucy Payne Washington, was the mistress. Harewood was one of many fine old estates in the area that suffered due to Civil War action. In August 1864, USA Gen. Philip Henry Sheridan's troops were defeated by CSA Gen. Jubal A. Early's men in fighting that swept over Harewood's neighboring farms, including Sulgrave, Tuscawillow, Cedar Lawn and Locust Hill.

A number of Jefferson County residents supported the Confederacy, and the town paid a heavy price at the hands of Union soldiers. Just before the Civil War, John Brown was tried in the Jefferson County Courthouse for his ill-fated raid on Harpers Ferry, found guilty and hanged in Charles Town. Charles Town was the home of W.L. Wilson, U.S. postmaster-general in the late 1800s. Wilson is credited with establishing the nation's first rural free mail delivery.

CHARLES TOWN CITY LIMITS TO THE JOHN BROWN GALLOWS SITE
Continue west on U.S. 340, which becomes W.Va. Highway 51 and then Washington Street. From the city limits, go west 0.3 mile to S. Samuel Street, turn left (south)

and go five blocks to the Gallows Site historical marker.

John Brown's Gallows Site
S. Samuel St., Charles Town, W.Va.

Following his trial and conviction in the county courthouse in Charles Town, John Brown was hanged at the gallows on present-day Samuel Street. There is a historical marker at the site. A Virginia militiaman, Maj. Thomas Jackson — later the prominent Confederate general "Stonewall" — commanded a howitzer unit that guarded the gallows site at the Brown hanging. John Wilkes Booth (T-13, T-15) was a member of that militia unit.

JOHN BROWN'S GALLOWS SITE TO THE JEFFERSON COUNTY COURTHOUSE
Return north on Samuel Street, which will become one-way before you reach Washington Street. Turn right on E. Congress Street, go one block, turn left on S. Mildred Street and go one block to Washington Street. Turn left (west) and go one block beyond Samuel Street to George Street and the Jefferson County Courthouse on the right.

Jefferson County Courthouse
George and Washington Sts.,
Charles Town, W.Va.

The restored 1836 courthouse still is used as a Jefferson County government building. Visitors can see the room where John Brown was tried, found guilty and sentenced to death

for leading the raid on Harpers Ferry. There is a marker outside on the curb.

◼◼◼◼◼◼◼◼◼◼

CHARLES TOWN TO
MARTINSBURG, W.VA.
From the Jefferson County Court-

Martinsburg Personality: Charles James Faulkner

Charles James Faulkner, son-in-law of Elisha Boyd, was born in 1806 in Martinsburg, when the town was a part of Virginia. A law school graduate of Georgetown University in Washington, D.C., Faulkner practiced law in Martinsburg. He served in the Virginia House of Delegates on and off from 1829 to 1849, and he was a Virginia member of a commission that debated a boundary dispute between Virginia and Maryland.

Faulkner was elected to the U.S. House of Representatives from Virginia and served from 1851 to 1859, when he was appointed U.S. minister to France by President James Buchanan. Returning to the United States in August 1861, Faulkner was detained by Federal authorities and charged with negotiating arms sales for the Confederacy while in Paris. Released in December 1861, Faulkner negotiated his own freedom after he suggested he be exchanged for a New York congressman who was taken prisoner by Confederates at the Battle of 1st Manassas.

Faulkner's son, also named Charles James Faulkner, was born at Boydville in September 1847. In 1859, the younger Faulkner accompanied his father to Paris, where the youth attended school. In 1862, Faulkner, 15, entered

Photo: Harpers Ferry National Historical Park

Charles James Faulkner served as an assistant adjutant general under CSA Gen. Jackson.

Virginia Military Institute (VMI), and two years later, in May 1864, he marched with the corps of cadets who fought in the Battle of New Market in Shenandoah County, Virginia (see T-3: New Market).

The elder Faulkner also joined the Confederacy during the Civil War and served as assistant adjutant general on the staff of CSA Gen. "Stonewall" Jackson. After the war, he returned to his Martinsburg law practice and served one additional two-year term in the U.S. House from West Virginia. He died at Boydville at the age of 78 and is buried in the family cemetery at the estate.

After the Civil War, the younger Faulkner graduated from the law school at the University of Virginia and began practicing law in Martinsburg. Elected a circuit court judge in 1880, he presided on the bench seven years until his election to the U.S. Senate, where he served for 12 more years.

Faulkner then retired from public life and practiced law in his hometown and pursued his agricultural interests at his estate. He died at Boydville in January 1929 and is buried at Old Norbourne Cemetery in Martinsburg.

house, leave Charles Town on George Street (W.Va. Highway 9), go west 3 miles, turn left, still on W.Va. 9, and go 11.3 miles to the Queen Street exit in Martinsburg, W.Va.

Berkeley County, W.Va.

This tour route, between Charles Town and Martinsburg, enters Berkeley County, West Virginia. The county was established by the Virginia General Assembly in 1772 and named for Norborne Berkeley, the Baron de Botetourt, who was governor of Virginia and died in office that year.

Berkeley County, like neighboring Jefferson and Morgan counties, was a Virginia county "annexed" by West Virginia in 1863. After the Civil War, these three counties that form the West Virginia panhandle along the Potomac River tried unsuccessfully to have their land retroceded to Virginia.

Martinsburg, W.Va.

Martinsburg is the seat of Berkeley County. Col. Bryan Martin, a wealthy landowner, established this community in 1778. Gen. Adam Stephen, George Washington's second-in-command during the French and Indian War and a Revolutionary War veteran, built his E. John Street home out of native limestone. The Baltimore & Ohio railroad reached Martinsburg in 1842. Seven years later, the railroad constructed a roundhouse and shops in the town. With the railroad, Martinsburg became a major valley supply and shipping center.

Martinsburg's loyalties were split during the Civil War. The town was raided in 1861 by CSA Gen. "Stonewall" Jackson, who burned the old roundhouse and rail shops, captured a number of locomotives and had them drawn by horse to Winchester, Virginia, 20 miles south.

Twice more, Martinsburg suffered intense Civil War action. Opposing forces fought in the vicinity in mid-June 1863 just before the Battle of Gettysburg (T-6), and again in August 1864 as part of USA Gen. Sheridan's Shenandoah Valley Campaign. After the war, the B&O Railroad constructed Martinsburg's present-day west roundhouse and two rail shops. The railroad built the present-day east roundhouse in 1872. These buildings are some of the last remaining examples of American industrial railroad architecture still in use.

MARTINSBURG TO THE BOYDVILLE HOUSE

From the Queen Street exit on W.Va. 9, turn left (west) on Queen Street toward downtown Martinsburg and go 0.6 mile to the Boydville House on the left.

Boydville House
Queen St., Martinsburg, W.Va.
• **(304) 263-1448**

Boydville, an elegant estate known for its fine workmanship, was built in 1812 by Elisha Boyd, a general in the War of 1812. The estate was constructed on land Boyd purchased from Gen. Adam Stephen. Boydville was the home of Elisha Boyd's son-in-law, Charles James Faulkner (see Martinsburg Personality in this chapter).

The estate was saved from destruction during the Civil War after President Lincoln, learning of Union occupation in Martinsburg, signed a presidential order in June 1863 to preserve the historic structure. Today, the house is operated as a historic inn: Boydville, The Inn at Martinsburg.

BOYDVILLE HOUSE TO BERKELEY COUNTY COURTHOUSE

Continue west on Queen Street for 0.4 mile to the intersection with King streets. Along the way, at the intersection of Stephen and E. Queen streets, are several old Martinsburg woolen mills buildings that have been converted into modern-day shopping outlets. The Berkeley County Courthouse is at the intersection of Queen and King streets.

Berkeley County Courthouse
King and Queen Sts., Martinsburg, W.Va.

Author Porte Crayon — Union Gen. David Hunter Strother's pen name — lived in Martinsburg. Crayon wrote his *Personal Rec-*

Martinsburg Side Trips: Jackson Headquarters, Sheridan Headquarters

From the Berkeley County Courthouse, walk west one block to the intersection of Queen and Burke streets.

In 1861, CSA Gen. Jackson made his headquarters at a house once located at Queen and Burke streets. USA Gen. Sheridan used the same house for his headquarters in 1864 during his Shenandoah Valley Campaign.

ollection of the War, in which he said the Martinsburg townspeople "kept their headquarters at the courthouse, sat up nights, arrested each other and everybody else they found prowling about." The Berkeley Courthouse was used as a prison for Confederate spy Belle Boyd, a Martinsburg native. The courthouse is still in use today, but there is no obvious Civil War damage.

From Queen and Burke streets, walk west another block to the intersection of Queen and Martin streets. St. John's Lutheran Church, at Queen and Martin streets, was used as a Union hospital during the war. From the church, return to the Berkeley County Courthouse at Queen and King streets.

Martinsburg to Winchester, Va.
From the Berkeley County Courthouse, take King Street (U.S. 11) south toward Winchester, Va. Go 0.3 miles to Winchester Street, turn left and go 13 miles to the Virginia-West Virginia state line.

Frederick County, Va.
This route crosses from West Virginia into Frederick County, Virginia, which was formed in 1738 and named for Frederick, England's Prince of Wales and the father of King George III.

Continue on U.S. 11 south of the state line 6 miles to the intersection with I-81. Take I-81 south 4

Martinsburg Personality: Belle Boyd

Belle Boyd, a noted Confederate spy, was born in Martinsburg in 1843. She was only 17 when she began running information on Union troop movements to CSA Gen. Jackson during his 1861 Valley Campaign. Boyd knew the terrain well. Besides Martinsburg, she lived in various other communities in West Virginia, as well as in Front Royal, Virginia. She was arrested twice, and twice released for lack of evidence.

Often, Boyd was imprisoned at the courthouse in Martinsburg. She escaped the country in 1863 and sailed to England, where she became a stage performer. Boyd returned to America after the war and went on tour, where she died, at Kibourne, Wisconsin, in 1900.

miles to exit 313-B in Winchester. (NOTE: An sign on I-81 directs travelers to use exit 315 — not 313 — for various historic Winchester sites. We recommend exit 313-B because it leads directly to the Winchester-Frederick County Visitor Center.)

Winchester, Va.

Winchester, the seat of Frederick County, is one of the oldest communities in Western Virginia. Originally known as Frederick Town, the town name was changed in 1752 in honor of Winchester, a city in England. Soon, Winchester, Virginia, became an important colonial transportation and commercial center, mainly because of the Great Wagon Road that spanned the length of the Great Valley.

The Winchester area is rich in Colonial history. A number of prominent military leaders — mainly Virginian George Washington and British Gen. Edmund Braddock — visited and headquartered in Winchester during the French and Indian War in the 1750s. Daniel Morgan, a wagoner who served in both the French and Indian War and the Revolutionary War, was a native of Frederick County and is buried in Winchester. George Washington was elected to the Virginia House of Burgesses as a representative of Frederick County and Winchester.

Winchester was also a prized location during the Civil War. Winchester is in the middle of the Great Valley, and during the Civil War it was a strategic location along the path of the old Great Wagon Road. To the north, the Potomac River flows east, cutting through the Blue Ridge at Harpers Ferry on its way to Washington, D.C., and beyond.

During the war, and still today, an important rail line followed the Potomac from upland West Virginia to eastern stations. Winchester lay in the path of a major route, the Valley Pike, often laden with grain and supply wagons. This path also was a major roadway for Confederates moving north and Federal troops moving south. From early 1862 to late 1864, Winchester changed flags no fewer than 70 times.

During the war, Winchester citizens generally remained loyal to the Confederacy; some remained neutral as the community frequently adjusted to changing occupation. Winchester was the scene of three significant Civil War battles: the First, Second and Third Battles of Winchester, in 1862, 1863 and 1864, respectively. All three engagements were strategically significant to the Confederacy, as they lured Union military might away from Richmond, the South's capital city.

The First Battle of Winchester was fought May 25, 1862. The battle took place just south of town, near Abram's Creek. CSA Gen. "Stonewall" Jackson, as part of his famed 1862 Shenandoah Valley Campaign, defeated USA Gen. Nathaniel Prentiss Banks, who was retreating north along the Valley Pike. Jackson's force of 17,000 Confederates outnumbered Banks' army two-to-one and drove the Union troops north (along present-day U.S. 11) and across the Potomac River.

The Second Battle of Winchester was fought June 14 and 15, 1863. This two-day battle took place around Winchester's northwestern area and is also known as the Battle of Stephenson's Depot. CSA Gen. Robert E. Lee, following action at Chancellorsville — and the loss of CSA Gen. Jackson — moved northwest across Virginia to invade Maryland and Pennsylvania. CSA Gen. Richard Stoddert Ewell, one of Lee's top commanders, defeated Federals in the command of USA Gen. Robert Huston Milroy. Milroy withdrew to the north and suffered losses on the way to the Potomac River. Following this engagement, Lee's army pushed north toward Gettysburg.

The Third Battle of Winchester was fought Sept. 19, 1864. This battle took place along the northeastern section of Winchester and was also known as the Battle of Opequon, after nearby Opequon Creek. USA Gen. Sheridan put a stop to CSA Gen. Early's Shenandoah Valley Campaign and the Confederate presence in the region. Sheridan's men moved along the Berryville Pike (present-day Va. Highway 7) and struck Early's troops in a day-long engagement. Early retreated south, along the Valley Pike (present-day U.S. 11). The opposing generals met again two days later at Fisher's Hill south of Strasburg, Virginia.

Photo: Library of Virginia

CSA Gen. Turner Ashby and his cavalrymen were among the first at the scene of John Brown's raid on Harpers Ferry.

WINCHESTER TO THE WINCHESTER-FREDERICK COUNTY VISITOR CENTER

From exit 313-B on I-81 go right on U.S. Highway 50 (Millwood Avenue) for 0.4 mile to the intersection of Millwood Avenue and Pleasant Valley Road. Turn right and go 0.1 mile to the Winchester-Frederick County Visitor Center on the right.

Winchester-Frederick County Visitor Center
1360 S. Pleasant Valley Rd., Winchester, Va. • (540) 662-4135, (800) 662-1360

The Winchester-Frederick County Visitor Center has a slogan: "Where the Shenandoah Valley Begins, and History Never Ends." It's a nice play on words that describes Frederick County's location in the northwestern part of Virginia. The center has an 18-minute video, *Welcome to the Top*, on city and county history and attractions, and it offers brochures and travel information on places to see in and around the Winchester and Frederick County area. In addition, the center sells booklets,

maps, a calendar of events and a community profile. Operated by the city, county and chamber of commerce, the center is open every day except Thanksgiving, Christmas and New Year's Day from 9 AM to 5 PM. It is handicapped-accessible and has restrooms. Tourists can call the center in advance for free copies of a dining and lodging guide and a calendar of area events.

WINCHESTER VISITORS CENTER TO JACKSON'S HEADQUARTERS

From the visitors center, return to Pleasant Valley Road, turn right (north), go 0.8 mile to the first traffic signal, turn left (west) and follow Cork Street for 0.8 mile into the Winchester historical district to Washington Street (U.S. 11). Turn right (north), go four blocks and turn left (west) on Piccadilly Street (U.S. Highway 522). The road immediately curves to the right (north) and becomes Fairmont Street. Continue north two blocks to North Avenue, turn right (east) and go one block, turn right (south) and go a half-block on N. Braddock Street to Jackson's Headquarters on the right. There is on-street parking.

"Stonewall" Jackson's Headquarters
415 N. Braddock St., Winchester, Va.
• (540) 667-3242

CSA Gen. "Stonewall" Jackson's headquarters was the home of Lt. Col. Lewis T. Moore, who invited Jackson to use the house as his headquarters prior to the Shenandoah Valley Campaign of 1862. Jackson used the house from November 1861 to March 1862. That winter, Jackson invited his wife to join him at the house, where the couple spent Christmas. A registered state and national landmark, this Gothic Revival-style house is open Monday through Saturday from 10 AM to 4 PM and Sunday noon to 4 PM from April 1 to October 31. From November 1 to March 31, the facility is available for tours by appointment. Call the Winchester-Frederick County

Historical Society, which administers the building, at (540) 662-6550 for more information. Admission is $3.50 for adults, $3 for seniors and $1.75 for children 6 through 12. A family rate of $8.75 is also offered. The house is not handicapped-accessible.

"STONEWALL" JACKSON'S HEADQUARTERS TO HANDLEY LIBRARY

From "Stonewall" Jackson's Headquarters, continue south 0.2 mile on one-way N. Braddock Street to the intersection of Braddock and Piccadilly streets. The Handley Library is on the northwest corner of the intersection.

Handley Library
100 W. Piccadilly St., Winchester, Va.
• (540) 662-9041

The Archives Room of the Handley Library contains volumes of newspapers, diaries, maps, correspondence, photographs, census records, books and original manuscripts related to Winchester and Frederick County history, particularly the Civil War period. Some of the materials date to the early 1700s. The Archives Room is open to the public Tuesday and Wednesday from 1 to 9 PM and Thursday through Saturday from 10 AM to 5 PM. It is closed Sunday and Monday. Admission is free and the facility is handicapped-accessible.

Winchester Personality: Hunter Holmes McGuire

According to historian Joseph W. A. Whitehorne, Winchester was filled with wounded soldiers following CSA Gen. Jackson's 1862 Shenandoah Valley Campaign. The wounded were hospitalized in various public buildings, including the old Union Hotel. They were treated by a group of Federal medical officers who volunteered to remain behind after their own forces withdrew. Up until this time, all enemy personnel were treated the same, regardless of their function. So, those doctors that remained in Winchester faced capture and the prospect of months in grim Confederate prisons.

Winchester native Hunter Holmes McGuire, Jackson's 26-year-old surgeon, urged Jackson to allow the Federal doctors to continue caring for their patients. Jackson agreed, so long as the doctors stuck to medical business and refrained from performing any hostile acts. Jackson instructed McGuire to formalize an accord with the Federal doctors, and the Union physicians were given their unconditional freedom. In exchange, the Union doctors agreed to work for the freedom of Confederate doctors when they got back to their own lines.

This sensible, merciful approach to medical care assured better patient treatment during the war, and it made an impression on the senior leaders of both the North and South. Within a month, both sides agreed that their medical officers should — in the words of USA Gen. George B. McClellan — "be viewed as non-combatants." This policy later was extended to include chaplains and any other individuals involved with medical work.

Thus, McGuire's practical suggestion established a practice that since has become global. McGuire benefited directly from the policy when he was captured at Waynesboro, Virginia, in March 1865, then released on orders of USA Gen. Philip Sheridan.

After the war, McGuire enjoyed a distinguished medical career in Richmond (see T-17), where he taught at the Medical College of Virginia. He founded St. Luke's Hospital and a nurses' training school. Later, he served as president of the American Medical Association. When he died in March 1900, he was one of the best-loved and well-known figures in Virginia. A statue of McGuire was erected in Capital Square in Richmond in 1904. Few of his distinguished contributions have had a more lasting effect on more people than his wartime establishment of medical non-combatant status. As historian Whitehorne once wrote, we know what one grateful Federal soldier meant when he said McGuire "humanized war."

Winchester Side Trip: Stonewall Cemetery, National Cemetery

Two blocks east of Kurtz Cultural Center is Mount Hebron Cemetery, which includes the Stonewall Cemetery. Just to the north on National Avenue is National Cemetery. There are 3,000 Confederate graves in Stonewall Cemetery, and an obelisk honors more than 800 unknown Confederates that were killed in battles in the vicinity. CSA Gen. Turner Ashby (see T-4) is buried in the cemetery. National Cemetery is one of the largest national cemeteries in Virginia and includes the bodies of more than 4,000 Union soldiers — half of them unidentified. Some of the action of the Third Battle of Winchester in 1864 was fought in the vicinity of this cemetery, along present-day Berryville Avenue (Va. 7) northeast of Winchester.

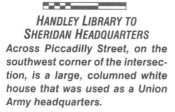

HANDLEY LIBRARY TO SHERIDAN HEADQUARTERS

Across Piccadilly Street, on the southwest corner of the intersection, is a large, columned white house that was used as a Union Army headquarters.

Sheridan Headquarters
Braddock and Piccadilly Sts., Winchester Va.

USA Gen. Sheridan used this attractive, columned house as his headquarters during the Third Battle of Winchester in 1864. Sheridan left the house on the morning of October 19, 1864, and rode south 8 miles along the Valley Pike (present-day U.S. 11) to rally his faltering troops at the Battle of Cedar Creek (see listing). The house now has a front-yard display of a large red apple, which symbolizes the city's dependence on the apple industry. The house is home to several commercial businesses and is not available for tours.

HANDLEY LIBRARY TO KURTZ CULTURAL CENTER

Continue south on one-way Braddock Street two blocks and turn left (east) on Boscawen Street four blocks — crossing over the attractive downtown pedestrian mall on former Loudoun Street. At the intersection of Boscawen and

Cameron streets is the old Winchester City Hall. Pay to park in one of several street or garage spaces available near this intersection. The Kurtz Cultural Center is across from City Hall at 2 N. Cameron Street.

Kurtz Cultural Center
2 N. Cameron St., Winchester, Va.
• (540) 722-6367

Kurtz Cultural Center boasts the Civil War Center, which includes an exhibit, "Shenandoah: Crossroads of the Civil War." This visit provides a thorough, interesting introduction to the Shenandoah Valley's important role during the war. The exhibit provides an overview of 15 military engagements, and it includes a summary of Valley campaigns conducted by CSA Gen. "Stonewall" Jackson and other leaders. Take advantage of the center's literature on Civil War attractions and sites as well as walking and driving tours. Admission is free. The center is open Sunday from noon to 5 PM and Monday through Saturday from 10 AM to 5 PM. It is handicapped-accessible.

After this side trip, return to downtown Winchester.

Harpers Ferry Tour Ends

Golf in the Carolinas

Covering courses in North and South Carolina

Other Tour Points of Interest

There is much to do in the Winchester area, Civil War-oriented and otherwise. For questions and assistance, ask for help at the Winchester-Frederick County Visitors Center (see listing).

Annual Events

Winchester is apple country, and the biggest event of the year is the **Shenandoah Apple Blossom Festival**, a 70-year-old, countywide event held for four days in late April or early May. Apples are the center of attention again in August at the annual, countywide **Apple Harvest Arts and Crafts Festival**. Other significant events include **George Washington's Birthday Celebration** (February), the **Frederick County Fair** (August), a Civil War skirmish sponsored by the **North-South Skirmish Association** (October) and historic holiday tours of museums and private homes (December).

Arts

Local artists are featured at **Kurtz Cultural Center**. The **Eugene B. Smith Gallery**, 156 N. Loudoun Street, (540) 667-6190, is on the mall in downtown Winchester and features the owner's art. **Gallery One**, 19 E. Boscawen Street, (540) 662-0233, features the work of local and regional artists. The **Shenandoah Fine Arts Gallery,** 1844 Valley Avenue, (540) 722-3855, sells prints, mainly Civil War-related art. In performing arts, **Shenandoah University** offers more than 300 performing arts programs during the year, and many are free. For more information, contact the box office at (540) 665-4569.

Historic Sites

Abram's Delight Museum, adjacent to the Winchester-Frederick County Visitor Center, was built with native limestone in 1754. The historic home gets its name from Abraham Hollingsworth, a Quaker who settled in Winchester in the early 18th century. Finding a suitable home site, complete with rich land and a clear, clean spring, he declared it, "A delight to behold." Abraham's son, Isaac, built the current house. In later days, the name was shortened from "Abraham's Delight." The house is open April 1 to October 31 from noon to 4 PM and Monday through Saturday from 10 AM to 4 PM. During the winter, tours can be arranged by appointment. For information, call (540) 662-6519.

George Washington's Office Museum, at the intersection of Braddock and Cork streets, is a registered state landmark. Washington used the little log building during the mid-1750s as a member of the Virginia militia. The museum is open daily from 9 AM to 5 PM. For information, call (540) 662-4412. The **Shenandoah Valley**

Discovery Museum is an exciting interactive science center for children and families. It features hands-on activities and exhibits, focusing on physical and natural sciences, along with other community and cultural exhibits. For more information, contact the Discovery Museum at (540) 722-2020.

Shopping

Try the **downtown mall** in Winchester for a variety of specialty shops and unique stores. The **Stone Soap Gallery**, 107 N. Loudoun Street, (540) 722-3976, offers country specialties, including food and crafts. It is open Monday through Saturday from 10 AM to 5 PM and Sunday 1 to 5 PM. It stays open an hour later on Fridays. Handcrafts are available at **Handworks Gallery**, 150 N. Loudoun Street, (540) 662-3927.

Winchester offers shoppers a wide variety of stores. Among the more prominent shopping areas is the **Apple Blossom Mall**, just off U.S. 50 near I-81. There is no greater enjoyment than a visit to the Frederick County countryside, where visitors can pick apples from any one of many orchards.

The **Blue Ridge Outlet Center** is in Martinsburg's old woolen mills buildings, at 315 W. Stephen Street. The buildings themselves date to the early 1900s. Inside are manufacturers' outlets including Anne Klein, Bass Shoe, Donna Karan, J. Crew, Jones New York and Woolrich. There are local treasures too, including a shop with West Virginia glass, and three places to snack. The outlet center is open Monday through Saturday from 10 AM to 6 PM and Sunday from 11 AM to 6 PM.

Tour 3
New Market

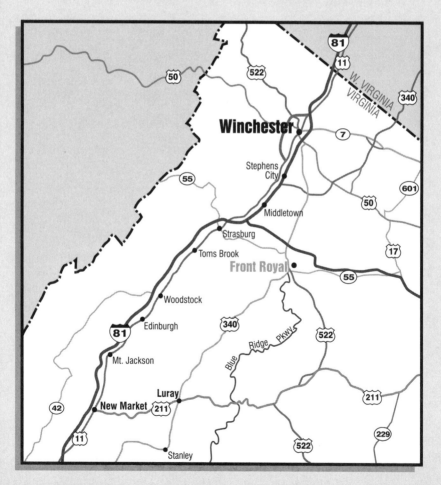

TOUR 3
New Market

About This Tour

This tour covers the Shenandoah Valley from Winchester, Virginia, to New Market, Virginia. The tour is the third of five in succession — from T-1: Sharpsburg through T-5: Lexington — that cover the long stretch of the Great Valley that runs through Pennsylvania, Maryland, West Virginia and Virginia. The route begins by exiting Winchester (see T-2: Harpers Ferry) and ends in New Market.

The Shenandoah Valley is part of the Great Valley, a natural trough that runs along the eastern slope of the Appalachian Mountains. Native Americans, the area's first inhabitants, used the Great Valley as a north-south route. The Great Wagon Road through the valley followed an old buffalo trail used by American Indians.

This region was settled by European pioneers, mainly German and Scotch-Irish, who landed at Philadelphia in the early 18th century and settled along the Appalachian Mountain highlands. German farmers established homesteads in the region in the early 1700s, followed within a few years by Scotch-Irish pioneers.

A word about the Shenandoah Valley's geography: This trough through the Great Valley is at its highest elevation near Roanoke, Virginia, about 175 miles south of Winchester. The valley floor descends in elevation nearer the Potomac River, north of Winchester. This means that travelers along the Valley Road — present-day U.S. Highway 11 or Interstate 81 — actually ascend "up" in elevation as they motor "down" — or south.

Civil War action took place throughout the Shenandoah Valley, beginning in June 1861 and continuing for the next three years. CSA Gen. Thomas Jonathan "Stonewall" Jackson fought his famous Shenandoah Valley Campaign in this region in 1862, and CSA Gen. Jubal Anderson "Old Jube" Early marched through the valley on his way to and from his attempted raid on Washington, D.C., in 1864.

Travel Tips

This tour route, from Winchester to New Market, follows U.S. 11 almost exclusively. Be alert to slow-moving farm vehicles along this route. Several small, local radio stations report weather conditions, but they only report traffic information in extreme circumstances. Citizens band radio users can find traffic information on Channel 19. State police usually monitor Channel 9. Mobile telephone signals are clear throughout the Shenandoah Valley.

This tour ends in New Market, where we suggest you plan evening dining and lodging. Recommended accommodations are listed in Chapter 22; dining suggestions are in Chapter 23. It is a good idea to review these recommendations before traveling this stretch of the Shenandoah Valley. In addition to our suggestions, there are the various expected fast-food facilities, gas stations, convenience stores and shops near Middletown, Strasburg and Mount Jackson, Virginia.

New Market Tour Begins . . .

WINCHESTER TO KERNSTOWN, VA.
From downtown Winchester, at the intersection of S. Braddock and Cork streets, exit the city south by Braddock Street (U.S. 11), and go 3.3 miles to Kernstown.

Photo: New Market Battlefield State Historical Park

The Hall of Valor Museum at New Market Battlefield Park features artifacts, models and films to relate the story of the battle.

Jackson held Winchester early in the war. Then, early in 1862, USA Gen. Banks moved south toward Winchester from the Potomac River, and Jackson moved south 40 miles to the village of Mount Jackson, Virginia. Nearly two weeks later, Jackson returned north on the Valley Road and met Union forces at Kernstown on March 23. Jackson was forced back south; the Union troops fell back north to Winchester. The enemy forces met again two days later in the First Battle of Winchester (see T-2).

In the second Kernstown battle, in July 1864, CSA Gen. Early pushed north through the Shenandoah Valley into Winchester and Frederick, Maryland, and moved northeast in an attempt to invade Washington. Meeting resistance near the nation's capital, Early fell back to near Winchester, only to face a Union force on July 24. The Federals, defeated in the battle, retired north and back across the Potomac River.

Abram's Creek, Va.

Along this route, at Abram's Creek, is the site of Civil War action during the First Battle of Winchester in 1862. On the morning of May 25, 1862, New England soldiers serving under USA Gen. Nathaniel Prentiss Banks held a position along the Valley Road, south of Winchester and north of Kernstown. The Union forces faced CSA Gen. "Stonewall" Jackson, who led his troops on an advance from the south. Later than morning, Jackson halted his advance guard at Abram's Creek to observe the Union position. Interestingly, in this same area a year later, June 1863, CSA Gen. Richard Stoddert Ewell instructed CSA Gen. Early to move around USA Gen. Robert Huston Milroy and attack a Union position west of Winchester.

Kernstown, Va.

Kernstown was the scene of two significant engagements in the Civil War. The First Battle of Kernstown was fought in March 1862 as part of CSA Gen. Jackson's Shenandoah Valley Campaign. The Second Battle of Kernstown was fought July 23 and 24, 1864, as part of CSA Gen. Early's raid on Washington, D.C.

KERNSTOWN TO STEPHENS CITY, VA.

Continue south on U.S. 11 for 3.5 miles to the community of Stephens City.

Stephens City, Va.

CSA Gen. Jackson's troops rested in the Stephens City vicinity in May 1862 on their way to the First Battle of Winchester. In May 1864, USA Gen. David Hunter ordered Stephens City burned to the ground, but a Union major in the 1st New York cavalry passionately pleaded with Hunter to not burn the town. USA Gen. Philip Henry Sheridan passed south through Stephens City in October 1864 on his way from Winchester to join his troops at the Battle of Cedar Creek.

STEPHENS CITY TO MIDDLETOWN, VA.

Continue south on U.S. 11 for 5.3 miles to Middletown.

Middletown, Va.

CSA Gen. Jackson and USA Gen. Banks fought a battle, related to the First Battle of Winchester, at Middletown on May 24, 1862.

MIDDLETOWN TO CEDAR CREEK BATTLEFIELD VISITOR CENTER

Continue south on U.S. 11 for 1.5 miles to the Cedar Creek Battlefield on the left (east) side of the highway.

Cedar Creek Battlefield Visitor Center
8437 Valley Pk., Middletown, Va.
• **(540) 869-2064, (888) OCT-1864**

The Cedar Creek Battlefield Visitor Center is on the east side of U.S. 11 and across the highway from the northernmost edge of the battlefield where Union and Confederate forces fought the Battle of Cedar Creek in October 1864. The visitors center is operated by the Cedar Creek Battlefield Foundation, a nonprofit organization that works to preserve land and promote the valor displayed at the Battle of Cedar Creek. Each year in October, the foundation conducts one of the nation's largest battle re-enactments. As of spring 1997,

the center will be open Monday through Saturday from 10 AM to 4 PM and Sunday from 1 to 4 PM. The center will feature exhibits on the 1864 Shenandoah Valley Campaign. The facility has restrooms and is handicapped-accessible.

Battle of Cedar Creek

USA Gen. Sheridan's army pushed south from Winchester toward Harrisonburg, Virginia, then turned back north toward Winchester, followed closely by a force under CSA Gen. Early. Along Cedar Creek, Early decided to attack Sheridan's men — Sheridan himself was in a conference in Washington. The engagement began a mile to the south near present-day Strasburg, Virginia, as Early's troops pushed north toward Belle Grove Plantation (see listing in this chapter).

Early moved out on the night of October 18, 1864, and was successful during the hours between sunrise and mid-morning. In fact, the Confederates roused Union soldiers from their campsites and captured 1,300 prisoners and a number of guns. But Early's efforts evaporated when he failed to continue his push against the enemy. Sheridan, meanwhile, had returned from Washington to Winchester. Hearing about his troops in battle, Sheridan rushed south along the Valley Pike (present-day U.S. 11) to rally his men and further destroy the Confederate chance of victory.

Both Union and Confederate armies suffered severe casualties. The Confederates, defeated in the battle, essentially lost control of the Shenandoah Valley, and the Union success helped bring an end to the war. A Union infantryman, Capt. S.E. Howard, wrote of the battle: "Never since the world was created was such a crushing defeat turned into such a splendid victory as at Cedar Creek."

CEDAR CREEK BATTLEFIELD TO BELLE GROVE PLANTATION

Continue south on U.S. 11 for 0.3 mile to the Belle Grove Plantation entrance road on the right.

Belle Grove Plantation
336 Belle Grove Rd., Middletown, Va.
• (540) 869-2028

This fine old plantation, built in the 1790s, was the home of Maj. Isaac Hite Jr. and his family for almost 75 years. Hite's grandfather, Joist Hite, was one of the first settlers in the Shenandoah Valley. The younger Hite married Nelly Conway Madison, sister of President James Madison. Madison reportedly enlisted the help of Thomas Jefferson in helping his brother-in-law design Belle Grove, an attractive architectural prize of the Shenandoah. Madison and his wife, the former Dolley Payne Todd, reportedly spent part of their honeymoon at the estate.

The building includes a limestone dressed south facade. During the Battle of Cedar Creek, Union troops camped on the grounds of Belle Grove. Today, the estate is operated by the National Trust for Historic Preservation. From mid-March to mid-November, the plantation is open Monday through Saturday from 10 AM to 4 PM and Sunday from 1 to 5 PM. There is a $5 admission charge for adults, $4.50 for seniors older than 65 and $2.50 for children 13 through 17. Children younger than 13 are admitted free. The plantation is closed for tours in the winter, but some special events are scheduled during the off-season. A gift shop is open throughout the year, but only on weekdays in the winter. The plantation is not handicapped-accessible.

BELLE GROVE PLANTATION TO HUPP'S HILL BATTLEFIELD PARK AND STUDY CENTER

Return to U.S. 11 (Valley Pike),

Cedar Creek Personalities: USA Gen. Philip Henry Sheridan, President Abraham Lincoln

USA Gen. Philip Sheridan was not at his headquarters at Belle Grove Plantation, as the Confederates thought, prior to the Battle of Cedar Creek in October 1864. He was off in Washington at a War Department strategy session. After his meeting, Sheridan rode back to Winchester to spend the night. Early the next morning, he was roused from his bed by the sound of cannon fire. His troops, he soon learned, were engaged in a fierce struggle at Cedar Creek against troops led by CSA Gen. Jubal Early.

Sheridan sped off down the Valley Pike and arrived in time to rally his men and turn the tide against Confederate advances. Sheridan eventually was victorious, and a short time later received a note, dated October 22, from the Executive Mansion in Washington.

President Lincoln wrote the Union general: "With great pleasure I tender to you and your brave army, the thanks of the nation, and my own personal admiration and gratitude, for the months' operation in the Shenandoah Valley, and especially for the splendid work of Oct. 19, 1864."

You can just **Visit**, or you can 'be an
Insider

Choose from
a variety of
guides to
interesting
places
in Virginia.

turn right (south) and continue for 3 miles to the entrance on the right to Hupp's Hill Battlefield Park.

Along this route make three notes. First, just south of Belle Grove, U.S. 11 crosses Cedar Creek. This was a significant river crossing during the Battle of Cedar Creek. Also at Cedar Creek, U.S. 11 moves from Frederick County to Shenandoah County. Shenandoah was established in 1772 and originally named Dunmore County in honor of John Murray, the Earl of Dunmore and the royal governor of Virginia at the time. In 1778, in the midst of the Revolutionary War, Dunmore's name was so unpopular in Virginia the state legislature renamed the county Shenandoah, a Native American word that means "Beautiful Daughter of the Stars." Third, in the distance to the southeast, the imposing Signal Knob first becomes evident. The knob is the northern face of the Massanutten Mountain range. It was used from time to time by both the Union and Confederacy as a signal station to relay information on troop movements.

Hupp's Hill Battlefield Park and Study Center
U.S. 11 N., Strasburg, Va. • (540) 465-5884

Hupp's Hill gets its name from the local Hupp family, whose members homesteaded in the Strasburg area in the mid-1750s. This battlefield park and study center feature hands-on exhibits. Visitors can see and feel Civil War uniforms and weaponry. Younger visitors are encouraged to try on uniforms and civilian clothing patterned after those of the Civil War era. A topographic map shows the scope of the Battle of Cedar Creek as well as the trenches and gun placements of Hupp's Hill, an entrenchment built during the Cedar Creek conflict.

From April to October, the park and study center are open Monday through Saturday from 10 AM to 5 PM and Sunday from noon to 5 PM. During winter months, the park and study center is closed on Tuesdays along with Thanksgiving and Christmas. All other days, it closes at 4 PM. There's a $3.50 admission fee, but seniors and children get reduced rates. Group tours of the study center and guided tours of the nearby Cedar Creek battlefield are avail-

able. The park also features benches, picnic tables, various historical markers and a walking trail. The park is handicapped-accessible.

HUPP'S HILL TO STRASBURG, VA.
Return to U.S. 11, turn right (south) and go 0.9 mile to the traffic signal in downtown Strasburg.

Strasburg, Va.
Earthworks southwest of Strasburg were built by USA Gen. Banks during CSA Gen. "Stonewall" Jackson's Shenandoah Valley Campaign of 1862. Strasburg was the starting point of CSA Gen. Early's attack on Union positions at Belle Grove in the Battle of Cedar Creek in 1864.

STRASBURG TO FISHER'S HILL BATTLEFIELD CIVIL WAR SITE
At the Strasburg traffic signal, turn right on U.S. 11 and go 1.9 miles to Va. Highway 601.

Along U.S. 11, leaving the south side of Strasburg, this route crosses a little creek. A bridge over this creek collapsed in October 1864 under the weight of retreating Confederate troops after the Battle of Cedar Creek. The bridge mishap delayed Southern troops and enabled USA Gen. Sheridan to recapture some of his wagons and cannon that had been taken by the Confederates.

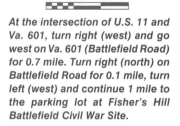

At the intersection of U.S. 11 and Va. 601, turn right (west) and go west on Va. 601 (Battlefield Road) for 0.7 mile. Turn right (north) on Battlefield Road for 0.1 mile, turn left (west) and continue 1 mile to the parking lot at Fisher's Hill Battlefield Civil War Site.

Fisher's Hill Battlefield Civil War Site
Fisher's Hill, Va.

Fisher's Hill was the site of a Civil War battle on September 22, 1864. CSA Gen. Early took a position on the hill after the Third Battle of

Winchester and was attacked by USA Gen. Sheridan. Early's adjutant-general, A.S. Pendleton, was killed during the conflict. The Civil War site is managed by the Association for the Preservation of Civil War Sites in partnership with the Strasburg Sons of the Confederate Veterans. The site, with an attractive view of the Shenandoah Valley landscape, has a historical marker. There are no facilities at this site. It is open during daylight hours.

FISHER'S HILL BATTLEFIELD CIVIL WAR SITE TO TOM'S BROOK, VA.

Return by Va. 601 to U.S. 11, turn right (south) and go 3.5 miles to Tom's Brook. Along this tour route, about 1 mile south of Va. 601 on U.S. 11, is a map and diagram with information on the Battle of Fisher's Hill.

Tom's Brook, Va.

Two weeks after the action at Fisher's Hill, on October 9, 1864, CSA Gens. Thomas Lafayette Rosser and Lunsford Lindsay Lomax lost a cavalry battle at Tom's Brook to USA Gen. Alfred Thomas Archimedes Torbert. Prior to the battle, USA Gen. Philip Sheridan, unhappy with his cavalry's performance, told Torbert, "Either whip the enemy or get whipped yourself." Union losses were 10 killed and 47 wounded, for a total of 57. Confederate losses were 20 killed, 50 wounded and 280 captured or missing, for a total of 350. The Southerners were pushed back so fierce and quick the Federals called the victory the Woodstock Races, referring to the Valley Pike route south to Woodstock, Virginia.

TOM'S BROOK TO EDINBURG, VA.

Continue south on U.S. 11, through Woodstock, for 11 miles to Edinburg.

Edinburg, Va.

Although this region was settled by Scotch-Irish, as well as German, pioneers, this town's name is not of Scottish origin. Rather, early townspeople considered this attractive area similar to the Garden of Eden, but they ended up spelling it incorrectly. This was the "Granary of the Confederacy," although a prominent mill, Edinburg Mills, was among the few buildings saved from the torches of USA Gen. Sheridan. A local legend says two local girls appealed to Sheridan's men to save the mill, which is still standing.

EDINBURG TO MOUNT JACKSON, VA.

Continue south on U.S. 11 for 7 miles to Mount Jackson.

Mount Jackson, Va.

No, this town is not named for the immortal CSA Gen. Thomas J. "Stonewall" Jackson. Legend says General — later President — Andrew Jackson was a frequent visitor to the area, and the community name of Mount Pleasant was changed in the 1820s to Mount Jackson to honor him. A number of buildings in downtown Mount Jackson were used as field hospitals for Confederate troops injured in battles throughout the Shenandoah Valley. There is a quaint Confederate cemetery along U.S. 11 in downtown Mount Jackson.

MOUNT JACKSON TO NEW MARKET, VA.

Continue south on U.S. 11 for 7 miles to the intersection with U.S. 211 in downtown New Market.

Along this tour route, 1 mile south of Mount Jackson, enemy cavalry units fought a battle in the vicinity of the roadway, then called the Valley Pike. A bridge over the Shenandoah River in this vicinity was burned by Union troops retreating from the Battle of New Market in May 1864.

New Market, Va.

This tranquil Shenandoah Valley community was struck by warfare in May 1864, when the Battle of New Market raged in and around the town. A Confederate force under CSA Gen. John Cabell Breckinridge arrived from Staunton and Lacey Spring, Virginia, just to the south, to face Union troops under the command of Union Gen. Franz Sigel. On May 15, 1864, Sigel pushed south with 6,500 troops on his way to destroy the railroad at Staunton.

He was met by Breckinridge, and a day-long battle was fought in a chilling spring rain.

The Southerners overran the Federals; one Pennsylvania regiment suffered 45 percent casualties. More than 200 cadets from Virginia Military Institute were part of Breckinridge's troop strength. The youngsters were not the principal part of the Confederate offensive, but they did take part in a portion of the battle and captured a Union battery. Sigel was pushed back north as far as Strasburg.

NEW MARKET TO SHENANDOAH VALLEY TOURIST INFORMATION CENTER
In downtown New Market, at the intersection of U.S. 11 and U.S. 211, turn right (west) on U.S. 211

and go 0.3 mile — beyond the I-81 interchange — to the Shenandoah Tourist Information Center on the left (south) side of the highway.

Shenandoah Valley Information Center
277 W. Old Cross Rd., U.S. 211 W., New Market, Va. • (540) 740-3132
This facility is operated by the Shenandoah Valley Travel Association. Travel counselors have brochures and general information about the entire Shenandoah Valley region, from Martinsburg, West Virginia, to Roanoke, Virginia. The facility is open every day but Christmas from 9 AM to 5 PM. It is handicapped-accessible, and there are restrooms.

New Market Personality: John C. Breckinridge

Photo: New Market Battlefield State Historical Park

CSA Gen. John C. Breckinridge led Southern troops at the Battle of New Market.

There is irony that General Breckinridge, a Kentucky native, saw Civil War action in the Great Valley of Virginia. That's where his family roots were. The general's great-grandfather was Robert Breckinridge, who married Lettice Preston near Staunton in 1758. Both Robert and Lettice were Irish natives, and both were members of families that were among the numerous Scotch-Irish who immigrated to the colonies in the 1730s and settled in the Virginia valley.

Robert and Lettice had six children, including two sons, John and James Breckinridge. James, the younger of the two, was born and raised in the newly created Botetourt County, Virginia, which he represented in the state legislature. He ran for governor of Virginia in 1799 but lost to fellow Virginian James Monroe.

John Breckinridge, grandfather of CSA Gen. John C. Breckinridge, was born near Staunton in 1760. He also represented Botetourt County in the Virginia legislature in Williamsburg, a service he provided while he simultaneously attended the College of William and Mary. Once, he was refused a seat in the General Assembly because he was under age.

— continued on next page

SHENANDOAH VALLEY TOURIST INFORMATION CENTER TO NEW MARKET HISTORICAL BATTLEFIELD PARK

From the information center, cross U.S. 211 to Va. Highway 305 (George Collins Parkway) and go 1 mile to New Market Historical Battlefield Park. (NOTE: There are two other museums and a motel along the George Collins Parkway prior to the New Market Historical Battlefield Park. Be sure to go the full mile to reach the New Market Historical Battlefield Park, operated by Virginia Military Institute.)

New Market Battlefield Park and Hall of Valor Museum

George Collins Pkwy., New Market, Va.

• (540) 740-3101

This museum features artifacts, murals, life-sized models and films to relate the story of the Battle of New Market. The museum is listed in the National Register of Historic Places and is open every day except Thanksgiving, Christmas and New Year's Day from 9 AM to 5 PM. The museum is handicapped-accessible. Adults admission is $5; children younger than 16 are $2.

New Market Tour Ends

— continued from previous page

In 1785, John Breckinridge married Mary Hopkins Cabell, the daughter of Joseph and Mary Cabell of Buckingham County, Virginia. John and his wife lived in Albemarle County, Virginia, where two of their nine children were born. John was elected to the U.S. Senate from Albemarle County in 1792, but he failed to take the seat. Instead, he and his family — along with his mother, aunts and uncles — moved to the newly established state of Kentucky.

John was active in Kentucky politics, serving as the new state's attorney general and in the legislature, as a U.S. Senator and eventually as President Thomas Jefferson's attorney general. His oldest son, Joseph Cabell Breckinridge, also took an active part in Kentucky politics. He married Mary Clay Smith in Kentucky in 1811. Joseph and Mary had only one child, John Cabell Breckinridge, who was born in Lexington, Kentucky, in 1821.

John carried on his family's political tradition, serving in the Kentucky legislature and as a congressman. In 1856, John was elected vice president on the ticket with President James Buchanan. In the U.S. presidential election four years later, John Breckinridge unsuccessfully opposed Abraham Lincoln. He then served as U.S. Senator from Kentucky.

In the Civil War, as a Confederate general, John Breckinridge saw action at Shiloh, Baton Rouge, Vicksburg, Chickamauga and Missionary Ridge. After serving in the Shenandoah Valley, he commanded his division at Cold Harbor and fought with CSA Gen. Early at Monocacy in Maryland. He was named the Confederate secretary of war just two months before the Confederate surrender at Appomattox in 1865.

Following the Civil War, Breckinridge went to Cuba, Europe and Canada before being returning to his native Kentucky. The Breckinridge family was seriously divided during the Civil War. The general and his three sons fought for the Confederacy, but two Breckinridge cousins supported the Union. One of the cousins had two sons who fought for the South and two who fought for the North. One of Breckinridge's cousins, Margaret Elizabeth Breckinridge, ministered to Northern soldiers in camps along the Mississippi River. She ran a relief boat between St. Louis and Vicksburg, but she contracted typhoid fever and died in 1864, just as she prepared to return to work on a battlefield in Virginia.

Photo: New Market Battlefield State Historical Park

New Market was the site of a day-long battle between the troops of USA Gen. Franz Sigel and CSA Gen. John Breckinridge on May 15, 1864.

New Market Personality: Franz Sigel

Franz Sigel, a native of Germany, was a graduate of the German Military Academy. He fled his home country in the 1840s, traveled to Switzerland and England, immigrated to the United States and became a school teacher in New York City and St. Louis.

Early in the Civil War, USA Gen. Sigel enlisted in the U.S. Army and served in the Trans-Mississippi Theater before leading a division against CSA Gen. "Stonewall" Jackson in the Shenandoah Valley Campaign of 1862. Sigel was defeated at the Battle of New Market in May 1864, after which he moved north to defend Harpers Ferry against CSA Gen. Jubal Early.

Sigel, according to Union military leaders, lacked aggression. He was dismissed from his command, but he didn't resign from the Union army until May 1865 — a year after New Market and a month after the Confederate surrender at Appomattox.

Photo: Library of Virginia

USA Gen. Franz Sigel was defeated at the Battle of New Market in May 1864.

He moved to Baltimore and then New York City, where he became known as a publisher, political activist and lecturer. He died in 1902 at the age of 86, more than three decades after the end of the war.

Other Tour Points of Interest

Annual Events

The annual Spring opening of **Belle Grove Plantation** is held in March. The **Cedar Creek Living History and Re-enactment Weekend** is held at the Cedar Creek Battlefield each year on the Saturday and Sunday closest to October 19, the anniversary of the 1864 battle. The weekend celebration includes dress parades, various military drills, a living history program at Belle Grove Plantation (see listing above) and a Sutlers Row. The event is one of the better-organized of various re-enactment programs throughout the country. An $8 fee is charged, with proceeds going to preserve the historic battlefield.

Arts

The **Wayside Theater** on U.S. 11 in Middletown provides live professional theater. For schedule information, call (540) 869-1776.

Historic and Natural Sites

Natural scenery is this region's most popular commodity. Nature lovers will enjoy the fine parks in the Shenandoah Valley region, including the **Shenandoah National Park** and the **George Washington National Forest**. Of course, there are the famous **Skyline Drive** and **Blue Ridge Parkway** that skirt across the tops of the Blue Ridge Mountain range. Don't miss the gorgeous Shenandoah River, and try fly fishing and view various wildflower exhibitions in the Shenandoah National Park. Among the most popular area attractions are natural caverns, including **Endless Caverns** near New Market, (540) 896-2283, and **Shenandoah Caverns** near Mount Jackson, (540) 477-3115.

Shopping

There are hundreds of small shops along U.S. 11 in the communities on the old Valley Pike. The drive is ideal for antique shopping or casual browsing. In Edinburg, **The Flea Market** is a popular stop — call (540) 984-8521 for more information. In Strasburg, visit **Emmart's Antiques, Flea Market and Museum**, (540) 465-5040. Woodstock has two shopping centers to complement its quaint downtown shops. In Mount Jackson, visit **Tuttle and Spice 1880 General Store and Museum**, (540) 477-9428.

Vineyards

There are several vineyards in the vicinity, including **Shenandoah Vineyards**, 3659 S. Ox Road, Edinburg, Virginia, (540) 984-8699, which is just a mile off I-81. The vineyard offers a tour and wine tastings. It is open from 10 AM to 6 PM every day except New Year's Day, Thanksgiving and Christmas. The winery is handicapped-accessible; its bathrooms are not.

Tour 4
Staunton

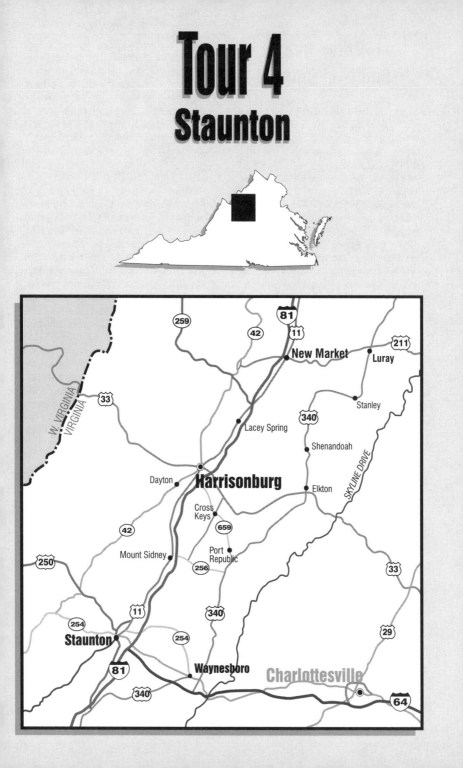

Staunton

About This Tour

This tour covers the Shenandoah Valley from New Market, Virginia, to Staunton, Virginia. The tour is the fourth of five in succession — along with T-1: Sharpsburg, T-2: Harpers Ferry, T-3: New Market and T-5: Lexington — that cover the long stretch of the Great Valley that runs through Pennsylvania, Maryland, West Virginia and Virginia.

The tour begins by exiting New Market and ends in Staunton. The Shenandoah Valley is part of the Great Valley, a natural trough that runs along the eastern slope of the Appalachian Mountains. Native Americans, the area's first inhabitants, used the Great Valley as a north-south route. The Great Wagon Road through the valley followed an old buffalo trail used by Indians.

This region was settled by European pioneers, mainly German and Scotch-Irish, that landed at Philadelphia in the early 18th century and made their homes along the Appalachian Mountain highlands. German farmers established homesteads in the region in the early 1700s, followed within a few years by Scotch-Irish pioneers. A major Scotch-Irish settlement was established near present-day Staunton, in Augusta County, in the 1730s.

Significant Civil War action took place throughout the Shenandoah Valley, beginning in June 1861 and continuing for the next three years. CSA Gen. Thomas Jonathan "Stonewall" Jackson fought his famous Shenandoah Valley Campaign in this region in 1862, and CSA Gen. Jubal Anderson "Old Jube" Early marched through the Valley on his way to and from his attempted raid on Washington in 1864.

Travel Tips

This tour route, from New Market to Staunton, follows U.S. Highway 11 and Interstate 81 almost exclusively. On U.S. 11, be alert to slow-moving farm vehicles; on I-81, watch for the heavy volume of tractor-trailer trucks. There are a series of small, local radio stations that report weather conditions, but these stations cover traffic conditions only in extreme circumstances. Citizens band radio users can find traffic information on Channel 19. State police usually monitor Channel 9. Mobile telephone signals are clear throughout the Shenandoah Valley.

The tour ends in Staunton, where we suggest you plan to eat and spend the evening. Recommended accommodations are listed in Chapter 22. Dining suggestions are itemized in Chapter 23. It is a good idea to review these recommendations before traveling this stretch of the Shenandoah Valley. In addition to our suggestions for Staunton, we also recommend locations to dine and spend the night in Harrisonburg, Virginia, in our Restaurants and Accommodations chapters. There are also the various expected fast-food facilities, gas stations, convenience stores and shops all along U.S. 11 and at most I-81 interchanges.

Staunton Tour Begins . . .

NEW MARKET, VA., TO
LACEY SPRING, VA.
Leaving New Market to the south on U.S. 11, go 8.8 miles to Lacey Spring, Va.

Rockingham County, Va.

Along this route, just south of New Market, U.S. 11 enters Rockingham County, which was established in 1778 and named for Charles Watson-Wentworth. Watson-Wentworth, the second marquess of Rockingham, was an enthusiastic supporter of American colonists in their struggle for independence from Great Britain.

Much of Rockingham County suffered the impact of CSA Gen. "Stonewall" Jackson's famous Shenandoah Valley Campaign of 1862. Jackson's campaign served as a diversionary tactic to prevent USA Gen. Irvin McDowell from pushing east toward Richmond and reinforcing the troops under USA Gen. George Brinton McClellan. From April to June 1862, Jackson and his 17,000 Confederate troops used their knowledge of the Shenandoah Valley to outmaneuver and confuse Union forces. Significant battles were fought in Rockingham County at Harrisonburg, Port Republic and Cross Keys.

Later, in 1864, CSA Gen. Early was in the Shenandoah Valley after his unsuccessful raid on Washington, D.C. Early and USA Gen. Philip Henry Sheridan fought a series of battles (see T-2 and T-3), including a final conflict in Augusta County near Waynesboro, Virginia.

Lacey Spring, Va.

USA Gen. George Armstrong Custer and CSA Gen. Thomas Lafayette Rosser fought a cavalry battle at Lacey Spring on Dec. 20, 1864. Rosser and Custer had been roommates at the U.S. Military Academy at West Point. Throughout the Civil War, the two former friends often engaged in cavalry action against each other.

After the war, Rosser went into railroading and was the chief engineer in the Indian Territory. He and Custer, his old adversary, again became friends when Custer's army unit was deployed to protect Rosser's railroad construction. Rosser later became a gentleman farmer in Albemarle County and died in 1910. (See more on CSA Gen. Rosser in T-10: Charlottesville.) Custer was killed at the Battle of Little Big Horn in Montana in June 1876.

LACEY SPRING TO HARRISONBURG, VA.
At Lacey Spring, continue south
on U.S. 11 for 5.1 miles, then take
I-81 south 3.5 miles to exit 247-A
(U.S. Highway 33) in Harrisonburg.

Harrisonburg, Va.

Harrisonburg, the seat of Rockingham County, was established in 1779, when farmer Thomas Harrison donated two acres of land for a county courthouse. Rockingham has been and remains largely agricultural. Farms in this region helped feed the Confederate Army. Today, Rockingham boasts more than 2,000 farms, with an average size of nearly 130 acres. The county ranks among the nation's top-ten turkey producers and leads the state in income from dairy, lamb, veal, beef and pork production.

Lacey Spring Personalities: Lincoln Family

On Feb. 12, 1809, Nancy Hanks Lincoln gave birth to a son in her Hardin County, Kentucky, cabin. She and her carpenter husband, Thomas, named the new child Abraham. Young Abraham's roots could be traced all the way to the Lacey Spring area of Virginia. John Lincoln — "Virginia John" — settled on 600 acres on Linville Creek in Rockingham County at Lacey Spring. Virginia John's son, Abraham L. Lincoln, was an officer in the American Revolution.

Capt. Abraham L. Lincoln and his son, Thomas, moved to Kentucky in 1782, a decade before the region was cut from Virginia for the creation of the new state. Virginia John remained in Rockingham County, near Lacey Spring, with a younger son, Jacob. On February 24, 1829, two decades after the future President Lincoln was born, Jacob's grandson, Franklin, carved his name and the date on the wall of Melrose Caverns, or Harrison's Cave, just north of Harrisonburg in the vicinity of Lacey Spring. Franklin Lincoln, President Lincoln's distant cousin, went on to serve in the Civil War as a soldier in the Confederacy.

HARRISONBURG TO THE HARRISONBURG ROCKINGHAM CONVENTION AND VISITORS BUREAU

Take exit 247-A off I-81, go west on U.S. 33 (E. Market Street) for 0.4 mile to Vine Street, turn right and go a quarter-block to the visitors bureau at the intersection of Vine Street and Country Club Road.

Harrisonburg Rockingham Convention and Visitors Bureau
800 Country Club Rd., Harrisonburg, Va.
• (540) 434-2319

This convention bureau and visitors center is operated by the Harrisonburg and Rockingham Chamber of Commerce. Travel counselors have information packets on area attractions and can help travelers plan accommodations and dining. This center is open Monday through Friday from 8:30 AM to 5 PM. It is closed on weekends and holidays. The center is handicapped-accessible and has restrooms. Check with counselors about Civil War booklets for sale and self-guided tour information.

HARRISONBURG VISITORS BUREAU TO ROCKINGHAM COUNTY COURTHOUSE

From the visitors bureau, return to U.S. 33 (E. Market Street), turn right on Market Street and go west 1 mile into downtown Harrisonburg to the Rockingham County Courthouse.

Rockingham County Courthouse
Main Street and Market Street, Harrisonburg, Va.

The imposing Rockingham County Courthouse was built in 1896 and is the fifth courthouse to occupy the 1.5-acre public square that was donated by Rockingham County's founder, Thomas Harrison, and his wife, Sarah. The building was one of more than 200 designed by architect T.J. Collins of Staunton, and it features the Romanesque and Renaissance Revival styles of architecture that were popular in the late 19th century. Constructed with rough-hewn sandstone blocks, the building has a lofty clock tower.

In June 1862, between 2,500 and 3,000 Union soldiers were taken prisoner after the Battle of Cross Keys, just east of Harrisonburg. These Union soldiers were transported to Harrisonburg and allowed to camp in a fenced enclosure that surrounded the Rockingham County Courthouse.

HARRISONBURG TO DAYTON, VA.

Continue west on Market Street (U.S. 33) around court square 0.2 mile to Va. Highway 42 (High Street), turn left (west) and go 4 miles west to the intersection of Va. 42 and Eberly Road in Dayton.

Dayton, Va.

This small valley community barely escaped being burned to the ground during the Civil War. In 1865, USA Gen. Sheridan sought revenge for the death of his staff officer, USA Lt. John Rodgers Meigs, the apparent victim of a Confederate guerrilla attack a few months earlier. Meigs was the son of USA Gen. Montgomery C. Meigs, the Union quartermaster-general (see more on USA Gen. Meigs in T-14: Northern Virginia). Sheridan ordered the burning of all houses within a 5-mile radius of Dayton, and USA Gen. Custer assumed the task with enthusiasm. But Sheridan had a last-minute change of heart. Instead, he ordered all able-bodied men in Dayton be taken prisoner.

DAYTON TO SHENANDOAH VALLEY FOLK ART AND HERITAGE CENTER

From Va. 42 in Dayton, turn right (north) on Eberly Road (Va. Highway 732), go 0.2 mile and follow signs across Cooks Creek to the Shenandoah Valley Heritage Museum on High Street. Along this route, Va. 732 changes from Eberly Road to Bowman Road to College Street.

Shenandoah Valley Folk Art and Heritage Center
382 High St., Dayton, Va. • (540) 879-2681

This attractive brick museum offers exhibits on the history of the Rockingham County and Shenandoah Valley region, including Civil War history. The museum also features seasonal exhibits and lecture programs. It has a gift shop and a book store. Hours vary: From April to October, the center is open Monday through Saturday from 9 AM to 4 PM and Sunday 1 to 4 PM. During winter, it is open Thursday through Saturday from 10 AM to 4 PM. A fee is charged.

right (south) on Main Street (U.S. 11) and go 0.6 mile to the intersection with Port Republic Road.

Along this section of U.S. 11 (Main Street) are a number of attractive buildings on the campus of James Madison University. Many of the campus buildings are constructed of native limestone.

DAYTON TO TURNER ASHBY MONUMENT
Return on College Street, Bowman Road and Eberly Road to Va. 42 (High Street), turn left (east) and go 3.6 miles to the intersection with Cantrell Avenue. (Look for Harrisonburg High School on the southwest corner of this intersection.) Turn right (east) on Cantrell Avenue, go 0.2 mile, turn

Turn right (east) on Port Republic Road and go 1.1 miles, crossing I-81, to Turner Ashby Lane. Look carefully for the Turner Ashby Lane road sign and a brown directional sign for the Ashby monument. At the directional sign, turn left (north) on Turner Ashby Lane and go 0.3 mile on the two-lane state route to the monument.

Harrisonburg Personality: Turner Ashby

CSA Gen. Turner Ashby was a dashing, colorful horseman who traced his roots to a long line of Virginia country gentlemen. His great-grandfather served with George Washington in the French and Indian War, and his father was a colonel in the War of 1812. Ashby was only 6 when his father died in 1834, and his mother, Elizabeth, made sure her son was properly educated by private tutors.

Ashby entered adulthood as an enviable gentleman whose days were filled with horse riding and hunting. A handsome man with dark hair, he never married. In 1855, at age 27, he formed a cavalry group to police the workers building the Manassas Gap Railroad. Four years later, when John Brown raided Harpers Ferry, Ashby's cavalrymen were among the first militia on the scene.

With the outbreak of the Civil War, Ashby became a daring Southern cavalry officer — some say he was as colorful as his friend "Stonewall" Jackson. Ashby became part of Jackson's Shenandoah Valley Campaign of 1862. According to legend, Ashby once disguised himself as an old horse doctor and rode a nag into Pennsylvania to spy on Union Army activities. Ashby's bravery was renown. During the retreat from Winchester in March 1862, he apparently was the last Confederate to leave town.

But Ashby's lack of military discipline led him to a confrontation with Jackson, who stripped Ashby of his command. Angered by Jackson's decision, Ashby said he would have challenged Jackson to a duel if the two were the same rank. Instead, Ashby threatened to resign his commission and remove his cavalry command from Jackson's army. In a rare move, Jackson backed down and reinstated Ashby.

A reckless cavalier, Ashby met his doom at Chestnut Ridge, leading a charge against Union soldiers. Jackson reacted to Ashby's death, saying "as a partisan officer I never knew his superior; his daring was proverbial; his powers of endurance almost incredible; his character heroic. . . ."

Turner Ashby Monument
Harrisonburg, Va.

CSA Gen. Turner Ashby took a battle position against Union forces at Chestnut Ridge, just east of Harrisonburg, on June 5, 1862. The next day, the Battle of Harrisonburg involved Ashby's cavalrymen — reinforced by the 48th Virginia Cavalry — against a Union force.

USA Gen. John Charles Fremont sent a group of sharpshooters, known as the Pennsylvania Bucktails, to attack the Confederate rear guard. To encourage his Southern troops, Ashby charged the front of the Union advance. Ashby's horse was shot out from under him, so he continued on foot until he was struck in the chest by a Union bullet and killed on the spot. His death rallied the Confederates, who eventually defeated the Northerners, including the Pennsylvania Bucktails. The monument at Chestnut Ridge reads, "General Turner Ashby, C.S.A., was killed on this spot, June 6, 1862, gallantly leading a charge."

TURNER ASHBY MONUMENT TO CROSS KEYS

From the Ashby Monument, return on Turner Ashby Lane to Port Republic Road, turn left (east) and go southeast 4.5 miles to the intersection with Va. Highway 276. The Battle of Cross Keys was fought just south of this intersection.

Cross Keys, Va.

The farms and fields in this vicinity look much as they did two centuries ago. The community gets its name from the early 19th century Cross Keys Tavern, which had two large crossed keys on its entrance sign. Today, there is little in the area to honor the Battle of Cross Keys, which was fought on June 8, 1862, two days after the Battle of Harrisonburg.

CSA Gen. Richard Stoddert Ewell's men were outnumbered by USA Gen. Fremont's troops by nearly two-to-one. Still, CSA Gen. Jackson ordered Ewell to attack Fremont to prevent Fremont from shifting north to Port Republic, Virginia, and reinforcing USA Gen. James Shields. During a morning battle, the

Union's 8th New York Infantry was forced to retreat and suffered the majority of the battle's casualties. A number of the wounded were taken to the Cross Keys Tavern, which was outfitted as a battlefield hospital.

CROSS KEYS TO PORT REPUBLIC, VA.
Continue southeast on Port Republic Road (Va. Highway 659) for 5.3 miles to Port Republic.

Port Republic, Va.

Port Republic is a quaint farm community in the picturesque flatlands along the base of the Blue Ridge Mountains in eastern Rockingham County. The village is at the confluence of the South and North rivers, which form the south fork of the Shenandoah River. Port Republic was settled by German pioneers in the 1730s and established as a town in 1802. In the 19th century, Port Republic was a thriving river port where the bounty from area farmers was loaded on flatboats and transported by the Shenandoah and Potomac rivers to Alexandria, Virginia. The town thrived until the 1890s, when river transport was replaced by the railroad.

On the evening of June 6, 1862, the body of CSA Gen. Ashby was transported from Chestnut Ridge, just east of Harrisonburg, to a house on the South River in the village of Port Republic. Women in the community prepared Ashby's body for burial. Legend says the women placed a red rose in his chest wound. With the pending battle in Port Republic, Ashby's body was hastily escorted out of the town on June 7 and taken to Charlottesville, across the Blue Ridge Mountains. Ashby later was interred at Stonewall Cemetery in Winchester (see T-3).

On June 9, 1862, the day after the Battle of Cross Keys, Civil War fighting shifted to Port Republic. Jackson shifted his forces across the North River and attacked USA Gen. Shields just northeast of town. Shields was forced to withdraw. Meanwhile, an advance by USA Gen. Fremont was thwarted when Jackson burned the town bridge over the North River. The Confederate victory marked the end of the Shenandoah Valley Campaign of 1862. After this series of battles, Jackson's troops

Photo: Library of Virginia

On Dec. 20, 1864, USA Gen. George Custer led a cavalry battle at Lacey Spring in Rockingham County.

moved east to Richmond and the Peninsula Campaign.

PORT REPUBLIC TO THE VILLAGE STORE
In downtown Port Republic, at the
North River Bridge, is the Village
Store.

Village Store
Port Republic Rd., Port Republic, Va.
• (540) 249-3096
The Village Store serves as the unofficial information center in Port Republic. The quaint country store offers the usual groceries and household items, plus canoe rentals, camping and fishing supplies and live bait. The store is open from 6:30 AM to 8 PM daily and remains open until 10 PM on summer Saturdays. Since there is no formal visitor information facility in Port Republic, the store passes out photocopies of historical information and maps related to the Battle of Port Republic.

PORT REPUBLIC TO STAUNTON, VA.
From Port Republic, return 10
miles on Va. 659 (Port Republic
Road) to I-81, and take the inter-
state south 20 miles to exit 225 in
Staunton.

Along this route is the community of Mount Crawford, where opposing cavalry forces fought an engagement on March 1, 1865. Also along this tour, the route crosses into Augusta County from Rockingham County. Augusta County was established in 1745, and it was named for England's Princess Augusta, the wife of Frederick, the Prince of Wales. Augusta was the mother of England's King George III.

Staunton, Va.
Staunton (pronounced "STAN-tun") was established in the 1730s by a group of Scotch-Irish settlers led by pioneer John Lewis. The Scotch-Irish clans in Augusta County included the Lewis, Patton, Preston, and Breckinridge families (see more on the Breckinridge family in T-3: New Market). The town was laid out in 1748 and likely named for Rebecca Staunton (pronounced "Staw-tun"), wife of Sir William Gooch, who was lieutenant governor of Virginia from 1727 to 1749. Staunton was established as a town in 1761.

Staunton was the headquarters of the Stonewall Brigade, a unit of the Virginia militia that dated its origin to the 1740s in the Shenandoah Valley. The Stonewall Brigade served in the Civil War under "Stonewall" Jackson. In 1865, USA Gen. Ulysses S. Grant, following the Confederate surrender at Appomattox, allowed members of the Stonewall Brigade band to take home their musical instruments. Ironically, the band played at Grant's funeral in July 1885 in New York City. Woodrow Wilson, later U.S. president, was born in antebellum Staunton.

STAUNTON TO MARY BALDWIN COLLEGE
From exit 225 off I-81, take Va.
Highway 275 (Woodrow Wilson
Parkway) west for 1.4 miles, turn
left (south) on U.S. 11 and go 0.4
mile to where the road splits. Take

the right fork, U.S. 11 Business, continue 0.7 mile, turn left (southeast) on Coalter Street and go 1.6 miles to Mary Baldwin College at the intersection of Sherwood Avenue.

Mary Baldwin College
Staunton, Va. • (540) 887-7000

Mary Baldwin College was established in 1842 as the Augusta Female Seminary. The school name was changed in 1895 to honor Mary Julia Baldwin, principal of the women's school in the difficult years following the Civil War.

▬▬▬

MARY BALDWIN COLLEGE TO STAUNTON VISITORS CENTER
Continue east on Coalter Street 0.2 mile, turn right (west) on Frederick Street (Va. Highway 254) and turn left immediately into the parking lot that services the Woodrow Wilson Birthplace and the Staunton Visitors Center.

Staunton Welcome Center
230 Frederick St., Staunton, Va.
• (540) 332-3865

Volunteers operate this small welcome center, which provides travelers with information on attractions in the Staunton vicinity. Counselors have brochures and general information about historic sites in the city. Except for Thanksgiving, Christmas and New Year's Day, the center is open daily from 10 AM to 4 PM. It is not handicapped-accessible but does have restrooms.

Woodrow Wilson Birthplace and Museum
18-24 N. Coalter St., Staunton, Va.
• (540) 885-0897

This 12-room Greek Revival manse was built in 1846 to serve ministers of Staunton's Presbyterian Church. Dr. and Mrs. Joseph Ruggles Wilson moved to the house in 1855, and young Thomas Woodrow Wilson was born at the manse the next year. The family moved south while young "Tommy" was still a baby.

As a college student, Wilson dropped his first name and used Woodrow, his mother's family name, instead. As an adult, Wilson often spoke of his remembrances of living in the South as a youth during and after the Civil War.

The historic house was dedicated as a museum in 1942 by President Franklin D. Roosevelt. Today, the Wilson house is open daily from 9 AM to 5 PM during the travel season of March to November. During winter, the museum is open from 10 AM to 4 PM, and it is closed on New Year's Day, Thanksgiving and Christmas. Admission is $6 for adults, $5.50 for seniors and AAA members, $4 for students and $2 for children 6 through 12. Kids younger than 6 get in free. The facility is handicapped-accessible, offers free parking and has a gift shop with period reproductions.

While the Woodrow Wilson Birthplace did not see any Civil War activity, it has some war-related information for visitors. The museum staff is well-versed in local war history. In addition, the museum offers a computer program, "History Harvest Archives," developed by the University of Virginia. The program compares two Great Valley communities, Staunton and Chambersburg, Pennsylvania (see T-1), during the period just before war. The rosters of local militia units are also available on computer at the museum.

The birthplace is one of several buildings incorporated in the Gospel Hill Historic District. The district showcases a variety of interesting residential architecture, ranging from simple pioneer houses to the elaborate work of Staunton architect T.J. Collins (see mention at Rockingham County Courthouse in this chapter). A stroll down E. Beverley and Kalorama streets reveals fine examples of Greek Revival, Italianate, Queen Anne and Colonial Revival architecture.

▬▬▬

WOODROW WILSON BIRTHPLACE TO THE HOTCHKISS HOUSE
From the Woodrow Wilson Birthplace and Museum walk south on Coalter Street a half-block, then walk east on Beverley Street four blocks to the Oaks.

Hotchkiss House
437 E. Beverley St., Staunton, Va.

This fine home, also known as the Oaks, is a private residence. The house was built in the 1870s by Jedediah Hotchkiss, a Confederate cartographer and aide to CSA Gen. "Stonewall" Jackson.

HOTCHKISS HOUSE TO MERRILLAT HOUSE
From the Hotchkiss House, continue on E. Beverley Street one block to the Merrillat House.

Merrillat House
521 E. Beverley St., Staunton, Va.

This fine house, a mid-19th century Gothic Revival cottage, is not open to the public. The house was built in 1851 for Dr. Jean Charles Martin Merrillat, a native of Bordeaux, France. Dr. Merrillat was appointed in 1839 to serve as the first director of the Department of the Blind at the Virginia School for the Deaf and Blind, also on E. Beverley Street. Dr. Merrillat was named administrator of the entire school in 1852.

During the Civil War, the Virginia School for the Deaf and Blind was used as a hospital, and Dr. Merrillat served as a surgeon.

Staunton Tour Ends

Other Tour Points of Interest

Annual Events

Mid-May brings the **Annual Outdoor Art Festival**, a juried art show featuring works by Staunton and Augusta County artists as well as music and dancing. Every Thursday from late May to Labor Day, enjoy **"Shakin,'"** a series of two-hour, family-oriented outdoor concerts featuring a variety of styles. The shows are at the Wharf parking lot on Johnson Street. During July and August, there is a **jazz festival** at Gypsy Hill Park, with performances following the Shakin' shows on Thursdays. There is an **African-American Heritage Festival**, exploring dance, art and cultural food offerings, in Staunton in September.

Arts

Mary Baldwin College provides a wealth of art and entertainment to the Staunton and Augusta County communities, with theater productions, exhibitions and visiting scholar presentations.

Historic and Natural Sites

Natural scenery is this region's most popular commodity. Nature lovers will enjoy the parks in the Shenandoah Valley region, including the **Shenandoah National Park** and the **George Washington National Forest**.

Staunton Personality: Jedediah Hotchkiss

Jedediah Hotchkiss was a New York native who moved to the Shenandoah Valley in 1847, at the age of 19, to teach school and follow his interest in geology. He made maps as a sideline.

In 1861, Hotchkiss closed his boys' school in Churchville, 7 miles west of Staunton, and began preparing military maps for the Confederacy. In 1862, he officially joined the Confederate Army and began preparing a detailed map of the Shenandoah Valley for CSA Gen. "Stonewall" Jackson. CSA Maj. Hotchkiss' work contributed greatly to Jackson's successful Shenandoah Valley Campaign of 1862.

Hotchkiss was considered the foremost mapmaker of the Civil War. His maps, now in the Library of Congress in Washington, D.C., are considered among the finest of their kind. After the Civil War, Hotchkiss was a successful land speculator and writer. He opened a boys' school in Staunton, where he died in 1899, at the age of 71.

Staunton Side Trip: Stuart Hall School

From the Staunton Visitors Center, walk three blocks west on Frederick Street to Stuart Hall School's central building, "Old Main."

Stuart Hall School
235 W. Frederick St., Staunton, Va.
• (540) 885-0356

This school was founded in 1843 as the Virginia Female Institute, which makes Stuart Hall the oldest preparatory school for girls in Virginia. The central building of the school, a Greek Revival structure, is called "Old Main." It was designed and built by Edwin Taylor in 1846. The school became affiliated with the Episcopal Church in 1856. It became known throughout Virginia and the nation in the period from 1880 to 1898, when Flora Stuart, widow of CSA Gen. James Ewell Brown "Jeb" Stuart, served as headmistress. The school was renamed Stuart Hall in 1907 in Mrs. Stuart's honor.

Staunton Side Trip: McDowell, Va.

Take U.S. Highway 250, 30 miles west of Staunton.

McDowell, Va.

The village of McDowell is high in the Appalachian Mountains west of Staunton. This trip is only for the avid Civil War buff — it takes 45 minutes or longer to reach McDowell along twisting, curvy U.S. 250. The town is 10 miles east of the Highland County seat, Monterey. In McDowell, the only attraction these days is the vast natural beauty of the mountains, which look much as they did during the Battle of McDowell in May 1862.

McDowell, the oldest town in Highland County, was named for former Virginia Gov. James McDowell, a native of nearby Rockbridge County. The Bullpasture and Cowpasture rivers, headwaters of the historic James River, spring from the ground near McDowell.

During his 1862 Shenandoah Valley Campaign, CSA Gen. "Stonewall" Jackson undertook what some historians consider one of the most difficult marches of the Civil War. In early May 1862, Jackson took a deceptive, roundabout route from Port Republic, in eastern Rockingham County, to McDowell. From Port Republic, Jackson marched his troops east across the muddy Blue Ridge Mountains, through Brown's Gap to the Mechum's River Rail Station in Albemarle County. There the Confederates boarded a Virginia Central Railroad train for a 25-mile ride west to Staunton. Near Staunton, Jackson met with reinforcements under CSA Gen. Edward "Allegheny" Johnson, and together the Confederate generals moved west on the village of McDowell. In all, Jackson marched his troops more than 90 miles in four days, not including the brief train ride.

The action at McDowell was relatively insignificant. The Confederates suffered more casualties than the Federals, but Jackson successfully held the Union force. The McDowell Presbyterian Church was used as a hospital after the fighting.

— Staunton Sidetrips continued on next page

— Staunton Sidetrips continued from previous page

Staunton Side Trip: Waynesboro, Va.

From Staunton, take U.S. 250 east 13 miles to Waynesboro.

Waynesboro, Va.

Here's another trek for the serious Civil War buff.

Waynesboro, nestled in the Blue Ridge Mountains in eastern Augusta County, was named for Gen. "Mad" Anthony Wayne, a Revolutionary War veteran. From 1847 until the outbreak of the Civil War, R.L. Dabney was the minister at Tinkling Spring church, just west of Waynesboro. Dabney went on to become a member of "Stonewall" Jackson's staff.

On March 2, 1865, in what was considered the last important Civil War battle in the Shenandoah Valley, CSA Gen. Early was driven from a ridge during USA Gen. Philip Sheridan's Valley Campaign. USA Gen. Custer's cavalry division led the Union attack and completely enveloped the enemy. Early escaped, but Custer captured about 1,600 Confederates, along with 17 flags, 11 guns and all of Early's supplies. Riverview Cemetery, at the intersection of U.S. 250 and U.S. Highway 340 in downtown Waynesboro, features a historical marker that honors Confederate soldiers from four states who were killed in the Waynesboro battle.

Staunton Side Trip: Mount Torry Furnace

From Waynesboro, go south 5 miles on Va. Highway 624 and Va. Highway 664 to the community of Sherando. Nearby, in the George Washington National Forest, follow the signs to the Mount Torry Furnace.

Mount Torry Furnace
Sherando, Va.

This trip is for the truly hardy. Mount Torry Furnace, a tapered stone structure, was established in 1804 as one of many iron furnaces in the mountains of western Virginia. The furnace ceased operations in 1854, but the Confederacy reopened it to supply pig iron to the Tredegar Iron Works in Richmond, a major arms manufacturer. Tredegar purchased the furnace in 1863, but Union troops raided the site in 1864 and put it temporarily out of business. After the Civil War, the furnace reopened and operated until 1892, when it was abandoned.

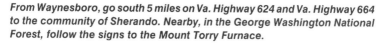

After these side trips, return to Staunton via U.S. 250.

The **Skyline Drive** and **Blue Ridge Parkway** skirt across the top of the Blue Ridge Mountain range.

The famous **Shenandoah River** offers plenty of entertainment and sport possibilities. During the colder months, try skiing at

Massanutten, 10 miles east of Harrisonburg on U.S. Highway 33. Call (540) 289-9441 for general Massanutten information; (540) 432-7000 for snow conditions. The **Daniel Harrison House**, (540) 879-2280, just north of Dayton, is the site of a house built in the

1740s, the front porch of which is incorporated in the present-day historic site. Daniel Harrison's brother, Thomas, was the founder of Harrisonburg. The Harrison house is open on Saturdays and Sundays from late May to late October.

The **Museum of American Frontier Culture**, just off I-81 at exit 222, (540) 332-7850, offers four authentic working farms that illustrate the European influence on American — particularly Shenandoah Valley — lifestyles. The museum is open 9 AM to 5 PM daily throughout the tourism season of March through November and daily from 10 AM to 4 PM during the winter. It is closed New Year's Day, Thanksgiving Day and Christmas Day as well as the first week of January. Admission is $8 for adults, $7.50 for seniors, $4 for children 6 through 12, and kids younger than 6 are admitted free. The museum is handicapped-accessible, and electric mobility carts are available for $2.50 a day.

Among the most popular area attractions are natural caverns, including **Grand Caverns** in Grottoes, Virginia, southeast of Harrisonburg, (540) 249-5705. Also visit **Natural Chimneys Regional Park**, featuring a collection of natural rock formations that are 120 feet in height. The park is just west of Harrisonburg at Mount Solon, Virginia. Call (540) 350-2510 for more information.

Shopping

The **Dayton Farmers Market**, just south of Harrisonburg on Va. 42, has 21 specialty shops offering local produce, bulk food, country hams, handcrafted furniture, jewelry, collectibles, art, books and antiques. The shops are open year round at the following hours: Thursday from 9 AM to 6 PM, Friday from 9 AM to 8 PM and Saturday from 9 AM to 5 PM. The **Staunton-Augusta County Farmers Market** on Johnson Street is another neat option, open 7 AM to noon each summer Saturday.

Staunton is a college town, so shoppers can find a number of cute, quaint apparel and gift shops in the downtown area. Harrisonburg too, as home to James Madison University, is a college town, but its major shopping area is the **Valley Mall** at the intersection of I-81 and U.S. 33 (Market Street). Antique shops are all along U.S. 11 in the vicinity of both Harrisonburg and Staunton.

Tour 5
Lexington

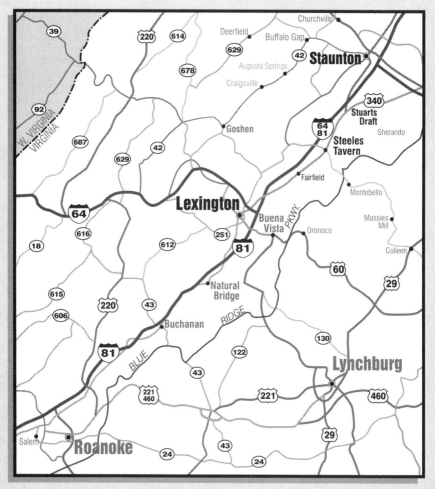

TOUR 5
Lexington

About This Tour

This tour covers the Great Valley of Virginia from Staunton to Lexington. It is the fifth of five tours — along with T-1: Sharpsburg, T-2: Harpers Ferry, T-3: New Market and T-4: Staunton — that cover the long stretch of the Valley that runs through Pennsylvania, Maryland, West Virginia and Virginia.

The Great Valley is a natural trough that runs along the eastern slope of the Appalachian Mountains. Along this route and to the southwest, the Great Valley stretches to the Virginia border with Tennessee. The Appalachians rise up dramatically to the west; the Blue Ridge Mountains form the valley's eastern side. Two major Virginia waterways, the James and Roanoke rivers, begin high in the Allegheny Mountains and cross the valley from west to east on their way to the Atlantic coast. Another, the New River, begins in North Carolina, flows north to near Radford, Virginia, and then flows west, not east, to become a part of the watershed of the Ohio River.

Native Americans, the area's first inhabitants, used the Great Valley as a north-south route, and the Great Wagon Road was built by European pioneers in the mid-18th century. This region, like the tour route areas in the four preceding chapters, was settled mainly by German and Scotch-Irish pioneers.

Civil War action took place in this region as early as June 1861, and it continued for the next three years. A number of communities in this southern valley section felt some impact of the conflict. Lexington has considerable Civil War history and was home to two Confederate heroes, Gens. Robert E. Lee and Thomas Jonathan "Stonewall" Jackson. Both are buried in the town.

Travel Tips

This tour route, from Staunton to Lexington, follows Interstate 81 between the two cities. Staunton is about 40 miles west of Charlottesville and 30 miles south of Harrisonburg, Virginia, at the intersection of two major interstate highways, I-81 and Interstate 64. Once in Lexington, the route winds through various town streets. Local radio stations report weather conditions. Citizens band radio users can find traffic information on Channel 19. State police usually monitor Channel 9. Mobile telephone signals are clear throughout this section of the valley.

The tour ends in Lexington, where we suggest you plan evening dining and lodging. Recommended accommodations are listed in Chapter 22. Dining suggestions are listed in Chapter 23. It is a good idea to review these recommendations before traveling throughout this stretch of the valley. Fast-food facilities and gas stations are scarce along this tour route, so look for interstate signs to point you to the services you want and need.

Lexington Tour Begins . . .

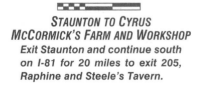

STAUNTON TO CYRUS MCCORMICK'S FARM AND WORKSHOP
Exit Staunton and continue south on I-81 for 20 miles to exit 205, Raphine and Steele's Tavern.

Along this section of the tour, the route crosses into Rockbridge County. Rockbridge was established in 1778 and named for the

Natural Bridge, a world-renowned natural arch in the county.

cessible and open daily from 8:30 AM to 5 PM. Admission is free.

Off the exit, turn left (east) on Va. Highway 606 and go 1 mile to Cyrus McCormick's Farm and Workshop on the left (north) side of the highway.

Cyrus McCormick's Farm and Workshop
Va. Hwy. 606, Steele's Tavern, Va.
• (540) 377-2255

This farm, near the Augusta-Rockbridge county line, is the birthplace of Cyrus McCormick, the inventor of the grain reaper. The farm is a mile west of Steele's Tavern, a settlement named for Daniel Steele, a Revolutionary War veteran who operated a tavern on the Great Wagon Road — present-day U.S. Highway 11.

Cyrus McCormick was born in 1809. His father, Robert McCormick, spent more than two decades experimenting with a grain-reaping machine. Picking up on his father's efforts, Cyrus successfully demonstrated a reaper in 1831. The invention, which enabled farmers to reap as much grain as they could plant, revolutionized agriculture. Cyrus patented the machine in 1834 and began commercial manufacture in the valley in the 1840s.

In 1847 he moved to Chicago and founded the McCormick Harvesting and Machine Company, the forerunner of International Harvester. In 1851, McCormick's "Virginia Reaper" won a gold medal at London's Crystal Place Exhibition. It was the highest award of the day, and it made McCormick a world celebrity.

During the Civil War, McCormick's invention had a profound impact on American manufacturing. His machine enabled Midwestern farmers to provide the grain necessary to feed the Union Army. McCormick died in 1884 after becoming one of the most successful manufacturers in the nation's industrial age. Today, the McCormick Farm is a National Historic Landmark and operated as part of the Shenandoah Valley Agricultural Experiment Station, a network managed by Virginia Polytechnic Institute and State University. The historic site is handicapped-ac-

MCCORMICK'S FARM AND WORKSHOP TO LEXINGTON, VA.
Return on Va. 606 to I-81 and continue south on I-81 for 16 miles to exit 188-B to Lexington.

Lexington, Va.

Lexington is the seat of Rockbridge County. The community was founded by Scotch-Irish pioneers in the 1770s and established as a town in 1778, not long after the famous Revolutionary War battle at Lexington, Massachusetts, for which the city is named. History comes alive during a stroll through Lexington amid authentic 18th and 19th century homes. It also is home of two top educational facilities, Washington and Lee University (W&L) and Virginia Military Institute (VMI).

A part of Lexington's history is based on its association with two Civil War greats — Robert E. Lee and Thomas "Stonewall" Jackson. Both Lee and Jackson were native Virginians, graduates of West Point, distinguished veterans of the Mexican War and college educators in Lexington. Both Lee and Jackson had homes in Lexington, attended church in the city and are buried in the city. The pair's birthdays — both in February — are celebrated by a joint observance in Virginia, Lee-Jackson Day.

During the Civil War, a corps of cadets from VMI began their march from Lexington in early 1864 for the Battle of New Market, 80 miles north (T-3). VMI was damaged by fire set in June 1864 by USA Gen. David Hunter. CSA Gen. Elisha Franklin Paxton, a commander of the Virginia militia's Stonewall Brigade and a victim in the 1863 Battle of Chancellorsville (T-16), lived near Lexington prior to the Civil War. Lexington also was the home of Virginia's wartime governor, John Letcher.

LEXINGTON TO THE LEXINGTON VISITOR CENTER
From the I-81 exit 188-B, turn right

HISTORIC LEXINGTON

Enjoy elegant dining in a restored 1820 Classical Revival town house in historic downtown Lexington

WILLSON-WALKER HOUSE
Restaurant

Creative American Cuisine
Deliciously Unique • Casually Elegant
Unexpectedly Affordable

Open for lunch and dinner
Tuesday - Saturday
Lunch   11:30 - 2:30
Dinner   5:30 - 9:00
Reservations required

Outdoor dining • Banquet rooms
Children's Menu
Famous $5.00 Lunch Special

30 North Main Street
540-463-3020   540-464-1635 (fax)
www.webfest-inc.com/lexington

STONEWALL JACKSON HOUSE

8 E. Washington St.
Lexington, Virginia
(540)463-2552

HISTORIC HOUSE, GARDEN AND MUSEUM SHOP

Guided tours daily,
Monday - Saturday, 9 until 5
Sunday, 1 until 5
Admission $5 adults, $2.50 youth

Stonewall Country

Created for LKA by Don Baker and
Robin & Linda Williams

As cannons blast and Robin & Linda Williams' music fills the night air, audiences relive the fascinating times of Thomas "Stonewall" Jackson and the Civil War.

Memorial Day to Labor Day
Plays Tuesday - Saturday
Concerts Sunday
(540) 463-3074

Stone ruins for a stage
Star-studded sky for a roof

* * * *
HISTORIC LEXINGTON
VIRGINIA

LEXINGTON VISITORS BUREAU
106 E. Washington Street
Lexington, Virginia 24450

Where your next
Civil War tour
should begin!

(540) 463-3777 (540) 463-1105 (Fax)
Open daily, 8:30 a.m. to 6 p.m.
(June, July and August)
Otherwise 9 a.m. to 5 p.m.
Handicapped accessible
Closed New Year's, Thanksgiving
and Christmas

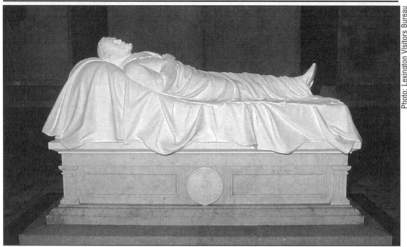

Photo: Lexington Visitors Bureau

The recumbent statue of R.E. Lee, designed by Edward Valentine, is the centerpiece of Lee Chapel at Washington and Lee University.

on U.S. Highway 60 and go west toward Lexington 2.4 miles to Lewis Street, turn right (north), go one block, then shift left to Washington Street. Continue west another 0.2 miles to the visitors center parking lot on the right.

Lexington Visitor Center
106 E. Washington St., Lexington, Va.
• **(540) 463-3777**

The Lexington Visitor Center is one of the nicest facilities of its kind in the mid-Atlantic, or anywhere else for that matter. Here, travel counselors greet you in a living room atmosphere. There's no counter between the hosts and guests. Rather, easy chairs, couches, exhibits and displays provide a cozy, comfortable setting. Still, the center is full of the usual, informative brochures, packets, tour maps and other travel information. The center offers restroom facilities, a water fountain and vending machines. It is handicapped-accessible.

An Accommodations Gallery has plenty of information of where to stay in the Lexington area, and it features a direct-dial telephone to some locations. The center is open daily from 8:30 AM to 6 PM during June, July and August; otherwise from 9 AM to 5 PM. It

is closed New Year's Day, Thanksgiving and Christmas.

LEXINGTON VISITOR CENTER TO STONEWALL JACKSON HOUSE
Walk one block west of the visitors center to the intersection of Washington and Main streets. The Stonewall Jackson House is at 8 E. Washington Street.

Stonewall Jackson House
8 E. Washington St., Lexington, Va.
• **(540) 463-2552**

CSA Gen. Thomas J. "Stonewall" Jackson, an instructor at VMI and one of Lexington's most celebrated former residents, lived in the community 10 years before going off to the Civil War. This house, made of brick and stone, was the only one Jackson owned. While living at the house, he married Elinor Junkin, suffered Elinor's death, travelled abroad, engaged in business, joined a debating society and worshiped at Lexington Presbyterian Church.

Jackson married a second time, to Mary Anna Morrison, and the couple moved into the house in 1859. Of her husband's home, Mary Anna Jackson once wrote: ". . . it was genuine happiness to him to have a home of his own: it was the first one he had ever possessed, and it was truly his castle. He lost no time in going to work to repair it and make it comfortable and attractive. His tastes were simple, but he liked to have everything in perfect order — every door 'on golden hinges softly turning,' as he expressed it; 'a place for everything, and everything in its place.' . . ."

Two years later, in 1861, Jackson rode off to war. The house was used as a hospital for a number of years before it was restored and opened to visitors. A national landmark, the house displays a number of Jackson's personal effects. It is open Monday through Saturday from 9 AM to 5 PM and Sunday from 1 to 5 PM. In the summer, it is open until 6 PM. A $5 admission fee is charged for adults; children and students pay $2.50. Tours begin on the hour and half-hour, with the last beginning at 4:30 PM (in the summer, the last begins at 5:30 PM). To keep young visitors involved, guides provide each child with a slate that lists items on the house tour, and the youngster can circle each item when they see the object. Accommodations are made for handicapped visitors.

STONEWALL JACKSON HOUSE TO LEXINGTON PRESBYTERIAN CHURCH
From the intersection of Washington and Main streets, go one block south on Main Street to the intersection of Nelson Street.

Lexington Presbyterian Church
Main and Nelson Sts., Lexington, Va.

Lexington Presbyterian Church, built in 1845, is where "Stonewall" Jackson worshiped, taught Sunday school and served as a deacon, all prior to the Civil War. The church is open for Sunday services.

LEXINGTON PRESBYTERIAN CHURCH TO STONEWALL JACKSON MEMORIAL CEMETERY
From the intersection of Main and Nelson streets, walk two blocks south on Main Street, beyond the intersection of McDowell Street,

to the Stonewall Jackson Memorial Cemetery.

Stonewall Jackson Memorial Cemetery
S. Main St., Lexington, Va.

"Stonewall" Jackson is buried here at the Stonewall Jackson Memorial Cemetery, as are a number of other Confederate veterans. Jackson's statue, sculpted by Richmonder Edward Valentine, was dedicated in 1891, 23 years after Jackson's death after the Battle of Chancellorsville (T-16). The cemetery's setting fulfills CSA Gen. Jackson's dying wish: "Let us pass over the river, and rest under the shade of the trees." Admission to the cemetery, open dawn to dusk, is free.

STONEWALL JACKSON MEMORIAL CEMETERY TO WASHINGTON AND LEE UNIVERSITY
From the cemetery, return north on Main Street to Washington Street, turn left (west) and go one block on Washington Street, just beyond Jefferson Street, to the Washington & Lee campus.

Washington & Lee University

The university was founded by Scotch-Irish pioneers in the 1740s as Augusta Academy. Later, renamed Liberty Hall Academy, it was just north of Lexington. The school was saved from bankruptcy when former President George Washington bequeathed $50,000. The school was renamed Washington University.

After the Civil War, CSA Gen. Lee accepted the university's presidency and infused new vitality into the school. After Lee died in 1870, the school name was changed to Washington and Lee to honor the two most prominent men in its history. The 55-acre campus has 30 principal buildings, including the historic Washington College group that forms the colonnade facing Lee Chapel. The following four-building cluster is worth noting:

Robert E. Lee Memorial Episcopal Church

This Episcopal church was founded in 1840, mainly through the efforts of Gen. Francis

H. Smith, the first superintendent of VMI and a colleague and friend of CSA Gen. Lee. Lee was a senior warden of Grace Episcopal Church. In 1870, a few days before his death, Lee approved plans for a new church building. This church was completed in 1883.

Lee House

Lee House, the college president's residence, is closed to the public. It was built for Gen. Lee while he was president of W&L. He died in a room on the first floor. The large porch was included for Mrs. Lee, who was confined to a wheelchair, and the garage was formerly used as a stable for Lee's famous horse, Traveller.

Lee-Jackson House

The Lee-Jackson House, also closed to the public, is where CSA Gen. "Stonewall" Jackson married Elinor Junkin, the daughter of George Junkin, then-president of W&L. The

Jacksons, married in 1853, lived in the north wing of the house for a number of years. Gen. and Mrs. Lee lived in the house after he became president of the college and before the adjacent Lee House was constructed.

Lee Chapel

Lee Chapel is a memorial to Gen. Lee and his family. The general and his father, Revolutionary patriot Henry "Light Horse" Harry Lee, are among several family members interred in a crypt beneath the chapel. *The Recumbent Statue of R. E. Lee*, by Edward Valentine, the centerpiece of the chapel, portrays Lee sleeping — not dead — on the field of battle. A plaque honors the Liberty Hall Volunteers of the Stonewall Brigade, a Virginia militia unit that fought in the Confederacy during the Civil War. From April to October, the chapel is open on Sunday from 2 to 5 PM and Monday through Saturday from 9 AM to 5 PM. During winter, the chapel closes daily at 4 PM. In the

VMI Personality: Matthew Fontaine Maury

In the decade prior to the Civil War, Matthew Fontaine Maury was one of the most famous men in the world. A Virginia native, Maury was a pioneer in oceanography, earning him dozens of international medals, honorary degrees and diplomas.

Today, ironically, his name is an enigma, even in his home state. He has been described as one of the most neglected figures in the history of America and science. Born in Spotsylvania County, Virginia, young Matt Maury was only four when his family moved west to Franklin, Tennessee. In 1825, at the age of 19, he turned down a future in farming, opting instead for a midshipman's warrant in the U.S. Navy.

Maury was determined to learn about the sea, ships and sailing, and for nearly a decade of cruises he conducted a detailed and exhaustive study of navigation. Taking a leave of absence in 1834, he married his cousin, Ann Herndon of Fredericksburg, Virginia. The couple made their home in Fredericksburg, where Maury published his study, *A New Theoretical and Practical Treatise on Navigation*.

In 1836, the newly promoted Lt. Maury was assigned to survey the harbors of towns along the Southeast coast. Two years later he became a strong advocate of a naval academy, eventually established at Annapolis, Maryland. Maury's break came when he was assigned to the Depot of Charts and Instruments in Washington, D.C., and he was named superintendent of the new Naval Observatory.

By 1847 he released his *Winds and Currents Chart of the North Atlantic*, a study that helped mariners cut two weeks off a ship's travel from New York to Rio de Janeiro. Maury conceived a universal system of oceanography, prompting an international congress in Brussels in 1853, where Maury was the U.S. representative. Two years later, during the Western gold rush, Maury's updated information helped sea captains

— continued on next page

chapel is Lee's office, preserved as he left it in 1870. It is open the same hours and admission to both locations is free. Lee's famous horse, Traveller, is buried outside the chapel.

LEE CHAPEL TO VIRGINIA MILITARY INSTITUTE

Just to the north of the W&L campus, along Letcher Avenue in Lexington, is VMI, founded in 1839 on the site of an arsenal.

Virginia Military Institute

VMI is known as the West Point of the South. It is the nation's oldest state-supported military school, and it has sent graduates to every American conflict since the Mexican War in the 1840s.

CSA Gen. "Stonewall" Jackson, a graduate of West Point, is the big hero at VMI, where he taught natural philosophy and artillery tactics. He was austere, and he chose to stand while preparing his school lessons. He also stood while he ate because he thought it was better for digestion. His cadets thought he was crazy; they called him "Tom Fool." A plain, silent, polite man, he was shabbily dressed, sucked on lemons, and believed passionately in the sternest aspects of Presbyterianism and predestination.

John Mercer Brooke, chief of naval ordinance for the Confederacy, also taught at VMI as did Matthew Fontaine Maury, the "Pathfinder of the Sea" (see listing below, T-10 and T-17). In May 1864, VMI cadets made up a portion of the Confederate strength at the Battle of New Market, north of Harrisonburg (see T-3: New Market). More information follows on several buildings of note clustered around the parade field at VMI.

Commandant's Quarters

Built in 1852, the Commandant's Quarters

— continued from previous page
cut a ship's average travel time from New York to San Francisco from 180 to 133 days. That same year, Maury prepared a report that proved the practicality — and assured the success — of the first trans-Atlantic cable between the United States and Europe.

In April 1861, after Virginia's secession from the Union, Maury joined the Confederate Navy. He tinkered with the concept of electric mines and was sent to England the next year on "special service" for the Southern cause, to test his plan. At war's end, Maury was among Confederate representatives abroad who were excluded from the pardon of the amnesty.

Exiled in Mexico, Maury was named imperial commissioner of immigration in an unsuccessful scheme to colonize former Confederates. Then he spent two years back in England, writing geography school books. With his exile order lifted, Maury returned to Virginia in 1868 to become professor of meteorology at VMI. Always the scientist, he published his *Physical Survey of Virginia*, and lectured on how farming could benefit from weather observations.

Maury died in Lexington in February 1873. His remains were removed to Richmond seven months later. VMI cadets escorted the cortege north out of Lexington along the North River. At Goshen Pass, his favorite retreat, his casket was covered with mountain laurel and rhododendron. At Goshen, Maury's body was put on the train for Richmond and a burial in Hollywood Cemetery.

The North River near Lexington was renamed Maury River, and a VMI building was given his name. In 1923, Virginia named Va. Highway 39 out of Goshen the "Maury Highway," and that same year, a monument in his honor was dedicated at Goshen Pass. In 1929, a sculpture was unveiled on Monument Avenue in Richmond (see T-17: Richmond) to honor the Virginian once known around the world as "Pathfinder of the Seas."

Photo: Lexington Visitors Bureau

Little Sorrel, Jackson's horse, is on display at VMI Museum.

Lexington Personality: Sam Houston

Sam Houston, a hero of Texas independence, was the Lone Star State governor who resigned rather than sign a Confederate oath of allegiance.

Houston was born in a log cabin just north of Lexington in Rockbridge County, Virginia, in March 1793. Following his father's death, young Sam moved with his family to Tennessee, where he spent much of his youth with Native Americans of the Cherokee tribe. After a career in Tennessee politics, including terms as governor and congressman, Houston moved to Texas.

In 1835, Houston assumed command of a 400-man army that eventually defeated Mexican Gen. Santa Anna at Buffalo Bayou in 1836 and gained independence for Texas. Two months later, Houston was chosen over another Texas hero, Stephen Austin, as president of the new Republic of Texas. Ironically, Austin also was born in western Virginia — 125 miles south of Lexington, near present-day Wytheville — and only eight months after Houston.

Houston went to the U.S. Senate from the new state of Texas and served from 1846 to 1859. On the eve of the Civil War, he was a pro-Union advocate — a posture challenged by the Texas legislature. He was not re-elected to the U.S. Senate, but he did garner enough votes to be elected Texas governor in 1859.

Houston took office in 1860 and tried unsuccessfully to prevent the state from a move toward secession. On February 1, 1861, the 25th anniversary of Texas independence from Mexico, the state seceded from the Union despite considerable opposition among the Texas citizenry. Six weeks later, on March 18, 1861, after refusing to swear allegiance to the Confederacy, Houston was declared deposed from the governorship. Afterward, Houston and his wife, Margaret Lea, lived in Huntsville, Texas, where he died on July 26, 1863 — less than a month after the Battle of Gettysburg in Pennsylvania. The city of Houston, Texas, was named in his honor.

Lexington Side Trip: Natural Bridge and points south

From Lexington, take either U.S. 11 or I-81 south for 50 miles to see a string of attractive and historic locations.

Natural Bridge, which the Monocan Indians called the "Bridge of God," is considered one of the seven natural wonders of the world. Thomas Jefferson once owned it. Today, U.S. 11 runs over the top of the natural bridge, a tourist attraction complete with motel accommodations, a restaurant and a gift shop. Admission is $8 for adults and $4 for children ages 6 through 15. Take exit 175 off I-81 to find Natural Bridge.

Buchanan, a community at the water gap of the James River, is named for John B. Buchanan, the son-in-law of prominent local landowner, Col. James Patton. The noted James River and Kanawha Canal, which originated in Richmond and was designed to cross the eastern continental divide to the Kanawha River in present-day West Virginia, ended at Buchanan in 1851. USA Gen. David Hunter, on his way to Lynchburg in June 1864, passed through Buchanan. It is at exit 167 of I-81.

In colonial times, the Great Wagon Road split at **Troutville**, with one fork leading south to the Carolinas and the other leading west, beyond the nearby Catawba Mountains, to the Cumberland Gap. You can reach Troutville by taking exit 150 or 156 off I-81.

Roanoke was originally called Big Lick, for the salt licks used by native fauna. The name was changed to Roanoke for the river of the same name. "Roanoke" is a word of Native American origin and is among the first Indian words used by Anglo pioneers in the late 16th century. Exits 146 and 143 off I-81 will take you there. **Salem** is southeast of Roanoke. In June 1864, CSA Gen. Jubal Anderson "Old Jube" Early traveled through Roanoke County in the vicinity of Salem as he pursued USA Gen. Hunter, who was retreating from Lynchburg. Early and Hunter fought a battle at Hanging Rock, south of Salem, in June 1864. I-81 exits 141, 140 and 137 will get you to Salem.

After completing this side trip, return to Lexington, where this tour route ends.

served as the home of VMI professor Matthew Fontaine Maury from 1868 to 1872. This building is closed to the public.

The Barracks

VMI cadets live in the Barracks, where one arch is named in honor of "Stonewall" Jackson. The Jackson statue in front of the arch depicts the general surveying the field at Chancellorsville, where he was mortally wounded in 1863. The cannons beside the statue were cast in 1848, and they were the ones used by Jackson to teach artillery at VMI. This building is closed to the public.

Jackson Memorial Hall-VMI Museum

VMI campus, Lexington, Va.
• **(540) 464-7232**

Jackson Memorial Hall, also named to honor Jackson, is the assembly hall for VMI cadets. Inside, the prominent oil painting depicts the VMI cadets who fought in the Battle of New Market in Shenandoah County in 1864. It was painted by Benjamin West Clinedinst, an 1880 VMI graduate.

The VMI Museum, downstairs in Jackson Memorial Hall, displays a variety of Jackson memorabilia. The remains of Jackson's horse, Little Sorrel, are preserved and displayed at

This cannon was used by Stonewall Jackson to teach artillery at VMI.

Photo: Lexington Visitors Bureau

Annual Events

The birthdays of both Robert E. Lee (January 19) and Stonewall Jackson (January 21, the two are honored by a Virginia state holiday) are celebrated annually in January. Special functions honoring the two Confederate heroes are conducted at Stonewall Jackson House, Washington and Lee University, and Virginia Military Institute. Sunrise **Easter services** are conducted at nearby Natural Bridge (see listing). The **Rockbridge Community Festival** is held in August each year. **Holiday in Lexington** is an annual event held the first weekend in December and includes a parade, house tours, a 10-kilometer race and a downtown open house.

Arts

The **Lime Kiln Theater** has been called "the most unusual theater setting in the United States." The summer outdoor theater is part of Lime Kiln Arts Inc., a nonprofit organization in Lexington. The site itself is historic. A.T. Barclay, a Confederate veteran who served with CSA Gen. "Stonewall" Jackson, began the kiln in 1896 to make lime. A highlight of each year's performances is *Stonewall Country*, a musical about the Confederate general.

Playgoers dress casual and have a chance to sit on the lawn in the Bowl, one of the three performance spaces at the 12-acre site. Plays are presented Tuesdays through Saturdays from Memorial Day to Labor Day; concerts are featured each Sunday. Performances begin at 8 PM. For more information, contact Lime Kiln Theater, P.O. Box 663, Lexington, Va. 24450, or call (540) 463-3074. To reach the theater, take Nelson Street (U.S. 60) west of Lexington 1 mile to Borden Road on the left, and follow signs to the entrance. The theater is handicapped-accessible, although the outdoor facility has some rough terrain.

Attractions/Historic Sites

Lexington Carriage Company, (540) 463-5647, offers tours of historic downtown Lexington. The 40-minute, narrated carriage rides are available from 10 AM to 4 PM and depart from the Lexington Visitor Center. For schedule and rate information, contact Lexington Carriage Company at P.O. Box 1242, Lexington, Virginia 24450.

the museum too. There is also a display of a typical VMI cadet's room. The museum is open every day from 9 AM to 5 PM. It is handicapped-accessible, and admission is free. Adjacent to Jackson Memorial Hall is a statue, *Virginia Mourning Her Dead*, which honors the VMI cadets who fought in the Battle of New Market. Six of the 10 cadets killed in the Battle of New Market are buried behind the monument.

Lexington Tour Ends

Other Tour Points of Interest

If you have questions or need more information on the events and sites listed below, ask for help at the Lexington Visitor Center (see listing in this chapter). Also, the entire area of this tour route is covered in exhaustive detail in *The Insiders' Guide® to Virginia's Blue Ridge,* a comprehensive guide to all there is to see and do in this beautiful part of the world. Pick up a copy at your favorite book store.

Photo: Lexington Visitors Bureau

The Stonewall Jackson House is the only house the general ever owned.

The **George C. Marshall Museum**, (540) 463-7103, at VMI highlights the life of the famous World War II general, a 1901 graduate of the institute. The museum details the course of World War II and includes an electronic map. It also has a treasure hunt for children, displays the general's Nobel Peace Prize and features a museum shop. The museum is open daily from 9 AM to 5 PM. Admission is free.

Goshen Pass, a 3-mile mountain gorge, provides the setting for canoeing, fishing, trail-walking and picnicking. The gorge is on Va. Highway 39, northwest of Lexington.

Shopping

Take a visit to the **historic downtown Lex-** **ington** area for a variety of specialty shops and unique stores. Bob Lurate at **Lexington Historical Shop**, (540) 463-2615, 9 E. Washington Street, offers a wide variety of used and rare books, local history items, and Civil War memorabilia, including first-edition materials, artifacts, prints and documents. The store boasts one of the largest collections of historical materials in the state. It is open Monday through Saturday from 11 AM to 6 PM, and at other times by appointment. Downtown Lexington also includes clothing stores, a coffee roaster (**Lexington Coffee Roasting Co.**, 9 W. Washington Street), local artisans — even **Sweet Things**, a parlor at 106 W. Washington Street that serves up homemade ice cream.

Tour 6
Gettysburg

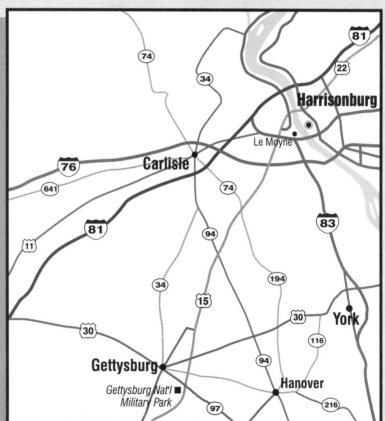

Harrisonburg

Le Moyne

Carlisle

York

Gettysburg

Hanover

Gettysburg Nat'l ■
Military Park

TOUR 6
Gettysburg

About This Tour

This route covers the community of Gettysburg, Pennsylvania, and its environs. The tour is the first of six in succession that cover a separate, distinct geographic feature of the Mid-Atlantic — the Piedmont — which runs north to south along the eastern slopes of the Appalachian Mountains. The other tour routes in this Piedmont series are T-7: Monocacy, T-8: Manassas, T-9: Brandy Station, T-10: Charlottesville and T-11: Lynchburg.

The area we concentrate on in this tour, the Piedmont of southern Pennsylvania, runs north-south along the eastern slopes of South Mountain and the Catoctin Mountains. To the north of Gettysburg, the rolling Pennsylvania farmland is part of the watershed for the great Susquehanna River. Native Americans lived and traveled in this scenic region long before Anglo pioneers arrived in the mid-18th century.

Europeans, mainly Germans and Scotch-Irish descendants, settled in the Pennsylvania Piedmont in the 1730s and 1740s. Most of these early pioneers, lured to the colonies by pacifist William Penn's advertisements, landed at Philadelphia and began a search for land where they could build homes and take up farming. As the population and land patents (similar to deeds) increased along the coastal plain, the Europeans pushed west, and their migration can be traced out of Philadelphia into this Piedmont region and eventually across the mountains into the Cumberland Valley.

Travel Tips

U.S. Highway 15 is a divided four-lane highway in this section of southern Pennsylvania. The Gettysburg area is farming country as the scenery attests. Be on the lookout for slow-moving tractors and other farm vehicles. Har-

risburg, Pennsylvania, and Washington, D.C., radio stations report traffic and weather conditions. Citizens band radio users can find traffic information on Channel 19, and state police usually monitor Channel 9. Motorists receive a strong mobile telephone signal throughout the Gettysburg vicinity.

This tour route concludes in Gettysburg, where we suggest you plan your evening dining and lodging. Recommended accommodations are listed in Chapter 22. Dining suggestions are listed in Chapter 23. It is a good idea to review these recommendations before traveling through the Gettysburg community. In addition to our suggestions, there are numerous fast-food facilities, gas stations, convenience markets and shops throughout the Gettysburg vicinity.

Getting Here

Gettysburg is 30 miles south of Harrisburg, Pennsylvania; 53 miles west of Lancaster, Pennsylvania; 118 miles west of Philadelphia; 65 miles east of Breezewood, Pennsylvania (the junction of Interstate 70 and Interstate 76, also called the Pennsylvania Turnpike); and 54 miles north of Baltimore. We suggest traveling to Gettysburg on U.S. 15 south out of Harrisburg.

Gettysburg Tour Begins . . .

HARRISBURG TO GETTYSBURG CONVENTION AND VISITORS BUREAU
Take U.S. 15 south out of Harrisburg toward Gettysburg.

LeMoyne, Pa.

Along U.S. 15, just across the

Photo: Gettysburg Convention & Visitors Bureau

Gettysburg National Cemetery was dedicated in November 1863, just four months after the battle.

Pennsylvania allocated funds for a courthouse for the new Adams County, the village was renamed Gettysburg. It was incorporated in 1806.

Gettysburg remained relatively obscure until the summer of 1863. The three-day Battle of Gettysburg, considered one of the most significant engagements in the Civil War, catapulted this obscure village into international, memorable fame.

GETTYSBURG TO GETTYSBURG CONVENTION AND VISITORS BUREAU

U.S. 30 becomes York Street. Continue 2 blocks on York Street to the main, downtown traffic circle, Lincoln Square. Turn right (north) at the circle onto Carlisle Street and go one block to the Gettysburg Convention and Visitors Bureau on the right. Parking is available adjacent to the building, and along the city streets.

Gettysburg Convention and Visitors Bureau
35 Carlisle St., Gettysburg, Pa.
- **(717) 334-6274**

The visitors bureau is a good place to start your experience in this historic community. It provides an opportune time to go over your lodging and dining arrangements and to get information on other sights and attractions in the vicinity. Also, ask travel counselors about special and discounted tickets to attractions. The center is open from 9 AM to 5 PM every day except major holidays. The facility offers restrooms and is handicapped-accessible.

Susquehanna River from Harrisburg, is Lemoyne, in Cumberland County, Pennsylvania. Lemoyne is named for an anti-slavery advocate, Francis LeMoyne. This town is the site of Fort Washington, the northernmost point Confederates reached during the Civil War. On June 29, 1863, two days before the Battle of Gettysburg, a Confederate cavalry unit exchanged shots with Union troops defending the state capital in Harrisburg. Today, Fort Washington is located at 8th and Ohio streets in Lemoyne.

Continue south on U.S. 15 for 30 miles to the Gettysburg exit for Lincoln Highway — U.S. Highway 30. Off the U.S. 30 exit go right (west) 2 miles to downtown Gettysburg.

Gettysburg, Pa.

Gettysburg was settled in the 1780s and originally called Marsh Creek Settlement. During the 1790s, Gen. James Gettys laid out a town that e called Gettys-town. In 1800, when

GETTYSBURG CONVENTION AND VISITORS BUREAU TO GETTYSBURG NATIONAL MILITARY PARK VISITORS CENTER

Return south on Carlisle Street one block to the downtown traffic circle, go halfway around the circle, then continue south on U.S. 15 (Bus.) or Baltimore Street, for five blocks. Shift right onto Steinwehr Avenue (U.S. 15 Bus.)

It's your move...
make it a good one.

In 295 pages, *The Insiders' Guide®
to Relocation* lends a helping
hand and offers tips that will go
a long way in reducing the
headaches commonly
attributed to moving.
Whether moving across
town or to another
country, this guide
covers many important
topics including:

   • relocation from a
   personal and corporate perspective
   • children's anxieties about moving and
   how to deal with them
   • organization for a successful, low-stress move
   • preparation for a partner's transfer
   • international business etiquette

The Insiders' Guide® to Relocation is available at your
local bookstore.

You can also order by calling (800) 765-2665 ext. 233 and
charging to your Visa or MC or by mailing the form below to:

The Insiders' Publishing Inc. • P.O. Box 2057
Manteo, NC 27954

Please send me a copy of *The Insiders' Guide® to Relocation*. I am enclosing $14.95 plus $3
shipping and handling for each book ordered. North Carolina residents add 90 ¢ sales tax.

Name: _____   Phone: _____

Address: _____

City/State/Zip: _____

and go two blocks to the Gettysburg National Military Park's Visitors Center on the left.

Gettysburg National Military Park Visitors Center
Steinwehr Ave., Gettysburg, Pa.
• (717) 334-1124

In early June 1863, a month after Chancellorsville in Virginia, CSA Gen. Robert E. Lee marched his Army of Northern Virginia west, through the gaps of the Blue Ridge Mountains, and north into Maryland and Pennsylvania. On his heels was the Union Army of the Potomac, commanded by USA Gen. Joseph "Fighting Joe" Hooker. The two armies met in the vicinity of Gettysburg quite by accident. The little village was home to a half-dozen tanneries, and a Confederate brigade was searching for new shoes and supplies when it chanced upon Union cavalry troops commanded by USA Gen. George Meade.

On the first day, July 1, Confederates attacked Northern troops on McPherson Ridge, just west of town. The outnumbered Union troops, commanded by Meade, were overpowered and driven to Cemetery Hill south of town.

During the second day at Gettysburg, the two armies were situated about a mile apart on parallel ridges — the North on Cemetery Ridge and the South on Seminary Ridge. Lee ordered an attacked against both Union flanks.

CSA Gen. James "Pete" Longstreet hit the Federal left, leaving the base of Little Round Top in shambles. At that point, Longstreet left Union dead strewn about the Wheatfield and he overran the Peach Orchard. To the north, CSA Gen. Richard Stoddert Ewell struck the Union right in the evening at East Cemetery Hill and Culp's Hill.

On the third day, July 3, Lee's artillery bombarded Federal lines on Cemetery Ridge and Cemetery Hill. This resulted in a thundering, two-hour duel by the cannon on both sides. Later in the day, Lee ordered some 12,000 Southerners to advance across a mile-long, open field toward the center of the Union line. This assault became known as "Pickett's Charge" — the namesake of CSA Gen. George Edward Pickett — in which an estimated 1,000 Confederates were killed.

Some consider Gettysburg the most significant battle of the Civil War. It certainly was costly — the North and South together suffered more than 50,000 killed, wounded or missing during the three days. The battle also is called the "High Water of the Confederacy," as it marked the end of the Confederate's second and final invasion of the North. After the three-day struggle, Lee's army moved south, and Meade later was criticized for failing to pursue the Southerners.

The Gettysburg Military Park Visitors Center is one of the best-equipped in the nation. It

Gettysburg Personality: USA Col. J. Lawrence Chamberlain

Joshua Lawrence Chamberlain, educated in Maine, was a 34-year-old professor at Bowdoin College in Maine in 1862 when he feigned a study trip abroad to join the U.S. Army. USA Col. Chamberlain fought at Antietam, then found himself at Gettysburg in late June 1863. For his leadership of the 20th Maine at Gettysburg's Little Round Top on July 2, he received a Congressional Medal of Honor.

Later in the war, he was shot in both hips, severely injured and not expected to live. However, he recovered and went on to see action at Spotsylvania, Cold Harbor and Petersburg. He was cited for bravery in action four times and wounded six times. He was promoted to brigadier general by a special order from USA Gen. Ulysses S. Grant, who gave Chamberlain the honor of accepting the Confederate surrender at Appomattox in April 1865. Chamberlain stunned friend and foe alike when he ordered his troops to attention at Appomattox to salute the defeated Southern troops. He went on to become governor of Maine and president of Bowdoin College. He died of his old war wounds in June 1914, at the age of 83.

has an information desk, a bookstore with ample materials for adults and children, and two floors of exhibits on uniforms, rifles, pistols, sabers, swords and cannon. The center has a simulated Civil War tent and field display. There is a large collection of Civil War memorabilia on display as well as a tribute to the African-American soldiers who fought in the Union Army.

A separate room houses an electronic map that vividly demonstrates troop movements during the Battle of Gettysburg (there is a $2.50 fee for the electronic map demonstration, which runs about every 45 minutes). The center's cyclorama has a free, 10-minute film, and a sound-and-light program is available. There are separate, informative brochures on the "High Water Mark" walking tour and the National Cemetery. Make sure you get the NPS brochure — it contains valuable information on how to get around the historic area as well as important rules and regulations.

The brochure also provides an excellent, capsulated rundown of the three important

Gettysburg Personalities: USA Gen. Winfield Scott Hancock and CSA Gen. Lewis Addison Armistead

Winfield Scott Hancock was born in Montgomery County, Pennsylvania, in February 1824. He graduated in 1844 from the U.S. Military Academy at West Point, and he served with honor in the Mexican War from 1846 to 1848. Appointed a brigadier general, he served in the Peninsular Campaign (T-18, T-19) of 1862.

Lewis Addison Armistead was born in North Carolina in 1817. He, too, attended West Point, where he was dismissed in 1836 for breaking a plate over the head of a classmate, Jubal Anderson Early. Armistead was commissioned an officer in the regular U.S. Army in 1839 and went on to gallantry in the Mexican War. He resigned

Photo: Antietam National Battlefield

CSA Gen. Lewis Armistead saw action in the Mexican War and in the Civil War's Peninsula Campaign.

from the Army in 1861 and joined the Confederacy as a major. Armistead was promoted to brigadier general in time to see action in the Peninsula Campaign.

A story is told of several U.S. Army officers, all old friends stationed in California, who met in 1861 for an emotional pre-Civil War farewell gathering. Armistead was among the Southern men who planned to leave the U.S. Army and join the Confederacy. It was particularly difficult for Armistead, for the farewell party broke up his close personal friendship with his host, Hancock.

At Gettysburg, Hancock was shot and injured at Seminary Ridge on July 3. Armistead was seriously wounded the same day while attacking the Union line at Seminary Ridge as part of Pickett's Charge. As he lay dying, surrounded by Union soldiers, Armistead asked about his friend, Hancock. Armistead requested that his personal belongings, including a Bible, be sent to Almira Hancock, the wife of his longtime friend.

After Gettysburg, Hancock participated in the Union drive on Richmond in 1865. After the war, he commanded the military division of Louisiana and Texas. His Reconstruction policies in the South endeared him to the Democratic Party, which made him their candidate for president in 1880. Hancock narrowly lost to James A. Garfield, returned to military life and died at Governor's Island, New York, in February 1886.

Photo: Gettysburg Convention & Visitors Bureau

A statue and an avenue in Gettysburg honor USA Gen. John Sedgwick.

days in Gettysburg's history — July 1-3, 1863. The visitors center is open daily from 8 AM to 5 PM, except on Thanksgiving, Christmas and New Year's Day. There is ample parking. For those who want to stroll the grounds, the battlefield is open from 6 AM to 10 PM.

Today, the Gettysburg battlefield is America's most tangible link to those three hot days in July 1863. Much of the landscape and park property looks just as it did 130 years ago. There is a self-guided auto tour book available at the visitors center, and the drive around the historic area includes numbered stops with markers that describe battle action. You can also take an auto tour with a licensed guide (there is a fee of $30 for up to five prople).

Walking about the battlefield, you can follow specially marked routes that include the High Water Mark Trail, Big Round Top Loop Trail, Billy Yank Trail, Johnny Reb Trail and paths to Devil's Den and Point of Woods.

The Gettysburg battlefield was used for the filming of the motion picture, *Gettysburg*, in the early 1990s. The film, based on the book *The Killer Angels* by Michael Shaara, immortalized a number of Civil War names, including CSA Gens. Lee, Longstreet and Pickett as well as USA Gens. Meade, Winfield Scott Hancock and Joshua F. Reynolds — and especially USA Col. Joshua Lawrence Chamberlain.

Gettysburg Personalities: Ghosts

During the first day's fighting at Gettysburg, Confederate troops under Gen. Alfred Iverson unwittingly exposed their flank and walked into a slaughter from Union troops hiding behind stone walls along today's Doubleday Avenue. The field was strewn with the bodies of more than 450 dead Confederate soldiers, who were hastily buried on the scene after the battle.

The bodies were exhumed in 1871. A farmer who owned the field said he was unable to get farmhands to work because of the "perturbed spirits" that were reported to be roaming in the area. It took years before crops grew on the sacred land. The farm owner later planted a vineyard in the depression left at the site, now known as "Iverson's Pit."

President Lincoln's Gettysburg Address

Following the three-day Civil War battle, Gettysburg was left in shambles. The townspeople were left to care for more than 50,000 dead, wounded and ill. Many of the casualties were put to rest in hastily dug graves; some were just not buried. The situation so distressed Pennsylvania Gov. Andrew Curtin that he convinced a Gettysburg attorney to buy land for a proper burial ground for Union dead. This became Gettysburg National Cemetery.

The cemetery was dedicated in November, just four months after the famous battle. The main speaker was Edward Everett, a politician, statesman and orator from Massachusetts. Everett's resume was awesome, and his list of experience was impressive: U.S. House member, governor of Massachusetts, U.S. minister to England, president of Harvard University, U.S. secretary of state, U.S. Senate member and an unsuccessful third-party vice presidential candidate in 1860. Everett delivered a two-hour address at Gettysburg. President Lincoln followed Everett at the podium to deliver a few appropriate remarks.

"Four-score and seven years ago," the President began his now-famous Gettysburg Address. He spoke just two minutes and uttered a mere 272 words. He considered the talk a failure. The world has judged it an eloquent masterpiece. The full text follows.

Photo: Harpers Ferry National Historical Park

President Lincoln considered his Gettysburg Address a failure.

"Four-score and seven years ago, our fathers brought forth on this continent a new nation, conceived in liberty and dedicated to the proposition that all men are created equal. Now we are engaged in a great civil war, testing whether that nation or any nation so conceived and so dedicated can long endure. We are met on a great battle field of that war. We have come to dedicate a portion of that field, as a final resting place for those who here gave their lives that this nation might live. It is altogether fitting and proper that we should do this.

But, in a larger sense, we can not dedicate — we can not consecrate — we can not hallow — this ground. The brave men, living and dead, who struggled here, have consecrated it, far above our poor power to add or detract. The world will little note, nor long remember, what we say here, but it can never forget what they did here. It is for us the living, rather, to be here dedicated to the unfinished work which they who fought here have thus far so nobly advanced. It is rather for us to be here dedicated to the great task remaining before us — that from these honored dead we take increased devotion to that cause for which they gave the last full measure of devotion —that we here highly resolve that these dead shall not have died in vain — that this nation, under God, shall have a new birth of freedom — and that government of the people, by the people, for the people, shall not perish from the earth."

Photo: Gettysburg Convention & Visitors Bureau

The 72nd Pennsylvania Infantry statue memorializes the soldiers who fought at Gettysburg.

Gettysburg Side Trip: Hanover, Pa.

This side trip is only for the most hardy Civil War enthusiast, because there is little evidence here of a June 30, 1863, battle — the first war action north of the Mason-Dixon line.

Hanover is 15 miles east of Gettysburg on U.S. 30 and Pennsylvania Highway 94. CSA Gen. James Ewell Brown "Jeb" Stuart's cavalry division faced Union cavalry troops under the command of USA Gen. Hugh Judson "Kill Cavalry" Kilpatrick. Stuart and his men captured a number of prisoners in the streets of Hanover before the Northerners mounted a counterattack. Stuart, riding his thoroughbred, Virginia, escaped almost certain capture by jumping a ditch.

The engagement kept Stuart from reaching Gettysburg on time. His arrival, a day after Gettysburg fighting began, meant that CSA Gen. Robert E. Lee was deprived of the "eyes of his army."

Gettysburg Tour Ends

Other Tour Points of Interest

Gettysburg is unique in that almost all its points of interest are related to the town's 1863 Civil War action. No question, Gettysburg is a tourist mecca, with sights and attractions to interest all ages. Try to stay several days here — Gettysburg grows on you. For questions or reservations, ask for help at the Gettysburg Convention and Visitors Bureau (see listing).

Annual Events

The **Apple Blossom Festival** is held the first weekend in May, and the **Apple Harvest Festival** is held the first two weekends in October. **Bluegrass festivals** are held in May and September. **Outdoor antique shows** are held annually in May and September.

Gettysburg Civil War Heritage Days are held annually the last weekend in June and the first week in July — coinciding with the actual dates of the 1863 battles. This event features living history encampments, band concerts, a lecture series and battle reenactments. And there's the annual observance of President Lincoln's Gettysburg Address, in November at the Gettysburg National Cemetery.

Antiques

Ask any Gettysburg local — for antiques, you can shop 'til you drop in the little Victorian village of **New Oxford**, 10 miles east of Gettysburg on U.S. 30. The Gettysburg Convention and Visitors Bureau can help you justify the trip to New Oxford — it's on the **Historic Conewago Tour**, a two-hour driving loop

Gettysburg Personality: Cornelia Hancock

Cornelia Hancock was young and attractive — two attributes that otherwise might have dissuaded Dorothea Lynde Dix, the Union superintendent of women nurses, from using Hancock to treat the sick and wounded at the Gettysburg battlefield. But Hancock was a hard-working Pennsylvania Quaker, and Dix overlooked her possibly distracting attributes. Hancock remained a nurse throughout the remainder of the war.

Gettysburg Side Trip: Cashtown, Pa.

Cashtown, 15 miles west of Gettysburg on U.S. 30, is in the South Mountains. Confederate troops, on the way over the mountains from Chambersburg, Pennsylvania, assembled in late June 1863 before advancing to Gettysburg. Just west of Cashtown is Caledonia Furnace. During a raid in 1863, CSA Gen. Jubal Anderson "Old Jube" Early destroyed the charcoal iron furnace — leaving only the stacks. The site now is a state forest park.

that passes by East Cavalry Battlefield, churches and farms in the Adams County area east of Gettysburg.

Arts

There are a number of galleries and print shops in and around the Gettysburg area. The **Gettysburg Dinner Theater**, complete with Civil War musicals and authentic period music, is near the entrance to the Gettysburg National Military Park on Steinwehr Avenue.

Historic Sites

Again, most of Gettysburg's historical sites relate to the community's rich Civil War history. Take advantage of auto and bus tours, particularly the **Gettysburg Battlefield Bus Tours**, (717) 334-6296. Also check into steam train rides and the diorama at **Battle Theatre**, a park-cyclorama with a sound-and-light program, (717) 334-6100.

See the **Confederate States Armory and Museum** on Baltimore Street, (717) 337-2340.

Gettysburg Personality: CSA Gen. George Edward Pickett

In 1851, a decade before the Civil War began, George Edward Pickett had reason to celebrate. He was 25 when he married his sweetheart, Sally Minge, who — like Pickett himself — was a Richmond, Virginia, native. But Pickett's marital bliss was short-lived. His wife died after only 11 months of marriage.

Photo: Antietam National Battlefield

An 1846 graduate of West Point, last in his class of 59 students, Pickett immediately saw action in the Mexican War. At the outbreak of the Civil War, Pickett was promoted to colonel and then brigadier general, and he saw action during the 1862 Peninsular Campaign against USA Gen. George Brinton "Young Napoleon" McClellan (T-18, T-19). Pickett was severely wounded at Gaines' Mill, east of Richmond, in June 1862.

The following year, at Gettysburg, Pickett's men took part in the famous "Pickett's Charge." Pickett didn't actually command the attack, and his troops didn't alone make up the largest part of the assault. Later in the war, Pickett saw action at Drewry's Bluff south of Richmond (T-20) in May 1864.

"Pickett's Charge" was named for CSA Gen. George Edward Pickett.

A dapper man, Pickett had shoulder-length hair worn in long, perfumed ringlets. He was a Norfolk insurance agent until he died in July 1875, a decade after Appomattox. The veteran's body was placed in a temporary vault until October that year, when his remains were borne to his native Richmond. He was buried at Hollywood Cemetery with full military honors.

The **National Civil War Wax Museum** is on Steinwehr Avenue, (717) 334-6245. The **Ghosts of Gettsburg Candlelight Tours,** (717) 337-0445, offers a unique way to see the town and experience the history.

Dale Gallon's Civil War artwork is displayed in more than 400 galleries nationwide, but (as you might expect) the best collection of his work is at **Dale Gallon Historical Art**, 9 Steinwehr Avenue, (717) 334-0430. The gallery, owned by Gallon, is open every day except winter Wednesdays, with extended hours during the summer season.

You'll have to search for something that's not Civil War oriented. One place is a gem — **Eisenhower National Historic Site**, where President Dwight Eisenhower and his wife, Mamie, retired after leaving Washington. The Eisenhower farm can be accessed only by shuttle buses from the Gettysburg National Park Vistitor's Center.

Shopping

There are countless shops that offer Civil War memorabilia and souvenirs. Countless. Pick up a Gettysburg travel guide book at the Gettysburg Convention and Visitor Bureau to get yourself started.

Tour 7
Monocacy

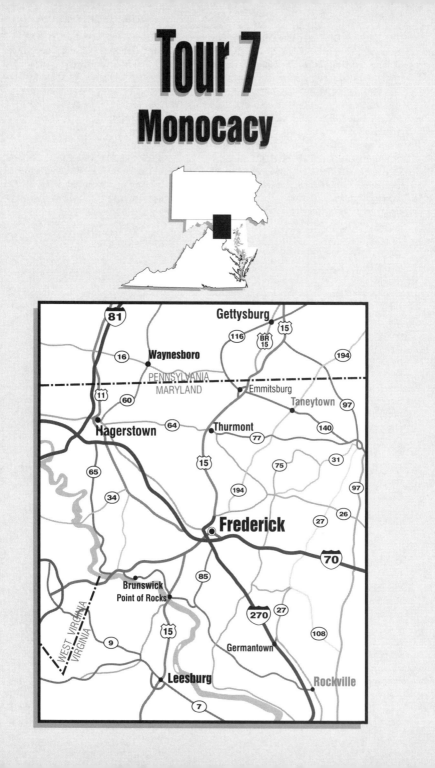

TOUR 7
Monocacy

About This Tour

This tour covers the Piedmont area of Pennsylvania, Maryland and Virginia. It begins in Gettysburg, Pennsylvania, and concludes 75 miles to the south, in Leesburg, Virginia. This route is one of six — from T-6: Gettysburg to T-11: Lynchburg — covering the Piedmont region of the Mid-Atlantic.

The geography and history of this tour are similar to the preceding Gettysburg route. Native Americans lived and traveled in this region long before Anglo pioneers arrived in the mid-18th century. The area was settled mainly by German and Scotch-Irish pioneers, who landed at Philadelphia and pushed west across the Piedmont to the Cumberland and Shenandoah valleys in the mountains. North of Gettysburg, the Piedmont region is a watershed for the Susquehanna River. South of Gettysburg, the Piedmont is drained by the Monocacy River, which flows through Frederick, beyond the site of the famous battle named for the river, then on to the Potomac River.

Travel Tips

This tour begins by leaving Gettysburg on U.S. Highway 15, which is a four-lane, divided highway in this section of southern Pennsylvania, central Maryland and northern Virginia. Frederick, Maryland, and Washington, D.C., radio stations report traffic and weather conditions. Citizens band radio users can find traffic information on Channel 19. State police usually monitor Channel 9. Motorists receive a strong mobile telephone signal throughout the Frederick and Leesburg areas.

The route ends in Leesburg, where we suggest you plan evening dining and lodging. Recommended accommodations are listed in Chapter 22; dining suggestions in Chapter 23. It is a good idea to review these recommendations before traveling through the region. In addition to our suggestions, there are the expected fast-food facilities, gas stations, convenience markets and shops along U.S. 15.

Monocacy Tour Begins . . .

GETTYSBURG, PA., TO THE MASON-DIXON LINE

Leaving Gettysburg, take U.S. 15 (Bus.) and U.S. 15 south to Maryland. A mile south of the U.S. 15 (Bus.) and U.S. 15 interchange is the Mason-Dixon Line (see T-1: Sharpsburg), the boundary between Pennsylvania and Maryland.

Mason-Dixon Line

This dividing line separated the North and South during the Civil War. The line was surveyed in the 1760s by two Englishmen, Charles Mason and Jeremiah Dixon. At the Mason-Dixon Line this tour enters Frederick County, Maryland's largest county and one of the state's most historic localities.

MASON-DIXON LINE TO EMMITSBURG, MD.

Continue south on U.S. 15 for 1 mile beyond Mason-Dixon Line to Emmitsburg.

Emmitsburg, Md.

Samuel Emmit, an Irishman, obtained a land patent in the mid-18th century and laid

Thurmont Side Trip: Catoctin Mountain Park

Catoctin Mountain Park offers walking trails, scenic drives, camping and watersports. Camp David is not visible from the roadway and is closed to the public. To reach the park visitor center, take the Md. Highway 77 exit off U.S. 15 at Thurmont and go west 2 miles to the center on the right.

out a town in the 1780s. Originally the community was known as Silver Fancy. Union forces moved through Emmitsburg in June 1863 just days before the Battle of Gettysburg.

EMMITSBURG TO THURMONT, MD.

Leaving Emmitsburg, continue south 8 miles on U.S. 15 to Thurmont, Md.

Thurmont, Md.

Thurmont is the gateway to Catoctin Mountain Park, a scenic and historic site that is home to Camp David, the U.S. Presidential retreat.

THURMONT TO CATOCTIN FURNACE, MD.

From Thurmont, continue south on U.S. 15 for 4 miles to Catoctin Furnace.

Catoctin Furnace

This furnace was established during the American Revolution. Iron from these mountains was used to produce arms during the Revolutionary War and the Civil War. Catoctin is an Algonquin word that means "speckled mountain," which accurately describes the rock from the region. Columns in Statuary Hall in the U.S. Capitol are made of Catoctin stone.

CATOCTIN FURNACE TO FREDERICK, MD.

From Catoctin Furnace, continue south on U.S. 15 for 6 miles to the northern limits of Frederick.

Frederick, Md.

Frederick is the seat of Frederick County. This village was settled by German immigrants who arrived in the mid-1700s. An Irishman, Daniel Dulaney, then laid out Frederick in 1745.

Photo: Antietam National Battlefield

Frederick, Md., was a bustling town when Civil War hostilities broke out in 1861.

A half-century later it was called Fredericktowne. Incorporated in 1817, Frederick was named either for Frederick Calvert, the sixth Lord Baltimore, or for Frederick, Prince of Wales, who was a friend of Lord Baltimore.

Frederick is conveniently located in the Maryland Piedmont. Several highways intersect here — Interstates 70 and 270, U.S. Highway 40, U.S. 15 and U.S. Highway 460. Frederick was also a strategic location in the 1860s, and that's one reason why it experienced considerable Civil War action.

CSA Gen. Robert E. Lee, following his victory at Manassas (T-8) in August 1862, marched his Army of Northern Virginia into Maryland to look for vitally needed men and supplies. USA Gen. George Brinton McClellan followed. In Frederick, McClellan fell upon a copy of a Confederate battle plan, known as "Lee's Special Order Number 191." McClellan pushed 12 miles farther west, to the passes through South Mountain, in pursuit of Lee. The Battle of Antietam was fought just southwest of Frederick (see T-1: Sharpsburg).

In June 1863, just before the Battle of Gettysburg, USA Gen. George Meade assumed command of the Army of the Potomac from USA Gen. Joseph "Fighting Joe" Hooker. The event took place at Prospect Hall, just west of Frederick. CSA Gen. Jubal Anderson "Old Jube" Early, on his march toward Washington in July 1864, paused in Frederick prior to the Battle of the Monocacy — the "Battle that Saved Washington." While in Frederick, Early demanded and received a $200,000 ransom from the townspeople (see "Old City Hall" listing in this chapter).

FREDERICK TO FREDERICK VISITORS CENTER

*U.S. 15 cuts through the heart of Frederick heading south. Take exit 6 for Patrick Street (U.S. 40-A, Md. Highway 144), then follow W. Patrick Street east to downtown — after 0.7 mile the street becomes one-way South Street. Continue 0.8 mile on South Street to the intersection with Market Street, turn left (north) onto one-*way Market Street (Md. Highway 355) and go 2 blocks. Turn right on Church Street; the visitor center is on the left, at 19 E. Church Street.*

Frederick Visitor Center
19 E. Church St., Frederick, Md.
• (301) 663-8687, (800) 999-3613

This visitor center is amid a host of downtown attractions, all within a 33-block historic district. The center has abundant information on attractions as well as dining and lodging facilities in the area. Group tours of the downtown historic area can be arranged, along with guided walking tours (April to December) and carriage rides. The only item you need to buy is a walking tour brochure of the Frederick historical sites, and it costs a mere 50 cents. Most all of Frederick's attractions can be observed by simply taking a casual stroll through the old town area. Only a few sites require motoring outside the downtown area. The visitor center is open from 9 AM to 5 PM every day except New Year's Day, Easter, Thanksgiving, Christmas, New Year's Day and Easter. It is handicapped-accessible.

FREDERICK VISITOR CENTER TO KEMP HALL

Begin your downtown walking tour with Kemp Hall, located across Church Street from the visitors center on the southeast corner of E. Church and N. Market streets.

Kemp Hall
E. Church and N. Market Sts., Frederick, Md.

Maryland was a border state during the Civil War, and there were factions in the state that supported both Union and Confederate interests. During the war's earliest days, newly elected President Lincoln asked the Maryland Civil War Legislature to vote on the issue of secession. He purposefully asked the legislature to leave Annapolis and meet in Frederick, so that a number of Maryland's southern delegates — proponents of secession — would be unable to attend. Frederick historians say Maryland may well have shifted its allegiance to the South had it not been for this early meeting at Kemp Hall. The building, which now houses various businesses, is marked with a bronze plaque.

KEMP HALL TO EVANGELICAL LUTHERAN CHURCH

Walk back across E. Church Street, and go just beyond the visitors center to Evangelical Lutheran Church.

Evangelical Lutheran Church
35 E. Church St., Frederick, Md.

This church was organized in 1738 by German Lutheran pioneers and built of logs. This particular, handsome German Gothic structure was constructed in 1854, less than a decade prior to the Civil War. The spires, outstanding Lutheran architecture, were among those referred to by John Greenleaf Whittier when he wrote the ballad of "Barbara Fritchie" (see Barbara Fritchie listing).

EVANGELICAL LUTHERAN CHURCH TO ST. JOHN THE EVANGELIST ROMAN CATHOLIC CHURCH

Continue walking 2 blocks east on Church Street, turn left (north) on Chapel Alley and go a short block to E. Second Street. The church is at 116 E. Second Street.

St. John the Evangelist Roman Catholic Church
116 E. Second St., Frederick, Md.

St. John's Church and Evangelical Lutheran Church are both good examples of the rich ethnic roots in old Frederick. The Catholic church was built by Irish immigrants in 1837, and it is the oldest of its faith in the nation, according to the Frederick Historical Society. During the 1860s, Civil War soldiers were held as prisoners in this church.

ST. JOHN CHURCH TO ST. JOHN CEMETERY

Walk north on Chapel Alley to E. Third Street, turn right (east) on Third Street and walk one block to East Street. The cemetery is on East Street between Third and Fourth streets.

St. John Cemetery
East and Third Sts., Frederick, Md.

St. John Cemetery includes the graves of Roger Brooke Taney, former chief justice of the Supreme Court, and a number of Maryland Civil War soldiers, including USA Pvt. George Washington of the 23rd U.S. Colored Troops. The cemetery is open dawn to dusk.

ST. JOHN CEMETERY TO OLD CITY HALL

Backtrack down Chapel Alley to E. Second Street and walk west toward Market Street. Old City Hall is at the intersection of Market and Second streets.

Old City Hall
124 N. Market St., Frederick, Md.

Old City Hall boasted a dubious Civil War distinction. CSA Gen. Early and his troops entered Frederick in July 1864 on their way to invade Washington, D.C. Early demanded $200,000 in cash — or its equivalent in supplies — or he threatened to torch the town. Local bankers scrambled to honor his request and paid Early at the Old City Hall. From Frederick, Early's men moved south and encountered Union troops in the noted Battle of the Monocacy (see listing).

OLD CITY HALL TO FREDERICK PRESBYTERIAN CHURCH

Continue west on Second Street, then cross Market Street to Frederick Presbyterian Church.

Frederick Presbyterian Church
115 W. Second St., Frederick, Md.

The Frederick Presbyterian Church was built in 1845, though the congregation dates to the American Revolution. This was a hospital during the Civil War. An interesting note — During the war, the Presbyterian minister's wife was a close friend of CSA Gen. Thomas Jonathan "Stonewall" Jackson's wife. Prior to the Battle of Antietam, Jackson stopped at the church to deliver a letter from Mrs. Jackson to the minister's wife.

FREDERICK PRESBYTERIAN CHURCH TO RAMSEY HOUSE

Continue west on Second Street and turn left on Record Street. Ramsey House is a quarter-block on the right.

Ramsey House
119 Record St., Frederick, Md.

USA Gen. George Lucas Hartsuff, recuperating from injuries he received at the Battle of Antietam, was a guest at Ramsey House in the fall of 1862. President Lincoln, after an inspection of the noted battlefield on Antietam Creek, returned east through Frederick in October 1862 and stopped at Ramsey House to visit the ailing Hartsuff. The president stepped outside and spoke to a small group assembled on Record Street. Today, the Ramsey House is a private residence that cannot be toured, but it is included as part of a downtown walking tour.

USA Gen. Joseph "Fighting Joe" Hooker was relieved of his command near Frederick, just prior to the Battle of Gettysburg.

RAMSEY HOUSE TO DR. JOHN TYLER'S HOME

Continue south down Record Street to Church Street. Across from City Hall and Courthouse Square is the site of Dr. John Tyler's home.

Dr. John Tyler's Home
108 W. Church St., Frederick, Md.

Dr. Tyler was a noted ophthalmologist. He had a pet dog, named Guess. Guess was the model for the black, cast-iron dog at the front of the Tyler House. This cast-iron model was stolen in 1862 by Confederate soldiers, who planned to melt down the statue to make bullets. But the plan went awry. Guess — the model — was found near the Antietam Battlefield and safely returned to his home on Church Street. The house is not open for tours, but you can still see the statue of ol' Guess as you pass by on a downtown walking tour.

DR. JOHN TYLER'S HOME TO COURTHOUSE SQUARE

Walk across Church Street to Courthouse Square.

Courthouse Square

City Hall was built in 1862, which means the Victorian building was in the square during Civil War action in Frederick. In the square are two busts — Thomas Johnson, Maryland's first governor, and Roger Brooke Taney, chief justice of the Supreme Court.

COURTHOUSE SQUARE TO EVANGELICAL REFORMED CHURCH

Continue east on Church Street, back toward Market Street, to the Evangelical Reformed Church.

Evangelical Reformed Church
15 W. Church St., Frederick, Md.

The Greek Revival church was built in 1848. Barbara Fritchie was a member of this church. CSA Gen. "Stonewall" Jackson worshipped at the church on the Sunday prior to the Battle of Antietam in 1862.

to March. Admission is $2, and the building is handicapped-accessible.

EVANGELICAL REFORMED CHURCH TO BARBARA FRITCHIE REPLICA HOUSE AND MUSEUM

Walk south on Market Street one block, turn right (west) and go two blocks on W. Patrick Street to the Barbara Fritchie House on the left.

Barbara Fritchie Replica House and Museum

154 W. Patrick St., Frederick, Md.
• (301) 698-0630

The Fritchie House is a reconstruction. Barbara Fritchie was immortalized in John Greenleaf Whittier's poem as the woman who challenged Confederate troops in Frederick in September 1862 during the Battle of Antietam. Whittier wrote that Fritchie said, "Shoot if you must, this old gray head, but spare your country's flag." From April to September, the house is open Monday, Thursday, Friday and Saturday from 10 AM to 4 PM and Sunday 1 to 4 PM. In October and November, the house is closed weekdays except by appointment, with operating hours Saturday from 10 AM to 4 PM and Sunday from 1 to 4 PM. Visitors see samples of Fritchie's clothes, furnishings and personal effects. It is closed from December

BARBARA FRITCHIE HOUSE TO B&O RAILROAD STATION

Backtrack on Patrick Street, turn right (south) and go one block to All Saints Street. The old B&O Station is on the southeast corner of S. Market and E. All Saints streets.

B&O Railroad Station

S. Market and E. All Saints Sts., Frederick, Md.

In October 1862, following his tour of the Antietam battlefield southwest of Frederick, President Lincoln spoke to a crowd from his train at the old station here. Following his speech, Lincoln returned to Washington. The old station now is the home of the Frederick Community Center.

B&O RAILROAD STATION TO NATIONAL MUSEUM OF CIVIL WAR MEDICINE

From S. Market and E. All Saints streets, backtrack on Market, turn right on Patrick Street and go one block to 48 E. Patrick Street.

Frederick Personality: Barbara Fritchie (Mary Quantrill)

Barbara Fritchie was 95 when John Greenleaf Whittier immortalized her name with the publishing of his poem, "Barbara Fritchie," in the October 1863 issue of *Atlantic Monthly*. But her instant fame may have resulted from a mistake. Civil War scholars think it was Mary Quantrill — not Fritchie — who was defiant with "Stonewall" Jackson's troops.

Mrs. Quantrill and her daughter stood at the gate of her house and waved several U.S. flags at Jackson's Confederates. Union troops, in town after the Confederates left, got word that Mrs. Fritchie — not Mrs. Quantrill — had challenged the Rebels. Someone gave Fritchie a fresh, new American flag, which she waved triumphantly at the Northern soldiers. USA Gen. Jesse Lee Reno tried to buy the flag from Mrs. Fritchie, but he was unsuccessful. Ironically, Gen. Reno was killed days later while fighting in the South Mountains west of Frederick. Meanwhile, through mistaken identity, Fritchie was the name passed on to the poet Whittier — and it was Fritchie, not Quantrill, who became a household word.

National Museum of Civil War Medicine
48 E. Patrick St., Frederick, Md.
• (301) 695-1864, (800) 564-1864

The city of Frederick recently converted the old Goodwin Building on E. Patrick Street into museum space and has leased the facility to the newly created National Museum of Civil War Medicine. Managed by a private board of directors, this new visitor facility details Frederick's role in caring for so many Civil War wounded after the battles at Antietam and the Monocacy. Its first phase exhibit opened in June 1996 and features five separate vignettes on Civil War medicine and medical care. The self-guided tour is free, but the museum requests a $2 contribution per visitor. In the future, the museum plans to develop two full floors of special exhibits. Currently, the museum has no restroom facilities; when it constructs restrooms, it will begin charging an admission fee. The museum is handicapped-accessible. In addition, the museum offers a Civil War walking tour of a 10-block area of downtown Frederick. Tour guides give a detailed account of sites associated with Civil War action. The tour costs $4.50 for everyone older than 12 and $3.50 for seniors. Children 12 or younger are admitted free.

NATIONAL MUSEUM OF CIVIL WAR MEDICINE TO FREDERICK VISITOR CENTER
Continue back north on Market Street one block, turn right on E. Church Street and return to the visitor center.

(See listing for visitors center, earlier in tour.)

FREDERICK VISITORS CENTER TO MOUNT OLIVET CEMETERY
In order to exit downtown Frederick by automobile, it is good to remember that E. Market Street in this area is one-way headed north. To exit to the south, drive east on Church Street three blocks, turn right on Carroll Street

— which runs parallel to Market Street — and go south three blocks. Turn right on South Street and return to Market Street. At this intersection, Market Street is two-way, and you can exit either north or south. Exiting to the south on Market Street, you will pass Mount Olivet Cemetery.

Mount Olivet Cemetery
515 S. Market St., Frederick, Md.

Among the notables buried at Mount Olivet Cemetery are Francis Scott Key, composer of *The Star Spangled Banner*, former Maryland Gov. Thomas Johnson, Barbara Fritchie and more than 800 Union and Confederate soldiers who fell in battle at Antietam and the Monocacy. The cemetery, established in 1852, is open dawn to dusk.

MOUNT OLIVET CEMETERY TO MONOCACY NATIONAL BATTLEFIELD
From downtown Frederick, take Market Street (Md. 355) south 0.5 mile across I-70 and continue 2 miles south on Md. 355 (Urbanna Pike) to the Monocacy National Battlefield Visitor Center.

Monocacy National Battlefield Visitor Center
4801 Urbana Pike, Frederick, Md.
• (301) 662-3515

The battle here on the Monocacy River on July 9, 1864, quite possibly saved the nation's capital from falling. For that reason — not because of the battle's size — this conflict is considered among the Civil War's more noted battles.

The visitor center at Monocacy is in an old mill. Operated by the National Park Service, the center offers a detailed brochure of the Monocacy battlefield area. It also has a brochure that outlines an automobile tour of the Monocacy area. The center is open daily from 8 AM to 4:30 PM during the tourist season from Memorial Day to Labor Day. During the off-season, the facility is closed Monday and Tuesday. There is no admission. The building is handicapped-accessible.

Gambrill's Mill Visitor Center is located at the Monocacy Battlefield.

Monocacy Battlefield

CSA Gen. Jubal Early was on his way east from the Shenandoah Valley to raid Washington, D.C. His troops were met at this site by Union solders under the command of USA Gen. Lewis Wallace. Essentially, the battle cost Early a day's march and a chance to capture Washington. Thwarted, the Confederates turned back to Virginia, thus ending the South's last big chance to carry the war above the Potomac.

Early's raid was part of a scheme to divert the North from CSA Gen. Lee's army at Petersburg, Virginia. Pushing north through the Shenandoah Valley, Early entered Winchester, Virginia, in early July, plundered federal stores at Harpers Ferry, crossed the Potomac River into Maryland at Sharpsburg — the site of a bloody battle two years before — and moved into Frederick. Early's threat to Washington forced USA Gen. Ulysses S. Grant to dispatch forces toward Frederick. Until these reserves arrived, however, the only barrier to Early was a force of 2,300 raw, unseasoned men under the command of USA Gen. Wallace.

Frederick Junction — or Monocacy Junction — was 3 miles southeast of Frederick. Wallace, a Union recruit trainer in Baltimore, was unsure whether Early would attack Washington or Baltimore. Frederick Junction was his logical choice as a place to defend either city. The Georgetown Pike to Washington, as well as the National Road to Baltimore, crossed the Monocacy River at this place. While a contingent of Union troops were rushed by rail out of Baltimore to back up Wallace, the Union officer stretched his small army over 6 miles of the river to protect the bridges of both turnpikes. On Saturday, July 9, the two armies collided along the banks of the Monocacy River, along the Georgetown Pike and on the National Road. It was only a matter of time before Early's 18,000 Confederates overpowered the 5,800 Union soldiers.

By late afternoon, the Federals began a retreat toward Baltimore, leaving behind more than 1,600 dead, wounded or captured. The Confederates reported 1,300 dead and wounded. Later, Wallace gave orders to collect the bodies of the dead in a burial ground on the battlefield where he proposed a monument to read: "These men died to save the National Capital, and they did save it." The next morning, Early was inside the District of Columbia at Fort Stevens. But having lost a precious day's time and leading exhausted men, Early could only watch as fresh Union troops arrived to thwart his advance on Washington. Early succeeded in drawing some of

USA Gen. Grant's forces away from CSA Gen. Lee, but he lost his chance to capture the capital city.

That night, Early and his men retreated to Virginia. Of the two days, Grant later wrote, "If Early had been but one day earlier, he might have entered the capital before the arrival of the re-enforcement I had sent." He added, "General Wallace contributed on this occasion, by the defeat of the troops under him, a greater benefit to the cause than often falls to the lot of a commander of an equal force to render by means of a victory." In time, Wallace went on to literary fame as the author of the book *Ben Hur*.

MONOCACY BATTLEFIELD TO POINT OF ROCK, MD.

From the Monocacy Battlefield Visitor Center, return north 2 miles on Md. 355 to I-70, go west on I-70 for two exits to exit 52 — follow the signs for the Catoctin Mountain Highway, U.S. 15-U.S. 340. From the exit, follow signs to the left for U.S. 15-U.S. 340. Four miles south, the highway splits. Take the left fork and continue south on U.S. 15.

To the west in this area is South Mountain. In the mountain gaps, in September 1862, CSA Gen. Lee tried to block the Federals pushing west out of Frederick. Battles took place at Turner's, Fox's, and Crampton gaps. Lee split his army in order to send "Stonewall" Jackson to capture Harpers Ferry, so Lee could only hope to delay the Northerners. USA Gen. McClellan forced his way through these gaps, and by the next afternoon both armies were established along battle lines west and east of Antietam Creek, near Sharpsburg (see T-1: Sharpsburg).

From the U.S. 15-U.S. 340 split, continue south on U.S. 15 for 7 miles to Point of Rock, Md.

Point of Rock, Md.

Alexander Brown opened a post office at Point of Rock in 1832. This place is a natural cut in the Catoctin Mountains, created by the Potomac River. In this general vicinity, Northern and Southern troops often forded the Potomac on their way into either Virginia or Maryland. Southern troops crossed the Potomac headed into Maryland in September 1862. CSA Gen. Early, on his return from raiding the outskirts of Washington in July 1864, passed this area too.

POINT OF ROCK TO BALL'S BLUFF NATIONAL CEMETERY

From Point of Rock, cross the Potomac River on U.S. 15 (Point of Rocks Turnpike) into Virginia and continue south.

Along the highway, just south of the Potomac River, are sites where Confederates often camped. CSA Gen. "Stonewall" Jackson camped in this vicinity in September 1862 prior to Antietam.

Ten miles south of the Potomac River, U.S. 15 splits — U.S. 15 (Bus.) continues straight, while the U.S. 15 bypass around Leesburg goes to the left. Take the bypass and continue south 1 mile to the Leesburg town limits. Follow signs for Balls Bluff Regional Park, turn left on Battlefield Parkway and go 0.3 mile into a subdivision to Balls Bluff Road, turn left on Balls Bluff Road and go an additional 0.3 mile to the road's end. Walk to the Balls Bluff Cemetery in Balls Bluff Regional Park.

Balls Bluff National Cemetery
Leesburg, Va.

On a ridge above the Potomac River, Balls Bluff is where Northern and Southern troops met on October 21, 1861. It was one of the Union's first disasters of the war. The Federal troops were led by President Lincoln's close friend and former Congressman, USA Gen. Edward D. Baker, who led his men into an ambush that claimed nearly 50 lives, including Baker's own. Some of the Union troops drowned in the Potomac, and a few bodies floated downriver to Washington, D.C. A national cemetery, open dawn to dusk, is at the battle site.

BALLS BLUFF NATIONAL CEMETERY TO LEESBURG, VA.
Backtrack on Balls Bluff Road and Battlefield Parkway to U.S. 15, turn left on the U.S. 15 bypass and go south 1.2 miles to the interchange

Leesburg Personality: CSA Col. John Singleton Mosby

Mosby's aggressiveness — and creativity — were demonstrated early in life. He shot and wounded a fellow student at the University of Virginia in Charlottesville, then made friends with his defense counselor and the judge by explaining his interest in studying law. That enabled him to escape the serious charges with a six-month jail sentence and a $1,000 fine.

Mosby was a Bristol lawyer when Virginia seceded in 1861, and he enlisted in the Confederate cavalry. CSA Col. Mosby participated in war action at 1st Manassas and then rode with CSA Gen. James Ewell Brown "Jeb" Stuart on the Virginia Peninsula and at Antietam. In 1863, he was allowed to organize a group known as "partisan rangers," who went on a guerrilla rampage in an area stretching through Virginia from Leesburg to Warrenton to Fairfax Courthouse. He also led forays into Maryland and Pennsylvania prior to Gettysburg and in the Shenandoah Valley in 1864.

Mosby, a 125-pound blond, wore a scarlet-lined gray cape that he draped over his shoulder and an ostrich plume in his hat. He was clean-shaven except during the war, when he wore a full beard. He became known as the Gray Ghost. In March 1863, he and his men crept inside Union lines near Fairfax County Courthouse and captured USA Gen. Edwin Henry Stoughton and 100 soldiers (see T-14: Northern Virginia).

Photo: Library of Virginia

CSA Col. John Singleton Mosby was a military man of legendary creativity.

Mosby and his men are credited with prolonging the Civil War — at least a little while. During the Wilderness Campaign near Fredericksburg, the Union wasted considerable time and energy in an attempt to track down the Gray Ghost. In April 1865, Mosby disbanded his troops rather than surrender. He returned to law practice and later supported his old adversary, Ulysses S. Grant, for president. It was a move that gained Mosby little popularity in the South. He served as consul in Hong Kong and later returned to Virginia to write his memoirs. He died in May 1916 in Washington and was buried in Warrenton (see T-9: Brandy Station).

with Va. Highway 7 (Bus.). Take the right exit ramp and turn right (west) toward downtown Leesburg at the traffic signal on Va. 7.

Leesburg, Va.

Leesburg is the county seat of Loudoun County, which gets its name from John Campbell, the fourth Earl of Loudoun, who was commander of British forces in North America during the early part of the French and Indian War. Loudoun was governor of Virginia from 1756 to 1759, during which time the county was founded. In 1758, a year after Loudoun County was cut from western Fairfax County, Francis Lightfoot Lee, one of several prominent and politically active brothers, inherited land in the new county.

Soon, "Frank" Lee was a member of the Colonial legislature from Loudoun. He was teased by his family and friends in the legislature for living so far from eastern Virginia, and they jokingly called him Francis Loudoun or Col. Frank Loudoun. Still, the House of Burgesses authorized a bill to establish a county seat in Loudoun and name it Leesburg in Frank's honor. He later served with his brother Richard Henry Lee in the Continental Congress, and he was a signer of the Declaration of Independence. CSA Gen. Robert E. Lee, a distant relative of Francis Lightfoot Lee, moved through the Leesburg area on his first march into the north in September 1862. CSA Gen. Early's troops passed this way in July 1864, headed for the Shenandoah Valley via the Snickers Gap Turnpike, after the attempted raid on Washington.

The road from Leesburg to Alexandria, now Va. 7, was a major route during the war. The single most active and partisan Confederate in this region was CSA Col. John Singleton Mosby. So popular were Mosby's exploits that the Loudoun area around Leesburg became known as "Mosby's Confederacy."

LEESBURG TO LOUDOUN VISITORS CENTER

Continue west on Va. 7 (Bus.) 2.7 miles, along the outskirts of Leesburg, to Loudoun Street, which veers to the left. Take

Loudoun Street 0.1 mile west, turn left (south) onto Harrison Street and into Market Station, the site of the Loudoun Visitors Center.

Loudoun Visitors Center
Loudoun and Harrison Sts.
(Market Station), Leesburg, Va.
• (703) 777-0519

The Loudoun Visitors Center offers exhibits, displays and general information on attractions in the Loudoun County vicinity. Ask about information on tours and literature related to local Confederate Civil War hero, Col. John Singleton Mosby. The center is open during the summer tourist season, June to September, from 9 AM to 6 PM daily. During the off-season it closes at 5 PM. There is no admission, and the center is handicapped-accessible.

LOUDOUN VISITORS CENTER TO LOUDOUN MUSEUM

From the visitors center at Market Station, walk west two blocks on Loudoun Street to 16 W. Loudoun Street.

Loudoun Museum
16 W. Loudoun St., Leesburg, Va.
• (703) 777-7427

A room in the Loudoun Museum is devoted to Loudoun County's Civil War history, and there are many artifacts and exhibits related to the war. Particular attention is given to Loudoun's war hero, Confederate "Gray Ghost" John Singleton Mosby. There is mention, too, of the Loudoun Rangers, a group of local German farmers recruited by the Union a few months after the Civil War began. Later in the war, in an attempt to field a regular force in pursuit of Mosby, the Union mobilized the rangers against the Gray Ghost, but they were unsuccessful in catching him. The museum is open Monday through Saturday from 9 AM to 5 PM and Sunday from noon to 5 PM. It is closed during the month of January. Admission is free. The museum is handicapped-accessible.

Photo: Antietam National Battlefield

CSA Gen. Jubal Early's march toward Washington was thwarted at Monocacy.

LOUDOUN MUSEUM TO LOUDOUN COUNTY COURTHOUSE

From the museum, walk north one block on Wirt Street then east one block on W. Market Street to the courthouse at the corner of King and Market streets.

Loudoun County Courthouse
King and Market Sts., Leesburg, Va.

The Loudoun County courthouse was built in 1759 and replaced in 1811 and again in 1894. A statue honoring Loudoun war veterans graces the front lawn.

LOUDOUN COUNTY COURTHOUSE TO LOUDOUN VISITORS CENTER

From the courthouse, walk east one block on E. Market Street and south one block on S. Church Street, returning to Market Station.

Monocacy Tour Ends

Other Tour Points of Interest

The Leesburg and Frederick areas boast three centuries of Anglo pioneer history. For questions, ask for help at the Loudoun Visitors Center or the Frederick Visitor Center (see listings).

Annual Events

Beyond the Garden Gates opens a number of historic and contemporary gardens in Frederick for tours in late May. Frederick also has an exceptional **Independence Day celebration** each year on the Fourth of July at Baker Park. **In the Street** is an annual downtown Frederick celebration held in early October: The city closes off nine blocks of Market Street for a day of family fun — children's events, food and entertainment aplenty.

Visitors to Loudoun County on Memorial Day weekend should take advantage of the **Hunt County Stable Tour**, an annual tour of stables at numerous well-known horse breeding farms. For more stable tour information, call (540) 592-3711. In late June, an annual **Celtic Festival** is held at historic Oatlands Plantation with Scottish games, dancing, music and living historic programs to celebrate the area's rich Celtic heritage. For more information, call Oatlands at (703) 777-3174. In late October (near Halloween), the Loudoun Museum in Leesburg (see listing) sponsors a three-day weekend tour of historic Leesburg homes and buildings that allegedly are haunted. This is a walking tour with guides and storytellers at each site. For more information, call (703) 777-7424.

And by all means, make every effort to attend the **Waterford Fair** in Loudoun County. The fair is held each year on the first full Friday-to-Sunday weekend in October, and it attracts upwards of 40,000 spectators to Waterford, a historic town that was settled in the 18th century by Quaker farmers. Today the town is protected by a number of historic and scenic easements that are financed by the proceeds from the fair. The fair was started in 1947 and draws 170 craftspeople annually. There is a crafts competition, food, entertainment and tours of some of Waterford's historic homes. For more information telephone (540) 882-3018.

Antiques, Shopping

Besides the downtown historic district, there are four other shopping areas of note in Frederick. **Everedy Square** and **Shab Row**, in a revitalized 19th century factory in the vicinity of St. John Cemetery (see listing), have 35 specialty shops including antiques, clothing, general merchandise, home furnishings and gifts. There are three dozen specialty shops clustered at **8 East Street**. The **Francis Scott Key Mall** has 75 stores on Buckeystown Pike in the vicinity of the Hampton Inn (see Chapter 23 for accommodations listing), and the **Frederick Towne Mall**, on U.S. 40 west of town, has more than 60 stores and shops. North of Frederick at Thurmont (see listing), the **Historic Cozy Village** has 12 specialty shops just off U.S. 15 on Md. Highway 806.

Arts

The **Delaplaine Visual Arts Center** is at 112 E. Patrick Street in Frederick. It offers displays and workshops. The **Weinberg Center for the Performing Arts**, at 20 W. Patrick Street in Frederick, is an old movie house redesigned to house year-round performing and visual arts programs .

Historic Sites

In Frederick, visit the **Hessian Barracks** on the grounds of the Maryland School for the Deaf at 101 Clark Place, four blocks south of downtown on S. Market Street. The stone building was built in 1777 during the American Revolution. German-Hessian mercenaries captured at Saratoga, New York, and Yorktown, Virginia, were imprisoned at the barracks. It was a hospital during the Civil War. The building is open only to groups by appointment.

Rose Hill Manor Museum, a mile north of downtown Frederick at 1611 N. Market Street, is the site of the home of Thomas Johnson, Maryland's first governor. Johnson lived at the house for a quarter of a century, beginning in 1794. It is open daily from April to October as a children's museum. The **Schifferstandt Architectural Museum**, 1110 Rosemont Avenue, just west of downtown Frederick off W. Second Street, is in a former 1756 manor house and is considered a fine example of German Colonial architecture.

Tour 8
Manassas

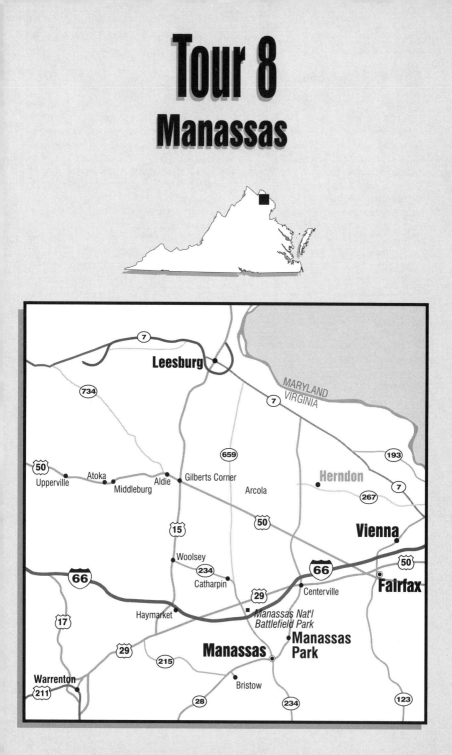

Manassas

About This Tour

This tour route covers the Virginia Piedmont from Leesburg, Virginia, to Manassas, Virginia. The route is one of six that covers the Piedmont region: T-6: Gettysburg, T-7: Monocacy, T-8: Manassas, T-9: Brandy Station, T-10: Charlottesville and T-11: Lynchburg.

The geography and history of this tour route is similar to that of T-7: Monocacy. Native Americans lived and traveled in this region long before Anglo pioneers arrived in the mid-18th century. The area was settled mainly by German and Scotch-Irish pioneers, who landed at Philadelphia and pushed west across the Piedmont to the Cumberland and Shenandoah valleys in the mountains.

There was considerable Civil War action in the area surrounding both Leesburg and Manassas.

Travel Tips

U.S. Highway 15, a continuation of T-7: Monocacy, is a multi-lane, divided highway in this section of Piedmont Virginia. Washington, D.C., radio stations report traffic and weather conditions. Citizens band radio users can find traffic information on Channel 19; state police usually monitor Channel 9. Motorists receive a strong mobile telephone signal throughout the region.

This tour concludes at Manassas, where we suggest you plan dining and lodging for the evening. Area accommodations and dining suggestions are listed in Chapters 22 and 23, and it's a good idea to review these recommendations before you begin the tour. In addition to our suggestions, there are numerous fast-food restaurants, gas stations and shops throughout the Northern Piedmont.

Manassas Tour Begins . . .

LEESBURG TO GILBERTS CORNER, VA.
Leaving Leesburg southbound on U.S. 15 (Aldie Pike), continue 10 miles to Gilberts Corner at the intersection of U.S. 15 and U.S. Highway 50.

Gilberts Corner, Va.

CSA Gen. Thomas Jonathan "Stonewall" Jackson's mother, Julia Beckwith Neale, was born in the vicinity of this crossroads on leap day, Feb. 29, 1798. She married Jonathan Jackson in 1818.

GILBERTS CORNER TO MANASSAS BATTLEFIELD
Continue south on U.S. 15 for 7 miles to the intersection at Va. Highway 234. Along this route, the tour enters Prince William County. The county was created in 1730 and was named for William Augustus, England's Duke of Cumberland and the third son of King George II. Turn left onto Va. 234 and proceed 6 miles to U.S. Highway 29. Cross over U.S. 29 and go a half-mile to the Manassas Battlefield Visitors Center entrance on the left.

U.S. 29 in this vicinity was known as the Warrenton Turnpike, which is noted in the following history of both 1st and 2nd Manassas. The stone house at the intersection of U.S. 29

Gilberts Corner Side Trip: Aldie, Va., and Middleburg, Va.

This is a side trip for avid Civil War buffs and anyone interested in seeing the gorgeous countryside that leads into Middleburg, the center of Virginia's hunt country.

From Gilberts Corner, go west on U.S. 50 (John S. Mosby-James Madison Highway) 0.8 mile to Aldie.

The Little River Turnpike — one of the nation's first turnpikes made of wooden planks — was built along this route from Aldie Mill east to Alexandria, Virginia. The roadway was named for Little River, which flows through Aldie, and today the pike follows U.S. 50, Va. Highway 236 and Duke Street through Fairfax County to the Potomac River port.

Aldie, Va.

Aldie is a community at the base of the Bull Run Mountains. A "run" is another name for a small creek. The Bull Run, which lent its name to the famous Civil War battles at Manassas junction just to the east, originates in these mountains. Virginia Congressman Charles Mercer laid out Aldie in the early 19th century.

The village is best known for the aforementioned mill on U.S. 50 at Little River. Union soldiers lodged inside the mill during their raids in this vicinity. A cavalry battle was fought near Aldie in October 1862. The next year, opposing cavalry and artillery fought a spirited battle here in June 1863, just prior to Gettysburg, as CSA Gen. James "Pete" Longstreet shifted northwest from Culpeper, Virginia, to the Shenandoah Valley prior to moving into Maryland and Pennsylvania.

From Aldie, continue west 5 miles on U.S. 50 to Middleburg.

Middleburg, Va.

This community is halfway between Winchester, Virginia, in the Shenandoah Valley and Alexandria, Virginia, on the Potomac, hence the name — Middleburg. The town and surrounding countryside is known for its horse breeding, fox hunting and steeplechase racing. In June 1863, more than 250 Union soldiers from Rhode Island were surrounded by Confederates near here in a series of Aldie-related clashes, and fewer than 25 fought their way out of town. There are no historic markers denoting the skirmish sites. The Red Fox at Washington and Madison streets is one of the oldest inns in the county.

From Middleburg, continue west 1 mile on U.S. 50 to Atoka.

Atoka, Va.

The intersection of U.S. 50 and Va. Highway 713 at Atoka, once known as Rectors Crossroads, is where CSA Col. John Singleton Mosby organized a company of his partisan rangers in 1863 (see T-7: Monocacy).

— continued on next page

— continued from previous page

From Atoka, continue west on U.S. 50 for 7 miles to Upperville.

Upperville, Va.

Upperville is in the upland foothills of Fauquier County, hence its name. In June 1863, after clashes in Aldie and Middleburg, federal troops put a push on Confederates, including CSA Gen. James Ewell Brown "Jeb" Stuart's cavalry. Stuart's back was to the Blue Ridge Mountains. Union forces tried driving his men into the Shenandoah Valley. This action was a prelude to Gettysburg a week later in Pennsylvania.

After completing this side trip, return on U.S. 50 to Gilbert's Corner.

and Va. 234 served as a field hospital during both engagements. The house is part of a driving tour of the 2nd Manassas battlefield described below.

Manassas National Battlefield Park Visitor Center

12521 Lee Hwy., Manassas, Va.
• **(703) 754-1861**

The National Park Service visitor center at Manassas has a museum, slide programs, maps and a publications display. There is a free brochure on Manassas that includes a walking tour of the 1st Manassas battlefield

and a driving tour of the 2nd Manassas battlefield. Follow the NPS-suggested routes for either the walking or driving tours. The center is open every day except Christmas from 8:30 AM to 5 PM. During daylight-saving time, the center stays open until 6 PM on weekends.

Manassas Battlefield

Let's cover two topics that raise questions: first, the origin of the name Manassas and second, the names of the two battles fought at the railroad junction. Historians aren't sure how Manassas got its name, but they think it comes from the word "Manassash" in the Bible.

Photo: Manassas Museum System

This illustration from the September 14, 1861, *Harper's Weekly* shows rebel troops near Manassas with captured Federal naval guns.

The North and South used different names for the battles fought at Manassas, just as they did at Antietam (T-2). The first battle at Manassas, a skirmish on July 18, 1861, was called the "Affair at Blackburn's Ford" by the North and the "First Battle of Bull Run" by the South. Three days later, the main engagement was called "1st Manassas" by the Confederates, and "1st Bull Run" by the Union. The North often used geographical features — in this case, the little Bull Run creek — to designate battles, while the South relied on familiar community names. In August 1862 the fighting was called "2nd Manassas" by the South, and either "2nd Bull Run" or simply "Manassas" by the North.

In the early 1860s, Manassas was a major rail stop, where lines from the Shenandoah Valley and central Virginia joined for a last leg into Alexandria and Washington, D.C. The rail routes were vital supply lines for whichever army could maintain control of them. Bull Run flows along the northern portion of the community.

A week prior to the first battle, USA Gen. Irvin McDowell received orders to force CSA Gen. Pierre Gustave Toutant Beauregard's troops out of the vital rail center at Manassas Junction. McDowell reached Centreville, just north of Manassas in Fairfax County, and led his troops into action at Blackburn's Ford, downstream on the Bull Run, east of Manassas.

CSA Gen. Joseph Eggleston Johnston was in the Shenandoah Valley when he received word of McDowell's advance. Starting out in the early morning, Johnston hurried his Confederates through Ashby Gap in the Blue Ridge Mountains to the west and then by rail to Manassas. It was an unusually quick response, and it was one of the first times in history that a rail line was used by a military force for mobility.

Fighting took place on a hot summer day, July 21, 1861, in an area bordered roughly by today's Gainesville, Sudley Springs and Manassas in Prince William County, and Centreville in Fairfax County (T-14). Both armies on the field at Manassas were mainly raw recruits or short-term soldiers whose release from the army was counted in days. The advantage went to the Southerners, who were less inexperienced. In late afternoon, McDowell's troops retreated from the field, moving north back to Centreville and then to the safety of Washington, D.C.

The Confederates were successful again a year later, in August 1862 at 2nd Manassas. The action was part of a three-pronged offensive designed by CSA Gen. Robert E. Lee. That offensive included CSA Gen. "Stonewall" Jackson's Shenandoah Valley campaign in the spring and Lee's own Seven Days' battles east of Richmond in late June. Again, the Southerners pushed the Federals back to Washington and proved the superiority of the Confederate leadership at this early stage of the war.

During the first day's fighting, USA Gen.

Manassas Personality: CSA Gen. Barnard Elliott Bee

CSA Gen. Barnard E. Bee was a South Carolina native and a graduate of the U.S. Military Academy at West Point. Bee, whose father was secretary of state in the new Republic of Texas, was wounded during the Mexican War in the mid-1840s. When the Civil War began, Bee resigned as a U.S. Army captain and became a Confederate major. He was promoted to brigadier general just a month before 1st Manassas.

At Manassas, Bee led a brigade of Confederates in a march to support Southerners embroiled in a struggle at Matthews Hill. There was disorder on the field. Bee was trying to rally his men when he spotted a freshly arriving Confederate brigade, led by CSA Gen. "Stonewall" Jackson. Pointing to Jackson, Bee yelled to his men: "There stands Jackson like a stone wall! Rally behind the Virginians!" In time, the Southerners held back the Union assault. However, Bee was seriously wounded that day on the battlefield. He died the next day, never realizing that his rallying call would immortalize Jackson with his famous nickname.

John Pope's troops outnumbered Jackson's men by three to one. Still, Pope could not move Jackson. The next day, Pope mistook Jackson's maneuvers as a retreat, and Pope's men were overcome by CSA Gen. Longstreet's troops and forced to retreat over the old stone bridge at Bull Run. The next day, the North suffered losses in a fight at Chantilly in Fairfax County, near Centreville. The victory at 2nd Manassas set the stage for CSA Gen. Lee's first push into the north.

MANASSAS BATTLEFIELD VISITOR CENTER TO MANASSAS MUSEUM

From the visitors center at the Manassas Battlefield, take Sudley

Road (Va. 234) southeast for 4.6 miles to Grant Avenue in downtown Manassas. Turn right on Grant Avenue (still Va. 234) and head south nine blocks to Center Street (Va. Highway 28).

Along Grant Avenue, on the right at the intersection with Lee Avenue, is the old Prince William County Courthouse. This red brick building was the site of a July 1911 celebration in honor of the 50th anniversary of 1st Manassas. With a theme of a Re-United States, President William Howard Taft was the main speaker. The cannon, anchor and monument commemorate the event, which was attended by both Union and Confederate veterans.

Manassas Personality: Kady C. Brownell

Born in Africa while her father was on duty as a British officer, Kady married an American named Brownell. She was only 19 when the Civil War began, and when her husband joined a Rhode Island regiment, Kady decided to go with him into battle. Observers noted she was proficient with both a sword and a rifle. She and her husband fought side by side at 1st Manassas — Kady carried the unit's colors into battle. When her husband's short enlistment was up, he re-enlisted in another Rhode Island unit and so did Kady.

In 1863, after her husband was discharged with a serious wound, Kady returned to the North and resumed housekeeping. She took along the unit colors she carried at Bull Run and a discharge signed by USA Gen. Ambrose E. Burnside.

A Civil War re-enactment near Manassas.

Photo: Manassas Museum System

Turn left (north) on Center Street and drive three blocks to Main Street, turn right and go one block to Prince William Street and the entrance to Manassas Museum.

Manassas Museum
9101 Prince William St., Manassas, Va.
• **(703) 368-1873**

The Manassas Museum is operated by the city government and managed by a professional staff and volunteers. The museum exhibits, which include Civil War materials, are frequently changed. The museum is open every day but Monday, but it is open on federal holidays that fall on Monday. It is closed on New Year's Day, Thanksgiving, Christmas Eve and Christmas. Admission is $2.50 for adults; $1.50 for seniors and children 6 through 17. Hours are 10 AM to 5 PM daily. The facility has restrooms and is handicapped-accessible.

MANASSAS MUSEUM TO MANASSAS VISITORS CENTER
Return to Center Street (Va. 28), turn right (north) and drive one block to the Manassas Visitors Center on the right side of the street.

Manassas Visitors Center
9025 Center St., Manassas, Va.
• **(703) 361-6599**

This visitors center is operated by Historic Manassas and managed by a staff and volunteers. There is travel information and an exhibit on Old Town Manassas, where the center is located. There are some Civil War artifacts displayed. It is not handicapped-accessible. The center is open 9 AM to 5 PM Monday through Friday, and Saturday and Sunday from 10 AM to 4 PM year round.

MANASSAS VISITORS CENTER TO MANASSAS CEMETERY
Continue north for one block on one-way Center Street and turn

Manassas Personality: CSA Gen. William Henry Fitzhugh "Rooney" Lee

The dedication of Manassas Cemetery featured an address by Virginia Congressman William Henry Fitzhugh "Rooney" Lee, son of CSA Gen. Robert E. Lee. Rooney was born in May 1837 at Arlington House in Arlington County (T-14), the third of Gen. Lee's seven children. Rooney attended private schools and Harvard University and served briefly in the U.S. Army. He made his home near White House, an estate in New Kent County, Virginia.

Rooney Lee raised a Confederate cavalry company in 1861, and during the Civil War he rose in rank from captain to major general. After the war, he lived at Ravensworth, an estate near present-day Burke, Virginia, in Fairfax County. A member of the state legislature, he was elected a Virginia congressman, serving in the U.S. House from March 1887 until his death in October 1891. Originally buried at Ravensworth, he was reinterred in the Lee Memorial Chapel family crypt at Washington and Lee University in Lexington, Virginia, in September 1922. William Henry Fitzhugh Lee is often confused with his cousin, Fitzhugh "Fitz" Lee, who was also a Confederate cavalry general.

Stonewall Jackson received his famous nickname on the Manassas battlefield.

left on Zebedee Street and left to Church Street (Va. 28), which runs one-way, parallel to Center Street. Go south seven blocks to the Manassas Cemetery on the left. The cemetery is near where Center and Church streets form two-way Va. 28 west of downtown.

Manassas Cemetery
Center St., Manassas, Va.

Two years after Appomattox, a Confederate veteran donated an acre of land south of Manassas for the creation of a cemetery, and within a year more than 250 Southern soldiers were reinterred at the site. In 1887, the Virginia General Assembly gave the Ladies Memorial Association funds to build a monument to Confederate dead. In 1889, a large red, sandstone marker was dedicated in a ceremony. The guest speaker for the occasion was CSA Gen. William Henry Fitzhugh "Rooney" Lee. The cemetery is open from dawn to dusk.

CSA Gen. P.G.T. Beauregard led troops at Manassas (Bull Run) in some of the war's earliest action.

Manassas Tour Ends

Other Tour Points of Interest

Annual Events

A **Civil War Weekend** is held in late July and again in late August at the Manassas Museum (see listing). The weekends, sponsored by the museum and free to the public, feature Civil War re-enactors in a living history environment that includes tents, camp scenes and sutlers. For more information, call the Manassas Museum at (703) 368-1873. Manassas also hosts the **Annual Manassas Railway Festival** — a day of railroad living history with memorabilia, exhibits, excursions and music. The event is held in early June in downtown Manassas — near the train depot, naturally — and is free. It's sponsored by Historic Manassas, a civic organization.

Manassas also hosts a **barbershop music show** in February; an **antique auto show** with rare cars on display in Old Town

Manassas in June; and the **Manassas Fall Jubilee**, held each year in Old Town in early October. An old-fashioned streetfest, the event includes live jazz music performances, food, rides and crafts. Sponsored by Historic Manassas, it is also free to the public.

Antiques, Arts

Old Town Manassas has a number of stores and several antique shops along Center Street. **Rohr's Museum and Store** is at the corner of Center and West streets downtown and has an extensive collection of antique cars and Americana. The **Hayloft Dinner Theatre**, 10501 Balls Ford Road off Sudley Road near Interstate 66, offers live theater with meal. The Hayloft is open every day except Monday, with cocktails and dinner beginning at 6:30 PM and performances at 8:45 PM. The fun begins one hour earlier on Sunday. There are a wide variety of price and show options and packages, so call for more details.

Historic Sites

Oatlands, an estate originally owned by George Carter, great-grandson of Virginia's famous Robert "King" Carter, is along U.S. 15 (Aldie Pike) between Leesburg and Gilberts

Corner. Oatlands escaped serious Civil War damage and today it is a popular historic attraction. It is open to the public (there is an admission charge) from April to December. Hours are 10 AM to 4 PM Monday through Saturday and 1 to 4 PM on Sunday.

Shopping

There are several shopping centers and countless stores, fast-food restaurants and shops along Sudley Road (Va. 234) between I-66 and downtown Manassas. Another strip of stores is north of downtown on Centreville Road (Va. 28) beyond Center Street. Pick up a Manassas travel guide book at the Manassas Museum or the Manassas Visitors Center (see listings above).

Tour 9
Brandy Station

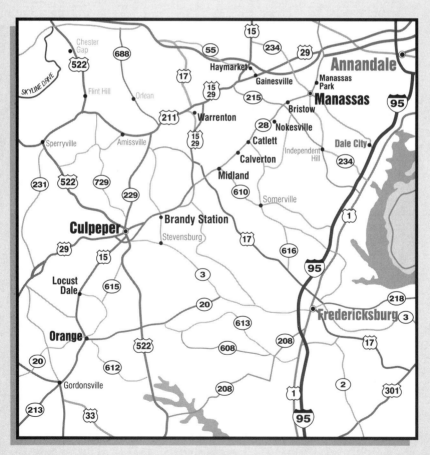

TOUR 9
Brandy Station

About This Tour

This tour route is a continuation of T-8: Manassas. Leaving Manassas, this tour includes visits to Warrenton, Virginia, the site of the Brandy Station cavalry battle, and Culpeper, Virginia, and ends in Orange, Virginia. Thus, this tour route is the fourth of six (T-6, T-7, T-8, T-9, T-10 and T-11) in succession that cover the Piedmont of Pennsylvania, Maryland and Virginia, along the eastern slopes of the Appalachian Mountains.

The main roads of this tour route are U.S. Highway 29 and U.S. Highway 15, which meander through a region known for its farms, vineyards and elegant estates. It ends at Orange, Virginia. This tour route runs north-to-south through a natural valley along the eastern slopes of the Blue Ridge Mountains.

This Piedmont region in Virginia was settled by western-moving settlers from the historic Tidewater region along the Atlantic coastline. Several rivers cross the Piedmont, flowing westerly from the mountains to the Coastal Plain, including the Rappahannock and Rapidan. This region was the home of many prominent Americans, including John Marshall, James Madison and Zachary Taylor.

The railroad arrived in the Piedmont in the 1840s. One line — the Orange and Alexandria — ran the length of the region, from Lynchburg, Virginia, north through Charlottesville and Orange, and on to Manassas and Alexandria near Washington.

Because of its central location, between eastern Virginia and the western mountains, Piedmont Virginia was the frequent scene of Civil War action. There was considerable action near Centreville, Virginia, associated with the two battles of nearby Manassas in July 1861 and August 1862. In the spring of 1862, CSA Gen. Thomas Jonathan "Stonewall" Jackson crossed Piedmont Virginia on his way west for his Shenandoah Valley Campaign.

The Battle of Brandy Station in Culpeper County, in May 1863, became known as the largest cavalry engagement fought in North America. Brandy Station was a prelude to the Battle of Gettysburg in 1863, after which the opposing armies fought battles at Bristoe Station and Rappahannock Station in Virginia.

The town of Orange offers several historic sites, and Orange County has significant war history, particularly as the site of the Wilderness Campaign, fought in May 1864. (The Wilderness is covered in more detail in T-16.) In 1864, the last full year of military action, the Wilderness Campaign began as both CSA Gen. Robert E. Lee and USA Gen. Ulysses S. Grant broke winter camp along the eastern fringe of the Piedmont.

Travel Tips

This tour route begins as you leave Manassas, Virginia, goes south on U.S. 29, turns onto U.S. 15 and winds its way through the Virginia hunt country of Fauquier, Culpeper and Orange counties. U.S. 29 is a busy divided highway; U.S. 15 is a well-maintained, well-traveled road, often four-lane but sometimes two-lane. Congestion is a problem only near Gainesville, Virginia, where U.S. 29 intersects with Interstate 66 — a major east-west interstate that connects Washington, D.C., with the Shenandoah Valley. Washington commuters pack eastbound I-66 in the early morning, and evening commuters bring westbound I-66 to a virtual standstill. So, plan accordingly.

In the Gainesville, Virginia, vicinity is Manassas (T-8). Use Washington, D.C., radio stations for traffic and weather reports. Citizens band radio users can find traffic information on Channel 19. There is a strong mobile telephone signal along the entire route except in the Orange, Virginia, vicinity.

This route ends in Orange, where we suggest you plan evening dining and lodging. Recommended accommodations are listed in Chapter 22: Accommodations; recommended dining selections are listed in Chapter 23: Restaurants. It is a good idea to review these chapters before traveling through this stretch of Piedmont countryside. In addition to our suggestions, there are numerous fast-food facilities, gas stations and shops throughout Fauquier, Culpeper and Orange counties.

Brandy Station Tour Begins . . .

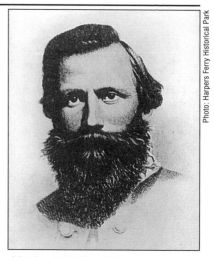

CSA Gen. "Jeb" Stuart's hat and cloak were swiped at Catlett's Station in 1862.

MANASSAS TO HAYMARKET, VA.

Exit Manassas from the Manassas National Battlefield Park, and go south on U.S. 29 (Lee Highway) for 1 mile to Gainesville, just south of I-66.

Gainesville, Va.

There was intense fighting in the Gainesville vicinity before both noted battles in nearby Manassas (see T-8), in 1861 and 1862, and during the Bristoe Campaign after Gettysburg in late 1863. Today, Gainesville is a growing community and boasts a collection of gas stations and fast-food marts that cater to motorists and commuters along U.S. 29 and I-66.

GAINESVILLE TO HAYMARKET, VA.

On U.S. 29 (Lee Highway) at Gainesville, turn right (west) on Va. Highway 55 and go 2 miles on Va. 55 (Washington Street) to downtown Haymarket.

Haymarket, Va.

There were numerous skirmishes in the Haymarket vicinity before both battles of Manassas (T-8). Haymarket was named for the town and famous race course of the same name near London, England. The small village became nationally known in the early

1990s, when the Walt Disney Company announced plans — later abandoned — to develop a historic theme park, Disney America, headquartered in Haymarket and taking in thousands of acres of land in the surrounding countryside.

HAYMARKET TO ST. PAUL'S CHURCH
Continue west on Va. 55 (Washington Street) in Haymarket, turn left (south) on Fayette Street and go one long block to St. Paul's Church.

St. Paul's Church
Fayette St., Haymarket, Va.
This red brick Episcopal Church was used as a hospital by both the Union and Confederacy during the Civil War. It looks much like it did more than 130 years ago. The church was built in 1801 as a district courthouse for four surrounding counties, and the building was converted to a church in 1822. Union troops then converted the church into horse stables in late 1862, and later they burned the building. The congregation rebuilt the church within the same walls in 1867. Today, the church is used for regular worship services and is open

Gainesville Side Trip: Bristow, Va., and Catlett, Va.

From the Va. 55 and U.S. 29 intersection in Gainesville, turn right on U.S. 29 (Lee Highway), go south a half-mile, go left on Va. 619 (Linton Hall Road) and 7 miles — cross over Va. Highway 28 (Nokesville Road) — to Bristow.

Bristow, Va.

There's little in Bristow today, but in 1863 the rail stop — known then as Bristoe or Bristoe Station — was the scene of action in the Bristoe Campaign. Located along the Orange and Alexandria rail line, Bristoe Station saw skirmishes in October and November 1863 after fierce summer fighting at Gettysburg, Pennsylvania (T-6). CSA Gen. Robert E. Lee took an offensive posture against a larger force under USA Gen. George Meade, who was forced to retreat.

Return a half-mile to Va. 28 (Nokesville Road), turn left and go south 7 miles — into Fauquier County — to Va. Highway 806 (Dumfries Road). Go left on Va. 806 and 0.1 mile to the railroad crossing at Catlett.

Catlett, Va.

Like, Bristow, there is little today in Catlett, known as Catlett's Station during the Civil War. In August 1862, Catlett Station was the scene of a dramatic event that became known as Stuart's Catlett Station Raid. First, USA Gen. John Pope captured one of CSA Gen. James Ewell Brown "Jeb" Stuart's aides and ran off with the Confederate's hat and cloak.

Stuart sought revenge. He found help from an old acquaintance, an unidentified African American, who helped guide Stuart to Pope's baggage trains. Stuart captured money, papers, clothes — even a handful of Pope's officers. Stuart felt repaid for his earlier loss. Confederate officials put Pope's uniform on display in a store front on Richmond's Main Street.

More important, Pope's stolen papers helped CSA Gen. Robert E. Lee successfully prepare for 2nd Manassas, which was fought the following week (T-8). A year later, on October 14, 1863, a light skirmish was fought on the rail line at Catlett's Station. Union soldiers beat back an advance by Stuart's cavalry.

After completing this side trip, return to U.S. 29 at Gainesville via Va. 28 and Va. Highway 619 (Linton Hall Road).

---

only on Sundays. The building is a registered state landmark.

ST. PAUL'S CHURCH TO GAINESVILLE, VA.

Return to Va. 55 (Washington Street), turn right and go back 2

miles to U.S. 29 (Lee Highway) in Gainesville.

GAINESVILLE TO BUCKLAND, VA.

From the intersection of U.S. 29 (Lee Highway) and Va. 619 (Linton Hall Road) in Gainesville, continue

Photo: Warrenton-Fauquier Visitor Center

The Old Jail Museum emphasizes Warrenton's Civil War heritage.

---

south on U.S. 29 for 3.2 miles to Buckland Mill.

Buckland, Va.

There's an old mill at Buckland aside Broad Run — a creek that crosses the highway — and visible from the roadway. This old mill has been restored and is a private residence. The Buckland vicinity was the scene of a cavalry clash in October 1863, when CSA Gen. Stuart's cavalry thoroughly defeated USA Gen. Hugh Judson "Kill Cavalry" Kilpatrick as part of the Bristoe Campaign. Stuart's men, who chased the Federals from the site, jokingly called it the "Buckland Races."

BUCKLAND TO FAUQUIER COUNTY AND WARRENTON, VA.

From Buckland, continue south on U.S. 29. Just south of Buckland this tour route crosses into Fauquier County.

Fauquier County, Va.

Fauquier — pronounced "Fawk-year" — was formed in 1759 and named for Francis

Fauquier, Virginia's royal governor at the time. Prior to the Civil War, the county was best known as the home of Kentucky pioneer Simon Kenton and Supreme Court Justice John Marshall. Today, it boasts large farms and horse-breeding estates. Its a rural haven for Washington-bound commuters who enjoy the country setting away from the city.

Continue south on U.S. 29 for 7 miles to Warrenton.

Warrenton, Va.

Warrenton, the Fauquier county seat, gets its name from Dr. Joseph Warren, a Revolutionary War hero killed at the Battle of Bunker Hill. Noted jurist John Marshall practiced law in Warrenton. Warrenton once was the home of two prominent Confederates: Gen. Eppa Hunton, later a U.S. senator and congressman, and Col. John Singleton Mosby, the "Gray Ghost of the Confederacy." CSA Gen. Stuart began his raid on Catlett Station from Warrenton in August 1862.

Today, Warrenton is a busy, prosperous

community. Local farmers and the "horsey set" visit downtown to conduct business or shop. Most travel-oriented businesses, mainly fast-food restaurants and motels, are crowded along the "old bypass," so the downtown courthouse area hosts a nice collection of many old, well-maintained homes and fine restaurants.

WARRENTON TO FAUQUIER COUNTY COURTHOUSE

From U.S. 29 (south), follow signs for U.S. 29/U.S. 15 Bus. (the old bypass), continue along U.S. 29/U.S. 15 Bus. for a half-mile to Blackwell Road (U.S. 15/U.S. 211 Bus.), turn left on Blackwell Road and go 1 mile to downtown Warrenton, turn left on Main Street to the front of the Fauquier County Courthouse. Because of the many confusing one-way streets in downtown Warrenton, it is best to park along Main Street in the courthouse area and walk to a few historic sites in the immediate vicinity.

Fauquier County Courthouse
Main St., Warrenton, Va.

Located in downtown Warrenton, the first Fauquier County Courthouse was destroyed by fire in the late 19th century after surviving the Civil War. It was rebuilt almost immediately, and the current courthouse looks much like the original. A statue of jurist John Marshall stands on the courthouse lawn. Adjacent to the courthouse is a stone marker that honors Col. John Singleton Mosby (see more on Mosby in T-7 and T-10).

FAUQUIER COUNTY COURTHOUSE TO OLD JAIL MUSEUM

Walk to the Old Jail Museum, located adjacent to the courthouse.

Old Jail Museum
Ashby and Waterloo Sts., at Court Square, Warrenton, Va. • (540) 347-5525

Portions of this structure date to the 1770s, and the two-part jail building was in use in

some form until the 1960s. A registered state landmark, the old jail building has been converted into a county history museum that emphasizes the area's Civil War heritage. Its exhibit area features material on CSA Col. John Singleton Mosby. The museum is maintained by the Fauquier Historical Society and is open every day except Monday from 10 AM to 4 PM. No admission is charged.

OLD JAIL MUSEUM TO WARREN GREEN HOTEL

From the Old Jail Museum, slip behind the courthouse on either Ashby Street or Court Street to Hotel Street, directly behind the courthouse to the old Warren Green Hotel.

Warren Green Hotel
Hotel Street, Warrenton, Va.

Once a hotel that predated the Civil War, this building now houses county government offices and, thus, is not available for visits inside. This stop enables you to see the building's exterior and its attractive 19th-century architecture. USA Gen. George Brinton "Young Napoleon" McClellan reportedly relinquished his command of the Army of the Potomac at the hotel in November 1862. Legend says McClellan delivered a farewell address to his troops from the hotel porch. This transfer of leadership from McClellan to USA Gen. Ambrose Everett Burnside, directed by President Lincoln, took place just after the Battle of Antietam in Maryland (T-1).

WARREN GREEN HOTEL TO WARRENTON/ FAUQUIER COUNTY VISITORS CENTER

From the Warren Green Hotel, walk back to Main Street. From this point, resume your motor tour. From Main Street, go east on Main Street for one block, turn right (south) on Second Street and go one block, turn right (west) on Lee Street and go three blocks, turn left (south) on Keith Street and go a long block — along the cemetery — to the Warrenton/

Fauquier Visitors Center.

Warrenton/Fauquier Visitors Center

183-A Keith St., Warrenton, Va.
• (540) 347-4414

The visitors center is in a professional office park complex on the left (east) side of Keith Street. The center has an ample supply of brochures on attractions, lodging, dining and other points of interest. Admission is free; there are restroom facilities. It is handicapped-accessible and is open every day from 9 AM to 5 PM.

WARRENTON/FAUQUIER VISITORS CENTER TO WARRENTON CEMETERY

From the visitors center, go back (east) on Keith Street to Lee Street, turn left (north) on Lee Street and go one block on Lee Street to the cemetery at the intersection of Lee and Chestnut streets.

Warrenton Cemetery

Lee and Chestnut Sts., Warrenton, Va.

CSA Col. Mosby, a Warrenton resident, is buried in the cemetery. Mosby's simple tombstone is located near the base of the tall shaft that honors hundreds of unknown Southern soldiers also buried in the town cemetery. The cemetery is open sunup to sundown. No admission is charged.

WARRENTON CEMETERY TO BRENTMOOR (SPILMAN-MOSBY HOUSE)

From the cemetery, drive north on Chestnut Street for one block to Waterloo Street, turn right (east) on Waterloo Street and go three blocks to the courthouse, shift right (east) on Main Street at the courthouse and go three blocks to Brentmoor (Spilman-Mosby House) on the left (north) side of Main Street.

Brentmoor (Spilman-Mosby House)

Main St., Warrenton, Va.

Brentmoor is private and not open to the public — so view the beautiful setting of this house from the street. The attractive white house, an example of the Italian Villa style of architecture, was once the home of both Eppa Hunton and John Singleton Mosby, two Confederate figures. The house was built just prior to the Civil War for Edward Spilman, a Fauquier County circuit court judge. Mosby purchased the house in 1875 and sold it two years later to Hunton, who was a member of the Congress at the time. A Hunton relative, Eppa Hunton III, was raised in the house and grew up to establish a Richmond law firm, Hunton & Williams, one of the largest and best-known firms in the South.

Warrenton Personality: Confederate Gen. Eppa Hunton

Born near Warrenton in September 1822, Eppa Hunton was the commonwealth's attorney in neighboring Prince William County for 12 years until the outbreak of the Civil War in 1861. Joining the Confederacy, Hunton was 40 years old and in frequent ill health by the time he saw action at Manassas (T-8) and Balls Bluff (T-7) in 1861 and at Antietam (T-1) in 1862. He was severely injured while leading a Virginia regiment during "Pickett's Charge" at Gettysburg (T-6) in 1863, but he survived the battle and the war, with action at the Wilderness (T-16) and Cold Harbor (T-18) in 1864 and at Petersburg (T-20) in 1865. Captured at Sayler's Creek (T-21) on April 6, 1865, while quite ill, he was held prisoner by the Union Army for three months. Later, Hunton served in the U.S. House from 1873 to 1881.

In 1877, he was appointed by the Congress to the Electoral Commission that helped decide the outcome of the 1876 presidential election between Rutherford Hayes and Samuel Tilden. Hunton was U.S. Senator from Virginia from 1892 to 1895, then he practiced law in Warrenton until his death in Richmond in 1908. He is buried in Hollywood Cemetery in Richmond (T-17).

BRENTMOOR TO RAPPAHANNOCK RIVER

From the former Mosby-Hunton home, continue east on Main Street for four blocks to Meetze Road (Va. Highway 643), turn left (north) on Meetze Road and go a half-mile to the U.S. 29 bypass, turn right onto the U.S. 29 bypass and go 13 miles south to the bridge over the Rappahannock River.

Rappahannock River

The Rappahannock — pronounced "Rap-ah-han-uk" — springs from the crest of the Blue Ridge Mountains, 40 miles to the west, flows east across the Virginia Piedmont to the "fall zone" at Fredericksburg, where it broadens on its way to the Chesapeake Bay. Old-line, tradition-oriented Virginians consider this river the unofficial boundary between "real Virginia" to the south and "foreign, Washington-oriented" Northern Virginia.

The Rappahannock River is the boundary of Fauquier and Culpeper counties. This tour enters Culpeper County, which was formed in 1748 and named for Thomas, the second Baron Culpeper, who was Virginia's Colonial governor in the 17th century.

The Rappahannock was a major river crossing during the Civil War. In early November 1863, this was the scene of a skirmish during the Bristoe Campaign. More than 60 Southerners were captured during the bayonet fight that occurred in a rare nighttime battle.

RAPPAHANNOCK RIVER TO KELLY'S FORD

Across the Rappahannock River

bridge, continue on U.S. 29 (south) for 1.7 miles to Va. Highway 674 (Kelly's Ford Road), turn left on Va. 674 and go 4 miles east to the parking area on left. Va. 674 is mainly unsurfaced, so skip this side trip during times of high water. Kelly's Ford is located down a mile-long, dirt-rutted path toward the Rappahannock River.

Kelly's Ford

In March 1863, Union cavalry under USA Gen. William Wood Averell marched toward Confederates positioned south near Culpeper. The Federals crossed the Rappahannock at Kelly's Ford. A Confederate hero, John Pelham, was killed in the all-day fight that followed. A marker at Kelly's Ford honors the fallen Pelham, although there's a debate about the exact site of his fatal injury.

Kelly's Ford was also the scene of action in June 1863, during fighting to the south at Brandy Station. And in November 1863, two Union regiments — 2,000 men — were captured by Southerners in an incident that thoroughly stunned Federal army leaders.

KELLY'S FORD ROAD TO PELHAM MARKER

From Kelly's Ford, return on Va. 674 (Kelly's Ford Road) to U.S. 29, turn left (south) on U.S. 29 and go south for a quarter-mile to Va. Highway 685.

Pelham Marker

At the intersection is a tall stone marker that honors Confederate hero John Pelham.

Kelly's Ford Personality: John Pelham

John Pelham was an Alabama officer. He resigned from West Point in May 1861, just after the Civil War began, and worked his way back through Federal lines to the Confederacy. He was described as blond, blue-eyed and handsome — an obvious sensation with Southern ladies. CSA Gen. Robert E. Lee once described Pelham as "gallant." Serving in CSA Gen. Stuart's cavalry, Pelham was struck by a shell fragment and killed near Kelly's Ford. Countless women went into mourning, and the "Gallant Pelham" was posthumously promoted to the rank of lieutenant colonel.

Photo: Orange County Visitors Bureau

While on the Brandy Station tour, visit Montpelier, home of President James Madison, near Orange, Virginia.

The marker is surrounded by weeds and underbrush and is easily missed.

PELHAM MARKER TO BRANDY STATION
From Va. 685, continue on U.S. 29 (south) and go 1 mile to Va. Highway 663 (Alanthus Road).

Brandy Station, Va.

Brandy Station got its name in the early 19th century, when a local inn served brandy, among other spirits. Legend says soldiers frequented the tavern, and when the bar ran out of brandy, the men got angry and wrote "BRANDY" on the outside wall. Just before the Civil War, when the rail line from Orange to Manassas was laid through the area, this area became known as Brandy Station.

A major Civil War battle — the largest cavalry battle in North American history — was fought at Brandy Station in June 1863. Today, only a few scattered highway signs mark the scene of the famous event. The battle was fought on the vast expanse of farmland in the Bailey's Store (see below) vicinity. The battlefield land is in private hands — there's no National Park Service facility at Brandy Station. Business developers and area preservationists are in constant debate concerning the battle site's fate.

In May 1863, on the heels of a victory at Chancellorsville (T-16), CSA Gen. Lee began moving his army northwest, from the "fall zone" near Fredericksburg to the Shenandoah Valley and into the rich farmland of southern Pennsylvania. USA Gen. Joseph "Fighting Joe" Hooker, who led his Army of the Potomac to defeat at Chancellorsville, learned that some of the western-moving Confederates were camped at Brandy Station, just north of Culpeper, on the Orange and Alexandria Railroad line.

On June 5, 1863, Hooker ordered a reconnaissance of the area around Deep Run, a creek that feeds the Rappahannock River in southeastern Fauquier County. Opposing forces fought a skirmish, and the Union soldiers took three dozen prisoners. USA Gen. John Sedgwick, located just to the east, made observations in the vicinity, leading the Union army to plan its Brandy Station attack.

Early on June 8, 1863, 11,000 Union cavalry troops left Falmouth near Fredericksburg (T-15) to attack the Confederates at Brandy Station. At 4 AM on June 9, under the cover of an early morning haze, the Union soldiers forded the Rappahannock River and struck the Southerners with a surprise, two-column attack. USA Gen. Buford assembled his troops northeast of the rail town at Beverly Ford, crossed the Rappahannock and struck CSA Gen. William Edmonson Jones' cavalry, push-

Brandy Station Side Trip: Stevensburg, Va.

From Bailey's Store, continue south on Va. 663 for 5 miles to Stevensburg.

There was a separate cavalry battle at Stevensburg in June 1863 during the Brandy Station action. USA Gen. Alfred Nattie Duffie, led a division that captured half a Virginia regiment. The battle took up precious time for the Northerners and delayed them from participating in the main part of the Brandy Station fight. Union cavalry troops reassembled at Stevensburg after Brandy Station. USA Gen. Grant camped his 2nd Corps at Stevensburg during the winter of 1863. And the next year, in May 1864, Union forces moved from Stevensburg to Germanna Ford, to the southeast, to begin the Wilderness Campaign near Fredericksburg (T-16).

ing the Confederates back from Fleetwood Hill toward Brandy Station. Fleetwood Hill changed hands several times.

Nine miles downstream, below Kelly's Ford, a Union cavalry division under USA Gen. Gregg circled south of Brandy Station and struck CSA Gen. Stuart's cavalry from the rear. Stuart drove Gregg back, while Fleetwood Hill was saved by a counterattack by CSA Gen. Wade Hampton.

Union cavalrymen, previously inferior to Southern horsemen, developed confidence early on that spring day in the Virginia Piedmont. The 11-hour battle ushered in the Gettysburg Campaign (T-6).

BRANDY STATION TO BAILEY'S STORE
From U.S. 29 at Va. 663 (Alanthus Road), turn left on Alanthus Road and go one block, zigzag left then right and go one block to Bailey's Store at Brandy Station.

Bailey's Store
Brandy Station, Va. • (540) 825-9169

The Brandy Station battlefield area has no visitors center facility, so Bailey's Store, a cute, two-story general store, serves as the unofficial information center for the area. The store is open Monday through Saturday from 6:30 AM to 8 PM and Sunday from 6:30 AM to 7 PM. It offers groceries, drinks, hardware, souvenirs and, of course, information.

BAILEY'S STORE TO FLEETWOOD HILL
From Bailey's Store, return on Va. 663 (north), across U.S. 29 and on to Frontage Road, turn right and go up the hill.

Fleetwood Hill
The memorial marker at Fleetwood Hill honors the cavalry action that was part of the Brandy Station battle.

BRANDY STATION TO CULPEPER, VA.
Return on the Frontage Road and Va. 663 to U.S. 29, turn right (south) on U.S. 29 and continue south 2.5 miles to the first Culpeper exit (U.S. 29/U.S. 15 Bus.).

Along this section of U.S. 29, just south of Brandy Station, is the site where CSA Gen. Lee reviewed his cavalry on June 8, 1863, just before the Battle of Brandy Station. This is the same place where USA Gen. Richard Ewell camped before beginning his post-Brandy Station march to Pennsylvania.

From U.S. 29, go right (west) on U.S. 29/U.S. 15 Bus. and go 4 miles into downtown Culpeper. This route becomes Main Street in the downtown area.

Culpeper, Va.

Culpeper is the county seat of Culpeper County. Among the county's many distinguished natives was Confederate Gen. Ambrose Powell "A.P" Hill. He was born in Culpeper on November 9, 1825. (See more on Hill in T-21.)

Like other communities along this tour route, Culpeper was frequently in the path of both Northern and Southern armies that shifted east or west during the Civil War. It, too, was a rail head of the Orange and Alexandria Railroad. Culpeper is sometimes called the "Cavalry Capital of the Civil War," mainly because of the action at nearby Brandy Station. A number of commercial buildings were used as hospitals for wounded soldiers, and soldiers — both Union and Confederate — are buried in downtown cemeteries. Today, Culpeper remains a quaint, charming community.

CULPEPER TO THE MUSEUM OF CULPEPER HISTORY

Continue south along Main Street in downtown Culpeper to one of the main intersections: Main and Davis streets. Turn left (east) on Davis Street and go a half-block to museum on the left.

Museum of Culpeper History

140 E. Davis Street, Culpeper, Va.
• (540) 825-1973

This community museum is a modest facility — the exhibits are few, but they are interesting. Civil War artifacts and memorabilia are part of its local history interpretation. It is open Monday through Saturday from 11 AM to 5 PM. There is no admission charge, although the museum welcomes contributions.

CULPEPER TO CEDAR MOUNTAIN, VA.

From the Culpeper Museum, continue east on Davis Street for a half-block to East Street, turn right (south) and go three blocks to Stevens Street, turn right (west) and go one block to Main Street, turn left (south) and go south for a half-mile to the traffic light and turn for U.S. 15 (south). Go left (south) on U.S. 15 (James Madison Highway) and zigzag right on U.S. 15, continuing south of Culpeper toward Cedar Mountain. Continue south through a rural area for 6 miles and observe Cedar Mountain in the distance to the east (left).

Cedar Mountain, Va.

There's no need to stop along the roadside. Observe Cedar Mountain in the distance to the east (left). The Battle of Cedar Mountain erupted on August 9, 1862, when CSA Gen. Jackson's troops fought with Union soldiers under USA Gen. Pope. Jackson was able to hold his positions until troops arrived to swing the tide to the Southern side, and Jackson drove the Union forces back to the northwest. This action, sometimes called "Slaughter Mountain" after a slurred version of the word "cedar," took place as both armies shifted into position for 2nd Manassas (T-8), later in August 1862.

CEDAR MOUNTAIN TO LOCUST DALE, VA.

Continue south on U.S. 15 (James Madison Highway) and go 4 miles to Locust Dale.

Locust Dale, Va.

There's no need to stop along the roadside. Observe the countryside where CSA Gen. Jackson crossed the Rapidan (pronounced "Rap-a-dan") River on his way north, August 9, 1862, hours before the Battle of Cedar Mountain.

LOCUST DALE TO WOODBERRY FOREST, VA.

Continue south on U.S. 15 (James Madison Highway) and go 3 miles to the intersection of Va. 622 and signs for Woodberry Forest School.

Woodberry Forest, Va.

There's no need to make a side trip. This community is the home of Woodberry Forest School, a boarding school founded in 1889 by Robert Stringfellow Walker. Walker was a

Confederate officer in CSA Col. Mosby's Rangers. The original Woodberry Forest estate was once owned by President James Madison's brother, William.

WOODBERRY FOREST TO THE RAPIDAN RIVER

Continue south on U.S. 15 (James Madison Highway) and go 1 mile to the Rapidan River crossing.

Rapidan River

Confederate veteran James Lawson Kemper is buried near where the highway crosses the river. Kemper was seriously wounded while leading his brigade of Southern troops in Pickett's Charge at Gettysburg (T-6) in July 1863. Later in the Civil War, he was promoted to major general, and he was governor of Virginia from 1874 to 1878.

Crossing the Rapidan River, this tour route enters Orange County, which was established in 1734. That year, Princess Anne, the eldest daughter of England's King George II, married William IV, the Prince of Orange-Nassau, so the county was named in William's honor.

Orange County, during the first decade of its existence, stretched west to the Appalachian Mountains. President James Madison made his home, Montpelier, in Orange County, and another president, Zachary Taylor, was born in Orange County.

RAPIDAN RIVER TO ORANGE, VA.

Crossing the Rapidan, continue south on U.S. 15 (James Madison Highway) and go 2 miles to the town of Orange.

Orange, Va.

The town of Orange is the county seat of Orange County. President James Madison was a resident of nearby Montpelier. The Wilderness battlefield (T-16) is located in Orange County, to the east of Orange.

ORANGE TO THE ORANGE COUNTY VISITORS BUREAU

U.S. 15 in downtown Orange be-

comes Madison Road. Continue along U.S. 15 (south), Madison Road, to just beyond Washington Street, to the Orange County Visitors Bureau center on the right (west).

Orange County Visitors Bureau
154 Madison Rd., Orange Va.
• (540) 672-1653

The Orange County Visitors Bureau is a county facility that assists travelers with information on county and state historic sites, accommodations, dining and shopping. It is open Sunday from noon to 5 PM and Monday through Saturday from 9 AM to 5 PM. (During the winter, from December 1 to April 1, it is open on Sunday from 1 to 4 PM, and Monday through Saturday from 10 AM to 4 PM.) The bureau has restroom facilities, and pets are welcomed. However, the bureau has no handicapped access.

The Orange County Visitors Bureau will move to a new location sometime in the 1997 tourist season. It will be relocated at the old downtown Orange train station, at the intersection of Main and Short streets. Directions to the new site: From the visitors bureau at 154 Madison Road, continue south on Madison Road for one block to Main Street, turn left (east) and go one block to Short Street. The bureau will keep the same operating hours at the new location.

ORANGE COUNTY VISITORS BUREAU TO ORANGE COUNTY COURTHOUSE

From the Orange County Visitors Bureau at 154 Madison Road, continue south on Madison Road for one block to Main Street, turn right (west) and observe the Orange County Courthouse on the right (south) side of Main Street

Orange County Courthouse
Madison Rd. and Main St., Orange, Va.

The Orange County Courthouse looks much as is did during the Civil War. Southerners used the basement of this old building as an arsenal during the war. A Confederate statue adorns the courthouse lawn.

Photo: Warrenton-Fauquier County Visitor Center

Warrenton native John Singleton Mosby is honored with this marker near the county courthouse.

Orange Side Trips: Lee's Camp, Jackson's Camp

Only an avid Civil War buff wants to take this side trip — where the landscape is the only attraction. Still, the rolling farmland northeast of Orange offers beautiful scenery. From St. Thomas Church, continue south on Caroline Street (Va. 20) for a quarter-mile to the Orange southern town limits and the intersection of U.S. 15 and Va. 20. At this intersection, turn left (northeast) on Va. 20 (north). A mile north is the area where CSA Gen. Robert E. Lee camped for the winter from December 1863 until May 1864 and the beginning of the Wilderness Campaign (T-16). Four miles farther north on Va. 20 is the area where CSA Gens. Thomas J. "Stonewall" Jackson, Richard Ewell and Ambrose Powell "A.P." Hill camped for a week, beginning August 15, 1862, between the battles of Cedar Mountain and 2nd Manassas (T-8).

ORANGE COURTHOUSE TO ST. THOMAS' CHURCH

From the courthouse, continue west on Main Street for two blocks to Caroline Street (Va. Highway 20), turn left (south) and go a half-block to St. Thomas' Church on the left (east) side of the street.

St. Thomas' Church
Caroline St., Orange, Va.

CSA President Jefferson Davis and CSA Gen. Lee occasionally attended services in this attractive old Episcopal church. A plaque beside the church reads: "General Robert E. Lee tied Traveller [his horse] to this tree regularly when he attended services in St. Thomas church in the Winter '63 -'64." The church remains open on Sundays.

Brandy Station Tour Ends

Other Tour Points of Interest

Annual Events

A partial listing of recurring events in Orange County includes the **James Madison's Birthday Celebration**, at his home, Montpelier (March), **Civil War Medical Living History** program, at the Exchange Hotel in Gordonsville (April), **Constitution Day**, at

Montpelier (September), **Gordonsville Street Festival** (October) and the annual **Orange Holiday Tour** (December).

Antiques

The Orange County Visitors Center has a list of nine antiques shops within the county boundaries, most in the town of Orange and some in out-of-the-way, rural locations. Check with travel counselors at the visitors center for specific directions.

Arts

There are three galleries in Orange County — one in each of the county's three principal communities. **Beth Gallery and Press** is in Barboursville, **Ed Jaffe Gallery** is on W. Main Street in Orange, and **Old Somerset Print Shop** is on Constitution Highway in Somerset.

Entertainment

Orange County and its county seat, the town of Orange, offer slim-pickin's when it comes to fancy nightlife, but the pastoral, Piedmont setting makes this region perfect for wholesome, outdoor recreation. **Clark Mountain** has a nature trail, picnic facilities and "pick-your-own" fruit in season. The **Orange County Airport** has airplane rides. You can fish at **Angler's Landing** at Lake Orange, and you can golf at **Meadows Farms Golf Course** or **Brownings Golf Course**. There's **Oakland Heights Farm Horseback Riding** in Gordonsville, and the **Oakland Farm Shooting Preserve** in Orange. Last, but not least, the Rapidan — a Virginia scenic river

— offers ample opportunity to fish, canoe, tube or raft.

Shopping

Despite its "small town" look, Orange is upscale in its choices of places to shop. Gift shops in the county are abundant. Looking for wine and related products? Visit the **Barboursville Vineyards** in Barboursville or **Horton Cellars** in Gordonsville.

Tour 10
Charlottesville

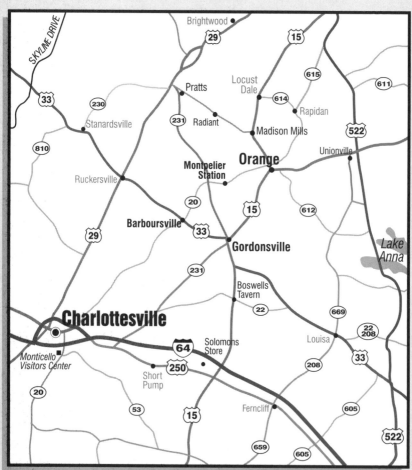

TOUR 10
Charlottesville

About This Tour

This tour route is a continuation of T-9: Brandy Station. Leaving Orange, Virginia, this tour includes a visit to Gordonsville, Virginia, and ends in Charlottesville, Virginia. Thus, this tour route is the fifth of six (T-6, T-7, T-8, T-9, T-10 and T-11) in succession that cover the Piedmont of Pennsylvania, Maryland and Virginia along the eastern slopes of the Appalachian Mountains. The main roads of this tour route are U.S. Highway 15, Va. Highway 231 and U.S. Highway 250, which meander through a region known for its farms, vineyards and elegant estates.

The Blue Ridge Mountains form the western boundary for this part of Virginia, just as they do for the four previous routes. Several prominent rivers cross the Piedmont, flowing east from the mountains to the Coastal Plain, including the Rappahannock, Rapidan, Anna,

Rivanna and James. The central Piedmont countryside, which spreads south along the eastern slope of the mountains, was settled mainly by early English pioneers who moved to the "upcountry" from the Tidewater area. This region was the home of many prominent Americans such as Thomas Jefferson, James Monroe, Meriwether Lewis and George Rogers Clark.

The railroad arrived in Piedmont Virginia in the 1840s. One line — the Orange and Alexandria — ran the length of the region, from Lynchburg, Virginia, north through Charlottesville, Gordonsville and Orange, and on to Manassas and Alexandria, Virginia, near Washington, D.C. At Gordonsville, the Orange and Alexandria met the Virginia Central rail line, which ran west from Richmond and Louisa County. There was significant Civil War action along these rail lines.

This section of Virginia's Piedmont, like

Monticello offers a fascinating side trip to the Charlottesville tour.

the section cited in T-9: Brandy Station, is centrally located between eastern Virginia and the western mountains. Thus, it was the scene of frequent Civil War action, although most events were small skirmishes rather than full-scale battles. Gordonsville experienced war action, particularly after the Wilderness Campaign (T-16).

Travel Tips

U.S. 15 is a well-maintained, well-traveled road, often four-lane but sometimes two-lane. U.S. 250 is a busy divided highway. Congestion is a problem only near Charlottesville, where U.S. Highway 29 and U.S. 250 connect with Interstate 64, a major east-west interstate that ties Richmond to the Shenandoah Valley.

Be alert in rural areas, particularly along U.S. 15 and Va. 231, for farmers on slow-moving tractors. Also watch out during the school year for school buses that make frequent morning and afternoon stops. Winter travel is dangerous only when there are heavy snows and icy highways. Summer, of course, is the time for most major highway construction and repair.

Listen to the radio for the latest traffic and weather conditions. Charlottesville radio stations come in clearly on this route. Citizens band radio users can find traffic information on Channel 19 along the U.S. 250 corridor. Car telephone users will have a strong signal all along the tour route except near Gordonsville. The tour ends in Charlottesville, where we suggest you plan evening dining and lodging. Recommended accommodations are listed in Chapter 22; dining suggestions are in Chapter 23. It is a good idea to review these recommendations before traveling through this stretch of countryside. In addition to our suggestions, there are numerous fast-food restaurants, gas stations and shops throughout Orange and Albemarle counties.

Charlottesville Tour Begins . . .

ORANGE TO GORDONSVILLE, VA.
Leave Orange on U.S. 15, which is a divided highway to Gordonsville.

Just south of Orange, CSA Gen. Thomas Jonathan "Stonewall" Jackson camped in August 1862 after the Battle of Cedar Mountain (T-9).

The Rotunda at the University of Virginia was designed by Thomas Jefferson.

Photo: Library of Virginia

Continue on U.S. 15 south for 8 miles to Gordonsville and the traffic circle at the intersection of U.S. 15 and U.S. 33. Go three-quarters around the roundabout and follow the signs for U.S. 33 east into the downtown area.

Gordonsville, Va.

Gordonsville traces its name to an inn built by Nathaniel Gordon in the late 18th century. By the 1840s, this little community was a regular stop on the Orange and Alexandria rail line that ran from Charlottesville north to Manassas. Another rail line, the Virginia Central, ran west out of Richmond and Louisa County and the two lines intersected at Gordonsville.

GORDONSVILLE TO GORDONSVILLE PRESBYTERIAN CHURCH

From the traffic circle at the intersection of U.S. 15 and U.S. 33, take U.S. 33 east about a quarter-mile toward downtown to the Gordonsville Presbyterian Church on the left (north) side of the street.

Gordonsville Presbyterian Church
U.S. Hwy. 33, Gordonsville, Va.

CSA Gen. "Stonewall" Jackson visited Gordonsville no fewer than 18 times during the Civil War, and he often worshiped at the Presbyterian church. The church is still open on Sundays.

PRESBYTERIAN CHURCH TO EXCHANGE HOTEL MUSEUM

Continue four blocks east on U.S. 33 to the Exchange Hotel Museum on the left (north) side of the street beside the railroad tracks.

Exchange Hotel Museum
U.S. 33, Gordonsville, Va. • (540) 832-2944

Originally a hotel for rail passengers on the Virginia Central Railroad from Richmond, this two-story building, with handsome Greek Revival architecture, now houses a museum with an exceptional Civil War exhibit. The old

Exchange Hotel was a hospital during the war. Wounded soldiers from Cedar Mountain (T-9), Chancellorsville (T-16), Brandy Station (T-9) and the Wilderness (T-16) were transported by train and treated at the hospital.

In 1864, after the Wilderness, no fewer than 6,000 men were taken to the hospital in a single month. Soldiers who died at the hospital were buried behind the building and later reinterred in nearby Maplewood Cemetery.

The museum is open Tuesday through Saturday from 10 AM to 4 PM and on summer Sundays from 1 to 4 PM. It is closed January 1 through March 15 and on Independence Day, Labor Day, Thanksgiving and Christmas. Admission is $4 for adults, $3 for seniors older than 60 and $1 for children 3 to 17. Anyone younger is admitted free.

EXCHANGE HOTEL MUSEUM TO MAPLEWOOD CEMETERY

From the Exchange Hotel Museum, return west on U.S. 33 back through downtown Gordonsville. At the traffic roundabout at U.S. 15, continue a half-mile west of the circle on U.S. 33 to Maplewood Cemetery on the right (north) side of the road.

Maplewood Cemetery
U.S. Hwy. 33, Gordonsville, Va.

A number of Civil War dead, especially those treated and buried at the Exchange Hotel hospital, were reinterred at the Maplewood Cemetery. More than 700 Southern soldiers, mainly from Georgia and North Carolina, are buried at the back of the cemetery, and a simple marker identifies the mass grave's location. It is open from sunup to sundown.

GORDONSVILLE TO MAURY'S SCHOOL SITE

Return east on U.S. 33 to the traffic circle. This time take Va. Highway 231 south. Just south of Gordonsville, this tour route crosses into Albemarle County.

Albemarle County Personality: Thomas Jefferson

The U.S. Congress adopted the Missouri Compromise on March 15, 1820. The legislation allowed Missouri's admission to the Union as a slave state, and Maine was cut from Massachusetts as a new state, thus balancing the U.S. Senate with representatives from both slave and free states. With the compromise, slavery was outlawed in the Louisiana Territory, north of Missouri's southern boundary. The issues evoked concern. "We have a wolf by the ears," Thomas Jefferson said, "and we can neither safely hold him, nor safely let him go."

A month after the bill passed Congress, on April 22, 1820, the retired President Jefferson wrote a letter to a friend, John Holmes. Jefferson wrote:

"This momentous question [the Missouri issue], like a fire-bell in the night, awakened and filled me with terror. I considered it at once as the knell of the Union. It is hushed, indeed, for the moment. But this is a reprieve only, not a final sentence. A geographical line [that divides free and slave territories] . . . once conceived and held up to the angry passions of men will never be obliterated; and every new irritation will mark it deeper and deeper.

Photo: Library of Virginia

Thomas Jefferson, who lived at Monticello near Charlottesville, saw the country headed for conflict as early as 1820.

. . . There is not a man on earth who would sacrifice more than I would to relieve us from this heavy reproach [of slavery], in any *practicable* way. The cession of that kind of property, for so it is misnamed, is a bagatelle which would not cost a second thought if, in that way, a general emancipation and *expatriation* could be affected; and, gradually, and with due sacrifice, I think it might be. But as it is, we have the wolf by the ears, and we can neither hold him, nor safely let him go. Justice is in one scale, and self-preservation in the other.

"Of one thing I am certain, that . . . their diffusion over a greater surface would make them individually happier, and proportionally facilitate the accomplishment of their emancipation. . . . An abstinence, too, from this act of power, would remove the jealousy excited by the undertaking of Congress to regulate the condition . . . of men composing a state. This is certainly the exclusive right of every state. . . . I regret that I am now to die in the belief that the useless sacrifice of themselves by the generation of 1776, to acquire self-government and happiness to their country, is to be thrown away by the unwise and unworthy passions of their sons, and that my only consolation is to be that I live not to weep over it. If they would but dispassionately weigh the blessings they will throw away, against an abstract principle more likely to be effected by union than by scission, they would pause before they would perpetrate this act of suicide on themselves, and of treason against the hopes of the world."

Jefferson lived six more years, and died on July 4, 1826 — on the 50th anniversary of the Declaration of Independence, which he wrote. He died having wisely sounded the alarm — like a "fire-bell" — on the issue of slavery in America. He was 40 years ahead of his time in warning of the Union's "scission," as he described it, which ultimately occurred in 1861.

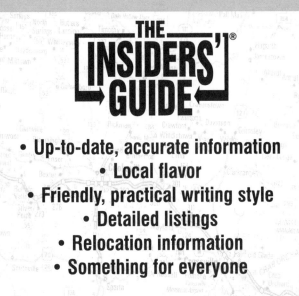

THE
INSIDERS'®
GUIDE

- Up-to-date, accurate information
- Local flavor
- Friendly, practical writing style
- Detailed listings
- Relocation information
- Something for everyone

YOUR COMPLETE TRAVEL, NEWCOMER AND BUSINESS GUIDES

Albemarle County

Pronounced "Al-ba-marle," this historic county was established in 1745 and named for Virginia's governor, William Keppel, the Earl of Albemarle. Thomas Jefferson was born in Albemarle County, and the region is affectionately known as "Jefferson's Country." He made his home at Monticello. James Monroe lived in Albemarle as well, at Ash Lawn-Highland. Jefferson designed the University of Virginia, and Presidents Jefferson, Monroe and James Madison served on the school's first board of visitors. Today, Albemarle County boasts countless horse farms and elegant estates. Four miles into Albemarle County, along U.S. 15, was the site of Maury's School.

Maury's School Site
Va. Hwy. 231, Albemarle County, Va.

There is no need to stop along the roadside: Maury's School is no longer in existence. The school was operated by the Rev. James

Maury, a Huguenot-turned-Episcopal minister. Rev. Maury taught science and mathematics in the mid-1700s to a number of local boys including Thomas Jefferson and John Walker, the son of explorer Thomas Walker. One of Rev. Maury's grandsons was Matthew Fontaine Maury, a Confederate veteran who was known as the "Father of Oceanography." (See Fontaine and Maury avenues in Charlottesville later in this tour route. Also, see more on Maury in T-5 and T-17.)

MAURY'S SCHOOL SITE TO CHARLOTTESVILLE
Continue on Va. 231 for 6 miles to Va. Highway 22.

Just before the intersection with Va. 22 is the site of Castle Hill, home of Thomas Walker. Walker was Thomas Jefferson's guardian and the explorer who discovered the Cumberland Gap to earn the nickname "Father of Kentucky." Castle Hill is privately owned and not open to the public.

Photo: Library of Virginia

The Exchange Hotel was a hospital during the war.

Continue on Va. 22 south 5 miles to U.S. 250, and proceed 2 miles to I-64. Along U.S. 250, between Keswick and Charlottesville, is the site of Shadwell, Thomas Jefferson's birthplace. Just west of Shadwell is Monticello Mountain, the site of Jefferson's home. Take I-64 West (follow signs for Staunton, Virginia) 2 miles to exit 121 (Va. Highway 20, Scottsville).

Charlottesville, Va.

Charlottesville is the Albemarle County seat. The town was established in 1763 and named in honor of England's new, 17-year-old queen, Charlotte of Mecklenberg-Sterlitz in Germany, who married George III. Today, Charlottesville is central Virginia's largest municipality, with about 100,000 people in its metropolitan area. Its cosmopolitan flavor can be attributed mostly to the University of Virginia, one of the nation's top institutes of higher learning, which draws an impressive faculty and bright student body.

As early as August 1861, Charlottesville was "a vast hospital for the sick and wounded," according to one newspaper. A number of public buildings and private homes in the downtown area were put to use to tend to Civil War casualties. During the four years of the war, nearly 23,000 were treated here. CSA Gen. Stonewall Jackson's troops were in the vicinity in 1862 during his Shenandoah Valley Campaign. Two years later on leap day, Feb. 29, 1864, there was a skirmish a few miles north of town at Rio Hill — or Rio Mill. USA Gen. George Custer led a small force south from Culpeper with a plan to destroy a bridge over the Rivanna River (site of today's Charlottesville Reservoir off U.S. 29 N.). A Confederate artillery unit, in winter camp on the south bank of the river, received an early warning. The battle was brief and somewhat uneventful, except that Custer's men succeeded in burning down the bridge.

CHARLOTTESVILLE TO THE MONTICELLO VISITORS CENTER

At the intersection of Va. 20 and I-64, follow the blue signs to the visitors center-museum. At the end of the exit ramp, turn left on Va. 20 (Scottsville Road) and head south a half-mile to the traffic light and the visitors center entrance on the right.

Monticello Visitors Center
600 College Dr. , Charlottesville, Va.
• **(804) 977-1783, (804) 293-6789**

The visitor facilities at this center are jointly operated by Monticello and the Charlottesville-Albemarle Convention and Visitors Bureau. The building was constructed in the 1970s as part of western Virginia's observance of the American Bicentennial. Monticello provides information and operates a gift shop. Tourists in need of general information can visit the section of the center operated by the city-county visitors bureau, where counselors dispense information on area attractions, including lodging and dining. Restrooms are available. Ramp access is provided for the disabled. The center is open every day from 9 AM to 5:30 PM. From November to February the center closes at 5 PM, and it is closed on New Year's Day, Thanksgiving and Christmas. There is no admission charge.

MONTICELLO VISITORS BUREAU TO DOWNTOWN CHARLOTTESVILLE

From the visitors center, turn left (north) on Va. 20 and follow it to downtown Charlottesville. Va. 20 becomes Monticello Avenue and then Avon Street. Continue 2 miles, cross Belmont Bridge over the railroad tracks and follow signs for Water Street, where you will find several blocks of municipal pay-to-park facilities. Park in one of the lots on Water Street.

Charlottesville Mall

A block north of the Water Street parking

areas is the Charlottesville Mall, formerly old Main Street. Stroll along the pedestrian walkway and experience the combination of old-town architecture and modern-day shopping amenities. This seven-block mall was dedicated in 1976, and it forever altered the city's downtown Main Street. The brick walkway is lined with trees, flower planters, art and benches.

CHARLOTTESVILLE MALL TO ALBEMARLE COUNTY COURTHOUSE

Two blocks north of the Mall, up either Fourth Street or Fifth Street, is the old Albemarle County Courthouse and historic Court Square. The courthouse is on Jefferson Street, between Fourth and Park streets.

Albemarle County Courthouse
Jefferson St., Charlottesville, Va.

Thomas Jefferson sometimes visited the old Albemarle Courthouse, which was used in

Charlottesville Personality: John West

One of Charlottesville's most prominent, early 20th century African Americans was a successful businessman named John West. A barber, West was the adopted son of Jane West, the community's richest free black in 1860. Young West inherited a house and $3,200 from his mother when she died in 1869. West died 60 years later in 1929, leaving a sizable estate that included 20 houses, 20 lots, several commercial buildings, thousands of acres of farmland throughout Albemarle County, more than $23,000 in cash and another $26,000 in bonds.

One afternoon in 1865, young West was standing outside a store on Main Street — today's Downtown Mall — when two strangers rode up, handed him the reins to their horses and went inside a tailor's shop. Moments later West was startled by a man running down the street, yelling for CSA Col. John Singleton "Gray Ghost" Mosby. Federal troops were invading Charlottesville from the north. Realizing he held the reins to Mosby's horse, West ran inside to alert the riders. The elusive Confederate rushed from the store, flipped West a silver dollar as thanks and headed west up Fifth Street on a dead run. West ran behind to make sure Mosby escaped and noticed the Confederate was able to "clear High Street at one jump with mud flying to heaven." In a flash, Mosby was gone; the Yankees, meanwhile, were too busy looting downtown to notice.

Forty years after the incident, in the early 20th century, Mosby was in Charlottesville and met West again. The barber showed the old Confederate the very silver dollar Mosby had given him and asked if he remembered the incident. Mosby replied that, while he had been busy looking at the endless number of Union blue coats, he had some recollection of the day.

Photo: Library of Virginia

In Colonial days, Sunday church services were held in the Albemarle County Courthouse.

Colonial days for Sunday church services. A Civil War statue of a Confederate soldier and a pair of cannons grace the courthouse lawn.

ALBEMARLE COUNTY COURTHOUSE TO JACKSON PARK
Adjacent to the Albemarle County Courthouse, at Fourth and Jefferson streets, is Jackson Park.

Jackson Park
Jefferson St., Charlottesville, Va.
Jackson Park is a small, urban plot that features a fine equestrian statue of CSA Gen. "Stonewall" Jackson by noted sculptor Charles Keck. There are benches at Jackson Park.

JACKSON PARK TO LEE PARK
Walk two blocks west on Jefferson Street to Second Street to Lee Park.

Lee Park
Jefferson St., Charlottesville, Va.
Lee Park, one square block of downtown Charlottesville, features an equestrian statue of CSA Gen. Robert E. Lee. Benches are available at Lee Park.

LEE PARK TO THE UNIVERSITY OF VIRGINIA
Walk three blocks south on Second Street and back across the

Charlottesville Personality: John Singleton Mosby

John Singleton Mosby grew up just south of Charlottesville, and he attended the University of Virginia. (See more on Mosby in T-7 and T-9.) A popular story is that, once in 1896, Mosby was visiting Charlottesville and was severely injured when he was kicked in the face by a horse. Unconscious, he was rushed to the University of Virginia infirmary. As Mosby returned slowly to consciousness, an intern leaned over to check him: "What's your name?" The old Confederate replied, "None of your damned business!" A surgeon in the room to operate on Mosby spoke up, "He's conscious all right."

Charlottesville Side Trip:
CSA Gen. Thomas L. Rosser Home

From westbound University Avenue in front of the Rotunda, turn right (north) on Rugby Road and go 0.7 mile to Rosser Lane on the right and Winston Road on the left.

CSA cavalry Gen. Thomas Lafayette Rosser lived in this vicinity. Rosser was born in October 1836 in Campbell County, Virginia, and moved with his family to Texas in 1842. A member of the West Point Class of 1861, Rosser resigned before graduation at the onset of the Civil War. He saw action at 1st Manassas (T-8), the Seven Days' Battles (T-18), 2nd Manassas (T-8), Chancellorsville (T-16) and Gettysburg (T-6). He served in CSA Gen. Jubal Early's Shenandoah campaign in 1864, earning the title "Savior of the Valley."

A recognized cavalry officer, Rosser rose in rank to major general. He regularly matched wits with his West Point classmate and erstwhile friend, USA Gen. George Armstrong Custer. After the war, Rosser became chief engineer of the Northern Pacific Railroad, and Custer commanded the U.S. Army unit that protected Rosser's project. Rosser later served in the Spanish-American War, and he was appointed the postmaster in Charlottesville.

Rugby Road in this vicinity is the namesake of Rosser's estate, Rugby, which can be found just off present-day Rosser Avenue, which is named, of course, for the general. Adjacent Winston Road is named for Rosser's wife, who was a Winston from Hanover County, Virginia.

After completing this side trip, return to University Avenue and the University of Virginia's Rotunda to continue the tour.

Mall to the municipal parking lots on Water Street. Resume a motor tour from the lot, continuing west on Water Street. At the convergence of Main and Water streets is a statue that honors Virginia explorers Meriwether Lewis and William Clark and their Native American guide, Sacajawea. Continue west 2 miles on Main Street (U.S. 250 W. Bus.), which becomes University Avenue as it enters the University of Virginia environs at the intersection of 14th Street NW. University Avenue. Continue west 0.3 mile on University Avenue un-til it passes in front of the Rotunda, the most prominent building at the University of Virginia.

University of Virginia

Take a few moments to visit the University of Virginia — known as "U-V-A." The buildings, including the Rotunda and the pavilions along the Lawn, were designed by Thomas Jefferson, the university's founder. The school's buildings are considered one of the best collections of architecture in the nation. The University of Virginia may be the only educational facility that avoids using the word "campus." Say "Grounds" instead. CSA Col. John Singleton Mosby made local history during his college days at UVa when he shot and injured a fellow student during a quarrel over a young lady friend. A sympathetic judge saved Mosby from a severe sentence.

UNIVERSITY OF VIRGINIA TO UNIVERSITY CEMETERY

From the Rotunda, continue west on University Avenue for 0.3 mile to the intersection of Emmet Street (U.S. 29 Bus.). Cross Emmet Street, and note that at this point University Avenue becomes Ivy Road (U.S. 250). Continue four blocks west on Ivy Road to Alderman Road, turn left (southeast) on Alderman and go a half-mile to University Cemetery at the intersection with McCormick Road.

University Cemetery
Alderman and McCormick Rds., Charlottesville, Va.

This cemetery, in the midst of student dormitories, features a large statue honor-

---

University Cemetery Personality: Thomas Staples Martin

Thomas Staples Martin, an Albemarle County native, attended Virginia Military Institute during the Civil War from 1864 to 1865. A severe cold landed him in the VMI infirmary, and that saved him from a march north with fellow cadets to the Battle of New Market in May 1864. Martin was the only Virginian who served as majority leader of the U.S. Senate. He was born in Scottsville, Virginia, in July 1842. Following the Civil War, from 1865 to 1867, Martin attended UVa, but he left school after his father died to support his mother, brothers and sisters.

Reading law mainly at night, Martin was admitted to the Virginia bar, set up his practice and soon became the local attorney for the C&O Railroad. Based mainly on his railroad connections, Martin began establishing political ties that in time evolved into a machine that ruled Virginia politics for a quarter-century. Martin engineered the 1887 Virginia election in which lawyer John Warwick Daniel defeated John Stroad Barbour Jr. in the U.S. Senate race. Barbour was a Culpeper lawyer and president of the Orange and Alexandria Railroad. Daniel, a Civil War veteran, had a limp caused by a war wound and was known as the "Lame Lion of Lynchburg." Two years later, in 1889, Barbour was elected to Virginia's other U.S. Senate seat. But Barbour died in 1892, and Virginia Gov. Phillip W. McKenney chose another Civil War veteran, Eppa Hunton of Warrenton (T-9), to fill Senator Barbour's seat until the legislature convened.

By early 1894, the U.S. Senate campaign narrowed to two candidates: lawyer Tom Martin and Confederate cavalry general and former Gov. Fitzhugh Lee. The nephew of Confederate Gen. Robert E. Lee, Fitzhugh Lee was one of the most popular men in the state. Having worked quietly behind the scene for months, organizing support and using railroad money to cover legislators' campaign expenses, the Virginia General Assembly chose Martin on the sixth ballot. Fitzhugh Lee bitterly blamed railroad money for his defeat. Martin took his seat in the U.S. Senate in March 1895. He was re-elected to each succeeding six-year term through 1918, serving until his death in 1919. He served nearly 25 years in the Senate, and his tenure ran during the administrations of five presidents, from Grover Cleveland to Woodrow Wilson. During his time in the Senate, he witnessed the advent of the automobile and the airplane, the beginning of popular elections for U.S. Senate candidates in Virginia, the Spanish American War and, ultimately, World War I. He was chosen majority leader of the Senate in March 1917; less than a month later, on April 4, the U.S. Senate passed a war resolution against the German Empire. Martin's term as majority leader ended in March 1919, and World War I officially ended just three months later, in June. Five months later, in November, the Senator died in Charlottesville.

Photo: Library of Virginia

Matthew Fontaine Maury created a universal system of oceanography.

ing more than 1,000 Confederate graves. The statue reads, "Fate denied them victory but clothed them with glorious immortality." Also buried in the cemetery is Thomas Staples Martin, a former U.S. senator from Virginia who attended Virginia Military Institute during the Civil War.

UNIVERSITY CEMETERY TO MAURY AND FONTAINE AVENUES
From University Cemetery at the intersection of Alderman and

McCormick roads, continue east on Alderman Road for 0.7 miles (Alderman will become Maury Avenue) to Fontaine Avenue.

Maury Avenue and Fontaine Avenue
Charlottesville, Va.

Fontaine Avenue is U.S. 29 Bus. and a continuation of Jefferson Park Avenue in western Charlottesville. Both Fontaine and Maury avenues are named for Matthew Fontaine Maury, a Confederate veteran known as the

"Pathfinder of the Seas" and the "Father of Oceanography." Maury was a grandson of the Rev. James Maury, who taught science to young Thomas Jefferson at Maury's School in eastern Albemarle County. (See more on Maury in T-5: Lexington.)

The Charlottesville tour ends at the intersection of Maury and Fontaine avenues.

Charlottesville Tour Ends

Other Tour Points of Interest

So, here you are in Mr. Jefferson's Country with a day or two to see all the sites and do a little shopping. You'll really need a week or two. Here is a thumbnail report on some of the area's other must-see attractions. For questions, information or reservations, ask for help at the Monticello Visitors Center (see listing, above).

Annual Events

The **Dogwood Festival** and **Garden Week** are both observed in April. The **Ash-Lawn Highland Summer Opera Festival** is conducted in July and August; for information, call (804) 293-9539. Late October brings the **Virginia Festival of American Film** to town — call (800) UVA-FEST for information. The **Foxfield Races** offer steeplechase and flat races annually on the last weekend in April and September. Of course, the **University of Virginia** provides exciting intercollegiate athletics.

Antiques

There are no fewer than two dozen antique shops in and around Charlottesville — far too many to single out one or two. Local tour guide books list many of these shops, along with their telephone numbers and addresses. Remember, though, that these shops vary in quality and service. Generally, really good antiques found in this community are expensive.

Arts

The **McGuffey Art Center**, housed in a former elementary school in the downtown historic area, has 20 working studios for artists and is open to the public. The **Bayly Art Museum** is near the grounds of the University of Virginia and offers ongoing art exhibits. The university's **Heritage Repertory Theater** rotates plays during the summer at Culbreth and Helms theaters. And the **Virginia Discovery Museum** offers a hands-on program that features history, art and science through interac-

Charlottesville Personality: Sarah Ann Strickler

Sarah Ann Strickler was only 19 when she traveled from her Madison County, Virginia, home to Charlottesville to attend the Albemarle Female Institute. The Civil War raged throughout Virginia, and young Miss Strickler was an avid Confederate. She wrote in her diary, "Oh, if I were only a boy, to fight [Sheridan's men] — it chafes me sorely to have to submit to their insolence."

No one was thinking of school, she wrote, and 2,000 Northern soldiers rode through her front yard at the school. She stood in her window and spoke to one of the enemy soldiers. He told her he was in town to "tear up the railroad." Then, he added, "If you live in Richmond you can go with us, we'll be there in a few days." Then, Strickler wrote, "I told him never, that if they fought 10 million of years they could not conquer us. He rode away, and some of them actually waived their hats at us." She and a fellow student clenched their fists and shook them at the soldiers.

In 1867, after having been severely chastised by townspeople for shaking her fists at the enemy, Sarah Ann Strickler married a Confederate veteran, Robert Herndon Fife. The Fifes lived in Charlottesville and raised nine children.

tive exhibits. This is an especially fun option if you are traveling with the kids. The Discovery Museum is on the Downtown Mall, across from City Hall.

Historic Sites

Monticello, the aforementioned residence of Thomas Jefferson, is one of the nation's premier presidential homes. But the wait for a tour is often long, especially during summer. The Monticello Visitors Center, operated by Monticello and the Charlottesville/Albemarle Convention and Visitors Bureau, has a Monticello exhibit and gift shop. Check in at the center at the Va. 20 exit off I-64 for tour times and availability at Mr. Jefferson's estate on top of Monticello Mountain. **Ash Lawn-Highland** is the restored summer home of President James Monroe. It is 2 miles west of Monticello. **Montpelier**, the home of President James Madison, is near Orange.

Shopping

You will find concentrated shopping areas downtown, uptown near the University of Virginia and northwest along the U.S. 29 (Emmet Street) corridor. The Charlottesville area has countless shops, boutiques and stores offering such specialty items as needlecrafts, jewelry, sports equipment, designer clothes, art and quilts. The area has three major shopping centers.

Vineyards

Albemarle County boasts several vineyards. Among the more popular ones in the region are Oakencroft, Montdomaine and Jefferson. **Oakencroft Vineyard** and Winery, (804) 296-4188, off Garth Road west of Charlottesville, was established by the late John Rogan, who built the lovely Boar's Head Inn. **Montdomaine Cellars**, (804) 971-8947, is 10 miles south of Charlottesville on the Scottsville Road. **Jefferson Vineyards**, (804) 977-3042, between Monticello and Ash Lawn, is at the former estate — Colle — of Jefferson's Italian friend Philip Mazzei, a wine connoisseur. All three vineyards offer tours, tastings and sales.

Tour 11
Lynchburg

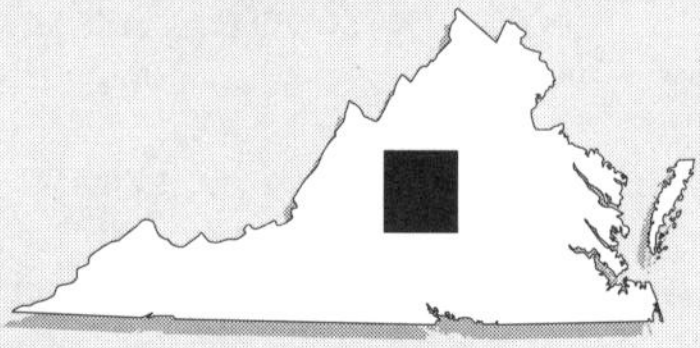

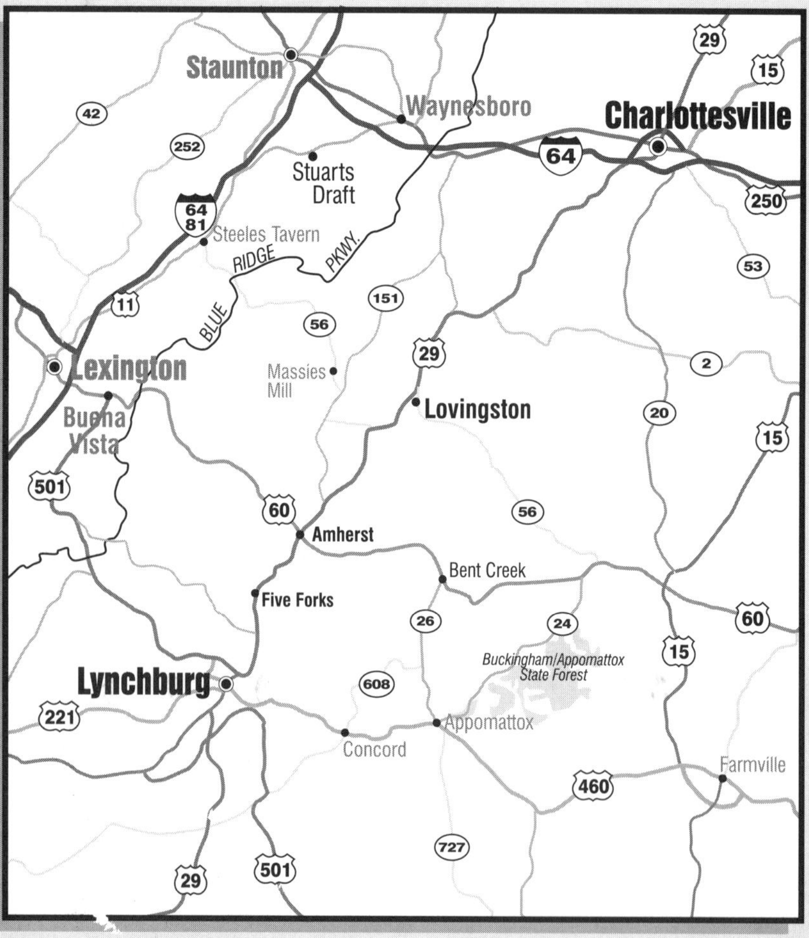

Staunton

42

252

Waynesboro

29

15

Charlottesville

64

250

Stuarts Draft

64 81

Steeles Tavern

RIDGE PKWY.

53

151

BLUE

56

11

29

2

Lexington

Massies Mill

Lovingston

20

15

Buena Vista

60

501

56

Amherst

Five Forks

26

24

60

15

Lynchburg

608

Buckingham/Appomattox State Forest

221

Concord

Appomattox

Farmville

460

29

501

727

TOUR 11
Lynchburg

About This Tour

This tour route is a continuation of the previous tour, T-10: Charlottesville, that concluded in Charlottesville, Virginia. This route begins as you leave Charlottesville, goes through Albemarle, Nelson and Amherst counties and concludes in Lynchburg, Virginia. The route stretches south through the fertile countryside and historic towns along the eastern slope of the Blue Ridge Mountains. The main route, U.S. Highway 29, take you through a region known for its rolling hills and small mountains. The tour includes stops in Lynchburg, which boasts multiple attractions. It also passes simple, undeveloped sites that contain a mere highway marker.

The Blue Ridge Mountains form the western boundary for this part of Virginia, just as they do for the five previous routes (T-6: Gettysburg, T-7: Monocacy, T-8: Manassas, T-9: Brandy Station and T-10: Charlottesville). Several prominent rivers cross the Piedmont, flowing westerly from the mountains to the Coastal Plain, including the Rivanna and James.

This central Piedmont countryside, which spreads south along the eastern slope of the mountains, was settled mainly by early English pioneers who moved to the "upcountry" from the Tidewater. The railroad arrived in Piedmont Virginia in the 1840s. One line, the Orange and Alexandria, ran from Lynchburg, Virginia, on to Manassas and Alexandria near Washington. There was significant Civil War action along these rail lines.

Travel Tips

U.S. 29 is a well-maintained, well-traveled, four-lane highway. Congestion is a problem near Charlottesville, where this tour begins, and Lynchburg, where the tour ends. Listen to the radio for the latest traffic and weather conditions. Charlottesville and Lynchburg radio stations come in clearly. Citizens band radio users can find traffic information on Channel 19 along the U.S. 29 corridor. Car telephone users will have a strong signal all along the tour route except near Gordonsville, Virginia.

The tour ends in Lynchburg, and we recommend accommodations in Chapter 22. We recommend dining selections in Chapter 23. Fast-food facilities, gas stations, shops and other amenities are sprinkled all along U.S. 29 between Charlottesville and Lynchburg.

Lynchburg Tour Begins . . .

▬▬▭▭▭▭

FONTAINE AVENUE IN CHARLOTTESVILLE TO NELSON COUNTY VISITORS CENTER
From Maury Avenue, turn right (south) on Fontaine Avenue (U.S. 29 Bus. south) and go 0.8 mile to the ramp to U.S. 29 south — follow signs for Lynchburg. Take U.S. 29 for 30 miles from Charlottesville to the Nelson County Visitors Center on U.S. 29 at Lovingston.

This route enters Nelson County, which was formed in 1807 from Amherst County and named in honor of Thomas Nelson Jr., governor of Virginia from June to November 1781.

Nelson County Visitors Center
8519 Thomas Nelson Hwy. (U.S. 29), Lovingston, Va. • (804) 263-5239
The Nelson County Visitors Center is small and relatively new. Travel counselors can help

with brochures and other information on area attractions. This center is operated by Nelson County, which also has a visitors center just off the Blue Ridge Parkway (near milepost 16), in the western part of the county. The Nelson County Visitors Center is open 9 AM to 5 PM daily. The center is handicapped-accessible, and there are restrooms.

NELSON COUNTY
VISITORS CENTER TO TYE RIVER
Continue on U.S. 29 south 8 miles to the Tye River.

Tye River

Just east of the highway along the Tye River, a Confederate unit called the Botetourt Battery attacked a group of Union raiders on June 11, 1864, and prevented the Federals from burning the Orange and Alexandria Railroad bridge over the Tye. The delay action enabled CSA Gen. Jubal Early to reach Lynchburg, just to the south, and save the town from capture by USA Gen. David Hunter.

At the Tye River, this tour route enters Amherst County, which was formed in 1761 and named for Major Gen. Sir Jeffrey Amherst, the British commander in Northern America during the latter part of the French and Indian War. Sir Jeffrey Amherst was also the royal governor of Virginia from 1759 to 1768, at the time the county was established.

TYE RIVER TO LYNCHBURG, VA.
Continue south on U.S. 29 for 20 miles, across the James River, to Lynchburg.

Lynchburg, Va.

Lynchburg was established in 1786 and named for John Lynch, who owned the site where the village was founded. Incorporated as a town in 1805, Lynchburg became a city in 1852. An important industrial center, it is strategically located on the James River, a major Virginia transportation thoroughfare in the 18th and 19th centuries. It became an important center of trade for tobacco, iron and agricultural products.

During the Civil War, Lynchburg was a

Nelson County Personality: Thomas Fortune Ryan

Thomas Fortune Ryan was born near Lovingston in October 1851, and was orphaned at the age of 14, in 1865, as the Civil War ended. A poor teenager who survived Reconstruction in southern Virginia, Ryan became a local — and national — legend after he moved to New York City and became a multi-millionaire. A wealthy financier, he built an empire with interests in streetcars, railroads, coal, diamonds, oil , rubber, tobacco, race horses and life insurance, among other ventures. He died in New York City in 1928, leaving a fortune of more than $200 million (in 1928 dollars). Before his death, Ryan returned to Nelson County and purchased a grand estate, Oak Ridge, near Shipman just east of Lovingston. Ryan visited his native county on numerous occasions. Despite his great wealth, he never forgot his early days of poverty in war-torn Nelson County.

Thomas Fortune Ryan escaped
Reconstruction in Virginia.

Tee Time!

This useful guide highlights course features such as par, yardage for men, women and pros, water holes, general course layout and playing tips.

major supply base and hospital center for the Confederate army. In June 1864, USA Gen. David Hunter's troops were pushed back by soldiers serving with CSA Gen. John Cabell Breckinridge. CSA Gen. Jubal Early's troops arrived from Charlottesville by train in time to assist Breckinridge in defending Lynchburg.

Riverside Park, along the James River, is hard to find, but a Civil War buff can see the *Marshall*, a passenger packet boat that plied the James River and Kanawha Canal in the mid-19th century. The *Marshall* carried CSA Gen. Thomas J. "Stonewall" Jackson's body to Lexington for burial in 1863. Pulitzer Prize-winning historian Douglas Southall Freeman, who wrote a biography of Robert E. Lee, was born in Lynchburg, and his home is on Main Street.

LYNCHBURG TO
LYNCHBURG VISITORS CENTER
Having crossed the James River on U.S. 29 into Lynchburg, go 0.1 mile

and take the Main Street exit (exit 1). Turn left (west) and go three blocks to 12th Street, turn left (south) and go one block to the Visitors Information Center at the corner of 12th and Church Sts.

Lynchburg Visitors Information Center

216 12th Street at Church Street, Lynchburg, Va. • (804) 847-1811, (800) 732-5821

The Lynchburg center is at the corner of 12th and Church streets. Despite its downtown setting, the center provides information about the city as well as the various outlying counties — Campbell, Bedford, Amherst and Appomattox. Travel counselors assist visitors with trip planning and can recommend places to spend the night, dine and shop. The center is open from 9 AM to 5 PM daily. There are restrooms, and the facility is handicapped-accessible.

display are personal papers, medical supplies, clothing and battle flags.

The museum is open daily from 1 to 4 PM, except New Year's Day, Thanksgiving, Christmas Eve and Christmas. There is a $1 admission fee. Children younger than 12, accompanied by an adult, are free.

Across the street is Monument Terrace, with sculptures and commemorative markers of the Civil War — as well as the Spanish-American War and World War I. Lynchburg natives who fought in these wars are honored by a 139-step staircase memorial.

A number of Confederate soldiers are buried in the cemeteries of Lynchburg.

LYNCHBURG VISITORS INFORMATION CENTER TO LYNCHBURG MUSEUM

From the visitors center, go east on one-way Church Street a half-block to 13th Street, turn right (south) and go one block. Turn right (west) on Court Street and go four blocks to Ninth Street and the Lynchburg Museum.

Lynchburg Museum at the Old Courthouse
901 Court St., Lynchburg, Va.
• (804) 847-1459

The Old Lynchburg Courthouse is a registered Virginia landmark, and it is on the National Register of Historic Places. Built in 1855 and designed as one of Virginia's outstanding Greek Revival civic buildings, the structure was restored in 1976 as part of Lynchburg's celebration of the American Bicentennial. The museum has two permanent exhibit galleries that relate Lynchburg's rich history. The museum also features a number of rotating exhibits on various historical eras, including the Civil War. Among the Civil War artifacts on

LYNCHBURG MUSEUM TO CITY CEMETERY

From the Lynchburg Museum at Ninth and Court streets, continue west on Court Street to Fifth Street (U.S. 29 Bus.), turn left (south) and go eight blocks to Taylor Street, turn right (west) and go one block to Fourth Street and into Old City Cemetery.

Old City Cemetery
Taylor and 4th Sts. Lynchburg, Va.

The Old City Cemetery is a Virginia landmark, and it is listed on the National Register of Historic Places. The first land for this cemetery was given by John Lynch, Lynchburg's founder. Established in 1806, the City Cemetery includes a section where 2,700 Confederate soldiers are buried. It is open from sunrise to sunset.

The Pest House Medical Museum, a white farm building, is on the grounds of Old City Cemetery. Built in the 1840s, it was the medical office of Dr. John Jay Terrell. "Pest" is short for "pestilence." A number of Dr. Terrell's medical tools and equipment are on display. The museum is open from sunrise to sunset. It offers self-guided tours, or special tours by appointment.

CITY CEMETERY TO SPRING HILL CEMETERY

Leave the Pest House Medical Museum and Old City Cemetery on the winding, one-way road that exits onto Wise Street at Fifth Street (U.S. 29

Bus.). Turn right (south) and continue 1.3 miles past E.C. Glass High School and Park Avenue to Oakley Avenue (U.S. Highway 221). Turn left (east) on Oakley Avenue and go one block to Fort Avenue and Spring Hill Cemetery. To enter the cemetery, turn left from Oakley Avenue onto Fort Avenue and go 100 yards to the cemetery entrance on the right.

Spring Hill Cemetery
Fort and Oakley Aves., Lynchburg, Va.

CSA Gen. Jubal A. Early, the man who helped save Lynchburg from USA Gen. David Hunter's attack in 1864, is buried at Spring Hill Cemetery. Early commanded the 2nd Corps of the Confederate Army of Northern Virginia. After the Civil War, he made his home in Lynchburg, where he died in 1904. A number of other Confederate heroes and soldiers are buried at Spring Hill. The cemetery is open from sunrise to sunset.

SPRING HILL CEMETERY TO FORT EARLY
Exit Spring Hill Cemetery and continue south on Fort Avenue (U.S. 29 Bus., U.S. 460 Bus.) for 0.6 mile to the intersection of Fort and Memorial avenues and the entrance to Fort Early.

Fort Early
Memorial and Fort Aves. Lynchburg, Va.

This is the site of the earthwork fortifications and command post used by CSA Gen. Jubal Early during 1864 action in Lynchburg. The grounds can be toured from 7 AM to 7 PM, but the building, a 20th century structure, is closed to the public. Access to the fort is free, and there is an information board to help you find your way around. Across the street from the fort entrance is an obelisk honoring Early.

Lynchburg Tour Ends

Other Tour Points of Interest

For questions, information or reservations at Lynchburg locations, ask for help at the Lynchburg Information Center.

Annual Events

Popular events in Lynchburg include the **Spring Garden Show** in April; **Festival by the James** and the **Bateau Festival**, both in June; **Kaleidoscope**, a three-weekend arts and crafts festival, in September; **Harvest Festival** in October; and **Christmas at Point of Honor** and **Christmas at the Market**, both in December.

Lynchburg Personality: Jubal Anderson "Old Jube" Early

Jubal Early, known as "Old Jube," was born in November 1816 in Franklin County, Virginia. A West Point graduate, Early practiced law in Rocky Mount, Virginia, from 1840 to 1860. He served a two-year term in the Virginia legislature in the 1840s as the youngest member of the House of Delegates. He was a veteran of the Mexican War, where he contracted rheumatism that left him with a lifelong stoop.

In the Civil War, Early saw action in nearly every engagement of the Confederacy's Army of Northern Virginia. His Shenandoah Valley campaign in 1864 included a victory at the Monocacy in Maryland (T-7), after which he raided close to Washington (T-13). He suffered defeats at Winchester (T-2), Fisher's Hill (T-3) and Cedar Creek (T-3), all in Virginia.

After the war, Early escaped to Mexico, then to Canada. Later, he returned to his native Virginia and resumed a law practice in 1869 in Lynchburg. He died in Lynchburg in March 1894.

Photo: Lynchburg Visitors Information Center

The Old Lynchburg Courthouse survived the war and now houses fascinating exhibits.

Arts

The **Lynchburg Fine Arts Center**, **Lynchburg Symphony Orchestra**, the **Virginia School of the Arts** — a private secondary school that prepares youths for dance, theater and visual arts careers — and the arts programs at four local colleges provide this community with a number of exceptional arts options.

Historic Sites

Point of Honor, at 112 Cabell Street, is an 1815 Federal-style house built by Dr. George Cabell, the personal physician to Virginia patriot Patrick Henry. **Poplar Forest**, Thomas Jefferson's "home away from home," is 3 miles west of Lynchburg in Bedford County. Patrick Henry's last home and burial site is at **Brookneal**, a small town 5 miles southeast of Lynchburg. Booker T. Washington, the noted African-American author and first president of Tuskegee Institute, was born on a small tobacco farm in Franklin County, about an hour's drive southwest of Lynchburg.

Shopping

Lynchburg offers six shopping centers and malls and an endless number of outlets and specialty shops. Two shopping areas, **River Ridge Mall** and **Candlers Station Shopping Center**, are just southeast of downtown Lynchburg on Candlers Mountain Road. The River Ridge Mall has 85 stores, and there are 12 shops in the Candlers Station center. Across town, on U.S. 501 (Boonsboro Road) is the **Boonsboro Shopping Center**, with its 25 businesses and stores.

Tour 12
Baltimore

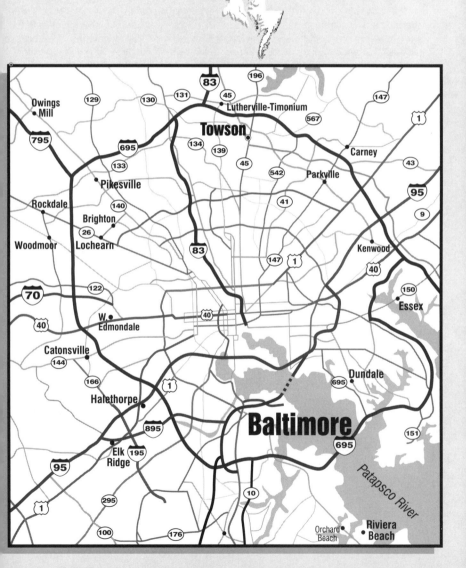

TOUR 12
Baltimore

About This Tour

This tour route is the first of eight that stretch north to south along the "fall zone" — a region along the imaginary line that separates the coastal plain region from the Piedmont. The seven other tours along the fall zone include T-13: Washington through T-18: Upper Peninsula, and T-20: Petersburg. This tour of Baltimore is also an alternative continuation of T-7: Monocacy, as Baltimore is a mere 47 miles east of Frederick, Maryland, on Interstate 70.

This tour concludes in Baltimore; the next tour, which features Washington, D.C., begins to the south. Baltimore is the largest city in Maryland, which was included in a charter granted by England's King Charles I to Cecil Calvert, who was the second Lord Baltimore and the man for whom the city was named. Cecil Calvert's younger brother, Leonard, founded the Maryland colony in 1634 at St. Marys City, which served as the colony's first capital. The Calvert family was Roman Catholic, and it offered a liberal policy of religious freedom in Maryland. Naturally, the colony became a safe haven for English Roman Catholics who opposed the Anglican (Protestant) Church of England.

Tobacco drove the economy of colonial Maryland. By the late 17th century, as more and more farms were cleared for tobacco production, the colonial capital was moved inland to Annapolis. Within a quarter-century, in the 1720s, Baltimore was established at the headwaters of the Patapsco River, along the fall zone some 15 miles from the Chesapeake Bay. Established as a port town, with access to the Chesapeake Bay and Atlantic Ocean, Baltimore was an outlet for Maryland-grown tobacco. Soon, it exported flour to England as well.

In 1745, Baltimore and a neighboring village, Jones-town, merged. The town was officially incorporated in 1797. Originally called Baltimore City, the name was shortened to Baltimore so it would not be confused with Baltimore County. The city and county were formally separated in 1851. The Baltimore area is rich in American history and offers countless attractions. Once the home of Native Americans, the land around the headwaters of the Patapsco River — a name of Native American origin — was surveyed by Anglo settlers almost immediately after the founding of Maryland in the mid-17th century. This land had been home to American Indians, particularly of the Algonquin tribe.

Once the nation's capital was established at Washington in the late 1700s, Baltimore grew to a size and stature that nearly equally its rival city on the Potomac. At the outbreak of the American Revolution, Baltimore was a bustling seaport and shipbuilding center. In fact, the U.S. Navy's first ship, *Constellation*, was launched in Baltimore (It is in dry dock for a two-year overhaul, after which it will return to its permanent mooring at Baltimore's inner harbor.) When the British occupied Philadelphia during the Revolutionary War, the Continental Congress met in Baltimore for three months beginning in December 1776.

In 1814, the British burned the U.S. Capitol and President's House in Washington, but the attackers were repulsed by the guns of Fort McHenry when they tried in September to crush Baltimore too. In 1827, the Chesapeake and Ohio Railroad was founded in Baltimore, and the rail line stretched from the city's Mount Clare Station west to the Appalachian Mountains. About the same time, the nation's first intercity telegraph was completed from Baltimore to Washington when Samuel F.B. Morse sent a message along the Baltimore and Ohio rail line from Mount Clare Station.

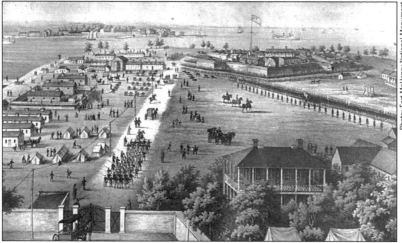

Photo: Fort McHenry National Monument

Confederate prisoners are marched into Fort McHenry in 1865.

On the eve of the Civil War, President-elect Abraham Lincoln passed through Baltimore in January 1861 on his way from Springfield, Illinois, to his Washington inaugural. When the war broke out, much of Baltimore — indeed, much of Maryland — remained loyal to the Union, although there were strong Southern sentiments in both the city and the state. As a result, the federal government imposed martial law in Baltimore and throughout Maryland.

A fire in February 1904 destroyed most of Baltimore's business district, but the community recovered quickly. At the outbreak of World War I, Baltimore began to develop industrially with the construction of steelworks, oil refineries and other war-related concerns. Following World War I, Baltimore acquired an intellectual aura from the work of H.L. Mencken, an essayist and editor, and his circle of friends, including journalists on the *Baltimore Sun* newspaper. Today, Baltimore is a major seaport with extensive shipbuilding and repair facilities and a highly diversified economy. More industrial and less imposing than Washington to the south, Baltimore is rich in cultural offerings as well.

Travel Tips

Baltimore is a big city, so expect big-city

problems when driving around it. If possible, avoid rush-hour traffic that clogs roadways into the city in the morning and out in the evening. Most of the downtown streets are one-way, which makes sightseeing a real problem. In the metro area, look for green "trail blazer" signs that provide directions to various points of interest and attractions. Radio traffic reports are helpful.

Baltimore does have a subway system, but it runs from downtown to northern Baltimore County and mainly serves commuters going to and from work. Baltimore also has a light-rail line, but it's not of much benefit to tourists either. Most of the stops on this tour route are most easily accessed by automobile. Another way to see Baltimore's historic attractions is Ed Kane's Water Taxi and Trolley (see listing below).

Baltimore is a tourist-conscious city. Still, travelers need to be cautious. When motoring or walking, go during daylight hours and take along companions. The tour ends in the city, where we suggest you plan dining and lodging for the evening. Recommended accommodations are listed in Chapter 22. Dining suggestions are in Chapter 23. It is a good idea to review these recommendations before striking out in Baltimore.

Getting Here

From Interstate 95 near the southern side of Baltimore, follow signs for downtown Baltimore via Md. Highway 295 (Baltimore-Washington Parkway), which becomes Russell Street inside the city limits. Continue north on Russell Street 1.1 mile into downtown Baltimore, passing Oriole Park at Camden Yards, to Pratt Street. Turn right (east) on Pratt Street and go 0.5 mile to Harbor Place at the Inner Harbor on the right (south) side of Pratt Street. There are a number of public parking garages and lots in the 10-square-block area in the vicinity of the Inner Harbor. Harbor Place also offers valet parking for motorists unfamiliar with the parking situation. Once safely parked, walk to Harbor Place. Your first stop, a Baltimore visitors center, is wharf-side in Harbor Place. .

Baltimore Tour Begins . . .

Baltimore Area Convention and Visitors Association Visitors Center
Inner Harbor, 301 E. Pratt St., Baltimore
• (410) 837-4636, (800) 282-6632

The visitors center is wharf-side at the Inner Harbor, accessed by Pratt Street, a major east-west artery through downtown Baltimore. The center helps visitors obtain information on Baltimore attractions, accommodations and dining as well as information on various points of interest. During the tourist season, the center is open Monday through Saturday from 9 AM to 5:30 PM and Sunday from 10 AM to 5:30 PM. In the off-season, the center closes at 4 PM on Sunday and other days at 5 PM. The center has no restroom facilities, but restrooms are available at various places throughout the Inner Harbor. The center is handicapped-accessible.

The USS *Constellation*, which is usually moored adjacent to the visitors center at the harbor wharf, is in dry dock for a two-year restoration. It will be returned to the Inner Harbor after the work is completed (estimated to be 1998 or '99). The *Constellation*, a 38-gun frigate, was the U.S. Navy's first ship and was built at Fell's Point in Baltimore. In 1854, the

old *Constellation* frigate was broken up, and the replacement *Constellation*, a 22-gun sloop-of-war, was constructed in Norfolk, Virginia. It is possible a few old timbers from the first *Constellation* were used in the newer ship's construction.

The second *Constellation*, the last all-sail ship constructed by the Navy, was commissioned in 1855 and saw action in the Civil War, intercepting slave ships off the coast of Africa. It also served in World War II. Later, it was restored to the appearance of the first *Constellation*. Now, it is again being restored to appear as the sloop-of-war commissioned in 1855.

Tickets to many Baltimore attractions and museums are available at the City Life Tickets kiosk at the Inner Harbor, (410) 396-8342. Look for the Downtown Partnership's "Clean and Safe" public safety guides — they wear black jackets with purple and gold shoulder patches. These guides can answer visitors' questions and provide directions to most Baltimore points of interest.

BALTIMORE AREA CONVENTION AND VISITORS ASSOCIATION VISITORS CENTER TO PRATT STREET RIOT SITE
From the Inner Harbor, go east on Pratt Street two blocks, at the National Aquarium, to the intersection of Pratt and Gay streets.

Pratt Street Riot Site
Pratt and Gay Sts., Baltimore

It's important to note that, in April 1861, Baltimore had two railroad stations — President Street Station, just east of the Inner Harbor, and Camden Station, just west of the Inner Harbor. Rail lines from the North ran into Baltimore and terminated at the President Street Station. Camden Station was a link to the B&O Railroad, which extended south to Washington, D.C., and west to the Appalachian Mountains. Rail passengers going through Baltimore were transported from one station to the other along Pratt Street by horse-drawn cars. Sometimes, horses simply pulled rail cars down Pratt Street to make the connection.

On April 15, President Lincoln issued a call

Inner Harbor Side Trip: Merchants Exchange Site

From the Inner Harbor, walk two blocks north on Gay Street to Water Street. At the corner, site of the present-day Custom House, stood the Merchant's Exchange, where President Lincoln's body lay in state in April 1865 (see Camden Station listing). The Merchant's Exchange no longer exists.

for 75,000 volunteers to guard against "insurrections," and the Sixth Massachusetts became the first regiment raised in response to the president's call. The regiment was dispatched to guard the nation's capital, Washington, D.C. The Sixth Massachusetts soldiers were shipped by rail and, of course, required to transfer between the two train stations in downtown Baltimore.

Arriving at President Street Station on April 19, the first seven companies of soldiers marched down Pratt Street to Camden Station without incident. A crowd assembled along Pratt Street, near present-day Gay Street, and it soon became unruly. After dumping a load of sand on the tracks in Pratt Street, the crowd threw down several anchors from boats moored in the Inner Harbor. Four companies of troops returned to the President Street Station, then turned and tried again to pass along Pratt Street. The mob pelted the troops with rocks and other debris. A gunshot cracked and the soldiers, alarmed, fired a volley into the mob.

Who were the rioters? Pro-secessionists or simply day workers, alarmed that the impending war might harm their chances of obtaining work? Baltimore, like Maryland, was full of Southern sympathizers, and many worried that Maryland might follow Virginia in seceding from the Union. The mob's identity remains a mystery. What is known is that four soldiers and 12 rioters were killed; 36 persons were injured. These unfortunate individuals were among the first casualties of the Civil War.

James Ryder Randall, a Marylander, was a school teacher in Louisiana when he read a newspaper account of the Pratt Street riot. One of Randall's close friends was killed in the melee. The story inspired Randall to write a nine-stanza poem he titled, *My Maryland*. He sent his poem to Jennie and Hettie Cary, sisters in Baltimore, who changed the poem title to *Maryland, My Maryland*. Later put to music, the song was a favorite of Maryland Confederate soldiers during the Civil War. It was declared the official state song of Maryland in 1939.

PRATT STREET RIOT SITE TO HISTORIC PRESIDENT STREET STATION

From the Inner Harbor, go east on Pratt Street for 0.3 mile to President Street, turn right (south) and go 0.2 mile to Historic President Street Station at the corner of President and Fleet streets.

Historic President Street Station
President and Fleet Sts., Baltimore

As noted, President Street Station was on the east side of the Inner Harbor and was the termination point for all rail lines to the north of Baltimore. Through-passengers between President Street Station and Camden Station were transported down Pratt Street by horse-drawn car. President-elect Lincoln arrived at President Street Station by train from Illinois in February 1861. From President Street, Lincoln was transferred by horse car down Pratt Street, beyond the Inner Harbor to Camden Station (see listing), the rail link to Washington. It was just two months later that Massachusetts troops en route to Washington arrived at President Street Station and became engaged in a riot (see Pratt Street Riot Site listing) as they marched to Camden Station.

Today, Baltimore is renovating the President Street Station as a tourist attraction that promotes the station's rail history. The project also will serve as a tribute to Frederick Douglass, a Maryland native and staunch abolitionist (see T-13: Washington). Douglass, a

The B&O Railroad Museum is one of the premier railroad museum facilities in the nation.

former slave, grew up in Baltimore, escaped slavery and eventually became the first African American to hold high rank in the U.S. government when he became an advisor to President Lincoln. Plans call for the restored President Street Station to open in mid-1997.

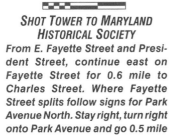

HISTORIC PRESIDENT STREET STATION TO SHOT TOWER PARK

From the President Street Station, return north on President Street, go four blocks, turn right on Baltimore Street and turn left into the Shot Tower Park parking area.

Shot Tower
801 E. Fayette St., Baltimore
• (410) 396-5894, (410) 396-3523

This 215-foot tall brick tower in Shot Tower Park once was one of the nation's largest suppliers of gun shot. Molten lead was poured through a hole-filled template, and then dropped down the tower's interior into a pool of cold water. A half-million 25-pound bags of shot were produced at the tower each year from 1828 to 1892, including all four years of the Civil War.

The tower has interactive exhibits and a sound-and-light show that illustrate the story

of how shot was made. Video cameras are mounted atop the tower, and monitors in the exhibit area below display pictures of the Baltimore skyscape. A national historic site, the tower is open 10 AM to 5 PM on Saturday and noon to 5 PM on Sunday. A $2 admission fee is charged, but if you visit the Baltimore City Life Museum at 33 S. Front Street — a half-block from the tower — you can get a free admission ticket as part of a tour package.

Just north of the shot tower, at the corner of Front and Low streets, once stood the Front Street Theater, where in 1860, Vice President John C. Breckenridge (see T-3: New Market) was nominated as a U.S. presidential candidate by Southern Democrats. Four years later at the theater, in 1864, President Lincoln was renominated as the Republican candidate for president. The building no longer exists.

SHOT TOWER TO MARYLAND HISTORICAL SOCIETY

From E. Fayette Street and President Street, continue east on Fayette Street for 0.6 mile to Charles Street. Where Fayette Street splits follow signs for Park Avenue North. Stay right, turn right onto Park Avenue and go 0.5 mile

Maryland Historical Society Side Trip: Lee and Jackson Statue

From the Maryland Historical Society, go west one block, turn right on Howard Street and go 20 blocks — about 2 miles — to the intersection of Howard Street and Museum Drive. On the east side of Howard Street at Museum Drive, across from the Baltimore Art Museum, is a fine equestrian state of CSA Gens. Robert E. Lee and Thomas Jonathan "Stonewall" Jackson. The statue, which depicts the two generals' last meeting at Chancellorsville (T-16), was sculpted by Laura G. Frazier and dedicated May 1, 1948. This statue reportedly is the only double-equestrian statue in world.

(six blocks) to the corner of Park Avenue and Monument Street. Use on-street parking on Monument Street.

Maryland Historical Society Museum and Library of Maryland History

201 W. Monument St., Baltimore
• **(410) 685-3750**

The historical society has an extensive, 200,000-item collection, including a number that relate to the Civil War. The library has 6 million books and manuscripts, Francis Scott Key's original *Star-Spangled Banner* manuscript and architectural drawings from the competition to design the U.S. Capitol in Washington.

The museum has a number of Civil War items, including period photographs, clothing items, medals, weapons and maps. Civil War-related publications are on sale in the museum's gift shop. The museum and library are open Tuesday through Friday from 10 AM to 5 PM, Saturday from 9 AM to 5 PM and Sunday from 1 to 5 PM. It is closed each Monday (except the library closes a half-hour earlier than the museum each day). Admission is $4, but free on Saturday from 9 to 11 AM. Both facilities are handicapped-accessible via an elevator at the Monument Street entrance.

MARYLAND HISTORICAL SOCIETY TO UNION SQUARE

From the historical society on

Monument Street, go west two blocks, turn left (south) on Eutaw Street, go 0.6 mile, turn right (west) on Lombard Street and go 1 mile to Gilmor Street. At the northwest corner of Lombard and Gilmor streets is Union Square.

Union Square

Lombard St., Baltimore

During the Civil War, Jarvis U.S. General Hospital was in the vicinity of Union Square. The site also was known as Camp Andrew. Both the hospital and the military camp were on the property of George Hume Steuart, who served as a general in the Confederate Army. There is no evidence of the hospital or camp today.

UNION SQUARE TO B&O RAILROAD MUSEUM

From Union Square, go south on Gilmor Street one block, turn left (east) on Pratt Street and go 0.4 mile to Poppleton Street and the B&O Museum parking lot on the right.

B&O Railroad Museum

901 W. Pratt St., Baltimore
• **(410) 752-2490**

Charles Carroll, the lone surviving signer of the Declaration of Independence at the time, was at this site on Pratt Street on July 4, 1828, to take part in the groundbreaking ceremonies for the new Baltimore and Ohio Railroad. The distinguished Marylander laid the cornerstone for the new venture, which eventually linked Baltimore with the Ohio River and opened a trade link between the Trans-Allegheny and the Atlantic coast.

Two years later in 1830, the B&O was completed with a rail stop at Mount Clare Station, the first rail station in the nation. Today, the B&O Railroad Museum incorporates the old Mount Clare Station site. The overall museum is one of the premiere railroad museum facilities in the nation. It has five buildings including a roundhouse and 120 pieces of "rolling stock" — locomotives, rail cars and the like. Civil War baggage cars and other war items are part of the large collection of railroad artifacts. The museum is open daily from 10 AM to 5 PM (closed only on Thanksgiving and Christmas). Admission is $6.50 for adults, $5.50 for seniors and $4 for students and children. The facility is handicapped-accessible, although some rail cars — part of interactive exhibits — are a bit difficult for the physically challenged.

B&O MUSEUM TO CAMDEN YARD
From Pratt and Poppleton streets, continue east on Pratt Street for 0.5 mile, turn right (south) on Eutaw Street and go one block to W. Camden Street — adjacent to Oriole Park at Camden Yards. Old Camden Station is at the corner of Camden and Howard streets.

Old Camden Station
Camden and Howard Sts., Baltimore

This old, historic train station was once a stop on the B&O Railroad, the lone rail connector between Baltimore and Washington, D.C. Originally, the rail connection to Washington began in Baltimore at the Mount Clare Station on W. Pratt Street. A spur of the line connected to Camden Station.

In 1861, President-elect Abraham Lincoln rode the train from Illinois into Baltimore to the President Street Station (see listing). President Lincoln was back at Camden Station in 1863 on his way from Washington to Gettysburg. He also used Camden Station when he visited Baltimore in 1864. In April 1865, President Lincoln's funeral train stopped at Camden Station on its way to Illinois. The president's body was escorted from Washington to Baltimore by John Garrett, president of the B&O. The casket was transported by hearse from the train station and down Pratt Street to the Merchant's Exchange (see listing) — site of the present-day Custom House — at Gay and Water streets.

A large contingent of dignitaries, including troops from nearby Fort McHenry, escorted the hearse down Pratt Street, which was lined by a throng of mourners. Lincoln's coffin was opened for public viewing as his body lay in state at the old Exchange. The coffin was then taken to President Street Station for transport to Harrisburg, Pennsylvania, and another public display of affection for the slain president.

The old National Hotel, which once stood

Union Square Personality: CSA Gen. George Hume Steuart

George Hume Steuart, also called "Maryland Steuart," graduated from the U.S. Military Academy at West Point in 1848 and immediately shipped out to serve on the American frontier. In 1861, at the onset of the Civil War, Steuart resigned his U.S. Army commission and joined the Confederacy as a captain. He saw action at Manassas (T-8), after which he was promoted to brigadier general.

Steuart fought with "Stonewall" Jackson in the 1862 Shenandoah Valley Campaign and was injured at the Battle of Cross Keys (T-4). He commanded an infantry brigade at Gettysburg (T-6), the Wilderness (T-16) and Spotsylvania (T-16), where he was captured. Sent to Charleston, South Carolina, Steuart was later involved in a prisoner exchange. He fought under CSA Gen. George Edward Pickett at Petersburg (T-20) in 1865. After the war, "Maryland Steuart" farmed in his native state.

Photo: Fort McHenry National Monument

This 15-inch Rodman gun at Fort McHenry is aimed toward Baltimore.

across Pratt Street from Camden Station, was used as a hospital during the Civil War. The old Fountain Hotel, at the corner of Howard and Camden streets, also was used as hospital. Both old hotels no longer exist.

OLD CAMDEN STATION TO FEDERAL HILL PARK

From the old train station at Camden and Howard streets, take Howard Street one block north, turn right (east) on Pratt Street and go 0.3 mile, turn right (south) on Light Street and go 0.5 mile, turn left (east) on Montgomery Street and go two blocks to Battery Avenue and the entrance to Federal Hill Park.

Federal Hill Park
Battery Ave., Baltimore

Overlooking the Inner Harbor, the steep-banked park was called Federal Hill during the Civil War, during which it was a natural observation point. Today, a 50-foot stairway ascends the embankment to the top. Open from 8 AM to midnight, the park is not handicapped-accessible.

FEDERAL HILL PARK TO FORT MCHENRY NATIONAL MONUMENT AND HISTORIC SHRINE

Go one block south on Battery Avenue, turn left (east) on Warren Avenue and then take an immediate right (south) on Riverside Avenue. Go two blocks on Riverside Avenue, turn left (east) on Cross Street and go two blocks, turn right (south) on Key Highway and go 0.5 mile, turn right (west) on Lawrence Street and go one block, turn left (south) on Fort Avenue and travel 1 mile to the entrance to Fort McHenry National Monument.

Fort McHenry National Monument and Historic Shrine
Fort Ave., Baltimore • (410) 962-4299

Five-sided Fort McHenry guards the mouth of the northwest branch of the Patapsco River. It forever will be linked to the War of 1812 and, specifically, to the unsuccessful British bombing in September 1814 that inspired a young Marylander, Francis Scott Key, to write a poem that became the national anthem. Seeing the American flag still flying at the fort after the

British shelling, Key wrote a poem that he originally titled, "Defence of Fort McHenry." It later was put to music and published. Key's poem-song came to be known as the *Star-Spangled Banner*, which later was adopted as the anthem. Thus, by the onset of the Civil War, Fort McHenry already was a historical site.

During the Civil War, the fort was used as a temporary prison for captured Confederate soldiers, Southern sympathizers and political prisoners. Among the military prisoners held at the fort during the Civil War were Francis Key Howard, the grandson of Francis Scott Key, and secessionist John Merryman.

From 1917 to 1923, Fort McHenry was used as a U.S. Army hospital to serve veterans of World War I. In 1925, Congress made the fort a national park and in 1939 it was declared a national monument and historic shrine — the only park in the nation to have the double distinction. The fort is operated by the National Park Service. It has a visitors center that includes information and a brief documentary film on the fort's history. Inside the fort complex are a parade ground, commanding officer's quarters, a powder magazine and a guardhouse. It is open 8 AM to 5 PM daily. Admission is $2 for everyone 16 or older. Those younger are admitted free. The visitors center is handicapped-accessible, and the informative film is captioned for the hearing-impaired.

Baltimore Tour Ends

Fort McHenry Personality: John Merryman

John Merryman was a farmer from Cockeysville, a village north of Baltimore. A Southern sympathizer, Merryman was a lieutenant in the local militia, and he allegedly took part in a gang's plot to burn several railroad bridges west of Baltimore. In May 1861, U.S. troops surrounded Merryman's farm, arrested him and put him in confinement at Fort McHenry without informing him of the charges against him.

The day after the incident, Chief Justice Roger B. Taney — a Marylander himself — issued a writ of habeas corpus and had it served on the commander at Fort McHenry, USA Gen. George Cadwalader. Habeas corpus is an age-old common-law writ that is issued by a court to direct one who holds another in custody to produce the individual in person for a specific purpose — usually to correct a violation of the individual's personal liberty or to determine the legality of the detention.

Judge Taney, sitting as a federal circuit court judge, issued his writ on the grounds that Merryman was improperly detained. But President Lincoln so feared the secessionist movement in Maryland he suspended habeas corpus. Given the president's actions, Cadwalader refused to obey Judge Taney's writ. This series of actions set off a conflict between the chief justice and the president. Taney cited Cadwalader for contempt of court, then wrote an opinion about the section of the U.S. Constitution that allows suspension of habeas corpus. Taney argued that Congress — not the president — had the power to suspend habeas corpus.

Lincoln justified his action in a message to Congress. In addition, the president ignored Taney's opinion and adhered to the writ's suspension throughout the Civil War. The man at the center of the controversy, John Merryman, was nearly forgotten in the public debate. Later, he was released from imprisonment.

By the end of 1861, Lincoln totally subjugated Maryland to military authority. The Baltimore mayor, chief of police, police commissioner and 31 members of the Maryland legislature as well as congressmen, judges and newspaper reporters were all held at Fort McHenry without charges because of their political views or actions. Meanwhile, the Constitutional question of who has the right to suspend habeas corpus, Congress or the president, was not — and never has been — officially resolved.

Photo: Library of Virginia

President Lincoln's 1861 call for troop volunteers precipitated a riot on Baltimore's Pratt Street.

Other Tour Points of Interest

There is much to see and do in Baltimore. Much of this activity is centered on the **Inner Harbor** and the **Baltimore Convention Center**, both on Pratt Street, and at **Fells Point**, which is east of the Inner Harbor.

Ask for details at the Baltimore Area Convention and Visitors Association Visitors Center at the Inner Harbor.

Annual Events

Baltimore celebrates hometown hero **Babe Ruth's Birthday** on February 6 at the Babe Ruth Birthplace and Baseball Center on Emory Street downtown. The **Maryland Day Celebration** in March observes Maryland's founding. The **Preakness**, the second jewel in horse racing's Triple Crown, is held in May. **Defenders' Day** is held at Fort McHenry the second Sunday of September each year. It's a celebration of the American victory over the British at the fort in 1814.

Arts

The **Baltimore Museum of Art**, Art Museum Drive (Charles Street at 31st Street), (410) 396-7101, is a nationally recognized museum of contemporary 20th-century art. The **National Aquarium** in Baltimore, adjacent to the Inner Harbor, (410) 576-3800, features more than 9,000 creatures representing more than 600 species of mammals, fish, birds, reptiles and amphibians in natural habitats. The **Baltimore Zoo**, Druid Hill Park, (410) 366-5466, is home to more than 1,000 animals and includes an innovative children's zoo.

The **Baltimore International Culinary College Cooking Demonstration Theater**, 206 Water Street at 31st Street, (410) 752-4983, features a 90-seat theater that offers step-by-step cooking demonstrations. Also, Baltimore has an opera, (410) 625-1600, a symphony, (410) 783-8000, and various theater companies. **Johns Hopkins University** also offers a variety of arts and cultural programs for Baltimore visitors. The **Walters Art Gallery**, 600 N. Charles Street, (410) 547-9000, houses one of the finest private art collections in the nation. Henry Walters donated his collection of more than 20,000 works to his native city in 1931.

Historic Sites

The **Babe Ruth Museum**, 216 Emory Street, (410) 727-1539, is where the birthplace of the baseball great once stood. The **Eubie Blake National Museum and Cultural Center**, 34 Market Place, (410) 625-3113, honors the life and music of the jazz great, a Baltimore native. **Homewood Museum**, 3400 N. Charles Street, (410) 516-5589, is the restored home of Charles Carroll (see B&O Railroad Museum listing).

Shopping

Harbor Place at the Inner Harbor is the place to begin your shopping spree. From elegant boutiques to souvenir shops, Harbor Place has two European-style pavilions on the water's edge with a variety of places to shop and eat. Unique businesses such as galleries, coffee shops, cozy pubs and restaurants are scattered all through **Fells Point**, the historic old town section of Baltimore, just east of the Inner Harbor. More than 100 merchants at **Lex-**

ington Market offer everything from authentic Maryland crab cakes to chocolate delights. Lexington Market is at Market Center, Lexington and Eutaw streets. For more information, telephone (410) 685-6169.

Sports

The **Baltimore Orioles**, including future Hall of Famer Cal Ripken Jr., are the toast of Baltimore. They play ball at **Oriole Park at Camden Yards**, off Pratt Street. For tour information, telephone (410) 685-9800; for tickets, telephone (410) 481-SEAT. The newest professional sports team in town is the **Baltimore Ravens** of the National Football League. For information, telephone (888) 9-RAVENS.

Tours

The best way to see Baltimore is the climb aboard **Ed Kane's Water Taxi**. Ed Kane is the owner and operator of the business. A Baltimore native, and self-proclaimed ol' salt, Kane

is the city's unofficial tour host. With automobile parking a premium, particularly in the tourist season, Kane's water taxi and land-side trolley are convenient ways to see 45 land and sea sites in the downtown vicinity. Water Taxi charges a $7 all-day fee ($6 for children younger than 10), which includes free reboarding on the taxi or the trolley throughout their entire tour routes. The water taxi operates all year; the trolley operates from May to October. Kane has special vehicles for the mobility-impaired.

If you get a chance, visit Kane's office — a white trailer off Browns Wharf on Thames Street at Fells Point. He knows more about Baltimore history, especially Civil War history, than all the city's travel counselors combined. Ed's personal guide service is available for advance group bookings. You can purchase a ticket at the Inner Harbor kiosk or on any trolley or water taxi. For details and information, call Ed Kane's Water Taxi at (410) 563-3901 or (800) 658-8947.

Tour 13
Washington, D.C.

TOUR 13
Washington

About This Tour

This tour route covers Washington, D.C., the nation's capital. Washington straddles the Potomac and Anacostia rivers, along the "fall zone" that separates Virginia's coastal plain from the rolling Piedmont region. It is rich in American history and offers countless attractions. Once the home of Native Americans, the land around the Potomac and Anacostia — both river names are of Native American origin — was surveyed by Anglo settlers almost immediately after the founding of Jamestown, Virginia, in 1607.

Near the end of the 18th century, with the formation of a new government in America, the new federal city was established on the Potomac. The legislatures of Maryland and Virginia contributed portions of their state land for the creation of the District of Columbia, a 10-square-mile, diamond-shaped territory. Creation of the capital city, named in honor of Virginian George Washington, transformed farmland, fields and river bottom land into a bustling community with a single commodity — politics.

By the time President Lincoln was inaugurated in 1861, the Washington population topped 60,000. Months later, Civil War-related activities swelled the city to twice its usual population. Naturally, Washington was a busy place during the Civil War. Federal troops guarded major buildings and roadways entering and leaving the city. From the war's beginning, there were threats and rumors of Confederate invasions, although Southern troops made only one major thrust, when CSA Gen. Jubal Anderson "Old Jube" Early's raid closed in on Fort Stephens, within the District of Columbia, in 1864.

Today, Washington's population is 10 times greater than it was in 1860. Its Metro-politan Statistical Area is the third-largest in the nation, stretching from the Pennsylvania border north of Baltimore, to Spotsylvania County, Virginia, near Fredericksburg, Virginia.

Travel Tips

Motoring into Washington is, at best, a tedious task. If possible, avoid rush-hour traffic that clogs roadways into the city in the morning and well into the evening. Radio traffic reports from Washington area stations are especially helpful. Remember, traffic can be particularly busy and often snarled during unusual weather conditions such as winter snows and heavy summer rains. Mobile telephone users will receive a strong signal throughout the Washington area. There is one consolation for visitors: Many Washingtonians leave town for their own vacations during the summer tourism season.

We strongly suggest that you avoid driving in Washington. If you have to drive, here are a few easy guidelines. The city's four quadrants — northwest, northeast, southwest, and southeast — are centered on the U.S. Capitol. Thus, the Capitol building is the point where the north-south and east-west axes meet. The dividing line for these four quadrants are North, South, and East Capitol streets and the Mall. Most places cited in this tour are in the vicinity of the Capitol in the northwest quadrant.

East-west streets run in alphabetical order, beginning with single letters. There is an A Street, a B Street and on through the alphabet to W Street — there is no X, Y or Z street. Then, east-west street names are two-syllable and alphabetical: Adams, Belmont and Chapin on through to Woodbine. Then, east-west street names become three-syllable and alphabetical: Albemarle, Brandywine, Chesapeake and on through to Worthington. Watch out near the

During the war, the U.S. Capitol was used as a hospital.

Capitol, as there are two A streets and two 1st streets. North-south streets are parallel and numbered, beginning with 1st Street. Diagonal streets are named for states of the union.

The best alternative to driving is the **Metro** rail system, a clean, efficient and safe way to see Washington without the confusing traffic patterns and motoring hassles, finding and paying for parking or getting lost. Each attraction listing on this route also includes the appropriate Metro stop. The Metro rail system has several rail lines that are color-coded and easy to decipher. The **Red Line** serves the northern section of the district and Montgomery County, Maryland. The **Green Line** serves the district's eastern section, including Prince George's County, Maryland (see also T-12). The **Orange Line** serves the eastern and western sections of the district, from Fairfax County, Virginia (T-14), to Prince George's County. The **Blue Line** runs from National Airport in Alexandria, Virginia (T-14), through the heart of the district to Capitol Heights, Maryland. The **Yellow Line** runs from the center of the city to Huntington, south of Alexandria (T-14).

The Metro has a $5 one-day, all-you-care-to-ride fare that is ideal for visitors. The special fare is good until midnight on weekdays, weekends and holidays, but you must board after 9:30 AM on weekdays because of morning commuter traffic volume. For information on Metro, call (202) 637-7000, a line available 6 AM to 11:30 PM every day. You can purchase the special ticket at Metro Center at 13th and F streets N.W. in Washington, and at the Concourse at the Pentagon in Arlington. It also is available at some grocery stores in the Washington metropolitan area. Up to two children younger than age 5 can ride free on Metro with an accompanying adult. All riders 5 and older must have their own Metro ticket.

Another way to see Washington's historic attractions is the **Tourmobile**, which provides transport to 18 major sites along Washington's Mall and into Northern Virginia. Tourmobile charges a fee, but it offers free reboarding throughout its tour route. Call (202) 432-SEAT for information.

Washington is a tourist attraction and visitors are welcome. Still, it makes good sense to be cautious, particularly outside the immediate downtown area. When motoring or walking, tour during daylight hours and take along companions.

Use interstate highways whenever possible to enter Washington, D.C. — Interstate 270 from the northwest, Interstate 95 from the northeast or south or Interstate 66 from the southwest. These routes converge at the Capital Beltway, which circles the district. This tour route is a natural continuation of either T-12: Baltimore or T-8: Manassas. Another route, T-7: Monocacy, concludes at Leesburg, Virginia, and from there, Washington is a brief, 30-mile jaunt along U.S. Highway 50. Another route, T-8: Manassas, concludes in Manassas, Virginia, which is a quick trip east on I-66 to Washington.

Washington Tour Begins. . .

This tour route begins in the vicinity of the U.S. Capitol. [Metro Blue-Orange lines: Capitol South stop; Metro Red Line: Union Station stop.]

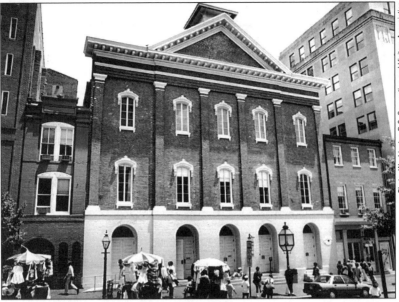

Ford's Theatre, site of President Lincoln's assassination, is still a popular Washington arts venue.

United States Capitol
1st and A Sts., Washington, D.C.
• **(202) 225-6827**

It is the most recognizable building in the nation; one of the most recognizable in the world. President Washington laid the cornerstone in 1793. In 1800, Congress moved into the first completed section, which is now the old Senate wing. Two years later, the House of Representatives met in a makeshift building erected on the foundation of its wing. By 1811, both the House and Senate wings were completed, and rebuilt, before they were damaged by the British during the War of 1812. The reconstruction led to several alterations and the construction of a wooden dome. In the 1840s, Congress moved to enlarge the Capitol, and by 1859, on the verge of the Civil War, both the House and Senate relocated into new wings. Plans were made to replace the old dome with a larger structure, and work continued on that project throughout the Civil War.

In the years preceding the Civil War, this remarkable building was forever linked with some significant national legislation and sig-

nificant lawmakers. Presidents were and are inaugurated here. Familiar legislators included South Carolina Sen. John C. Calhoun; Kentucky Sen. Henry Clay, called the Great Compromiser; Illinois Sen. Stephen Douglas, known as the Little Giant; and Massachusetts Sen. Daniel Webster. Pre-Civil War congresses debated major issues and legislation including the Missouri Compromise, the compromises of 1833 and 1850, nullification, secession, the Fugitive Slave Act and the Kansas-Nebraska Bill. The 13th Amendment, which prohibited slavery in the nation, was adopted in 1865. The U.S. Supreme Court, known for its famous Dred Scott Decision in March 1857, met in the Capitol until its own building was constructed across 1st Street in 1935.

Beginning in the 1850s, arguments over slavery intensified. Members of Congress began carrying pistols and canes; fights broke out. As Southern states seceded, their representatives fled the Washington madness. The Capitol became a Union Army barracks, and troops camped in the Rotunda. Supplies were stored in the legislative chambers, and an oven was set up in the basement to bake the Union

Interestingly, The Lincoln Memorial, dedicated in 1922, faces across the Potomac toward Robert E. Lee's Arlington House.

---

soldiers' daily 10-ounce bread ration. Soldiers drilled on the East Lawn. During the war, the Capitol was used as a hospital. All the while, work continued on the 250-foot dome, and the famous crowning statue, *Freedom,* was installed in December 1863. The statue was refurbished in 1993. There are a number of statues of Americans associated with the war at the Capitol, especially in Statuary Hall and the Rotunda.

Free tours are conducted from 9 AM to 3:45 PM every day except New Year's Day, Thanksgiving and Christmas. The line forms on the East Front. The Capitol also offers a variety of places to dine and shop, and hours vary according to the Congressional schedule and season of the year.

UNITED STATES CAPITOL
TO LIBRARY OF CONGRESS
From the East Front, cross 1st Street SE to the corner of 1st Street and Independence Avenue SE [Blue-Orange Line: Capitol South stop].

Library of Congress
101 Independence Ave. SE, Washington, D.C. • (202) 707-5000

This is the nation's foremost library and collector of important manuscripts and papers, including materials related to the Civil War. The main building of the library complex was constructed in 1896. Before that, the library housed its vast collection in the U.S. Capitol. Today, the library is housed in three separate buildings — called Jefferson, Madison and Adams. The Jefferson Building underwent extensive renovation in 1993 and 1994, and the Adams Building is used solely for research purposes. Visitor services are centered at the Madison Building. Its entrance is on Independence Avenue SE.

A variety of exhibits are offered at any given time and usually are free. Free tours are conducted Monday through Friday at 10 AM and 1 and 3 PM, except on federal holidays. Groups of more than nine should check in advance to be accommodated, as tours are restricted to 50 visitors. A free orientation film is shown every half hour from 9 AM to 9 PM, Monday through Friday; Saturday from 8:30 AM to 5 PM; and Sunday from 1 to 4:30 PM. A gift shop is off the Madison Building lobby and is open Monday through Saturday from 9 AM to 5 PM. The library cafeteria is open for lunch Monday through Friday from 12:30 to 3 PM.

LIBRARY OF CONGRESS
TO OLD CAPITOL PRISON SITE
Go west on 1st Street to the present-day site of the U.S. Supreme Court [Blue-Orange lines: Capitol South stop; Red Line: Union Station stop].

Old Capitol Prison Site
1st and A Sts. NE, Washington, D.C.

It's the present-day site of the U.S. Supreme Court, but it used to be home to the Old Brick Capitol used by Congress after the British trashed the Capitol building during the War of 1812. Afterwards, with the Capitol under reconstruction, President James Monroe was inaugurated in 1817 on a platform outside the Brick Capitol. The structure also was used as a hotel, and it was converted to a prison during the Civil War. Among its more

Capitol Side Trips: Seward Square, Garfield Park, Lincoln Park, Stanton Park

There are several places in the Capitol area with Civil War-related names. Seward Square, at Pennsylvania and North Carolina avenues SE, honors William Henry Seward, President Lincoln's secretary of state during the Civil War. Seward, a New Yorker, was injured by an accomplice of John Wilkes Booth during the Lincoln assassination in 1865. A Whig, Seward was a former governor of New York and twice was passed over by Republicans as a possible presidential candidate.

Garfield Park, at New Jersey Avenue and F Street SE, honors President James A. Garfield, a Civil War veteran. Later, of course, Garfield was assassinated during his term as U.S. president (see listing at the White House in this tour).

Lincoln Park, at E. Capitol Street and 11th Street NE, features the Emancipation Statue, which honors Lincoln's freeing of the slaves. The statue was dedicated in April 1876, and those attending included President Ulysses S. Grant and noted African-American leader Frederick Douglass.

Stanton Park, at Maryland and Pennsylvania avenues NE, honors Edwin McMasters Stanton, who was President Lincoln's secretary of war during the Civil War. Stanton, an Ohioan, previously served as U.S. attorney general under President James Buchanan. Serving through Lincoln's two administrations, Stanton also was secretary of war briefly under President Andrew Johnson. When he opposed Johnson's reconstruction plans, he was asked to resign. He refused, and President Johnson suspended him.

After Johnson replaced him with former USA Gen. Ulysses Grant, the U.S. Senate named Stanton back to the old post of war secretary. Again the president tried to remove him, and the Senate again overruled the president. Stanton resigned after President Johnson was impeached. In 1869, newly elected President Ulysses Grant appointed Stanton to the U.S. Supreme Court, but the jurist died only four days later. Stanton, a town in northwest Pennsylvania, is named in his honor.

famous prisoners was Belle Boyd, a Confederate spy (T-2: Harpers Ferry).

OLD CAPITOL PRISON SITE TO DOUGLASS HOME SITE

The Douglass Home Site is one block directly behind the present Supreme Court building. From 1st Street, go to E. Capitol Street, then left one block to Second Street. Go left one block to A Street and turn right onto A Street [Red Line: Union Station stop].

Douglass Home Site
300 block, A St. NE, Washington, D.C.

This is the site of Frederick Douglass' first Washington residence. A former slave from Maryland, this famous abolitionist was a min-

ister to Haiti. He lived in the neighborhood six years, beginning in 1871. Today, there is nothing to distinguish the residence.

DOUGLASS HOME SITE TO GARFIELD MONUMENT

Return to 1st Street and go around the U.S. Capitol to the Southwest Front. The Garfield Monument is near the Reflecting Pool at 1st Street and Maryland Avenue [Blue-Orange lines: Federal Center stop].

Garfield Monument
Maryland Ave. and 1st St. SW, Reflecting Pool, Washington, D.C.

This monument honors President James A. Garfield, who was a Civil War veteran. (See more on President Garfield in the White House section of this tour.)

GARFIELD MONUMENT TO GRANT MEMORIAL
The Grant Memorial is on the opposite side of the Reflecting Pool from the Garfield Monument [Blue-Orange lines: Federal Center stop].

Grant Memorial
1st Street SW, Reflecting Pool, Washington, D.C.
This equestrian statue is one of the largest in the world. It was dedicated in April 1922, on the centennial of USA Gen. Ulysses S. Grant's birth. The memorial's sculptor took more than 22 years to complete this tribute to Grant, which includes a dozen horses, nearly as many soldiers and four lions. (See more on Grant in T-16: Spotsylvania.)

REFLECTING POOL TO SMITHSONIAN INSTITUTION
Go west from the U.S. Capitol on the Mall to the Smithsonian Institution [Blue-Orange lines: Smithsonian stop].

Smithsonian Institution
1000 Jefferson Dr. SW on the Mall, Washington, D.C. • (202) 357-2700
This is America's attic. The Smithsonian offers an array of exhibits, places to dine and shop and other visitor amenities. There is a wealth of American history depicted in the Smithsonian. Of particular interest, the Museum of American History, at the corner of Constitution Avenue and 14th Street NW, has an exhibit on the Civil War. The Smithsonian's facilities are open free every day except Christmas from 10 AM to 5:30 PM. There are extended hours in the summer tourism season.

GRANT MEMORIAL TO PENNSYLVANIA AVENUE
From the West Front of the U.S. Capitol, walk northwest down

USA Gen. George Brinton McClellan — called "Young Napoleon" early in his career — is honored with an equestrian statue in Washington.

Photo: Library of Virginia

Constitution Avenue to Pennsylvania Avenue [Green-Yellow line: Archives-Navy Memorial stop].

Pennsylvania Avenue
In May 1865, along Pennsylvania Avenue and in front of the White House, more than 150,000 Union soldiers marched in review before President Andrew Johnson and Northern generals. The parade included the armies of the Potomac, Tennessee and Georgia (named for where they fought, not where they were from). Soldiers marched 12 abreast for more than eight hours straight.

PENNSYLVANIA AVENUE TO MEADE STATUE
The Meade Statue is at the intersection of Constitution and Pennsylvania avenues.

Meade Statue
Pennsylvania and Constitution Aves., Washington, D.C.
In front of the U.S. Courthouse, this statue honors USA Gen. George Meade. A son of Ameri-

Meade Statue Side Trip: Judiciary Square

Judiciary Square is between 4th and 5th streets NW, and between D and G streets [Red Line: Judiciary Square stop].

There are three sites of note in the area of Judiciary Square.

The Lincoln Statue, at Judiciary Square and D Street NW, honors President Abraham Lincoln. The National Building Museum, formerly the Pension Building, at F and 4th streets NW, has a frieze that depicts Civil War troops.

The National Portrait Gallery, at 7th and G streets NW, formerly the U.S. Patent Office and a fine example of Classical Revival architecture, was used as a Civil War hospital. Today, it is open free from 10 AM to 5:30 PM every day except Christmas.

can parents, Meade was born in 1815 in Spain. He was appointed to the U.S. Military Academy at West Point from Pennsylvania and participated in the Peninsular Campaign, 2nd Manassas, Antietam, Fredericksburg and Chancellorsville. He then commanded the Army of the Potomac from just prior to Gettysburg until the end of the war. He died of pneumonia in 1872 at the age of 57, having never fully recovered from a wound he received at White Oak Swamp just east of Richmond during the Seven Days' Battles of the Peninsular Campaign (T-18).

MEADE STATUE TO HANCOCK STATUE
Walk west on Pennsylvania Avenue to 7th Street NW [Green-Yellow lines: Archives-Navy Memorial stop].

Hancock Statue
7th and Pennsylvania Aves. NW, Washington, D.C.

USA Gen. Winfield Scott Hancock was born in 1824 and entered the U.S. Military Academy at West Point from Pennsylvania. During the Civil War, he participated in USA Gen. George McClellan's Peninsular Campaign in 1862 (T-18, T-19) and saw action at Chickahominy, Golding's Farm, Savage's Station and White Oak Swamp (T-18). Hancock also fought at Antietam (T-1), Fredericksburg (T-15), Chancellorsville (T-16) and Gettysburg (T-6), where he was seriously injured. After

the war, Hancock was an unsuccessful candidate for president in 1880, losing to President James Garfield. He died in 1886. (See more on Hancock in T-6: Gettysburg.)

HANCOCK STATUE TO NATIONAL ARCHIVES
National Archives is on Pennsylvania Avenue at 7th Street NW [Green-Yellow lines: Archives-Navy Memorial stop].

National Archives
8th St. and Pennsylvania Ave. NW, Washington, D.C. • (202) 501-5400

The National Archives displays both the Declaration of Independence and the U.S. Constitution — the nation's two most precious documents. The Archives is open free from 10 AM to 9 PM during the peak tourist season, April 1 to Labor Day. Off-season, it is open from 10 AM to 5:30 PM. The National Archives has an extensive collection of military service records, but call in advance to check the latest information on hours available for research work.

NATIONAL ARCHIVES TO J. EDGAR HOOVER FBI BUILDING
The J. Edgar Hoover FBI Building is between 9th and 10th streets on Pennsylvania Avenue [Blue-Orange lines: Federal Triangle stop].

J. Edgar Hoover FBI Building

9th St. and Pennsylvania Ave. NW, Washington, D.C.

Completed in 1975, this building cost $126 million dollars. The Pennsylvania Avenue facade of the building features a block-long, 10-foot-tall exhibit honoring eight American presidents and their relationship with the "Main Street of America." President Lincoln is among the eight presidents featured.

J. EDGAR HOOVER FBI BUILDING
TO FORD'S THEATER
NATIONAL HISTORICAL SITE

From the J. Edgar Hoover FBI Building, walk a block north on 10th Street to E Street NW [Blue-Orange and Red lines: Metro Center stop].

Washington Personality: John Wilkes Booth

John Wilkes Booth was born and raised near Baltimore (T-12). In 1859, as a member of a Virginia militia, Booth took part in the arrest and execution of John Brown, the abolitionist who raided Harpers Ferry (T-2). A year before the Civil War ended, Booth apparently developed his daring plan to kidnap President Lincoln. Such an event, he figured, might bring about the war's end or at least an exchange of prisoners. Booth sought out two former schoolmates, ex-Confederates Samuel Arnold and Michael O'Laughlin.

During the last two months of 1864, Booth surveyed the roads of southern Maryland and those leading out of Washington. Booth also made friends with John Surratt, a Confederate dispatch rider who operated between Richmond and Washington. John Surratt brought in two more accomplices: an unbalanced 19-year-old named David Herold, and a coach-maker and Confederate sympathizer named George Atzerodt. In March 1865, Arnold and O'Laughlin moved to Washington, and Booth lined up another conspirator, Lewis Powell Payne, a poor teenage Confederate veteran who was injured at Gettysburg and later escaped the military.

On March 20, 1865, the wild band tried to capture Lincoln as he rode by carriage near the Old Soldier's Home north of the city. But the president didn't make the trip that day, and Booth's party was foiled. Thinking their plot was suspected, the group split up, with Arnold and O'Laughlin heading back to Baltimore and Surratt scattering to Richmond and then Canada. Early the next month, the North invaded Richmond, and the Confederates surrendered at Appomattox. Five days later, on April 14, the conspirator made his final plans after he heard the president planned to attend a performance at Ford's Theater, five blocks east of the White House.

Booth planned to assassinate the president himself. Atzerodt would kill Vice President Johnson in his Kirkwood Hotel room, and Payne and Herold would assassinate Secretary of State Seward at home. Having rigged the president's box at the theater, Booth slipped in during the performance and shot Lincoln in the head. He stabbed USA Maj. Henry Rathbone, who was in the box with the president and their two wives. Then Booth leaped onto the stage, shouting "Sic semper tyrannis" — the Virginia state motto. "The South is avenged," he added. His spur caught in the folds of the flag draping the president's box. Booth fell and broke his left leg.

Atzerodt, assigned to Vice President Johnson, became frightened and never took part in the plot. Herold deserted Payne, who succeeded in wounding Seward. Herold, meanwhile, met up with Booth as he escaped the city on horseback. The pair met at the Anacostia River bridge near the Navy Yard and headed southeast out of the city. Booth and Herold were hunted down in Caroline County, Virginia. (See more on Booth's escape in T-15: Fredericksburg.)

Photo: Washington D.C. Convention and Visitors Association

The White House became a quasi-barracks for the Union Army in 1861.

Ford's Theater National Historical Site
511 10th Street NW, Washington, D.C.
• **(202) 426-6927**

President Lincoln was shot at Ford's Theater on Good Friday, April 14, 1865, five days after the Confederate surrender at Appomattox. He was attending a performance of *Our American Cousin* and was shot just before 10 PM by John Wilkes Booth. The president died the following morning. Booth masterminded the plot the previous year with several accomplices. The theater has been recreated to look as it did the night Lincoln was fatally wounded. Performances are still held in the theater section, and it sometimes closes briefly for pre-performance set up. Ford's Theater National Historic Site is open free from 9 AM to 5 PM every day except Christmas. There is a museum of assassination-related memorabilia in the basement of the theater. Adjacent to the museum is a book store, open from 9:30 AM to 4:15 PM.

FORD'S THEATER TO PETERSEN HOUSE
The Petersen House is across the street from Ford's Theater [Blue-Orange and Red lines: Metro Center stop].

Petersen House
516 10th St. NW, Washington, D.C.
• **(202) 426-6830**

This house is where President Lincoln was taken after being shot. The president died the next morning in a back bedroom. The house has been preserved and restored to its 1865 appearance as a boarding house owned by William Petersen, a German tailor. It is open free from 9 AM to 5 PM every day except Christmas.

PETERSEN HOUSE TO WILLARD HOTEL
From 10th Street, return to E Street NW, turn right (west) and go five blocks west to 14th Street NW and the Willard Hotel [Blue-Orange lines: Federal Triangle stop].

Willard Hotel
14th St. and Pennsylvania Ave. NW, Washington, D.C.

This is where President-elect Lincoln lived before his inaugural ceremony in March 1861. Lincoln and his wife, Mary, accompanied by President James Buchanan, left the Willard Hotel on the morning of the inauguration and rode by open carriage up Pennsylvania Avenue to the Capitol for the ceremony. During

Willard Hotel Side Trip: Treasury Department Building

The Treasury Department building is at 1500 Pennsylvania Avenue, adjacent to the White House [Blue-Orange lines: McPherson Square stop].

Treasury Building

The Treasury Department is housed in the third-oldest building in Washington. Construction began in 1836 at a site chosen by President Andrew Jackson. The building ruined the view of the long vista between the Capitol and the White House. In 1861, after word spread of possible Confederate attacks, the building was put under heavy Union guard.

the war, a Union vigilante group was stationed here. A popular myth is that Julia Ward Howe composed the "Battle Hymn of the Republic" at the hotel, but she probably wrote her classic while visiting a Union campsite somewhere in the Washington vicinity (see Richmond Personality: William Steffe in T-17).

WILLARD HOTEL TO SHERMAN STATUE
From the Willard Hotel, walk a block west to 15th Street NW and the Ellipse behind the White House [Blue-Orange lines: McPherson Square stop].

Sherman Statue
President's Park, Ellipse, Washington, D.C.

USA Gen. William Tecumseh Sherman, a native of Ohio, saw action in the Civil War's Western Theater. He is also known for his march on Atlanta and his "March to the Sea" and Carolina campaigns. In 1869, Sherman succeeded USA Gen. Ulysses Grant as commander in chief of the Army, a position he held for 14 years. He died in 1891.

SHERMAN STATUE TO AMERICAN NATIONAL RED CROSS BUILDING
Walk to the west side of the Ellipse and 17th Street NW. The American

National Red Cross building is at 17th and D sts. NW [Blue-Orange lines: Farragut West stop].

American National Red Cross Building
17th and D Sts. NW, Washington, D.C.
• (202) 737-8300

This building was completed in 1929. It has an inscription over the portico, "In Memory of the Heroic Women of the Civil War." The Red Cross has exhibits on the first and second floors. The building is open free Monday through Friday from 9 AM to 4 PM and closed on federal holidays.

AMERICAN NATIONAL RED CROSS BUILDING TO THE WHITE HOUSE
Walk north on 17th Street NW four blocks to Pennsylvania Avenue, turn right (east) and go a half-block to the White House [Blue-Orange lines: Farragut West stop].

White House
1600 Pennsylvania Ave. NW, Washington, D.C. • (202) 456-7041

This is the official residence of the president and first family. Construction on the building began in 1792, and President John Adams' family was the first to live here. Originally called the President's House, it was painted to hide evidence of the fire set by the British during the War of 1812. It was then renamed White House.

President Lincoln moved here in 1861. Within months, the official residence was turned into an army barracks as war fever hit Washington. Union soldiers drilled and slept in the East Room. From here, Lincoln issued his famous Emancipation Proclamation in September 1862 after the Battle of Antietam. The president prepared the proclamation's final draft at his summer cottage on the grounds of the U.S. Soldiers' Home, 2 miles north of the U.S. Capitol on N. Capitol Street. The official document ap-

Washington Personalities: Noted Women

Susan Brownell Anthony, a reformer in her 40s, was a teacher, lecturer and suffragette. She was an organizer of the Women's Loyal League that supported President Lincoln.

Mrs. Stephen Barker was a nurse who went to Washington from Massachusetts in 1861 with her husband, a Union chaplain. She worked her way up to become

Photo: Library of Virginia

superintendent of several Washington infirmaries. A lecturer who traveled throughout New York to raise funds for the Sanitary Commission, she stayed in Washington after the war's end to aid returning Union veterans.

Clara Barton, also in her 40s, was a Massachusetts woman working at the U.S. Patent Office in Washington when the war began. She helped get medicine and care to Union soldiers. An active philanthropist, she became the first president of the American Red Cross in 1882. (See more on Clara Barton at Fairfax Station in T-14: Northern Virginia.)

Dorothea Lynde Dix was the Union superintendent of women nurses during the war. She organized the women's nurse corps for the Union Army and performed her work in Washington. Born in 1802, Dix was active in movements to reform prisons and asylums.

Clara Barton became the first president of the American Red Cross in 1882.

A native of Maine, **Isabella Fogg** became a nurse after her son enlisted in the Union Army. Going to work in Washington, she later saw action during the Peninsular Campaign (T-18, T-19), Fredericksburg (T-15), Chancellorsville (T-16), Gettysburg (T-6) and the Wilderness (T-16). She collapsed from overwork after nursing her son, a war casualty, back to health. In January 1865, four months before Appomattox (T-21), Fogg fell and was permanently crippled.

Harriett Hawley was a Union army nurse from Connecticut. Working mainly in the South, she moved to Washington in 1864 when her husband was assigned to USA Gen. Benjamin Franklin Butler's command on the James River in Virginia.

Mary Morris Husband, a Pennsylvania native, worked on hospital boats operated by the Sanitary Commission. She helped care for Union soldiers injured on Virginia's Peninsula (T-18, T-19) then worked in Washington until May 1865.

plied only to areas still in rebellion, where the Union government had no authority. It said that, beginning January 1, 1863, ". . . all persons held as slaves within any State, or designated part of a State, the people Whereof shall then be in rebellion against the United States, shall be then, henceforward, and forever free."

Tours are free at the White House on Tuesday through Saturday from 10 AM to noon. Tickets, however, are required and may be obtained at the ticket booth on the Ellipse beginning at 8 AM the morning of the tour. White House tickets are easier to get than one might expect. Call your congressional representative for tickets.

WHITE HOUSE TO BLAIR HOUSE
Walk across Pennsylvania Avenue to the Blair House at 1651 Pennsylvania Avenue [Blue-Orange lines: Farragut West stop].

Blair House
1651 Pennsylvania Ave. NW, Washington, D.C.

Adjacent to Lafayette Park, this is the guest quarters for the White House. The home of Francis Preston Blair, President Lincoln's postmaster general, this is the place where the president offered Robert E. Lee the command of the Union army. This building is closed to the public.

WHITE HOUSE TO LINCOLN MEMORIAL
Before getting started, remember that Pennsylvania Avenue is closed to all vehicle traffic between 15th and 17th streets in front of the White House. So take Pennsylvania Avenue east from 17th Street to Washington Circle at 23rd Street. Go three-quarters around the circle, then south on 23rd Street for 10 blocks, through Foggy Bottom, to the Lincoln Memorial at the end of the Mall and Memorial Bridge.

Lincoln Memorial
On the Mall at the end of Memorial Bridge

The Lincoln Memorial is one of Washington's most recognizable attractions. An appropriate memorial to President Abraham Lincoln began to be debated almost immediately after his assassination. There was talk of a memorial roadway between Washington, D.C., and Gettysburg, Pennsylvania, and of monuments near the Capitol and Union Station. Finally, a site was chosen in the swampy overgrowth along the Potomac River, and the monument was dedicated in 1922.

Outside, the 36 columns signify the number of states in the Union during Lincoln's presidency. The columns tilt inward to avoid the

White House Personality: Elizabeth Keckley

Born into slavery, Elizabeth Keckley purchased her freedom and served as a seamstress for both Mrs. Jefferson Davis (Varina Howell Davis) and Mrs. Abraham Lincoln (Mary Todd). In 1868, she published *Behind the Scenes*, about her experiences in Lincoln's White House. She wrote about a "sad, anxious day" in 1863 when the Confederates — obviously before Gettysburg — were "flushed with victory." She wrote:

"One day [President Lincoln] came into the room where I was fitting a dress on Mrs. Lincoln. His step was slow and heavy, and his face sad. Like a tired child he threw himself upon a sofa, and shaded his eyes with his hands. He was a complete picture of dejection. Mrs. Lincoln, observing his troubled look, asked, "Where have you been father?" "To the War Department," was the brief, almost sullen answer. "Any news?" "Yes, plenty of news, but no good news. It is dark, dark everywhere." He reached forth one of his long arms, and took a small Bible from the stand near the head of the sofa, opened the pages of the holy book . . . . I discovered that Mr. Lincoln was reading the divine comforter, Job."

USA Gen. William Tecumseh Sherman is remembered for his march on Atlanta.

illusion of bulging at the top. Inside, on the south wall, Lincoln's Gettysburg Address is carved into the marble. Interestingly, this memorial faces across the Potomac toward Arlington House, Robert E. Lee's former residence (T-14). The memorial is open daily from 8 AM to midnight. There is no admission charge. A gift shop and book store operate on an abbreviated schedule, depending on the season.

This concludes the tour of Washington, D.C. See the next chapter, T-14: Northern Virginia, for a natural continuation of the Washington tour, beginning at Memorial Bridge adjacent to the Lincoln Memorial.

Washington Tour Ends

Other Tour Points of Interest

There is much to see and do in Washington, D.C. What follows is a brief rundown of a few of the most popular annual events, arts locations and shopping destinations in the city. For a complete, thorough listing of attractions in the nation's capital, see *The Insiders' Guide® to Metropolitan Washington, D.C.*, which covers annual events, arts, historical sites and places to shop, dine and stay the night.

Annual Events

The **Cherry Blossom Festival** is a citywide event in early April that includes a parade down Constitution Avenue. Other activities take place at various locations in the city, mainly along the Mall and the Tidal Basin,

White House Personalities: President-Veterans

Besides Ulysses Grant, four other U.S. presidents were veterans of the war. All four were Union officers from Ohio.

Rutherford Hayes saw action at Winchester (T-2), Cedar Creek (T-3) and South Mountain (T-7), where he was wounded in the arm. He served in Congress from Ohio and supported President Andrew Johnson's impeachment. He was elected twice as governor of Ohio. In 1876, he became the 19th president, succeeding President Ulysses Grant, after a disputed vote count and a special electoral commission awarded him a razor-thin victory. President Hayes ended Reconstruction in the South by withdrawing the last of Union troops. He served one term in the White House and died in Ohio in 1893.

James Garfield saw action in the war's Western Theater. A member of Congress, he was on the special electoral commission that voted for Hayes in 1876. Elected president in 1880 to succeed Hayes, he was inaugurated in March 1881 and shot three months later by a mentally disturbed office seeker while entering a Washington train station. He died in September 1881 in New Jersey and was buried in Cleveland.

Benjamin Harrison, like Garfield, saw action in the Western Theater. He was the great-grandson of a Virginia signer of the Declaration of Independence and the grandson of President William Henry Harrison. An attorney and U.S. senator, Harrison defeated incumbent President Grover Cleveland in 1888. Cleveland received more popular votes than Harrison but fewer electoral votes. Harrison lost to Cleveland in the presidential race four years later. He died in Indianapolis in 1901.

William McKinley enlisted in Rutherford Hayes' 23rd Ohio Regiment at the age of 18. He served in the West Virginia and Shenandoah Valley (T-2, T-3, T-4) campaigns. After the war, McKinley served in Congress and as governor of Ohio. He was elected president in 1896, and re-elected in 1900. McKinley was shot by an anarchist at the Pan-American Exposition in Buffalo in September 1901, and he died a week later.

USA Gen. Philip Henry "Little Phil" Sheridan is memorialized by Washington's Sheridan Circle.

Photo: Library of Virginia

Smithsonian Institution's **Folk Life Festival**. Other major holidays, including Memorial Day and Veterans Day, mean a grand parade, usually along Constitution Avenue. In December, as the nation's capital celebrates the holiday season, the **Pageant of Peace** features a giant evergreen tree on the Ellipse at the White House.

Arts

Washington is the nation's center for museums and galleries. Some of the most popular ones include the **Corcoran Gallery of Art**, **National Air and Space Museum**, **National Gallery of Art**, **National Museum of American History**, **National Museum of American Art** and much, much more.

Some of the newest arrivals on the arts scene include the **U.S. Holocaust Memorial Museum**, at Independence Avenue and 14th Street NW, and the **National Postal Museum**, at 2 Massachusetts Avenue NE. Also new are the **Navy Memorial**, between 7th and 9th streets on Pennsylvania Avenue NW, and a statute honoring women veterans at the **Vietnam Veterans Memorial** near the Lincoln Memorial.

which is ringed by cherry trees. For more information on the festival, call (202) 789-7000. The **Easter Egg Roll** is held on the South Lawn of the White House on the Monday after Easter. For more information, call (202) 456-2200. **Independence Day** on the Mall in July is spectacular, and it's accompanied by the

Entertainment

Washington is also home to the **Kennedy Center**, **Arena Stage**, **National Theater**,

Blair House Personality: Francis Preston Blair

Francis Preston Blair descended from a long line of prominent Virginians. His great-grandfather, family progenitor John Preston, was one of the earliest Irish settlers of Virginia's Shenandoah Valley. Preston's daughter, Anne, married Francis Smith of Orange County, Virginia. The Smith's daughter, Elizabeth, married a western Virginia attorney, James Blair. Their son, Francis Preston Blair, was born in Abingdon, Virginia, in April 1791.

A Kentucky lawyer turned journalist, Blair strongly opposed nullification. In 1830, he was invited to Washington by President Andrew Jackson to start a pro-administration newspaper. In 1836, he purchased a President's Square residence. Blair also had a summer home in the country outside Washington that he named Silver Spring — the origin of the name of today's Maryland suburb.

Active in Republican politics, Blair presided over the 1856 meeting that organized the new party. In January 1865, he met with Confederate President Jefferson Davis, Blair then initiated plans for a peace conference held in the Hampton Roads area of Virginia and attended by President Lincoln and Confederate Vice President Alexander Stephens.

White House Side Trip: Squares and Circles of Interest

Start this side trip by observing Lafayette Square, across Pennsylvania Avenue from the White House.

Lafayette Square

Lafayette Square was home to a number of Washington personalities including Lincoln's Secretary of State William Henry Seward and South Carolina Senator John C. Calhoun.

The Hay-Adams Hotel, at 1 Lafayette Square (800 16th Street NW), was the residence of John Milton Hay, who was in his 20s when he served as President Lincoln's assistant private secretary. Hay later wrote a 10-volume biography of the president, and he served as ambassador to Great Britain and secretary of state under Presidents William McKinley and Theodore Roosevelt respectively. Hay died in 1805.

From Lafayette Square, walk north on 17th Street NW two blocks to Farragut Square (K and 17th streets NW).

Farragut Square

The Farragut statue, square and park honor USA Adm. David Glasgow Farragut, a Tennessee native. In 1812, while still a pre-teen, he was prize master of a ship captured in the Pacific during the War of 1812. A Union sympathizer, Farragut married twice (both times to Norfolk, Virginia, natives) and left his home in Tidewater Virginia when the South began secession talks.

Farragut was a hero of naval battles in the South during the war. In 1864, returning to a hero's welcome in New York City, he received $50,000 from city officials to buy a home and a promotion to the newly created rank of vice admiral. In 1865, he was one of the first Union men to enter Richmond when it fell, and the next year he became the first person in U.S. Navy history to be promoted to admiral. He died in 1870.

From Farragut Square, walk east on K Street NW for two blocks to McPherson Square (K and 15th Streets NW).

McPherson Square

This statue and square honor USA Gen. James Birdseye McPherson, a native of Ohio. He was first in his class of 52 at the U.S. Military Academy at West Point in 1853 and commanded the USA Army of Tennessee in the Western Theater. He was just 35 when he was killed in the Battle of Atlanta.

From McPherson Square, walk north on Vermont Avenue for two blocks to Thomas Circle (Vermont and Massachusetts avenues NW).

— continued on next page

— continued from previous page

Thomas Circle

This statue and circle honor USA Gen. George Henry Thomas. The junction of four major Washington streets, the circle now has a traffic tunnel underneath.

Thomas was known as the Rock of Chickamauga. A Virginia native and graduate of the U.S. Military Academy at West Point, he remained loyal to the North. He saw action in the Western Theater and was one of only 15 Union officers to receive Thanks of Congress for his war action and heroism. He died on active duty in 1870.

From Thomas Circle, walk west two blocks to Scott Circle (Massachusetts Avenue and 16th Street NW).

Scott Circle

This circle and statue honor USA Gen. Winfield Scott. The statue, cast from cannon captured in the Mexican War, was erected in 1874. Scott, a Virginian, was a hero of the Mexican War and general-in-chief of the U.S. Army at the beginning of the Civil War. He was born in 1786, a year before the U.S. Constitution was adopted. He died at West Point just two weeks shy of his 80th birthday, and he was the only Southern non-West Pointer who remained loyal to the North.

Also in Scott Circle is the Daniel Webster Statue, honoring the noted pre-Civil War-era senator from Massachusetts. The statue was cast in bronze and erected in 1900.

From Scott Circle, walk west three blocks to DuPont Circle (Connecticut Avenue NW at P Street).

DuPont Circle

This circle has a fountain that honors USA Rear Adm. Samuel Francis duPont. Originally Pacific Circle, DuPont Circle was graced with a statue of duPont in 1884. Later, his family moved the statue to Delaware and commissioned Daniel Chester French to design the fountain.

DuPont was a veteran of war action in the South. He was president of a board that met in Washington in June 1861 to plan the North's naval operations. He died in June 1865, two months after the war's end, while still on active duty.

From DuPont Circle, walk north on Connecticut Avenue for seven blocks to the McClellan Monument (Connecticut Avenue and California Street NW).

McClellan Monument

This equestrian statue honors USA Gen. George Brinton McClellan. A Pennsylvania native, McClellan succeeded the venerable Winfield Scott as commander and chief of the U.S. Army.

McClellan was widely referred to as "Young Napoleon" during the early stages of the war. But after Antietam, McClellan was replaced by USA Gen. Ambrose E. Burnside as commander of the Army of the Potomac. McClellan ran unsuccessfully against Lincoln for president in 1864. (See more on USA Gen. McClellan in T-18: Upper Peninsula and T-19: Lower Peninsula.)

— continued on next page

— continued from previous page

From the McClellan Monument, return south on Connecticut Avenue for five blocks, turn right on R Street NW and walk four blocks to Sheridan Circle (Massachusetts Avenue and 23rd Street NW).

Sheridan Circle

USA Gen. Philip Henry Sheridan, known during the war as "Little Phil," was a New Yorker of Irish descent. Sheridan saw action at the Wilderness and Spotsylvania. He conducted a raid on Richmond in May 1864, during which time CSA Gen. J.E.B. "Jeb" Stuart was killed. Sheridan's Shenandoah Valley Campaign raged from August 1864 until nearly the end of the war. He was with USA Gen. Ulysses Grant at Appomattox in 1865 (see T-21: Appomattox).

Warner Theater, **Ford's Theater** (see listing), and **Folger's Shakespeare Library**. For the latest in political parody and satire, take in **Capitol Steps**, a group of current and former Capitol Hill employees that performs weekends at Chelsea's Restaurant in Georgetown. There is no greater national treasure to the folks in this area than the beloved **Washington Redskins**. The Redskins, often a title contender in the National Football League, currently play at RFK Stadium, but the team plans to move to a new stadium facility in the Washington suburbs of Maryland. Meanwhile, the team's home games have been sold out since the Lincoln administration — so your only hope of seeing a game live is by knowing and/or marrying a season-ticket holder. For RFK Stadium information, call (202) 547-9077.

The nation's capitol is home to the **Washington Bullets**, a National Basketball Association franchise that currently makes its home at the USAir Arena in Landover, Maryland. For information, call (301) 622-3865. USAir Arena is also home of the **Washington Capitals**, members of the Eastern Division of the National Hockey League. For Caps information, call (301) 386-7080.

Then there's harness racing at **Rosecroft Raceway** in Fort Washington, Maryland, near the Indian Head Highway exit on the Capital Beltway near Woodrow Wilson Bridge. **Avenel Golf Course** in Potomac, Maryland, is a popular tour stop for professional golfers, and the **Marine Corps Marathon** is held each year in late October or early November. The 26-mile route begins and ends at the Iwo Jima Memo-

Washington Personalities:
Dr. Edward Maynard, Mathew Brady, John Ericsson

Dr. Edward Maynard, a Washington dental surgeon, obtained a patent in 1845 for a "primer tape," similar to the caps used in toy cap guns. Rifles used in the war were made or modified to accommodate this tape, which became known as Maynard tape.

Mathew Brady, the noted war photographer, was an astute entrepreneur who created a mobile darkroom for his assistants who worked various battlefields. Brady was quite nearsighted and seldom did much negative work himself. In fact, he rarely stepped foot out of his two studios, located in New York City and in Washington.

John Ericsson, a Swede, invented the screw propeller and designed the *Monitor* ironside in 1861 (see more on the *Monitor* in T-19: Lower Peninsula). A memorial in West Memorial Park is dedicated to Ericsson.

rial near Arlington Cemetery and winds its way through downtown Washington.

Shopping

The nation's capital is a shopper's paradise. From elegant boutiques to souvenir shops, Washington has it all. For starters, there are three prominent shopping areas: **Georgetown Park** in Georgetown, the **Shops at National Place** (adjacent to the downtown Marriott on Pennsylvania Avenue) and the old **Post Office Pavilion** (also on Pennsylvania Avenue).

Each section of Washington offers a unique shopping experience such as **Filene's Basement**, a bargain-hunter's delight across the street from the Mayflower. Go exploring! Near Capitol Hill, the renovated **Union Station** rail center has a number of fancy shops and restaurants. The building itself is worth a visit.

Tour 14
Northern Virginia

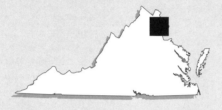

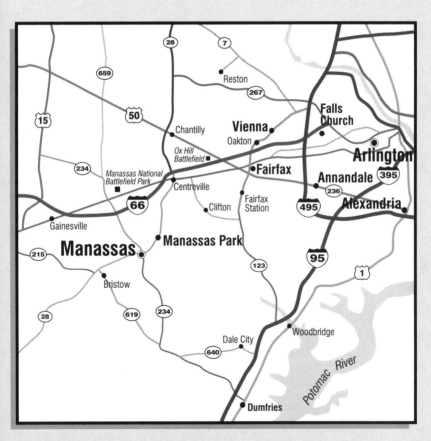

Northern Virginia

About This Tour

This tour route covers Arlington and Fairfax counties and the cities of Fairfax and Alexandria — all modern-day Northern Virginia suburbs of Washington, D.C. It is a natural continuation of either T-13: Washington or T-8: Manassas.

Before the Civil War, Northern Virginian society was more oriented to things Southern — toward Richmond. During the war, all the localities in this region were occupied by Union forces. After the war's conclusion the area saw population grow with an influx of new residents that included Union sympathizers from the North and African Americans from the liberated South. Northern Virginia become more associated with the whims and politics of Washington, D.C.

This region traces its origins to Anglo pioneers from Virginia's coastal Tidewater area. In 1649, King Charles II of England granted land patents between the Potomac and Rappahannock rivers to a handful of Englishmen, particularly Thomas, sixth Lord Fairfax, for whom Fairfax County is named.

In time, the Virginia area along the Potomac River was settled by a number of illustrious families including the Washingtons, Masons, Carters, Fitzhughs and Lees. Mount Vernon, on the Potomac, was the home of Lawrence Washington, and it later passed to Lawrence's half-brother, George Washington. Nearby was Belvoir, the home of George William Fairfax, who was a cousin of Lord Fairfax. Gunston Hall was the home of George Mason, one of many Virginians involved in the American struggle for independence. Arlington was the estate of George Washington Parke Custis, the step-grandson of George Washington.

Tobacco was the principal crop of Colonial Northern Virginia, and warehouses were all along the Potomac. Roads leading from the hinterland farms, including the now-famous Little River Turnpike, led from inland east to the river. These port sites became the locations of such prominent communities as Alexandria in Fairfax County and Dumfries, Occoquan and Woodbridge in Prince William County. The main route between Northern Virginia and Richmond generally followed the "fall zone" — the geographic division between the Coastal Plain and the rolling Piedmont. The fall zone marks the end of tidal movement and the head of navigation for the rivers of the Coastal Plain.

In the late 18th century, a portion of Northern Virginia land was donated by the state for the establishment of the new American governmental seat, the District of Columbia. The new federal city, which bore the name of Virginian George Washington, was a 10-mile square overlapping portions of Maryland, Virginia and the Potomac River. The Virginia portion of the district took in the community of Alexandria, which was then the county seat of Fairfax. With this land division, the county seat was moved west to Providence, which is present-day Fairfax. In 1846, Virginia retroceded — took back — its portion of the land within the District of Columbia. This area was named Alexandria County then renamed Arlington County in 1920.

In the 1850s, two major rail lines were constructed in Northern Virginia. One ran from Alexandria, Virginia, to Leesburg, Virginia. The other ran from Alexandria to Gordonsville, Virginia, and through a small Prince William County community known as Manassas Junction. The railroad greatly reduced Alexandria's prestige as a major river trading center. By this time, Richmond and Baltimore already were drawing business away from Alexandria, and tobacco and wheat were dropping in

Photo: Virginia Department of Historic Resources

Robert E. Lee spent his early years in this house in Alexandria.

popularity. Alexandria developed the dubious distinction as being a major trade center for African-American slaves.

When Virginia seceded from the Union in spring 1861, Union soldiers poured into Northern Virginia to occupy jurisdictions along the Potomac River. Skirmishes were less prevalent here, thanks in part to a series of forts, including Fort Ward in Alexandria, that encircled the nation's capital. In 1863, when the new state of West Virginia was established, Alexandria became the location of the restored, federally controlled government of Virginia. Because of this "occupation," Northern Virginia recovered more quickly than other Southern locales after the surrender at Appomattox.

Travel Tips

This section of the Metropolitan Washington area is heavily congested, especially during morning and evening rush hour periods. Be particularly careful on the highways and roads of Northern Virginia, especially the Washington Beltway, Interstate 395 and Interstate 95. Washington radio stations report traffic and weather conditions. Citizen band radio users can find traffic information on Channel 19; state police usually monitor Channel 9.

Motorists receive a strong mobile telephone signal throughout the vicinity.

This tour begins and ends in Northern Virginia. See Chapter 22 for recommended accommodations and Chapter 23 for dining suggestions. It's a good idea to review these recommendations before ending the tour. In addition to our suggestions, there are numerous, varied places to spend the evening, dine and shop throughout Northern Virginia.

Northern Virginia Tour Begins...

LINCOLN MEMORIAL TO ARLINGTON NATIONAL CEMETERY
Cross the Potomac River from Washington, D.C., into Virginia on the Memorial Bridge and Memorial Avenue.

Memorial Bridge symbolically links the North and the South. The bridge is the northern terminus of the Mount Vernon Memorial Highway, which extends south along the Virginia and District shore of the Potomac to the home of George Washington.

Arlington Cemetery Side Trip: Freedman's Village

Arlington National Cemetery once was the site of Freedman's Village, a flourishing town for 10,000 freed African-American slaves. The village, complete with houses, farms, businesses, school and hospital, was built in 1863 on land that was part of Robert E. Lee's estate, Arlington. Originally, Freedman's Village was developed to house the thousands of former slaves that crowded into Washington after President Abraham Lincoln abolished slavery in the city — a year before the Emancipation Proclamation freed slaves nationwide. The village, located just north of the present-day visitors center, grew to major proportions. This section of the cemetery was later dedicated to U.S. Colored Troops and the residents of the village. Two African-American churches in Arlington County trace their roots to Freedman's Village, but there's very little other evidence of the town. Arlington National Cemetery includes the graves of 3,800 freed slaves and 1,200 African Americans who fought in the Union Army.

MANASSAS (T-8) TO ARLINGTON NATIONAL CEMETERY

To access this tour from Manassas, take I-66 east from Manassas to exit 72, Spout Run Parkway. Off the exit ramp turn right (north) onto U.S. Highway 29 (Lee Highway) and go one block to Va. Highway 124. Turn left onto Va. 124 (Spout Run Parkway) and proceed 1 mile to merge with southbound George Washington Memorial Parkway. Take the George Washington parkway south for 1.8 miles to the exit for Memorial Bridge and Arlington Cemetery. The exit ramp makes a 180-degree loop to Memorial Drive. Turn left on Memorial Drive and go one block to Arlington Cemetery entrance.

Arlington National Cemetery

Virginia Hwy. 110 at Memorial Dr., Arlington, Va. • (703) 692-0931

More than 225,000 American war veterans and their family members are buried at Arlington, the best-known of the country's 100-plus national cemeteries. The cemetery traces its origins to the Civil War and the efforts of USA Gen. Montgomery Cunningham Meigs, the quartermaster general who schemed to use 200 acres of CSA Gen. Robert E. Lee's family property to bury Washington's overwhelming Civil War casualties. By 1865, more than 16,000 graves were scattered about Arlington House, the Lee mansion overlooking the Potomac River.

In 1882 Lee's son, George Washington Custis Lee, successfully sued the federal government for having taken the Arlington House property from his family during the Civil War. However, the estate by 1882 was covered with graves, so young Lee accepted a $150,000 government offer for the property and renounced any thought of living at Arlington House. The cemetery includes the Tomb of the Unknown Civil War Dead, the remains of more than 2,000 Union soldiers, a Confederate monument and a section for the burial of Confederate soldiers. Oliver Wendall Holmes Jr., a U.S. Supreme Court Justice and a Civil War veteran (see Hagerstown, Maryland, in T-1: Sharpsburg), is buried at Arlington as are Presidents John F. Kennedy and William Howard Taft. The cemetery has memorials to the crew of the space shuttle *Challenger*, servicemen killed in the hostage rescue attempt in Iran and nurses from the Spanish-American War to the present.

Arlington National Cemetery is open every day October to March from 8 AM to 5 PM and from 8 AM to 7 PM from April to September. There is a parking facility at the cemetery where you can park for a fee, but Arlington can also be reached by the Washington Metro blue line.

A visitors center is open every day. Handicapped visitors and persons who want to visit a private grave site may get a temporary pass to drive into the cemetery; otherwise, vehicle traffic is prohibited.

Arlington House, the Robert E. Lee Memorial

Arlington, Va. • (703) 693-0931

In 1824, the Marquis de Lafayette visited Arlington House and described the view across the Potomac to Washington, D.C., as the finest in the world. George Washington Parke Custis, President Washington's step-grandson, built Arlington House in the early 1800s, and it was named for the Custis family homestead on Virginia's Eastern Shore.

Robert E. Lee married Custis' daughter, Mary Anna Randolph Custis, at Arlington House in 1831, and the estate became their

Arlington House Personality: Robert E. Lee

Photo: Harpers Ferry National Historical Park

The young Robert E. Lee lived in Alexandria until leaving for West Point.

Robert E. Lee was born January 19, 1807, at Stratford in Westmoreland County, Virginia, on the Northern Neck, a peninsula sandwiched between the Potomac and Rappahannock rivers in Tidewater country. Lee likely never remembered Stratford Hall in Westmoreland, however, because he was just 3 when he moved to Alexandria with his mother, two brothers and sister. Young Robert lived in Alexandria until he left home to attend the U.S. Military Academy at West Point in June 1825. A few miles up the Potomac from Alexandria was Arlington estate, home of George Washington Parke Custis. Custis was like a father to Robert E. Lee, who married Custis' daughter in 1831 at the estate.

Throughout Lee's career in the Army and until the beginning of the Civil War, Arlington remained his home. It was a haven where he could lay down his disappointments, frustrations and anxieties. In 1861, Lee was forced to decide between his nation and state. On April 18, he rode from Arlington into Washington to visit Virginian Winfield Scott (see Petersburg Personality in T-20: Petersburg), general in chief of the U.S. Army, and Francis Blair (see Blair House Personality in T-13: Washington), President Lincoln's advisor.

— continued on next page

— continued from previous page

Blair told Lee that Lincoln was willing to give him command of a 100,000-man federal army. The next day, a Baltimore mob killed three Union soldiers, and by 2 PM their bodies were lying in state at the Capitol. That afternoon Lee received news from Richmond that a Virginia convention had voted to secede from the Union. War was imminent.

Sitting alone at Arlington, Lee resigned his U.S. Army commission. The next day he attended church in Alexandria, where a Richmond contingent arrived to say Virginia wanted him to be major general of the state's army. On April 22, Lee left for Richmond, never to return to Arlington. Later, he commented on his resignation from the U.S. Army: "I did only what my duty demanded."

home for the next 30 years. Lee was living here when he received word of Virginia's secession from the Union in April 1861. At Arlington, Lee decided to resign his U.S. Army commission to join the Confederate army. Soon, federal troops occupied the house.

In 1864, the 1,100-acre Arlington estate was designated a national cemetery. Ironically,

Lee Home Personalities:
Henry "Light-Horse Harry" Lee, Ann Carter Lee

January 1807 was not the best of times for Ann Hill Carter Lee. She had just lost her father, Charles Carter of Shirley Plantation (see T-18: Upper Peninsula), and her husband, "Light-Horse Harry" Lee, was known to disappear frequently. Ann, who was pregnant, caught a bad cold riding a coach through wet and cold weather from Shirley to her Westmoreland County, Virginia, home. Alone at Stratford, she gave birth to a son on January 19 and named the new baby after her brothers Robert and Edward — Robert Edward Lee.

The boy was the fourth child for Ann and her husband, whose real name was Henry Lee, but who was better known as Light-Horse Harry, a veteran of the Revolution, a member of the Continental Congress and Virginia governor. He commanded U.S. soldiers in the Whiskey Insurrection in 1794 and delivered President Washington's eulogy before both houses of Congress. Light-Horse Harry also suffered financial reversals, and he reportedly spent time in jail twice for debt.

In 1813, during the War of 1812, Light-Horse Harry sailed to the Caribbean, either to relieve his family of the burdens of his illness (brought on by a Baltimore fight and a malignancy in the lower abdomen) or to avoid public embarrassment for his poor finances. Five years later, on his way home, he died at Cumberland Island in Georgia. The Lee children — Charles Carter, Anne Kinloch, Sydney Smith, Robert Edward and Mildred — were raised by their mother, who was forced to use her family trust income to sustain the household. During the economic depression following the War of 1812, Ann ran the family on about $600 a year.

Ann Hill Carter Lee hosted the Marquis de Lafayette at her home during the Frenchman's visit to America in the 1820s. George Washington Parke Custis, the man who built Arlington House, married Mary Lee Fitzhugh in the drawing room. Later, the Custises daughter married Robert E. Lee at Arlington House. Ann Lee lived long enough to see her children grow to adulthood. When she died in 1829, Carter was an attorney, and Anne was married to William Marshall, a clergyman-turned-lawyer. Smith was in the Navy, and Robert had only recently graduated second in his class at the U.S. Military Academy at West Point. Mildred later married and settled in Europe.

Arlington Cemetery would be the final resting place for many federal solders who opposed Lee. Interesting as well, Arlington estate was never actually located in its namesake, Arlington County. The mansion was a part of the Virginia land ceded in the late 1700s to the District of Columbia. Later, it was located in Alexandria County — the portion of Virginia land returned to the Commonwealth by the District in 1846. It was a part of federal property in 1920, when Alexandria County was renamed Arlington by the Virginia General Assembly to honor Lee and his estate. One of the smallest counties in the nation, Arlington covers just 24 square miles, one-fifth of which is federal property occupied by the cemetery, Washington National Airport, Fort Myer, the Pentagon and other governmental offices.

In 1925, Congress designated Arlington House and its grounds as the Robert E. Lee Memorial, with Memorial Bridge to link memorials to Lee and President Lincoln. An Arlington House tour includes most of the estate's 26 rooms, including bedrooms, the Morning Room, the family dining room, the guest chamber and Lee's Chamber, where the general wrote his U.S. Army resignation. Arlington House is open from 8:30 AM to 6:30 PM from April to September and from 8:30 AM to 4:30 PM October through March. Admission is free. Parking at the cemetery is $1.25 an hour for the first 3 hours, but this involves a steep hike. For $4, Tourmobile will pick you up at Arlington National Cemetery and take you to the Arlington House as well as the Tomb of the Unknown Soldier and the gravesite of John F. Kennedy.

ARLINGTON NATIONAL CEMETERY TO LEE'S BOYHOOD HOME
Return north on Memorial Drive to the traffic roundabout at Memorial Bridge. Go three-quarters of the way around the circle, then take the left exit ramp (signs for I-395, Alexandria and Mount Vernon) that loops back onto the George Washington Memorial Parkway south toward Alexandria and National Airport. Continue south on the parkway 5.5 miles —

past the I-395 interchange and the National Airport entrance — to the northern city limits of Alexandria. At the first traffic signal in Alexandria, the parkway becomes Washington Street through the downtown area. Proceed through six more traffic signals (0.8 miles) to Oronoco Street. Turn left, across northbound parkway traffic, onto Oronoco. The Boyhood Home of Robert E. Lee is in the first block.

Boyhood Home of Robert E. Lee
607 Oronoco St., Alexandria, Va.
• **(703) 548-8454**

Beginning about 1810, Robert E. Lee lived with his mother, brothers and sisters in several Alexandria houses including this stately, brick Federal-style home owned by William Henry Fitzhugh, a relative. The house is listed in the National Register of Historic Places and as a Virginia Highway Historic Landmark. It is furnished with authentic period pieces. Lee's boyhood home is open Monday through Saturday from 10 AM to 4 PM and on Sunday from 1 to 4 PM. It is closed Easter, Thanksgiving and for a rare wedding reception or other social function. Also, the house is open only by appointment from December 15 to January 31. Admission is charged.

LEE HOME TO CHRIST CHURCH
From Oronoco Street, turn left on Washington Street and go three blocks to Cameron Street. Christ Church is at the corner of Washington and Cameron streets. Turn right on Cameron Street and go one block to Columbus Street, where you will find a public parking lot and on-street parking. Enter the church grounds from Columbus Street.

Christ Church
118 N. Washington St., Alexandria, Va.
• **(703) 549-1450**

This attractive, 18th-century Episcopal

Photo: Library of Virginia

Robert E. Lee received word of Virginia's secession while living at Arlington House.

Church is one of Alexandria's, and Virginia's, most famous landmarks. Many of Alexandria's famous families, including the Washingtons and Lees, worshipped at the church. The cemetery was the town burying ground until 1815. Robert E. Lee was confirmed at Christ Church, and he attended services at the church as a youth and young adult.

On the third Sunday in April 1861, the day after Lee resigned his commission in the U.S. Army, he was at Christ Church services when he was met by a Richmond contingent that asked Lee to be major general of the state's Confederate forces. Within days, Lee was on his way to Richmond and the Civil War. The church is open on Sunday from 2 to 4:30 PM and Monday through Saturday from 9 AM to 4 PM.

CHRIST CHURCH TO INFANTRY MONUMENT

From Christ Church, go south one block on Columbus Street, take a left onto King Street and go one block to Washington Street. Turn right on Washington Street and go one block to Prince Street. The

Infantry Monument sits in the middle of this intersection.

Infantry Monument
Washington and Prince Sts., Alexandria, Va.

The Confederate monument in the middle of Washington Street honors the men of Alexandria's 17th Virginia Infantry Regiment. This is the place where nine units of the Confederate infantry assembled before marching down Duke Street to board an Orange and Alexandria Railroad train headed for Manassas Junction. At Manassas, they joined Confederate forces for the Battle of 1st Manassas.

The statue was dedicated in a ceremony in 1889. The address was delivered by Virginia Gov. Fitzhugh Lee, a former Confederate officer in the Army of Northern Virginia and CSA Gen. Robert E. Lee's nephew. The area around the monument once measured 40-by-60 feet, and it included a fence with ornamental gas lamps. The statue's island was reduced in size as automobile traffic increased along Washington Street, especially in 1932 after construction of the George Washington Memorial Parkway. Since then, the statue has been struck by errant automobiles on several occasions.

INFANTRY MONUMENT TO THE LYCEUM

The Lyceum is on the southwest corner of the intersection of Washington and Prince streets. It has a parking lot entrance off Washington Street.

The Lyceum

201 S. Washington St., Alexandria, Va.
• (703) 838-4994

The Lyceum, a good example of Greek Revival architecture, was established in 1839 as a cultural and scientific center. Its origins are traced to the efforts of Quaker educator Benjamin Hallowell, who ran an Alexandria school a decade earlier and helped Robert E. Lee prepare for West Point. During the Civil War, the Lyceum was used as a hospital. After being used as a private residence and for offices, it became a state center for the American Bicentennial celebration in the 1970s. Today, the old Lyceum is home of Alexandria's History Museum. And it looks more like it did in 1839. The Lyceum has visitor information, a gift shop and a small permanent exhibition area that includes Civil War material. It is open Sunday from 1 to 5 PM and Monday through Saturday from 10 AM to 5 PM. It is closed New Year's Day, Thanksgiving and Christmas. Admission is free, and the building is handicapped accessible.

THE LYCEUM TO THE STABLER-LEADBEATER APOTHECARY SHOP

Park your vehicle at the Lyceum and walk for the next portion of this tour. Head north one block to Washington and King streets, turn right (east) on King Street, walk four blocks, take a right (south) on Fairfax Street and go a quarter-block to the Stabler-Leadbeater Apothecary Shop.

Stabler-Leadbeater Apothecary Shop

107 S. Fairfax St., Alexandria, Va.
• (703) 836-3713

The pharmacy was founded in 1792, the year the cornerstone was laid at the President's House (later called the White House) in Washington, D.C. The shop is named for Edward Stabler, a young Quaker who started a family pharmacy business in Alexandria. Stabler's daughter, Mary, met and married an Englishman, John Leadbeater, in the 1830s. The shop's original furnishings and glassware remain intact today. In the fall of 1859, CSA Gen. James Ewell Brown "Jeb" Stuart, then a U.S. Army lieutenant, went to the apothecary shop to find another U.S. Army officer, Col. Robert E. Lee. Stuart was to deliver a message from the Secretary of War telling Lee to rush to Harpers Ferry to put down a disturbance started by abolitionist John Brown (see T-2: Harpers Ferry). The shop is open Monday through Saturday from 10 AM to 4 PM and Sunday from 1 to 5 PM. It is closed on major holidays. Admission is $2 for adults, $1 for students and free for children younger than 11.

Return to the northeast corner of the intersection of King and Fairfax streets.

Ramsey House

221 King St., Alexandria, Va.
• (703) 838-4200

On the northeast corner of King and Fairfax streets is the William Ramsey House, built in 1724 by Ramsey, who was Alexandria's first mayor. The building now serves as Alexandria's official visitors center. Note that the Ramsey House is not handicapped-accessible. That makes the Lyceum on Washington Street a better alternative for handicapped visitors. The Ramsey House sells block tickets to various Alexandria historic attractions.

Continue walking north on Fairfax Street for a half-block to the Carlyle House, at the intersection with Cameron Street.

Carlyle House

Fairfax and Cameron Sts., Alexandria, Va.
• (703) 549-2997

The Carlyle House was built by John Carlyle in 1753 and served as the headquar-

Old Town Personalities: USA Col. Ephraim Elmer Ellsworth and Secessionist James William Jackson

From the Carlyle House, return to King Street, turn right (west) and go two blocks, past the Alexander City Hall, to Pitt Street. At the corner of King and Pitt streets is the site of the former Marshall House Hotel and a famous incident in 1861.

USA Col. Ephraim Elmer Ellsworth organized the Chicago Zouave Cadets, a group of soldiers who modeled themselves after the French Algerian infantrymen (known as Zouaves) of Colonial days. A New York native, Ellsworth moved to Chicago in the 1850s, a time when newspapers reported on the exploits of the French Zouaves in the Crimean War. He was fascinated with the North African uniforms and the Zouave reputation for drill and weapons precision.

Ellsworth and his Chicago group put on a number of exhibitions including visits to West Point and the White House. President Abraham Lincoln was once quoted as saying Ellsworth was "the greatest little man I ever met." In the first year of the Civil War, Ellsworth and his men were organized as a U.S. Army regiment and stationed at the U.S. Capitol in Washington. Soon the regiment was part of a 13,000-man Union contingent ordered across the Potomac River to occupy Alexandria, Virginia.

As the regiment crossed the river, Ellsworth spotted an exceptionally large Confederate-like flag that flew from the Marshall House, a hotel then located at King and Pitt streets in Alexandria. The Marshall House manager, Virginian James William Jackson, was an ardent secessionist. Ellsworth decided to capture the flag, so he and a group of followers entered the Marshall House, went to the roof, hauled down the flag and began their escape. But Jackson, armed with a double-barrelled shotgun, met the group in the stairway. USA Cpl. Francis E. Brownell used his rifle to deflect Jackson's shotgun, but the Secessionist's weapon discharged, striking Ellsworth and killing him instantly. In turn Brownell fired his rifle at Jackson, who was struck in the head and fatally injured.

The incident was witnessed by a New York newspaper correspondent, and soon the two deaths were sensationalized by both Northern and Southern sympathizers. Souvenir seekers stole pieces of the Marshall House stairway where the two men died. Ellsworth's funeral, held in the East Room of the White House, was attended by a bereaved President Lincoln. The Marshall House incident inspired patriotic poems and songs, and Ellsworth was hailed in the North as "the first to fall." The 44th New York Regiment, known as "Ellsworth's Avengers," was raised in his honor. The regiment adopted a commemorative ballad, of which a stanza said:

First to fall, thou youthful martyr,
Hapless was thy fate;
Hastened we, as thy avengers,
From thy native State,
Speed we on, from town and city,
Not for wealth or fame,
But because we love the Union,
And our Ellsworth's name."

ters for British Gen. Edward Braddock during the French and Indian War. Braddock, an associate of Virginia militia member George Washington, summoned five Colonial governors to the Carlyle House to discuss ways to induce colonists to pay for his military campaign in the French and Indian War. The resulting Stamp Act helped provoke the Revolutionary War.

Return by King and Washington streets to the Lyceum to continue this tour by automobile.

THE LYCEUM TO ALEXANDRIA NATIONAL CEMETERY

Go south on Washington Street one block, turn right (west) on Duke Street, go four blocks to U.S. Highway 1 (S. Henry Street, one-way south) and turn left. Go one block on U.S. 1, turn right (west) on Wilkes Street and go six blocks to the gates of Alexandria National Cemetery.

Alexandria National Cemetery
Wilkes St., Alexandria, Va.

Nearly 4,000 Civil War dead, mostly Union soldiers, are buried in this, one of the nation's first national cemeteries. It is open from dawn to dusk.

ALEXANDRIA NATIONAL CEMETERY TO UNION STATION, KING STREET

Backtrack east on Wilkes Street for six blocks to Patrick Street (U.S. 1, one-way north). Turn left (north) on Patrick Street and go three blocks, turn left on King Street (Va. Highway 7) and go west for 0.5 mile to Union Station, Alexandria's main railroad station.

Union Station
King St., Alexandria

The 88-year-old Union Station is the only surviving rail station of four that once served Alexandria. Just north of Union Station is Potomac Yard, nearly a century old, which traces its origins to Alexandria's emergence as a regional railroad center.

Beginning in the 1840s, and continuing through the Civil War, Alexandria's reputation as a major river port declined as it became known as a national rail center. Alexandria became directly involved in construction projects for five major railroad lines — some that vanished in time, others that formed the foundation for such prominent rail companies as the Southern, C&O, Pennsylvania and the Richmond, Fredericksburg and Potomac (RF&P). A north-south rail link between Washington, D.C., and Richmond was completed in 1872, within a decade of the end of the Civil War. The Pennsylvania Railroad took over the old Alexandria and Fredericksburg Railroad and built a line to Quantico, connecting with the RF&P to Richmond.

By the turn of the century, both Alexandria and Washington were important railroad centers. Alexandria was filled with remnants of classic old rail lines — the Alexandria and Harpers Ferry, which grew to become the Washington and Old Dominion; the Orange and Alexandria, which later merged with the Manassas Gap to become the Orange, Alexandria and Manassas; and the Alexandria and Fredericksburg, which merged with the Alexandria and Washington to become the northernmost part of the RF&P.

In Washington, from the northern end of the Long Bridge over the Potomac to the Capitol, there were freight yards, a freight station, a passenger depot and grade crossings for the Pennsylvania, Southern and B&O railroads. In 1907, Washington opened its new Union Station. To eliminate the number of freight yards previously located through Washington, a major new rail yard was built south of the Potomac. Situated between the Long Bridge and Alexandria's northern city limits, it was called Potomac Yard. It opened in August 1906, and by World War II it was the busiest rail classification center in the nation.

Carlyle House was built in 1753 in Alexandria.

*UNION STATION TO FORT WARD
MUSEUM AND HISTORIC SITE*

*Beyond the railroad station, past
the underpass on King Street, turn
left (south) on Callahan Road.
Observe the Washington Masonic
Temple across Callahan Road
from the railroad station. The
temple is a monument to President Washington. Continue south
on Callahan Road for one block to
Duke Street, turn right (west) on
Duke Street (Va. Highway 236) and
proceed west 1.3 miles, turn right
(north) on Quaker Lane and go 1.2
miles to Braddock Road.*

Observe the Fort William historical marker
on the west side of Quaker Lane, just 0.2 mile
from Duke Street. Fort William was one of the
earthworks built as a circle of defense around
Washington during the Civil War.

*At Braddock Road, turn left (west)
and go 0.7 mile to Fort Ward Museum and Historic Site on the right.*

Fort Ward Museum and Historic Site

4301 W. Braddock Rd., Alexandria, Va.
• **(703) 838-4848**

Fort Ward was the fifth-largest of more than
150 earthwork forts and batteries that formed
the defenses around Washington, D.C.. This
fort, like numerous others, was constructed
soon after Virginia voted in early 1861 to secede from the Union. It guarded Alexandria's
western approaches such as the Alexandria-
Leesburg Turnpike and the Little River Turnpike. The fort was named for Commander
James Harmon Ward, the first Union naval officer killed in the Civil War. The museum is
patterned after a Union headquarters building. It houses a collection of Civil War artifacts. A self-guided tour (it is suggested that
you allow about 45 minutes to complete it)
leads along the fort's preserved earthwork
walls, 95 percent of which are visible.

The fort is among the best preserved of all
that formed a ring around Washington. The
45-acre historic park site is open daily from 9
AM to sunset. The museum is open Sunday
from noon to 5 PM and Tuesday through Saturday from 9 AM to 5 PM. The museum is
closed Mondays and on New Year's Day,
Thanksgiving and Christmas. The facility is
owned and operated by the city of Alexandria,

Fairfax Personalities: Antonia Ford Willard, Laura Ratcliffe

Antonia Ford was just 19 when Union soldiers searched her father's house (present-
day 3977 Chain Bridge Road) and hauled her off to prison on charges of being a
Confederate spy. Antonia was sent to the Old Capital Prison (see T-13: Washington).
The story has a happy ending: USA Maj. Joseph C. Willard, a former provost marshall
at the Fairfax Courthouse, fell in love with Antonia, negotiated her release from prison
and married her. Maj. Willard was co-owner of the famous Willard Hotel in Washington,
D.C. (see T-13: Washington). He and Antonia had just one child, a son, Joseph E.
Willard, who served as lieutenant governor of Virginia and U.S. minister to Spain. The
younger Joseph Willard was considered by many the most influential political figure in
Fairfax County in the early 1900s.

Laura Ratcliffe was born in 1836 in Fairfax County and was in her mid-20s when the
Civil War erupted in Northern Virginia. Ratcliffe befriended CSA Col. John Singleton
Mosby and alerted him to a Union plan to capture him. She and Mosby became close
friends, and he often used her western Fairfax County home as a headquarters during
the war. Once he trusted her with thousands of federal dollars he captured from Union
troops. Despite her aggressive Confederate activity, Laura Ratcliffe was always able to
avoid Union arrest.

Fairfax Courthouse Side Trip: Fairfax Station

From the Fairfax Courthouse, return to Va. 123 (Chain Bridge Road), turn right (south) and go 3.3 miles on Va. 123 to Fairfax Station Road (Va. Highway 660).

Fairfax Station

Fifty yards south of Fairfax Station Road on Va. 123 is the original rail bed of the Orange and Alexandria Railroad, which served as a link between Alexandria and Manassas Junction, Virginia. A quarter-mile west on Fairfax Station Road (Va. 660) is St. Mary's Church, the oldest Roman Catholic church in Fairfax County. The church was built in 1758 for the Irish immigrants who came to the area to build the railroad line. In August 1862, after 2nd Manassas, wounded Union soldiers were brought to the church by rail on their way to Alexandria. Here, nurse Clara Barton, founder of the American Red Cross, tended to the war wounded (see Women Nurses in T-13: Washington).

Two miles north of Fairfax Station is Burke's Station, the next stop on the Orange and Alexandria Railroad. CSA Gen. J.E.B. "Jeb" Stuart captured a telegraph station operator at Burke's Station in December 1862 (see Occoquan in T-15: Fredericksburg).

---

which charges no admission but gladly accepts donations.

FORT WARD TO FAIRFAX MUSEUM
Leaving Fort Ward, turn right (west) on Braddock Road and go a half-block to Howard Street, turn left (south) on Howard Street for four blocks then take a right on Seminary Road and go 4 blocks to I-395 (Shirley Highway). Turn left and take I-395 south (toward Richmond) for 4 miles to I-495 (Washington Beltway), then take I-495 north (exit 1-C for Rockville) and go 4 miles on the beltway's inner loop to exit 6 (Va. Highway 236, Little River Turnpike). Follow signs for Va. 236 to Fairfax and continue west on Va. 236 for 4.5 miles to the Fairfax Museum. Va. 236 becomes Main Street in the vicinity of downtown Fairfax, and the Fairfax Museum is just beyond Locust Street. Turn left into the museum parking lot.

Fairfax Museum
10209 Main St., Fairfax, Va.
• **(703) 385-8414**

This attractive museum is in one of Fairfax's oldest buildings. A Virginia landmark, it was constructed in 1873 and is the oldest two-story brick schoolhouse in Fairfax or Fairfax County. The museum has detailed exhibits of eras in Northern Virginia history, and it includes personal items of various local heroes including CSA Col. John Singleton Mosby. Also included are items from the Battle of Chantilly (Ox Hill), fought just west of the town of Fairfax in September 1862. The museum is a private, volunteer operation. It is open daily from 9 AM to 5 PM (excluding Thanksgiving, Christmas and New Year's Day), but Sunday visitors should call in advance to determine the exact closing time. There's no admission fee, but there is a contribution basket for donations.

FAIRFAX MUSEUM TO
FAIRFAX COUNTY COURTHOUSE
From the museum parking lot, turn left (west) onto Main Street (Va. 236), drive one block to the traffic

signals and zig-zag right and left (follow Va. 236 signs) onto one-way westbound North Street. Proceed two blocks to Va. Highway 123 (Chain Bridge Road), turn left (south) and go two blocks, crossing over Main Street, before turning right into the Fairfax Courthouse parking lot.

Along this route, between North and Main streets on Chain Bridge Road, is the old Ford residence at 3977 Chain Bridge Road (see Fairfax Personality: Antonia Ford Willard).

Fairfax County Courthouse
4000 Chain Bridge Rd., Fairfax, Va.

The historic community around the courthouse was the scene of numerous skirmishes during the Civil War. Some historians say a battle at the courthouse on June 1, 1861, was technically the first battle of the war (also see Big Bethel in T-19: Lower Peninsula). It hap-pened when future Virginia Gov. William "Extra Billy" Smith took charge of the Warrenton Rifles from Fauquier County, Virginia, after their commander, CSA Capt. John Q. Marr, was killed during a Union cavalry raid. Marr is honored by a plaque on the courthouse grounds. Another Southerner, CSA Lt. Col. Richard Stoddert Ewell — later a lieutenant general — was injured in the skirmish. There was another significant battle in the Fairfax vicinity in late June 1863, just days before the Battle of Gettysburg in Pennsylvania.

George and Martha Washington's wills were recorded at the courthouse, which showed up often in Matthew Brady's photographs of Civil War sites. The courthouse was used as a Union signal post and headquarters throughout the war. The building is now on the National Register of Historic Places.

Across Main Street, on Chain Bridge Road, was the home of Antonia Ford Willard, an alleged Confederate spy.

Fairfax Personalities:
USA Gen. Philip Kearny, USA Gen. Isaac Ingalls Stevens

USA Gen. Philip Kearny, a native of New York, joined the U.S. Army in 1837 at the age of 23 after studying law at Columbia University. He lost his arm while fighting with USA Gen. Winfield Scott in the Mexican War and resigned from the Army in 1851 to travel in Europe. A decade later, with the onset of the Civil War, he was commissioned a brigadier general. He saw action at Seven Pines during the Peninsula Campaign (T-18) and at 2nd Bull Run (T-8). At Ox Hill in September 1862, Kearny rode into a line of soldiers led by CSA Gen. Thomas Jonathan "Stonewall" Jackson. The Union officer tried to fight his way out of the trap and was fatally injured. Later that year, the officers who served under Kearny devised a gold medal — the "Kearny Medal" — to award those who honorably served in Kearny's command. The next year, another medal — the "Kearny Cross" — was designed for Union enlisted men who distinguished themselves in battle. More than 300 Kearny Medals were awarded; two women were among the recipients of the Kearny Cross. Kearny led the 1st New Jersey Brigade, and Kearny, New Jersey, bears the general's name.

USA Gen. Isaac Ingalls Stevens was a U.S. Army engineering officer from Massachusetts. A graduate of the U.S. Military Academy at West Point, Stevens resigned from the U.S. Army in 1853 and served as governor of the Washington (state) Territory until 1857. He served in the U.S. House of Representatives from March 1857 to March 1861, representing the Washington Territory. During the Civil War, he led the 79th New York Highlanders and rose in rank to major general. Stevens' son, USA Gen. Hazard Stevens, was twice injured at Ox Hill.

FAIRFAX COURTHOUSE TO THE DR. WILLIAM GUNNELL HOUSE

From the Fairfax County Courthouse parking lot, exit on West Street, go north one block to Main Street, turn left and go a half-block to the Truro Episcopal Church parking lot on the right at 10520 Main Street. The Dr. William Gunnell House, now a private residence, is near the back section of the lot.

Dr. William Gunnell House
10520 Main St., Fairfax, Va.

This private residence was once the home of Dr. William Gunnell, and it was the place where CSA Col. John Singleton Mosby captured USA Gen. Edwin Henry Stoughton, a youthful 25 years at the time, in March 1863. Born in 1838 in Vermont, Stoughton saw action in USA Gen. George McClellan's Peninsula Campaign and was promoted to brigadier general in 1862 at the age of 24.

On March 9, 1863, the Union officer and a number of his men were captured by a 29-man Confederate force led by Mosby (see Leesburg Personality in Tour 7: Monocacy), who crept inside Union lines near the courthouse. The sleeping Stoughton was awakened when Mosby slapped him on his backside.

Mosby said, "Get up, general, and come with me."

Stoughton replied, "What is this? Do you know who I am, sir?"

Mosby answered: "I reckon I do, general. Did you ever hear of Mosby?"

"Yes," said Stoughton, then asked, "Have you caught him?"

Mosby answered, "No, but he has caught you!"

Mosby also stole away with two other officers, 30 soldiers and 58 horses. When President Lincoln learned of Stoughton's capture, he reportedly commented in disgust that he could create another general with the stroke of a pen, but he hated to lose the horses. Mosby escorted Stoughton to Culpeper, well behind CSA lines. The Union officer was shipped to Richmond, where his brigadier general commission expired while he was held in Libby Prison.

The Mosby incident led to the Union search of the Ford House in Fairfax (see Fairfax Personality: Antonia Ford Willard). The Gunnell House is not open to the public.

DR. WILLIAM GUNNELL HOUSE TO CONFEDERATE CEMETERY

From the Dr. William Gunnell House and the Truro Episcopal Church, go west on Main Street (Va. 236) four blocks to the Confederate Cemetery.

Confederate Cemetery
Main St., Fairfax, Va.

A handful of monuments at the Confederate Cemetery signify the place where a number of Southern soldiers, known and unknown, are buried. The cemetery was the site of a Union stockade during the Civil War.

CONFEDERATE CEMETERY TO OX HILL BATTLEFIELD

Continue west on Main Street (Va. 236) and follow signs for U.S. Highway 50 (Lee-Jackson Highway). Go west 3 miles on Va. 236 and U.S. 50 and take the second exit for West Ox Road south. Proceed for 0.4 mile to Monument Drive, turn right (west) on Monument Drive and go 0.1 mile to the Ox Hill Battlefield Park. To reach the park, continue west on divided Monument Drive for a half-block to Fair Ridge Drive, make a U-turn and return east on Monument Drive to the parking pull-off.

Ox Hill Battlefield Park
Monument Drive, Chantilly, VA

A Civil War battle was fought at Ox Hill on September 1, 1862, just after 2nd Manassas. CSA Gen. Robert E. Lee, maintaining an offensive posture after the Manassas battle, clashed with Union forces just west of Centreville. Two prominent officers, USA Gen. Philip Kearny and USA Gen. Isaac Ingalls Stevens, were killed in the battle. The battlefield park, operated by the Fairfax County Park

Authority, offers a small bit of park space in the midst of the thick urban sprawl in western Fairfax County.

Northern Virginia Tour Ends

Other Tour Points of Interest

There is much to see and do in Northern Virginia. For a more comprehensive list of area attractions, see the *Insiders' Guide® to Metropolitan Washington, D.C.*, which covers, among other topics, annual events, arts, historical sites, kidstuff and places to shop, dine and stay overnight. The following is an abbreviated list of options.

Annual Events

George Washington is Alexandria's most famous local hero. The city hosts a parade each February in honor of Washington's birthday. Alexandria is rich in Scottish and Irish history, and the city features a great St. Patrick's Day parade in March and an exciting Scottish Christmas program in December.

Antiques

There are a number of antique shops in Northern Virginia, particularly on the back streets of Old Town Alexandria. This is an affluent community, so don't be surprised if prices are higher than what you're used to.

Arts

The top arts attraction in Northern Virginia is **Wolf Trap Farm Park**, off the Dulles Toll Road near Tyson's Corner in western Fairfax County. A nationally famous center for the performing arts, Wolf Trap offers big-name entertainers throughout the year, but the specialties are featured during the summer. The park's annual concert series is virtually free of musical boundaries. The Smashing Pumpkins may perform on a Friday night, followed by a Saturday afternoon Cajun music festival, a Sunday journey through Lake Wobegon with Gar-

rison Keillor and a Monday evening with Peter, Paul and Mary. Patrons often take blankets and picnic dinners to lounge on the grassy lawn and enjoy. The **Patriot Center** at George Mason University in Fairfax features a number of popular attractions each year as well.

Historic Sites

Besides Civil War attractions, Northern Virginia has a number of prominent historical sites. Remember, Alexandria is George Washington's hometown. His famous estate, **Mount Vernon**, is just 8 miles south of the city at the end of the George Washington Memorial Parkway along the Potomac River. Nearby are **Woodlawn Plantation**, which was carved about 3 miles west of Mount Vernon property, and **Gunston Hall**, the home of George Mason, at Mason Neck National Park at Lorton 15 miles south of Alexandria. **Sully Plantation**, the home of Richard Bland Lee ("Light-Horse Harry" Lee's brother and Robert E. Lee's uncle), is at Chantilly near Dulles Airport. It is a fine example of an 18th-century county farmhouse.

There is a convenient way to see some of Northern Virginia's historic attractions: **Tourmobile**. The 18-site tour includes stops at the White House, Washington Monument, the National Air and Space Museum, Union Station, the U.S. Capitol, the National Gallery of Art, the American History Museum and other popular attractions. Tourmobile costs $12 for adults and $6 for children 3 to 11. It offers free reboarding throughout its route and special vehicles for the mobility impaired For information, call (202) 432-SEAT.

Shopping

The urban sprawl of Northern Virginia offers the unique advantage of a proliferation of top-quality shopping malls. In Arlington, enjoy **Ballston Common**, Glebe Road at Wilson Boulevard, and **Fashion Centre** at Pentagon City, just off I-395 near the Pentagon.

In Fairfax County, shop at **Seven Corners Shopping Area**, U.S. 50 and Va. 7; **Fairfax Square**, Va. 7 at Tysons Corner; **Tysons Corner Center**, Va. 7 and Va. 123; **Galleria at Tysons II**, Va. 7 and Va. 123; **Reston Town Center**, Reston; **Fair Oaks Mall**, U.S. 50 and I-66; and **Springfield Mall**, Franconia Drive at I-95.

On Interstate 95, 20 miles south of Alexandria, is **Potomac Mills Mall**, one of the top outlet mall attractions in the nation. Considered by everyone we know as the ultimate in outlet shopping, Potomac Mills is north of Fredericksburg on I-95 (exit 156).

Tour 15
Fredericksburg

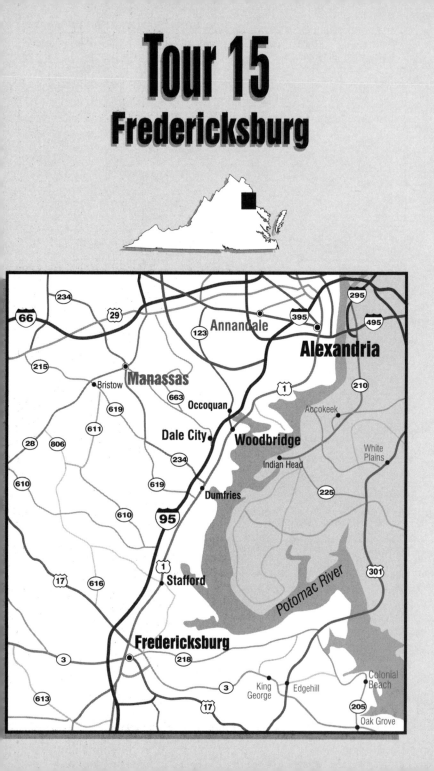

TOUR 15
Fredericksburg

About This Tour

This tour route is a continuation of Tour 14: Northern Virginia. The route begins in Northern Virginia and runs the length of Interstate 95 from the Washington Beltway in Northern Virginia 40 miles south to Fredericksburg, Virginia.

The stretch between Washington and Fredericksburg was originally settled by Native Americans, and the names they used for places are still in evidence today: the town of Occoquan, Aquia Creek, the Potomac and Rappahannock rivers. Jamestown's Capt. John Smith explored the upper reaches of the Rappahannock and Potomac as early as 1608. English settlers in Virginia's Tidewater began pushing west in the late 17th century, and they settled a number of communities along the "fall zone" of Virginia's principal rivers.

Note that this tour covers only Fredericksburg and the area east of I-95. The next route, T-16: Spotsylvania, covers Spotsylvania County and the area west of I-95.

Travel Tips

I-95 is part of the busy north-south corridor of Virginia that stretches along the fall zone. Be on the lookout for heavy, fast-moving traffic along this major interstate route, and be especially alert to traffic along the beltway and I-95. Avoid rush-hour traffic that clogs the southbound interstate in the evening. Since peak traffic times often vary by the day of the week or season of the year, radio traffic reports are especially helpful. Washington stations will also report weather information. Remember that traffic can be particularly heavy and often snarled during unusual weather conditions such as winter snows and torrential summer rains.

During heavy congestion, consider using U.S. Highway 1 southbound, parallel to I-95, as an alternate route. U.S. 1 has a number of traffic signals, but it can be a wise choice when I-95 becomes a parking lot. Again, Washington radio stations can be helpful in recommending alternate routes. Citizens band radio users can find traffic information on Channel 19. State police usually monitor Channel 9. Motorists receive a strong mobile telephone signal all along the I-95 corridor.

This tour concludes in Fredericksburg, where we suggest you plan evening dining and lodging. See Chapter 22 for our recommendations on accommodations and Chapter 23 for dining suggestions in the Fredericksburg area. It's a good idea to review these recommendations before traveling the tour route. In addition to our suggestions, there are various fast-food facilities, gas stations and shops throughout the Fredericksburg area.

Fredericksburg Tour Begins...

ALEXANDRIA TO OCCOQUAN, VA.
From Alexandria, take U.S. 1 to the Washington Beltway (Interstate 495 west, I-95 south). Take the beltway south (follow signs for Richmond) for 6 miles to the junction of I-495, I-95 and Interstate 395. This is one of the busiest intersections along the East Coast. At exit 167, take I-95 south and continue south through Fairfax County into Prince William County.

Photo: Library of Virginia

Soldiers dug trenches in the front lawn of Brompton House during the battle of Fredericksburg.

Occoquan, Va.

At the Occoquan River, I-95 enters Prince William County. This county was established in 1730 and named for William Augustus, England's Duke of Cumberland and the third son of King George II.

Just west of the I-95 bridge is the town of Occoquan. The town dates to 1736 as the site of a tobacco warehouse. In December 1862, CSA Gen. Wade Hampton led raids against Union wagon trains, capturing prisoners and wagons near Occoquan and Dumfries to the south. CSA Gen. James Ewell Brown "Jeb" Stuart then joined Hampton to lead raids on Dumfries and Occoquan, beginning the day after Christmas 1862. After a successful operation, Stuart moved just west to Burke's Station on the Orange and Alexandria Railroad and captured the telegraph station operator before an alarm could be tapped out to Union authorities in Washington, D.C. According to

one of several conflicting stories, Stuart had one of his men, an accomplished telegraph operator, tap out a message to USA Gen. Montgomery Cunningham Meigs, the Union quartermaster-general, to complain about the quality of mules furnished for his men. Stuart, it is said, told Meigs the mules were so inferior they were embarrassing.

Today, Occoquan boasts a sizeable historic district with homes and business structures that date to the late 19th century.

OCCOQUAN TO STAFFORD COUNTY, VA.

Continue south on I-95, crossing into Stafford County near exit 148.

Stafford County, Va.

Stafford County, named for Staffordshire, England, was established in 1664. Stafford, the county seat, is off I-95 at exit 140. Between

Stafford and Fredericksburg is Falmouth, Virginia, which was laid out as a village in 1727 at the westernmost navigable point on the Rappahannock River. Falmouth and the entire northern bank of the Rappahannock often were occupied by opposing forces during the Civil War.

STAFFORD COUNTY TO FREDERICKSBURG, VA.

Continue south on I-95, crossing the Rappahannock River into Fredericksburg. Continue 2 miles and take exit 130 to Va. Highway 3 (east), then follow the signs for downtown Fredericksburg.

Fredericksburg, Va.

Fredericksburg was established in 1728 on the Rappahannock River and named, like Frederick County, Virginia, for Frederick Louis, England's Prince of Wales and the oldest son of King George II.

As a youth, George Washington lived at Ferry Farm, just across the Rappahannock from Fredericksburg in Stafford County. Washington's only sister, Betty Washington Lewis, lived with her husband, Fielding Lewis, at Kenmore in Fredericksburg. Washington's mother, Mary Ball Washington, lived in Fredericksburg until her death in 1789. During the American Revolution, the community bustled with activity.

After the war, James Monroe was an attorney in Fredericksburg prior to moving to Washington, D.C., to begin a lengthy service in the federal government.

In 1861, Fredericksburg was a quiet community of about 5,000. But its strategic location, midway between Washington and Richmond, made it a critical focal point during the Civil War. More than 100,000 soldiers were killed or wounded in four Civil War campaigns associated with the Fredericksburg area. Today, the Fredericksburg and Spotsylvania National Military Park commemorates the Battle of Fredericksburg in 1862 as well as the Chancellorsville Campaign in April and May 1863, the Battle of the Wilderness in early May 1864 and the Battle of Spotsylvania Court House in mid-May 1864 (all in T-16).

Fredericksburg is like a natural amphitheater, with the land rising up on either side of the Rappahannock River. USA Gen. Ambrose Everett Burnside set up a position east of town on Stafford Heights in mid-November 1862. A month later, on December 11, Union troops crossed the Rappahannock on pontoon bridges to attack Confederates set on the high ground west of Caroline Street in town. The Federals pushed west through the town and beyond the north-south tracks of the Richmond, Fredericksburg and Potomac Railroad. Moving uphill, Burnside attacked twice. USA Gen. George Meade made an assault on the left, attacking CSA Gen. Thomas J. "Stonewall" Jackson at Prospect Hill. Jackson eventually pushed Meade back.

The other Union assault struck at CSA Gen. Robert E. Lee's main defense at Marye's Heights. Northerners were slaughtered by artillery fire and by thousands of Confederate infantrymen behind a stone wall in the vicinity of the "sunken road." It was a devastating loss for both armies; thousands of men were killed or wounded. The battle was Lee's most one-sided victory of the Civil War. Fighting again flared in Fredericksburg 1863 as part of the Chancellorsville Campaign (T-16).

Today, the historic district in downtown Fredericksburg covers a 40-block area that includes the 50 acres of the 1728 town site and land added in 1759. More than 200 historic buildings remain in this historic area. Amazingly, despite the heavy Civil War fighting in Fredericksburg, much of downtown was spared any loss.

FREDERICKSBURG TO FREDERICKSBURG VISITOR CENTER

From I-95, take Va. 3 east for 1.2 miles to Va. 3 E. Bus. (William Street), and curve left onto William Street east. Proceed 1.3 miles to Princess Anne Street (U.S. 1, U.S. Highway 2, U.S. Highway 17), turn right and go three blocks to Charlotte Street. Turn left (east) on Charlotte Street, and you will find parking areas on both sides of the street for the Fredericksburg Visitor Center. The center is at the

Photo: Library of Virginia

Due to its strategic location, Fredericksburg was ravaged by Civil War action.

intersection of Charlotte and Caroline streets.

Fredericksburg Visitor Center
706 Caroline St., Fredericksburg, Va.
• (540) 372-1216, (800) 260-3646,
(800) 678-4748

This visitors center is operated by the Fredericksburg Department of Tourism. There are a number of historic attractions in the downtown Fredericksburg area (see listings at end of this chapter for points of interest not related to the Civil War), and travel counselors here can help you with information and materials. Ask about a "Hospitality Pass," which is a combined admission to various downtown historic sites and the Fredericksburg Area Museum and Cultural Center. Ask about carriage tours of the historic district. The handicapped-accessible center is open 9 AM to 5 PM daily except New Year's Day, Thanksgiving and Christmas. There are snack machines and restrooms.

Before touring downtown Fredericksburg, stop in at the Fredericksburg Battlefield Visitor Center, a National Park Service facility.

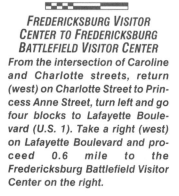

FREDERICKSBURG VISITOR CENTER TO FREDERICKSBURG BATTLEFIELD VISITOR CENTER
From the intersection of Caroline and Charlotte streets, return (west) on Charlotte Street to Princess Anne Street, turn left and go four blocks to Lafayette Boulevard (U.S. 1). Take a right (west) on Lafayette Boulevard and proceed 0.6 mile to the Fredericksburg Battlefield Visitor Center on the right.

Fredericksburg Battlefield Visitor Center
1013 Lafayette Blvd. (U.S. Hwy. 1 Bus.),
Fredericksburg, Va. • (540) 373-6122

The National Park Service (NPS) operates

THE INSIDERS' GUIDE TO
Golf in the Carolinas

You can just **Visit**, or you can be an **Insider**

a complex, 7,700-acre battlefield system in the Fredericksburg and Spotsylvania County area. This national military park system includes battle sites in and around Fredericksburg, with four significant locations — Fredericksburg, Chancellorsville, the Wilderness area and Spotsylvania Courthouse. All but Fredericksburg are covered in T-16: Spotsylvania. In addition, the NPS incorporates information on Chatham (an estate just east of town), Old Salem Church (west of Fredericksburg, see T-16) and Guinea Station (a shrine to Stonewall Jackson south of town, see T-16). The Park Service has a brochure that offers a tour of the Fredericksburg and Spotsylvania County battlefields, and a cassette tape of the tour is available. Our tour generally follows the NPS recommendations, but we do offer a few variations along the way.

The Fredericksburg Battlefield Visitor Center is open 9 AM to 5 PM daily except New Year's Day and Christmas. From June to September, hours are extended to 6 PM on Saturdays and Sundays. Park rangers are on duty to provide information. There are restroom facilities. In addition, the center sells regional history publications and offers picnic tables and facilities to assist handicapped visitors.

FREDERICKSBURG BATTLEFIELD VISITOR CENTER TO FREDERICKSBURG PRESBYTERIAN CHURCH

Return to downtown Fredericksburg 0.7 mile on Lafayette Boulevard (U.S. 1), turn left (north) on Caroline Street and go to George Street. Turn left (west) on George Street and go one block to Princess Anne Street.

Fredericksburg Presbyterian Church

Princess Anne and George Sts, Fredericksburg, Va.

The Fredericksburg Presbyterian Church, built in 1833, was a hospital during the Civil War for soldiers from both the Union and Confederacy at various times. Clara Barton (T-13) went to the church in 1862 to nurse Union soldiers after the Battle of Fredericksburg.

PRESBYTERIAN CHURCH TO CONFEDERATE CEMETERY

From Princess Anne Street, return to Caroline Street and go north to Amelia Street (Va. 3). Turn left (west) and drive six blocks to Washington Avenue. The cemetery is at Amelia Street and Washington Avenue.

Confederate Cemetery

Amelia St. and Washington Ave., Fredericksburg, Va.

In 1865, the year the Civil War ended, the Fredericksburg Ladies Memorial Association established the Confederate Cemetery. More than 2,000 Southern soldiers, most unidentified, are buried in the cemetery. It is open from sunup to sundown with no admission charge.

CONFEDERATE CEMETERY TO KENMORE

From the intersection of Amelia Street and Washington Avenue, turn right (north) on Washington Street and go one block to Lewis Street. Kenmore is at this intersection.

Kenmore

1201 Washington Ave., Fredericksburg, Va. • (540) 373-3381

Kenmore is one of Fredericksburg's most attractive and charming sites. It was the home of Fielding Lewis and his wife, Betty, who was George Washington's only sister. The Georgian mansion was built in 1775. Kenmore was used as a Union field hospital during the Battle of Fredericksburg, and the estate still shows scars of the war in its plaster walls. Kenmore is open Monday through Saturday from 10 AM to 5 PM and Sunday from noon to 5 PM. Admission is $5 for adults, $2.50 for students ages 6 through 18 and $12 for a family. It is closed Thanksgiving, Christmas Eve, Christmas and New Year's Day.

KENMORE TO CHATHAM

From Kenmore, continue east on

Lewis Street, turn right (south) on Princess Anne Street and go to William Street (Va. 3). Turn left (east) on William Street, go two blocks, cross the Rappahannock River bridge and turn left (north) on White Oak Road (Va. Highway 218). It is 0.1 mile to the entrance to Chatham on the left and the entry road to the estate is a half-mile.

Chatham
120 Chatham Ln., Falmouth, Va.
• **(540) 373-4461**

Chatham, a fine old Georgian mansion, once was the home of wealthy Virginian William Fitzhugh. Interestingly, Fitzhugh, one of CSA Gen. Robert E. Lee's ancestors, was the father of Mary Fitzhugh Custis, the first mistress of Arlington House (T-13). Lee courted his wife, the former Mary Custis, at Chatham. By the 1860s, J. Horace Lacy owned Chatham, so it became known as the Lacy House when Union officers used it as a headquarters in 1862. It also was used as a Union hospital. Clara Barton (see T-13) and poet-essayist Walt Whitman — whose brother was injured during the Battle of Fredericksburg — were among those who helped treat the war-wounded at Chatham.

Once encompassing more than 1,000 acres, the estate declined after the Civil War to barely 30 acres. It was donated to the National Park Service (NPS) in the 1970s. There is a great view of Fredericksburg from the front lawn. Park rangers are on duty to provide information and interpretation of the overall battlefield park story. The NPS has historical publications for sale and picnic tables are available. The handicapped-accessible estate is open from 9 AM to 5 PM every day except New Year's Day and Christmas.

Fredericksburg Tour Ends

Other Tour Points of Interest

Annual Events
President's Day and **Washington's Birthday** are celebrated with special events in Fredericksburg in February. The **Market Street Fair** is a springtime celebration in May. The **Fredericksburg Art Festival** is held in June, and **Kenmore's gingerbread house contest** and exhibit is conducted in December.

Antiques
Caroline Street in downtown Fredericksburg is an antique lover's heaven. No fewer than 20 shops offer antiques and memorabilia, much of it Civil War-related. Browse along the stores and window-shop for brief, unexpected history lessons.

Historic Sites
Many buildings in downtown Fredericksburg are on the list of state or national landmarks. These include the **Mary Washington House**, 1200 Charles Street, where George Washington's mother lived for 17 years until her death in 1789; **Rising Sun Tavern**, 1306 Caroline Street, built in the 1760s by George Washington's younger brother, Charles; and the **James Monroe Law Office**, 908 Charles Street, which houses a number of Monroe's personal possessions. **Ferry Farm**, George Washington's home when he was a youngster, is across the Rappahannock River in Stafford County.

Shopping
Caroline Street in downtown Fredericksburg is a bustling, active place with dozens of shops and stores. The ultimate in outlet shopping, **Potomac Mills**, is 22 miles north of Fredericksburg on I-95 (exit 156). This is the known as the No. 1 attraction in Virginia and the largest outlet center in the world. It offers more than 200 stores.

Fredericksburg Side Trips: King George County, Westmoreland County

From Chatham, return to Va. 3 (King's Highway) and turn left (east). Stay on Va. 3 for 19 miles from Chatham to the intersection of U.S. 301.

Along this route, the tour enters King George County, which was established in 1720 and named for England's King George I.

U.S. Highway 301

Today's U.S. Highway 301 follows the route of a Colonial road between Richmond and Baltimore. In April 1865, after assassinating President Lincoln in Washington (T-13), John Wilkes Booth escaped and fled south through eastern Maryland (T-12), across the Potomac and Rappahannock rivers and into Caroline County, Virginia. Booth's route roughly followed present-day U.S. 301.

Continue east on Va. 3 for 7 miles into Westmoreland County, Virginia. Continue east on Va. 3 for 2 miles to Oak Grove.

Westmoreland County was formed in 1653 and named for an English shire. The county boasts the birthplaces of George Washington, CSA Gen. Robert E. Lee and James Monroe.

Oak Grove, Va.

This community where George Washington attended school was raided by Union cavalry troops in 1863. In the Oak Grove vicinity are various historic sites.

Ingleside Plantation Vineyards
Va. Hwy. 638, 2 miles south of Oak Grove, Va. • (804) 224-8687
Ingleside Plantation Vineyards is on the site of a Virginia plantation built in 1658 on the Rappahannock River. Old Washington Academy of Westmoreland was established at the estate, but it closed in the 1840s and the farm was renamed Ingleside. Today, the working plantation includes a vineyard and a winery where tours are offered.

Westmoreland Berry Farm and Orchard
Va. Hwy. 634, 4 miles south of Va. Hwy. 3
• (800) 997-BERRY
Once known as Leesville, this estate was shelled and burned by Union gunboats on the Rappahannock River. Now, the berry farm and orchard produces 16 separate crops year round.

Continue east on Va. 3 for 8 miles to Va. Highway 214, turn left (north) and proceed to the entrance of Stratford Hall Plantation.

— continued on next page

— continued from previous page

Stratford Hall Plantation
Stratford, Va. • (804) 493-8038

Stratford Hall is the birthplace of CSA Gen. Robert E. Lee. This grand old estate was built in the second quarter of the 18th century by Thomas Lee and was the birthplace of the only pair of brothers who signed the Declaration of Independence: Richard Henry Lee and Francis Lightfoot Lee. Stratford is open from 9 AM to 4:30 PM daily for tours, and the grounds of the estate include a reception center and a gift shop. Admission is $7 for adults 18 or older, $6 for seniors and $3 for ages 6 through 17. The plantation dining room is open all year.

Robert Edward Lee was born January 19, 1807, at Stratford, the fourth child of Col. Henry "Light-Horse Harry" Lee and Ann Hill Carter. Despite his family's rich ancestry, Lee lacked the advantages of wealth. His father was a poor financial planner who died when Lee was a child. Ann Carter Lee, an ailing widow with seven children, was closest to her youngest son, Robert. In turn, Lee was influenced greatly by his mother's character and morality. Young Lee escaped the family's cash-poor, near-poverty conditions by gaining admission to the U.S. Military Academy at West Point. (See more on Lee in T-14: Northern Virginia.)

After completing this side trip, return by Va. 3 to Fredericksburg.

Tour 16
Spotsylvania

TOUR 16
Spotsylvania

About This Tour

This tour is a natural continuation of Tour 15: Fredericksburg. The route begins at the Spotsylvania Visitors Center on Interstate 95 southwest of Fredericksburg.

Spotsylvania County was established in 1720 and named for Alexander Spotswood, Virginia's lieutenant governor from 1710 to 1722. In 1861, Spotsylvania was a quiet, rural county. The Civil War spoiled the serenity. Today, the Fredericksburg and Spotsylvania National Military Park commemorates the county's rich Civil War heritage, which includes the Chancellorsville Campaign (including Chancellorsville Battlefield and Old Salem Church) in April and May 1863, the Battle of the Wilderness in early May 1864 and the Battle of Spotsylvania Court House in mid-May 1864.

Travel Tips

I-95 is part of Virginia's busy north-south corridor that stretches along the "fall zone." As you'll remember from Tour 14: Northern Virginia, the fall zone is the geographic division between the Coastal Plain and the rolling Piedmont. Be on the lookout for heavy, fast-moving traffic along this major interstate route. If possible, avoid rush-hour traffic in the Fredericksburg-Spotsylvania County area, particularly on Va. Highway 3 west of I-95, which clogs with morning and evening commuters. Radio traffic reports are especially helpful. Remember that traffic is very busy and often snarled during unusual weather conditions such as winter snows and heavy summer rains. Citizens band radio users can find traffic information on Channel 19. State police usually monitor Channel 9. Motorists will receive a strong mobile telephone signal all along the I-95 corridor.

This tour route concludes in southern Spotsylvania County, and we suggest you return to the area near the visitors center to dine and spend the evening. We recommend accommodations in Chapter 22 and dining suggestions in Chapter 23. It's a good idea to review these recommendations before traveling throughout the Spotsylvania County area. In addition to our suggestions, there are the usual fast-food restaurants, gas stations and shops throughout Spotsylvania County.

Spotsylvania Tour Begins . . .

Spotsylvania Visitors Center
4704 Southpoint Pkwy., Fredericksburg, Va. • (540) 891-TOUR, (800) 654-4118

This visitors center is operated by the County of Spotsylvania. It has a display of Civil War memorabilia, maps and a complete supply of brochures and travel materials. As this route also concludes in Spotsylvania County, you can reserve your accommodations and set dining plans from here.

The center has a National Park Service brochure with information on touring Civil War battlefields in Spotsylvania County and neighboring Fredericksburg, and a cassette tape of the tour is also available. Our tour generally follows NPS-recommended sites, but we do offer a few variations along the way. In addition, the center has information about Civil War-related attractions and points of interest west and south of Spotsylvania, in Caroline and Hanover counties near Richmond and in Orange and Culpeper counties in the Piedmont. The staff at this particular center is especially helpful. Travel counselors know the area and can give visitors good information, including

Photo: Library of Virginia

This photo was taken on May 21, 1864, at Massaponax Church, a temporary headquarters for USA Gen. Grant.

printed lists, on places to spend the night, dine and shop.

Various localities in Virginia have joined together to develop a number of special Civil War tours, complete with points of interest, trail signs and a corresponding brochure. These tours are packaged as Virginia Civil War Trails, and the program boasts a distinctive sign-logo program. One tour, "Lee vs. Grant: The 1864 Campaign," covers sites from Orange County (west of Spotsylvania County) through Spotsylvania itself and south as far as Richmond and Petersburg. This tour — T-16 — covers some but not all of the locations cited in the "Lee vs. Grant" brochure. The visitors center is open 9 AM to 5 PM daily.

SPOTSYLVANIA VISITORS CENTER TO OLD SALEM CHURCH
Exit the visitors center and return on Southpoint Parkway 0.2 mile to U.S. 1, turn right (north) and go 0.2 mile to I-95 North. Take I-95 north for 4 miles to exit 130-B (Va. Highway 3 W.). Drive west on Va. 3

for 1.6 miles to Va. Highway 639 (Salem Church Road), turn left (south) and immediately turn left into the church parking area.

Old Salem Church
Spotsylvania County, Va.

Old Salem Church was built just two decades before the Civil War. During the Battle of Fredericksburg (T-15) in December 1862, a number of women and children escaped the battle-torn village and sought refuge in the church west of town. During the Chancellorsville Campaign in May 1863, fighting raged in the vicinity of the church, and Confederate surgeons treated soldiers at this site after the fight subsided. The church is not an active house of worship today.

OLD SALEM CHURCH TO CHANCELLORSVILLE VISITOR CENTER
From Old Salem Church, take Va. 3 west 6.6 miles to the Chancellorsville Visitor Center on the right.

WHETHER YOUR OUTLOOK IS BLUE OR GRAY, YOU'LL FIND COLORFUL HISTORY HERE.

Grant, Lee, Lincoln, Davis, Clara Barton, Walt Whitman. These are just a few of the thousands who played a part in Fredericksburg's illustrious history during the Civil War.

The stories and places are still here today for you and your family. Just off I-95. That's 50 miles south of Washington, or 55 miles north of Richmond — depending on which side you're coming from.

Virginia's Fredericksburg, Spotsylvania and Stafford

Call for a visitor guide, 800-654-4118 or fax 540-891-2605

Chancellorsville Visitor Center
Va. Hwy. 3, Chancellorsville, Va.
• **(540) 786-2880**

At this center, the National Park Service offers information on sites related to the Chancellorsville Campaign. The NPS self-guided tour, including the tape cassette tour, includes the Chancellorsville site. The Chancellorsville Visitor Center has a museum (no admission is charged), auditorium for programs and presentations, restrooms and a picnic area. There are special facilities for handicapped visitors. Publications can be purchased. It is open every day from 9 AM to 5 PM except New Year's Day and Christmas.

After suffering serious losses at the Battle of Fredericksburg (T-15) in December 1862, the Union Army welcomed a new commander when President Lincoln dismissed USA Gen. Ambrose Everett Burnside and replaced him with USA Gen. Joseph "Fighting Joe" Hooker. In the spring of 1863, USA Gen. Hooker moved his army west upriver on the Rappahannock to near the crossroads at Chancellorsville —

not a town, but a brick estate complete with a veranda — in the area known as the Wilderness. CSA Gen. Robert E. Lee moved his Confederate troops into positions to thwart a Union attack. Hooker's men were struck on May 2 in a surprise flank attack led by CSA Gen. Thomas Jonathan "Stonewall" Jackson. The day ended in tragedy when Jackson was accidentally shot by a group of Confederate soldiers. Jackson's arm was amputated and buried near this site. Lee sent word to Jackson, "You have lost your left arm; I have lost my right." Jackson died several days later of the wounds he suffered. Lee, meanwhile, struck repeatedly at the Federals and drove the enemy back across the Rappahannock after three long days of fighting.

CHANCELLORSVILLE VISITOR CENTER TO GERMANNA FORD
From the Chancellorsville Visitor Center, turn right (west) onto Va. 3 and go 9.3 miles west, through

the traffic signal at Va. Highway 20, to the Rapidan River crossing. After crossing the river bridge, make a U-turn and return east on divided highway Va. 3, cross the river and turn right (south) just before the entrance to Germanna Community College.

Germanna Ford
Orange County, Va.

At this point on the Rapidan River, Union forces crossed on May 4, 1864, prior to the battle at the Wilderness. A small kiosk has information on this important river ford and its role in the Civil War.

GERMANNA FORD TO THE WILDERNESS EXHIBIT SHELTER
Continue east on Va. 3 for 4.8 miles back to the traffic signal at Va. 20. Turn right (west) on Va. 20 and go 1.7 miles to the Wilderness Exhibit Shelter on the right.

Wilderness Exhibit Shelter
Orange County, Va.

The wooded area near the Spotsylvania-Orange county line was so thick it became known as the Wilderness. The trees in the Wilderness were literally set on fire by the volume of bullets fired through them in early May 1864 when CSA Gen. Lee met USA Gen. Ulysses S. Grant in the Battle of the Wilderness. This was the first of the many renowned encounters between these two military titans. The opposing armies fought along the Orange Turnpike (present-day Va. 20) for the better part of two days. Fighting to a draw, with no land changing hands, USA Gen. Grant moved his army southeast toward the Spotsylvania County Courthouse. Having suffered more than 17,000 casualties, Grant wept. Lee suffered about half that amount.

The Wilderness Exhibit Shelter is exactly that: a covered shelter with a display exhibiting the details of the Wilderness battle.

WILDERNESS TO SPOTSYLVANIA COURTHOUSE
From the Wilderness Exhibit Shelter, continue west on Va. 20 for 0.1 mile, then turn left (south) on Hill-Ewell Drive. Continue south 3.3 miles to Va. Highway 621 (Orange Plank Road), turn left (east) and go 0.7 miles to the intersection with Va. Highway 613 (Brock Road). This point is known as the Brock Road-Plank Road intersection. Turn right (south) on Va. 613 (Brock Road) and go 8.5 miles to the Spotsylvania Exhibit Shelter.

Spotsylvania Exhibit Shelter
Spotsylvania Courthouse, Va.

"Fight it out on this line if it takes all summer," wrote USA Gen. Ulysses S. Grant to his chief of staff, USA Gen. Henry Wagner Halleck. The phrase was part of a communication written May 11, 1864, from Spotsylvania. Grant was determined to move on to Richmond despite the heavy losses his army received at this old county courthouse. Both armies dug in at the courthouse after the Wilderness. The day after Grant wrote Halleck, two Union corps charged Confederates in a dense fog. The Southerners had wet gunpowder, enabling the Union soldiers to complete a successful initial assault. Confederate reinforcements moved in, and the opposing troops fought a fierce, 20-hour battle, often resorting to hand-to-hand combat. Much of this fighting took place at the now famous "Bloody Angle." Grant abandoned the field on May 21. Visitors to the exhibit shelter will see a story plaque with information on the battle.

SPOTSYLVANIA EXHIBIT SHELTER TO MASSAPONAX CHURCH
From the Spotsylvania Exhibit Shelter, continue south on Va. 613 (Brock Road) for 1.8 miles to Spotsylvania Courthouse. Continue past the courthouse on Va. 613 for 0.7 mile, turn left (east) on Va. Highway 608 (Massaponax Church Road) and drive 4.7 miles

Wilderness Personality: USA Gen. Ulysses S. Grant

Ulysses Simpson Grant was born in April 1822 at Point Pleasant, Ohio, a community east of Cincinnati just across the Ohio River from Kentucky. His father, tanner Jesse Root Grant, and his mother, the former Hannah Simpson, baptized him Hiram Ulysses Grant. Later, when he registered as a young cadet at U.S. Military Academy at West Point, he inverted his name — to Ulysses Hiram Grant — because he thought the initials "H.U.G." would be ridiculed. Days later, he learned his congressman had listed his name as Ulysses Simpson Grant, which erroneously incorporated his mother's maiden name, so Grant lived with the name change.

He was the best horseman at West Point, but nothing else distinguished him at the service academy. He asked for a commission in the cavalry, but there were no vacancies,

Photo: Library of Virginia

USA Gen. Ulysses S. Grant matched wits with CSA Gen. Robert E. Lee in Spotsylvania's bloody battles.

so he ended up in the infantry. During the Mexican War, Grant served with two distinguished generals, Zachary Taylor and Winfield Scott, both of whom were Virginia natives. Later, stationed in California, Grant survived dreary military conditions alone and took up drinking. Chastised by his commanding officer for consuming alcohol in excess, Grant resigned his commission. Ironically, his resignation was accepted by the Secretary of War, Jefferson Davis, the future president of the Confederacy.

Following a decade of insignificant business dealings, Grant rejoined the U.S. Army at the outbreak of the Civil War and was sent to duty in Missouri and Illinois. Slowly, Grant worked his way up the Army hierarchy and saw extensive action in the Western Theater. In spring 1864, President Lincoln promoted Grant general-in-chief of the Union Army. It was left to Grant to establish a concerted effort of all Union forces. He set about a three-pronged attack against the Confederates — USA Gen. George Meade's Army of the Potomac against CSA Gen. Robert E. Lee; USA Gen. Benjamin Butler's Army of the James against Confederate communications and Richmond; and USA Gen. William Tecumseh Sherman's Army of Tennessee against Atlanta and CSA Gen. Joseph Johnston's army.

Grant himself took up headquarters with the Army of the Potomac and encountered his first head-on collision with Lee at the Wilderness. A year later in April 1865, Grant accepted a surrender from Lee at Appomattox. Three years after Appomattox, Grant gave up a comfortable Army position and its $25,000 annual salary to enter politics. He was the Republican party's nominee for the presidency, and he took the electoral votes of all but eight states. Grant's White House was filled with a number of his military cronies. His father-in-law, Col. Frederick Dent, an unreconstructed Southerner, visited often.

Grant served two terms as president, took his family on a two-year whirlwind tour of Europe and settled in New York City. Overcome by throat cancer, he earned an income writing his personal memoirs, which he finished just before he died. He was buried in a granite mausoleum on New York's Riverside Drive. President Abraham Lincoln once summed up Grant's service, simply saying, "He fights".

to the intersection with U.S. 1 and the Massaponax Baptist Church on the left.

This section of Va. 608, from the Spotsylvania Courthouse to Massaponax Church, is the route taken by CSA Gen. "Stonewall" Jackson's ambulance wagon when it transported him from the Chancellorsville area to Guinea Station.

Massaponax Baptist Church
Spotsylvania, Va.

Massaponax (Mass-ah-pon-ex) Baptist Church was built just before the Civil War on the main route between Richmond and Washington — present-day U.S. 1. Thus, the church was on the path of major troop movements by both armies. A famous Civil War photograph shows USA Gen. Ulysses Grant and several of his officers sitting on church pews in the yard at Massaponax Church. The church is still used for Sunday services, but it is not open as a tourist attraction.

MASSAPONAX CHURCH TO STONEWALL JACKSON SHRINE
From the intersection of U.S. 1 and Va. 608, turn right (south, away from Fredericksburg) on U.S. 1, go 0.6 mile to Va. Highway 607 and turn left (east). Drive 3.6 miles to the point where Va. 607 curves right, continue an additional 2.1 miles to Va. Highway 606, turn left (east), cross the railroad tracks and turn immediately left into Jackson Shrine.

This was the continuation of the route used by CSA Gen. "Stonewall" Jackson's ambulance wagon when it transported the general to Guinea Station after Chancellorsville.

Along this route, the tour enters Caroline County. The county was established in 1727 and named for Caroline of Anspach, the consort of England's King George II.

Stonewall Jackson Shrine
Guinea Station, Caroline County, Va.

After being accidentally wounded at Chancellorsville on May 2, 1863, CSA Gen. "Stonewall" Jackson was removed to a field hospital near Wilderness Tavern to have his arm amputated. Two days later, he was taken overland by an ambulance wagon to the house at Guinea Station (then known as Guiney's Station) on the RF&P (Richmond, Fredericksburg and Potomac) Railroad. Jackson was placed in a field office. His wounds were complicated by pneumonia, and he died at Guinea Station on May 10.

The Jackson Shrine is open 9 AM to 5 PM every day except Wednesday and Thursday. The shrine offers walking tours, living history talks and other interpretive programs. There is no admission, but a variety of Civil War history publications are available for purchase. The site has picnic tables and restrooms, and it is handicapped-accessible.

This tour route ends at Guinea Station. Return to Spotsylvania via Va. 606, Va. 607, U.S. 1 or I-95. This back-track is clearly marked.

Spotsylvania Tour Ends

Other Tour Points of Interest

Annual Events

During the entire month of May, take in

Spotsylvania Personalities: Mountain Rifles

The Mountain Rifles was a unique Confederate unit. Mustered in 1861 at Green Bank in Pocahontas County, West Virginia, its 100-plus recruits were all over 6-feet tall. Most of these mountaineer giants were killed at the Bloody Angle at Spotsylvania Courthouse.

Feel the Fury, a walking and riding living history with soldiers who served at Chancellorsville, Wilderness and Spotsylvania. Tours are by reservation, and there is a $20 hourly fee with a minimum of two hours. Also enjoy *Return to Spotsylvania*, a living history program that is held the last weekend of May each year. The program features authentic camps, a working field hospital, a skirmish, period entertainment and a service at the Spotsylvania Confederate Cemetery on Sunday. For more information, call (540) 582-1016. There is no fee, but donations are requested.

Attractions

Lake Anna State Park offers 13,000 scenic acres for sailing, canoeing, waterskiing and sport fishing, not to mention a beach for sun worshippers and trails for hikers. The park is adjacent to Va. Highway 601 off Va. Highway 208, about 15 miles south of Fredericksburg. In addition, take in the **Lake Anna Winery**, located in a renovated barn on Courthouse Road (Va. 208) 13 miles southwest of Fredericksburg near Lake Anna State Park. The winery offers tours and tastings on Sunday from 1 to 7 PM and Wednesday through Saturday from 11 AM to 5 PM. For more information, call (540) 895-5085.

Shopping

Suburban shoppers converge at **Spotsylvania Mall**, just west of I-95 on Va. 3 (Plank Road). Value shoppers go to Southpoint, just off I-95 at exit 126-B, to the **Massaponax Outlet Center**, which offers a wide variety of discount outlet stores.

Guinea Station Personality:
CSA Gen. Thomas J. "Stonewall" Jackson

Thomas Jackson was born January 21, 1824, near Clarksburg, Virginia, which is in present-day West Virginia. He was the third child and second son of Julia Beckwith Neale Jackson (T-8) and lawyer Jonathan Jackson. Tom's parents died in poverty while he was still young, and he was raised by an uncle, Cummins Jackson. As a young adult, Thomas honored his late father by taking Jonathan as his middle name.

One of the most noted Southern generals, Jackson was nicknamed "Stonewall." It was at the Battle of 1st Manassas in July 1861 (see T-8: Manassas), during an attempt to rally Southern troops, that CSA Gen. Barnard Elliott Bee spotted an arriving Confederate brigade led by Gen. Jackson. Pointing to Jackson, Bee yelled to his soldiers: "There stands Jackson like a stone wall! Rally behind the Virginians."

On April 20, 1863, in the midst of an afternoon downpour at Guinea Station south of Fredericksburg, CSA Gen. Jackson rushed aboard the train from Richmond to greet his family. The general's wife, Anna, traveled from her parent's home in North Carolina for him to see their 5-month-old daughter, Julia, for the first time. Jackson was excited to see his "little angel." He had been orphaned at age 7 and spent his youth crisscrossing Virginia, living with relatives and dreaming of a family of his own. Young Julia was named for his late mother. After being shot by friendly fire at the Battle of Chancellorsville, Jackson was taken to the rail head, where he developed pneumonia. On May 9, 1863, the general called for his little Julia, and his wife and daughter returned to be at his side. He caressed Julia with his wounded right hand and prayed while the little girl cooed. Jackson died the next day. Julia Jackson grew up, married a Richmond newspaperman, William Edmund Christian, and had a son and a daughter. She died at the age of 27, leaving her mother to raise the two children. (See more on Jackson in T-5, T-11 and T-17.)

Tour 17
Richmond

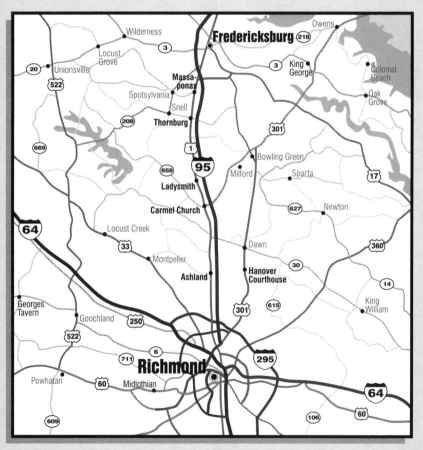

TOUR 17
Richmond

About This Tour

This tour route is a natural continuation of Tour 16: Spotsylvania. It begins outside Fredericksburg, Virginia, and ends in Richmond, Virginia. We suggest you plan staying the night and dining in the Richmond area. Chapter 22 has a list of suggested accommodations, and Chapter 23 has some good options for dining. It's a good idea to review these recommendations before traveling the tour route. For a complete, comprehensive guide to the city, including attractions, shopping, nightlife, history, kidstuff, and much more, pick up a copy of *The Insiders' Guide® to Greater Richmond*. In addition to our suggestions, there are the expected fast-food eateries, gas stations and various shops along the Interstate 95 corridor between Fredericksburg and Richmond.

Richmond is located at the James River on the "fall zone," which separates Virginia's coastal plain from the rolling Piedmont area. It was named by William Byrd II after the borough of Richmond, England. Byrd himself laid out the village in 1737. More than 40 years later, in 1779, Richmond was designated the Virginia state capital. Richmond experienced action during the American Revolution.

In 1785, the James River Company was established for the purpose of building a 200-mile canal from Richmond to the Appalachian highlands. George Washington was honorary president of the effort that later became known as the James River and Kanawha Canal project. Chief Justice John Marshall was a longtime resident of Richmond, which was the site of Aaron Burr's famous treason trial in 1807.

Richmond was the primary objective of the Union army for four years. Their cry was "On to Richmond!" After all, Richmond was the Confederate capital, and it served as the South's main manufacturing and medical center. The supply depots in Richmond served the entire Eastern Theater. Twice, Union forces advanced dangerously close to the Capitol. There was USA Gen. George Brinton McClellan's Peninsula Campaign (T-18, T-19) and USA Gen. Ulysses S. Grant's assault in 1864. Barely a business or residence in Richmond escaped the horrors of war.

Today, the state capital is rich in Civil War heritage, but business and government leaders spend too much time debating their differences, such as what to promote and how. As a result, this former Confederate capital lacks a cohesive strategy for developing and promoting its Civil War history. As of now, and until a cooperative spirit emerges, the Civil War traveler is the one that suffers.

Travel Tips

I-95 is the main artery of the busy north-south corridor of Virginia that stretches along the fall zone. Be on the lookout for heavy, fast-moving traffic along this major interstate route. If I-95 seems particularly congested, try U.S. Highway 1 (Jefferson Davis Highway) as an alternative. U.S. 1 runs parallel to I-95. Richmond radio stations can keep you up-to-date on traffic and weather conditions. Citizens band radio users can find traffic information on Channel 19. State police usually monitor Channel 9. Motorists receive a strong mobile telephone signal throughout the Fredericksburg and Richmond vicinity.

Richmond Tour Begins . . .

Driving south from the Fredericksburg area, the I-95 cor-

ridor to Richmond has a number of historical sites related to the Civil War. The first location of note is Ladysmith, on U.S. 1, just off exit 110.

Ladysmith, Va.

Confederate troops often camped near Ladysmith as they traveled either north or south during the war. It is in Caroline County, which was established in 1727 and named for Caroline of Anspach, consort of England's King George II.

The statue of Robert E. Lee was the first to be erected on Monument Avenue.

LADYSMITH TO CARMEL CHURCH

Continue south on I-95 to exit 104 and follow the signs for Carmel Church. Off the exit ramp at Va. Highway 207, turn right (west), go 0.4 mile and cross U.S. 1, then immediately turn left into the Carmel Church parking area.

Carmel Church
Caroline County, Va.

USA Gen. Ulysses S. Grant moved through the area in May 1864, taking Confederate earthworks and establishing his headquarters in the church. Following the Battle of North Anna River, just to the south of Carmel Church, Union forces moved in the church vicinity prior to maneuvering toward Cold Harbor, northeast of Richmond. The church still has an active body of worshippers today.

Photo: Library of Virginia

CARMEL CHURCH TO OX FORD BATTLEFIELD (NORTH ANNA)

Continue south on U.S. 1 for 4.5 miles, turn right on Va. Highway 684 and go 2.5 miles to Ox Ford Park on the right. Follow the entrance road a half-mile to the parking area.

Ox Ford Battlefield
Hanover County, Va.

A small county park commemorates the Battle of Ox Ford, which was fought on the nearby North Anna River in May 1864. USA Gen. Grant, moving south after Spotsylvania Courthouse, struck Confederate troops under CSA Gen. Robert E. Lee, who was entrenched at Hanover Junction to the south. The Northern and Southern armies suffered equal losses, but the Federals withdrew without success.

The Ox Ford Battlefield Park is not staffed and is open only during daylight hours. A walking trail of about 1 mile leads to the North Anna River, where a small kiosk has an illustration and some general information on the small battle. For more detailed information and a park map, contact the Hanover Visitors Center in Ashland, Virginia, (804) 752-6766.

The North Anna River forms the boundary

of Caroline and Hanover counties. Hanover County was established in 1720 and named for England's King George I, who was an elector of Hanover in Germany.

OX FORD BATTLEFIELD TO OLD HANOVER JUNCTION
Return on Va. 684 to U.S. 1, turn right (south) and go 0.4 mile to Va. Highway 688 (Doswell Road). Turn left (east) on Doswell Road and go 0.3 mile to Old Hanover Junction.

Old Hanover Junction
Hanover County, Va.

This site was an important railroad junction of two Confederate rail lines — the Richmond, Fredericksburg and Potomac (RF&P), which ran north to Fredericksburg, and the Virginia Central, which ran west to Louisa and Orange counties. This critical junction was where CSA Gen. Lee established his troops to

thwart a southern movement by USA Gen. Grant just prior to the Battle of Ox Ford. Lee nearly trapped Grant during this two-day action in May 1864. Today, the Hanover Junction community, called Doswell, has a small collection of attractive old homes.

HANOVER JUNCTION TO ASHLAND, VA.
Return on Doswell Road to U.S. 1, turn left (south) and go 7.2 miles to the intersection of Va. Highway 54 (England Street) in Ashland, Virginia.

Ashland, Va.

Both CSA Gen. Thomas J. "Stonewall" Jackson and CSA Gen. James Ewell Brown "Jeb" Stuart camped in the Ashland vicinity in June 1862.

ASHLAND TO ASHLAND VISITORS CENTER
At U.S. 1 and the Va. 54 intersec-

Hanover County Personality: Henry Clay

Five miles east of Ashland is the birthplace of Kentucky statesman Henry Clay. Clay was born on April 12, 1777, during the earlier days of the American Revolution. Clay traced his family roots to English settlers who arrived in the Virginia colony shortly after the Jamestown settlement. The area of his birthplace in Hanover County was known as "the Slashes" — a term describing wet, swampy terrain that often is overgrown with scrub pines and bushes. With the aid of his stepfather, Henry Watkins, Clay took a job in 1792 in Richmond, where he soon caught the attention of jurist George Wythe.

By 1797, Clay was practicing law and feeling the lure of the new state of Kentucky. Settling in Lexington, he became a prominent criminal lawyer and quickly climbed the ladder of political success. In 1803, at the age of 26, he was elected to the Kentucky legislature. Three years later he was elected to the U.S. Senate to fill the unexpired term of John Adair, taking office in November despite being younger than the minimum Constitutional age limit of 30. In and out of both houses of Congress, including a tenure as Speaker of the House of Representatives, Clay also was secretary of state under President John Quincy Adams and an unsuccessful candidate for president in 1824, 1832 and 1844.

Clay was the chief architect of the Compromise of 1850 (see our "Prelude to War"), and for this he became known as the Great Compromiser. He also was known, at various times, as the Mill Boy of the Slashes, Prince Hal (for having a personality similar to Shakespeare's King Henry V), Harry of the West and the Great Pacificator (for his efforts to wrangle peaceful relations among his fellow legislators). Clay died in Washington, D.C., on June 29, 1852, and funeral services were held in the old U.S. Senate chambers.

*tion, turn right (west) on Va. 54
(England Street) and go 0.5 mile
to N. Railroad Avenue. Turn right
on N. Railroad Avenue and go 0.1
mile and cross over the western
side of the railroad tracks to the
Ashland Visitors Center (railroad
depot) at 112 N. Railroad Avenue.*

Ashland Visitors Center
112 N. Railroad Ave., Ashland, Va.
• (804) 752-6766
The small community visitors center in Ashland is in the railroad depot, situated adjacent to the railroad tracks. The railroad runs through the heart of Ashland, adding to the community's charm. Several nice homes and businesses are situated along both sides of the tracks in the downtown vicinity. The visitors center offers travel information and recommendations for lodging and dining and has restrooms. The facility is operated by the town of Ashland, Hanover County and the area chamber of commerce. It is open 9 AM to 5 PM every day except major holidays. The depot is handicapped accessible except for a small step at the depot-visitor center front door.

ASHLAND TO YELLOW TAVERN, STUART MONUMENT
From the Ashland Visitors Center, continue south on S. Railroad Avenue-S. Center Street for 0.9 mile, along the western side of the railroad tracks, to Ashcake Road (Va. Highway 657). Turn left (east), go 0.8 mile to U.S. 1 (Washington Highway), turn right (south) and go 5.5 miles to Virginia Center Parkway. Turn left (east), go 0.5 mile to Telegraph Road, turn right and go 0.2 mile to the monument on the right.

Yellow Tavern, Stuart Monument
Henrico County, Va.
Yellow Tavern was a stop on the main thoroughfare (present-day U.S. 1) between Richmond and Fredericksburg. On May 12, 1864, CSA cavalry Gen. "Jeb" Stuart was shot here by a Union marksman. Stuart died in Richmond the next day of the wound he received. A monument to Stuart was dedicated in June 1888 by Virginia Gov. Fitzhugh Lee, a Civil

Hanover County Personality: USA Lt. Thomas Farrell

A historic Southern church, destroyed by Confederate cannon fire in 1864, may be rebuilt from the sketches of Union spy and artist Thomas Farrell.

Hanover County's Polegreen (or Pole Green) Church, built in the 1740s, was the home pulpit of Samuel Davies, a Presbyterian who protested against the Virginia colony's church policies. In 1862, Farrell was a young Union Navy lieutenant and busy at work on a spying mission in Hanover Courthouse, drawing sketches in preparation of USA Gen. George McClellan's pending Peninsula Campaign. Farrell, 17, was President Lincoln's bodyguard at the beginning of the Civil War.

USA Lt. Farrell sketched the Hanover landscape and took time to draw a few exterior and interior scenes of Polegreen Church. But his efforts were useless, because the Union never struck Hanover during the campaign. In 1864, the historic church was struck instead by Confederate cannon fire during the Battle of Cold Harbor. It burned to the ground. William S. White, a member of the 3rd Richmond Howitzers during the June 1864 battle, wrote in his diary that it was his cannon that struck the famous, simple, box-shaped church.

In the early 1990s, a printer found Farrell's faded church sketches in a grocery bag stored in the basement of the Philadelphia row house owned by the printer's grandfather. Now the artwork may fulfill a purpose. The Polegreen Foundation plans to use the drawings as part of an effort to rebuild the historic building.

The White House of the Confederacy was the home of
CSA President Jefferson Davis during the war.

War veteran himself. The monument is just 30 feet from the place where the cavalry general was shot.

Stuart was born in Virginia on February 6, 1833. Known by his West Point classmates as Beauty, the handsome Confederate officer had a long beard that concealed his youthful image. He was just 31 when he died.

YELLOW TAVERN, STUART MONUMENT TO METRO RICHMOND VISITOR CENTER

From Yellow Tavern, Stuart Monu-

ment, backtrack on Telegraph Road and Virginia Center Parkway to U.S. 1, turn left and go 0.1 mile to Interstate 295. Follow the signs for Richmond from I-295 to I-95. Continue on I-95 for 11 miles to exit 78, Boulevard. Turn right (west) on Boulevard, then turn left (south) at the first traffic signal at Robin Hood Road, adjacent to the stadium complex. Go 0.1 mile to the Metro Richmond Visitor Center on the left.

Richmond Personality: CSA Capt. Sally L. Tompkins

Sally Louisa Tompkins, a native of Mathews County in Tidewater Virginia, was just 28 years old when the Civil War erupted. In 1861, Sally converted a private home into a hospital to treat Confederate soldiers. She used her own money to equip and maintain the house throughout the four-year war.

Confederate President Jefferson Davis gave Tompkins a cavalry officer's commission in order to retain her work after his government took control of Southern hospitals for military use. "Captain Sally," the only woman commissioned in the Confederate Army, served without officer's pay and retained her captain rank until she died in Richmond in July 1916. She was buried with full military honors.

Metro Richmond Visitor Center
1710 Robin Hood Rd., Richmond, Va.
• **(804) 358-5511**

This visitors center is operated by the Metro Richmond Convention and Visitor Bureau, and it offers brochures and maps on attractions, lodging, dining and shopping in the greater Richmond area. The center occasionally offers special discount rates for some accommodations. Specialty gifts and souvenirs are sold at the center. The center is open daily from 9 AM to 5 PM except for major holidays. Hours are extended in the summer months. It is handicapped-accessible, and there are restrooms.

METRO RICHMOND VISITOR CENTER TO MONUMENT AVENUE
From the Metro Richmond Visitor Center, backtrack on Robin Hood Road to Boulevard, turn left (west) and go 1 mile to Monument Avenue.

Monument Avenue

Designed in 1889, Monument Avenue is a leading symbol of Richmond's heritage. The broad avenue offers an architecturally diverse mix of Classic Revival buildings, constructed in harmony with rows of maples and oaks. Since 1907, the roadway has been paved in asphalt block. The avenue has provided a ceremonial entry to downtown Richmond, with such notables as William Howard Taft, Winston Churchill and Charles Lindbergh entering the city by this boulevard. Here's a list of the six significant monuments along the avenue:

Boulevard leads directly to Monument Avenue and a statue of **CSA Gen. Thomas J. "Stonewall" Jackson**. This statue was unveiled in 1919.

From Boulevard, turn right (north) and go 0.2 mile to N. Belmont Avenue. At the intersection is a monument to oceanographer **Matthew Fontaine Maury**, known as the "Pathfinder of the Sea" (See more on Maury in T-10: Charlottesville and T-5: Lexington). The statue was dedicated in 1929. Maury, a Civil War veteran, taught at Virginia Military Insti-

tute after the war. He is buried in Hollywood Cemetery in Richmond.

From N. Belmont Avenue, continue north on Monument Avenue to Rosneath Road. At the intersection is a statue of tennis legend **Arthur Ashe**, a Richmonder. The Ashe statue, unveiled in 1996, is the first on Monument Avenue to honor an African American and a non-Confederate hero. The statue caused some controversy in Richmond.

At Rosneath Road, make a U-turn and backtrack south on divided Monument Avenue. Go 0.2 miles south of the statue of CSA Gen. Thomas J. "Stonewall" Jackson to Davis Avenue. At Davis Avenue is a monument to **CSA President Jefferson Davis**. The statue of Davis was designed by Richmond's Edward Virginius Valentine and unveiled in 1907. The statue is near the location of the northern edge of the outer defenses of Richmond during the Civil War. Valentine's studio was on E. Clay Street, site of the present-day Valentine Museum. Valentine also designed the statue of Thomas Jefferson in the lobby of the Hotel Jefferson in Richmond.

From Davis Avenue, continue south on Monument Avenue for 0.4 mile to Allen Avenue. At Allen Avenue is a monument to **CSA Gen. Robert E. Lee**. A 60-foot monument, it has a simple inscription: "Lee." It was unveiled in 1890, when the area was an open field. During the Civil War, Lee's family rented a house in downtown Richmond.

From Allen Avenue continue south on Monument Avenue for 0.2 mile to Lombardy Street. At Lombardy Street is a monument to **CSA Gen. J.E.B. "Jeb" Stuart**, who was considered the best cavalry officer in America. He was just 31 when he was wounded at the battle of Yellow Tavern north of Richmond in Hanover County. He died the next day at his brother-in-law's home on nearby Grace Street. The statue was dedicated in 1907.

MONUMENT AVENUE TO ST. PAUL'S CHURCH
From Boulevard and Monument Avenue, go south on Monument Avenue, which becomes Franklin Street as it winds through the campus of Virginia Commonwealth

ASSOCIATION FOR THE PRESERVATION
OF VIRGINIA ANTIQUITIES

Founded in 1889, our association was the first statewide preservation organization in the nation. Today, thanks to the continuing efforts of our members, a rich heritage is yours to share. A part of our effort is devoted to Civil War history. Join the APVA — the foundation on which America was built.

204 W. Franklin Street
Richmond, Va. 23220

(804) 648-1889
email: apva@apva.org

Monument Avenue Side Trip: Virginia Historical Society

From the intersection of Boulevard and Monument Avenue, take the Boulevard east two blocks to the Virginia Historical Society on the right. Parking is available in front of the society building.

Virginia Historical Society

The Virginia Historical Society, 428 N. Boulevard, is the oldest continually operating cultural institution in Virginia, and it has the largest collection of materials related to Virginia history anywhere. It boasts more than 7 million processed manuscripts, more than 125,000 books, 5,000 maps and nearly 800 portraits. Founded in 1831, the society conducts programs, conferences and lectures around the state for schools, museums, libraries and local historical societies. In addition, it has sponsored more than 100 teacher recertification workshops, seminars and conferences in the past three years.

The state headquarters, built in 1912 and refurbished in 1992, was originally a memorial to the Confederate soldier. Battle Abby, as the building is sometimes called, is well-known for its monumental murals called "Seasons of the Confederacy." These were developed by Frenchman Charles Hoffbauer in the 1920s. A fee of $4 for adults, $3 for seniors and $2 for students is charged for non-members. The society is open Sunday from 1 to 5 PM and Monday through Saturday from 10 AM to 5 PM. Access for the handicapped is provided through a separate entrance on the building's south side. Call (804) 358-4901 for more information.

Belvidere Street Side Trip: Hollywood Cemetery

At N. Belvidere Street, turn right (south) and go 0.5 mile to Spring Street. Turn right (west), go three blocks, turn right (north) on Cherry Street and go one block to the entrance to Hollywood Cemetery at 412 S. Cherry Street.

Note that the route to Hollywood Cemetery is through a neighborhood that, while appearing unkempt, is safe. Remember, though, to practice safety precautions while motoring in the area.

Hollywood Cemetery, (804) 648-8501, is an elegant cemetery established in 1847 and named for its prolific holly trees. More than 100 acres, the cemetery includes the burial site of CSA President Jefferson Davis and his family, and CSA Gen. "Jeb" Stuart and CSA Gen. George Edward Pickett. Two Virginia-born U.S. presidents, James Monroe and John Tyler, are buried here as well. More than 18,000 Confederate soldiers are buried in Hollywood Cemetery including many who were removed from Gettysburg. There is no admission fee. The cemetery is open Monday through Saturday from 7 AM to 6 PM and on Sunday from 8 AM to 6 PM.

Leaving Hollywood Cemetery, backtrack to Belvidere and the intersection with Franklin Street.

University. Continue on Monument Avenue-Franklin Street for 0.6 mile to N. Belvidere Street.

N. BELVIDERE STREET TO ST. PAUL'S CHURCH

At N. Belvidere Street, return to Franklin Street, turn right (east), go 1 mile, turn left (north) on Ninth Street and go one block to the intersection of Ninth and E. Grace streets. St. Paul's Church is at this intersection. Pay parking is available in various lots within a one-block radius of the church.

St. Paul's Episcopal Church
815 E. Grace St., Richmond, Va.
• (804) 643-3589

CSA President Jefferson Davis and CSA Gen. Lee attended this Episcopal church of Greek Revival architecture, so it became known as the Cathedral of the Confederacy. During worship services the first Sunday in April 1865, Davis received a note that Lee's lines were broken at Petersburg — the Confederate president was advised to evacuate Richmond immediately. Today the church has a large, active congregation. Pews used by both Davis and Lee are marked. The church is open daily from 10 AM to 4 PM. A brief church tour is offered each Sunday following the 11 AM worship service. St. Paul's Church is across the street from Capitol Square, the site of the Virginia State Capitol.

ST. PAUL'S CHURCH TO THE VIRGINIA STATE CAPITOL
Walk across Ninth Street to Capitol Square.

Virginia State Capitol
Capitol Square, Richmond, Va.
• (804) 786-4344

The Virginia State Capitol was the headquarters of the Confederacy. This is the meeting place of the Virginia General Assembly, the oldest lawmaking body in the Western hemisphere. The building was designed by Thomas Jefferson, while he was minister to France. For his model, Jefferson chose La Maison Carree, a Roman temple built in Nimes, France, in the first century of the Christian era. He called the structure "the best morsel of ancient architecture now remaining." The Capitol cornerstone was laid in August 1785, and the assembly held its first session in the state's third capital city in 1788.

The portico was added in 1790, and the walls were stuccoed in 1800. The marble statue of George Washington in the Capitol's rotunda, sculpted by Jean Antoine Houdoun, is considered one of the most precious statues in the nation. The Hall of the House of Delegates was restored in 1929. It contains numerous pieces of statuary, including depictions of CSA Gens. "Stonewall" Jackson, "Jeb" Stuart, Joseph E. Johnston and Fitzhugh Lee. There is also a statue of Matthew Fontaine Maury and busts of CSA President Davis and CSA Vice President Alexander H. Stephens.

The statuary on the Capitol grounds include statues of CSA Gen. "Stonewall" Jackson; Dr. Hunter Holmes McGuire, the surgeon who served as Jackson's medical director (see T-2: Harpers Ferry); and William "Extra Billy" Smith, a brigadier general in the Confederacy and governor of Virginia during the Civil War. The statue of Jackson was the first Confederate hero's monument erected in Richmond. Also on the Capitol grounds is another statue of George Washington. CSA President Davis delivered his inaugural address from this statue. The old bell tower on the Capitol grounds was completed in 1824.

Next door, the Executive Mansion has been the official residence of Virginia governors since 1813. It is the oldest continuously occupied governor's residence in the nation. The body of Jackson was taken to the Executive Mansion to lie in state after the general's death in May 1863.

Capitol tours are given on Sunday from 1 to 5 PM and Monday through Saturday from 9 AM to 5 PM. Groups are asked to make reservations. The Executive Mansion also offers tours, but hours vary, and reservations are required. For more information on tours of the governor's residence call (804) 371-2642.

VIRGINIA STATE CAPITOL TO THE LIBRARY OF VIRGINIA

Walk from the Virginia State Capitol to the Library of Virginia on E. Broad Street at Capitol Square. If you choose to drive to the library, park along E. Broad Street or in public parking lots in the vicinity.

Library of Virginia

E. Broad and Ninth Sts., Richmond, Va.
• **(804) 786-8929**

This library has a vast collection of books and artifacts. In addition, it frequently offers exhibits on various Virginia history topics. The library has an extensive collection of state government records, including those related to the Civil War.

LIBRARY OF VIRGINIA TO MUSEUM AND WHITE HOUSE OF THE CONFEDERACY

Return to your car, and from Broad Street continue north on Ninth Street for three blocks, turn right (east) on Leigh Street and go three blocks, turn right (south) on Twelfth Street and drive two blocks to Clay Street. Turn left (east) on Clay Street and go a half-block to the Museum of the Confederacy. Park in the lot at the end of Clay Street.

Museum and White House of the Confederacy

1201 E. Clay St., Richmond, Va.
• **(804) 649-1861**

The Museum and the White House of the Confederacy are in Richmond's historic Court End district. Clay Street is a gorgeous site amid the tall, overpowering structures of the Medical College of Virginia. The Museum of the Confederacy offers self-guided tours of exhibits on the South's role in the Civil War. The museum has CSA Gen. E. Lee's surrender sword from Appomattox, CSA Gen. "Jeb" Stuart's plumed hat and the coat worn by CSA President Davis when he was captured in 1865. The museum's collection of Civil War art includes the original oil titled *The Last Meeting of Lee and Jackson*. The museum is open

Monday through Saturday from 10 AM to 5 PM and Sunday from noon to 5 PM. It is open every day except New Year's Day, Thanksgiving and Christmas. Dual admission to the museum and the White House is $8 for adults, $7 for seniors and $5 for children 7 to 17. The museum has a small gift shop.

MUSEUM OF THE CONFEDERACY TO CHURCH HILL NEIGHBORHOOD
From the Museum of the Confederacy at 12th and Clay streets, go south on 12th Street two blocks, turn left (east) on E. Broad Street, drive 0.7 mile and turn right (south) on 23rd Street. Proceed one block to E. Grace Street, turn left (east) and go to the Beleview School in the 2300 block of E. Grace Street in the Church Hill neighborhood. The school is on the right (south) side of E. Grace Street and occupies the site where Elizabeth Van Lew lived during the Civil War.

Church Hill Neighborhood
E. Grace St., Richmond, Va.

Beleview School sits on a bluff overlooking the James River. Few visitors realize the school once was the site of the home of Elizabeth Van Lew — alias "Crazy Bet" and "Miss Lizzie" — a Union spy during the Civil War. Van Lew was from a well-known Richmond

family. She was called Crazy Bet because she is said to have acted rather nutty, probably to disguise her spy work. She frequently helped Northern soldiers escape Richmond during the war. After the war, Van Lew was appointed Postmistress of Richmond by President Ulysses Grant. She is buried in Richmond.

VAN LEW HOMESITE TO CONFEDERATE SOLDIERS AND SAILORS MONUMENT
From Beleview School continue east on Grace Street for five blocks to 29th Street.

Note that at the intersection of 24th and E. Grace streets, between E. Grace and E. Broad streets, is St. John's Church. This was the site of Patriot Patrick Henry's famous "Give me liberty" speech. The church is a popular Richmond tourist attraction.

From E. Grace and 29th streets, turn right (south) on 29th Street and go two blocks to the Confederate Soldiers and Sailors Monument.

Confederate Soldiers and Sailors Monument
29th St., Richmond, Va.

The Confederate Soldiers and Sailors Monument is the centerpiece of Libby Hill Park in Richmond's far east end. The monument,

Virginia State Capitol Personality: CSA Gen. Robert E. Lee

The Virginia secession convention was held in the Virginia State Capitol in 1861, and CSA Gen. Robert E. Lee appeared before the session to accept command of the armed forces of Virginia. CSA Gen. Lee delivered a brief speech in accepting his command, saying:

"Mr. President and Gentlemen of the Convention. Profoundly impressed with the solemnity of the occasion, for which I must say I was not prepared, I accept the position assigned me by our partiality. I would have much preferred had your choice fallen on an abler man. Trusting in Almighty God, an approving conscience, and the aid of my fellow-citizens, I devote myself to the service of my native State, in whose behalf alone will I ever again draw my sword."

Lee's remarks are inscribed on the base of his statue in the old Hall of the House in the Capitol.

Virginia State Capitol Side Trip: Tredegar, Belle Isle

From Ninth and Grace streets, take Grace Street west one block to Eighth Street, turn left (south) and go four blocks to Canal Street, turn right (west) and go three blocks. Turn left (south) on Fifth Street, drive one block to Byrd Street, turn left (east) and go two blocks to Seventh Street. Turn right (south) on Seventh Street and go 0.5 mile, following the signs for Belle Isle parking lot. On the way to the parking area is the site of the old Tredegar Iron Works.

Old Tredegar Iron Works

The Tredegar Iron Works was owned by Joseph Reid Anderson, a graduate of the U.S. Military Academy at West Point. Anderson built the Valley Turnpike between Staunton and Winchester (T-2). Commissioned a Confederate brigadier general and wounded during the Peninsula Campaign, Anderson returned to work at Tredegar in 1862 and stayed. Tredegar, along with the Richmond Armory and Arsenal, accounted for half of the ordnance issued by the Confederacy. The old Tredegar buildings last housed a defunct Civil War exhibit.

Park in the Belle Isle parking lot and take the foot bridge across the James River to Belle Isle.

Belle Isle

Belle Isle was the site of the infamous Bell Isle Prison, one of two, along with the Libby Prison, located in Richmond during the Civil War. The prison was operated from 1st Manassas until mid-1863. At one time, Belle Isle's prison housed as many as 10,000 enlisted Union soldiers, but the operation was a drain on Richmond's food supply, and the prisoners eventually were shipped to Andersonville, Georgia.

From Belle Isle and the Tredegar Iron Works, return northeast on Seventh Street, crossing over Canal, Cary and Main streets to Franklin Street. Turn right on Franklin Street, go two blocks, turn left on Ninth Street and go one block back to Capital Square.

situated on a bluff overlooking the James River, was constructed between 1887 and 1894 as a tribute to Confederate veterans and victims.

CONFEDERATE SOLDIERS AND SAILORS MONUMENT TO THE RICHMOND NATIONAL BATTLEFIELD PARK VISITORS CENTER
Return north on 29th Street to E. Broad Street, turn right (east) and go four blocks to 33rd Street and the entrance to the Richmond National Battlefield Visitors Center.

Richmond National Battlefield Park Visitor Center
3215 E. Broad St., Richmond, Va.
• **(804) 226-1981**

The battlefield park is at the site of the Confederate's Chimborazo General Hospital. The hospital, built in 1862, served more than 75,000 sick and wounded Confederate soldiers during the Civil War. A model of the hospital is on display in the visitors center.

This National Park Service visitors center offers tour information, exhibits, a slide presentation and a movie. There are also living history programs. The NPS has a brochure

Photo: Library of Virginia

The Virginia State Capitol is the meeting place of the Virginia General Assembly.

here that covers a number of Civil War sites. The brochure includes a self-guided, 80-mile tour running throughout the eastern outskirts of the city. It has color-coded sites to associate them with either the campaigns of USA Gen. George McClellan in 1862 or USA Gen. Ulysses Grant in 1864. There are taped audio tours of some sites available for rent or sale. Our tour route in T-18: Upper Peninsula follows much of the NPS route with some minor alterations. The NPS tour route and park system feature distinctive brown signs.

The visitors center is accessible to the handicapped and is open from 9 AM to 5 PM every day except New Year's Day and Christmas. There are restroom facilities.

Richmond Tour Ends

Other Tour Points of Interest

For questions, information or reservations, ask for help at the Metro Richmond Visitors Center (see listing in this chapter). The convention and visitors bureau also operates a booth at the Sixth Street Marketplace, 550 E. Marshall Street, Richmond. You can write the bureau at Box C-250, Richmond, Virginia 23219, or call (800) 365-7272 or (804) 782-2777.

For a comprehensive look at the Richmond area — including restaurants, accommodations, shopping, attractions, kidstuff, nightlife, history and more — pick up a copy of *The Insiders' Guide® to Greater Richmond*.

Virginia State Capitol Personality:
Gov. William "Extra Billy" Smith

Smith acquired the nickname "Extra Billy" from his days running a mail-coach service from Washington, D.C., to Georgia. As business grew, Smith demanded and got extra payment from the government. A lawyer-turned-politician, he served in the Virginia legislature, then as a Congressman before his election as governor in 1845. Smith served three years before moving to California in 1849. Out west, Smith refused to run for state office because he would not give up his Virginia residency.

Upon his return to Virginia, Smith again was elected to Congress — a position he held nine years until Virginia's secession in 1861. He served at 1st Manassas (see Fairfax Courthouse in Tour 14: Northern Virginia) and then was elected to the Confederate Congress. He attended political meetings when his military schedule permitted. Appointed a brigadier general, Smith was elected governor of Virginia in May 1863, but he decided to fight at Gettysburg the next month and waited until January 1864 to take office. After the war, Smith lived near Warrenton, Virginia. He served in the Virginia Assembly into his 80s, and he died in 1887 at the age of 91.

Confederate White House Personality: Jefferson Davis

Jefferson Davis was born June 3, 1808, in Christian County (now Todd County), Kentucky. He was the 10th child of Jane Cook Davis and her husband, Samuel, who was the son of a Welsh emigrant and a Revolutionary War veteran. Jefferson Davis moved with his family to Mississippi during his boyhood. Nominated for an appointment to West Point, Davis graduated from the academy in 1828. He had the distinction of attending the U.S. Military Academy with Robert E. Lee, a fellow cadet. Later, Davis took part in the Black Hawk War with Abraham Lincoln, a fellow officer.

In 1833, Davis was stationed at a Wisconsin fort commanded by Col. Zachary Taylor of Orange County, Virginia. Davis fell in love with Taylor's daughter, Sarah Knox Taylor, and despite her father's disapproval, the pair was married in Mississippi. Three months

later, however, Sarah died of malarial fever. Davis remarried, was elected to the U.S. House of Representatives and served in the Mexican War under his former father-in-law — and later president — Gen. Zachary Taylor. In the mid-1840s, Gen. Taylor appointed his former son-in-law as one of the commissioners to negotiate the surrender of Monterey.

In time, Davis returned to Washington as a U.S. Senator, with a break in service for a stint as secretary of war in President Franklin Pierce's cabinet. After Mississippi's secession, which Davis announced on the Senate floor, he retired to the South and was elected president of the Confederate States of America.

On February 11, 1861, Jefferson Davis said goodbye to his family at Brierfield Plantation and began his trip to Montgomery, Alabama, for his inauguration as president of the Confederacy. Traveling alone, Davis took a boat to Vicksburg, Mississippi, but due to the lack of direct railroad lines in the South, he went through Jackson, Mississippi, Chattanooga, Tennessee and Atlanta on his way to Alabama. Ironically, on the same day he left home, a crowd of 1,000 supporters rallied in a morning drizzle at the train station in Springfield, Illinois, as President-elect Abraham Lincoln, on the eve of his birthday, departed for his inaugural in Washington, D.C. Lincoln told the crowd, "I now leave, not knowing when, or whether ever, I may return, with a task before me greater than that which rested upon Washington. Without the assistance of that Divine Being, who ever attended him, I cannot succeed. With that assistance I cannot fail."

On April 30, 1864, Jefferson Davis' 5-year-old son, Joe Davis, died after falling off the veranda of the Confederate White House. Thus, the presidents of both the South and the North, Lincoln and Davis, lost sons while in the service of their countries. Davis eventually relocated to a home in Richmond.

Jefferson Davis announced Mississippi's secession on the U.S. Senate floor, then, in 1861, became CSA president.

Photo: Harpers Ferry National Historical Park

A statue on Monument Avenue memorializes CSA Gen. J.E.B. Stuart.

Annual Events

A partial listing of recurring events in the Richmond area includes the **Virginia State Horse Show**, held in early April at the Virginia State Fairgrounds. The Virginia State Fairgrounds also hosts the **Virginia Food Festival** in late August. The **Winston Cup NASCAR race weekend** roars into town every March at Richmond International Raceway, also at the state fairgrounds. And in September, the fairgrounds hosts the **Virginia State Fair**, with exhibits, displays, food, rides and fun for the entire family! For these events, contact the fairgrounds office at (804) 228-3200.

A number of historic Richmond homes and gardens are open in late April during **Historic Garden Week** in Virginia. The state office for the event is in Richmond at (804) 644-7776. The **Richmond Craft Show** is held each November at the Richmond Centre. For more information, call (804) 783-7300.

Arts

Cultural and performing arts abound in the Richmond area. There's the **Richmond Ballet**, **Richmond Symphony**, the **Virginia Opera**, **Theatre IV**, **TheatreVirginia** and Hanover County's **Barksdale Theatre**. The **Virginia Museum of Fine Arts** is at Boulevard and Grove Avenue and is open every day but Monday. The **Valentine Museum**, near the Museum of the Confederacy, depicts the life and history of Richmond and is open daily. The convention and visitors bureau has telephone numbers and schedules for these and other arts activities.

Photo: Library of Virginia

The statue of Stonewall Jackson on Monument Avenue was unveiled in 1919.

Richmond Personality: Association for the Preservation of Virginia Antiquities

The Association for the Preservation of Virginia Antiquities (APVA), headquartered in Richmond, has a separate branch to identify and preserve endangered Civil War sites. This subgroup is named for noted historian Douglas Southall Freeman (see more on Freeman in T-11: Lynchburg). The APVA branch works with other historical organizations, individuals and local governments and agencies to identify significant Civil War sites in the state. The APVA was founded in 1889. Today it has more than 5,000 members and owns or administers 35 historic properties (Jamestown Park and the Cape Henry Lighthouse at Fort Story are two others) in Virginia. For more information on the APVA, write them at 204 W. Franklin Street, Richmond 23220; or call (804) 648-1889.

Entertainment

Looking for something else fun to do? Try a cruise down the James River on the *Annabel Lee*, a riverboat that carries up to 350 passengers and features a variety of luncheon and dinner trips on the historic river. The riverboat docks at 4400 E. Main Street at Intermediate Terminal. For more information on times and rates, call (804) 222-5700. Then there's the **Science Museum of Virginia** at 2500 W. Broad Street in the historic Broad Street Train Station. The museum has more than 250 hands-on exhibits and participatory programs to encourage visitors to explore science history. For more information, call (804) 367-1013.

Or, pack up the kids and spend a weekend at **Paramount's Kings Dominion**, 15 miles north of Richmond on I-95 at Doswell. Kings Dominion is a 400-acre family entertainment theme park with water rides, roller coasters and a Nickelodeon hands-on "mess-a-mania" section. For more information, call (804) 876-5000. In you've got a hankering for some educational fun, the **Lora Robins Gallery** has a top-notch collection of fine minerals, gems, fossils and rare seashells. The gallery is at the University of Richmond. For more information, call (804) 289-8237.

Historic Sites

Pick from a list of dozens of important sites in Richmond. There's the **Maggie Walker National Historic Site, Maymont**, the **John Marshall House, Black History Museum and Cultural Center of Virginia, Agecroft Hall, Wilton House** and the **Edgar Allan Poe Museum** and **Old Stone House**, to name only a few. Various tours are available. Ask for details at the convention and visitors bureau.

Shopping

Downtown Richmond's **Sixth Street Marketplace** covers three city blocks and features a wide variety of stores and shops, restaurants and entertainment. It is at Sixth Street between the coliseum and Grace Street. The shops at Libbie and Grove avenues in Richmond's west end include a number of specialty shops that offer jewelry, antiques and gift items. Also in Richmond's west end is **Carytown**, a long stretch of Cary Street near Interstate 195, with blocks of unique stores and shops. **Regency Square**, in Richmond's west end, and **Willow Lawn**, on Broad Street nearer downtown, are two shopping malls with hundreds of places to browse and dine.

Bizarre Bazaar is held at the Virginia State Fairgrounds the first weekend in December. Hundreds of exhibitors from throughout the country — selling everything from food products to bird houses to household items — have made this a growing pre-holiday draw. For information on attending or being a vendor, call (804) 288-9467.

Richmond Personality: Sallie Putnam

Sallie Putnam lived in Richmond throughout the war. On April 3, 1965, as Union forces moved in on Richmond, she wrote:

"As the sun rose on Richmond, such a spectacle was presented as can never be forgotten by those who witnessed it. . . . All the horrors of the final conflagration, when the earth shall be wrapped in flames and melt with fervent heat, were, it seems to us, prefigured in our capital. . . . The roaring, crackling and hissing of the flames, the bursting of shells at the Confederate Arsenal, the sounds of the instruments of martial music, the neighing of the horses, the shouting of the multitudes. . . . gave an idea of all the horrors of Pandemonium. Above all this scene of terror, hung a black shroud of smoke through which the sun shone with lurid angry glare like an immense ball of blood that emitted sullen rays of light, as if loath to shine over a scene so appalling. . . . [Then] a cry was raised: 'The Yankees! The Yankees are coming.'"

Tour 18
Upper Peninsula

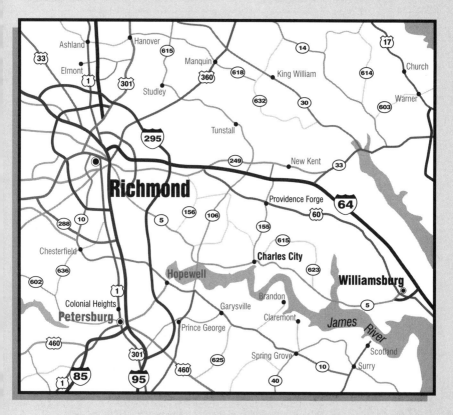

TOUR 18
Upper Peninsula

About This Tour

The long stretch of land known as the Virginia Peninsula stretches from Richmond east to Hampton Roads and the Atlantic Ocean. This route begins in Richmond and ends at Williamsburg, Virginia. The tour covers the upper half of the Peninsula as far east as Williamsburg. The next tour, T-19: Lower Peninsula, covers the eastern portion of the Peninsula including Yorktown, Newport News and Hampton.

In 1862, USA Gen. George Brinton McClellan began his Peninsula Campaign by ferrying a 100,000-troop force down the Potomac River from Washington, D.C., into the Chesapeake Bay and on to Hampton, where he began a move upland toward Richmond. McClellan left Alexandria with his troops on March 17 and arrived at Fort Monroe in time to start the assault on April 3. CSA Gen. Joseph Eggleston Johnston, who commanded the Southern troops, was injured near Fair Oaks, and CSA Gen. Robert E. Lee was placed in command of the army. Lee led the Confederates against the invading Northerners in what has become known as the Seven Days Battles. In the end, following 35,000 casualties suffered by the two opposing armies, McClellan retreated east after getting within 10 miles of the capital city.

Two years later in 1864, USA Gen. Ulysses S. Grant assumed command of the Union forces and began a relentless push to take Richmond. He inched his way south and east from Fredericksburg to the outskirts of Richmond, fighting Lee at every opportunity. In early June, in a fierce battle at Cold Harbor, the Federals lost 7,000 men in less than a half-hour. Afterwards, Grant pushed south across the James River toward Petersburg and dug in for the last winter of the war.

Richmond was protected by a ring of fortifications that nearly encircled the town. An outer ring, about 16 miles from downtown, stretched more than 65 miles. Another ring of defenses was inside that circle, about four miles from downtown. Forts, trenches and earthworks helped protect the capital of the Confederacy.

Travel Tips

Va. Highway 5 is the principal roadway for this tour, but we include a number of back roads as well. Be on the lookout for heavy, fast-moving traffic along the major routes. Many of the smaller state roads you will use are narrow and less-traveled, so use caution. Various Peninsula radio stations report traffic and weather conditions. Citizens band radio users can find traffic information on Channel 19. State police usually monitor Channel 9. Motorists receive a strong mobile telephone signal throughout the Peninsula area.

We suggest you plan evening dining and lodging in Williamsburg. See Chapter 22 for our recommendations on accommodations and Chapter 23 for dining suggestions. It's a good idea to review these recommendations before traveling through the Peninsula. In addition to our suggestions, there are the expected fast-food eateries, gas stations and shops along the Va. 5 corridor between Richmond and Williamsburg.

Upper Peninsula Tour Begins . . .

This tour route begins at the junction of Interstate 95 and Interstate 64 in downtown Richmond.

RICHMOND TO CHICKAHOMINY BLUFF
From 1-95 and I-64 in downtown Richmond, take I-64 east (follow signs for Norfolk) 1 mile, then take U.S. Highway 360 east (exit 192, follow signs for Mechanicsville) east for 2 miles to the Chickahominy Bluff park entrance on the right.

Chickahominy Bluff
Henrico County, Va.

This site was part of the ring of outer defenses of Richmond during the Civil War. CSA Gen. Lee watched the beginning of the Seven Days' Battles from this spot, which offers a nice view of the Chickahominy River to the north and Mechanicsville beyond. The National Park Service (NPS) offers interpretive information, exhibits and a short self-guided trail. There are no restrooms. The exhibit is open dawn to dusk.

CHICKAHOMINY BLUFF TO BEAVER DAM CREEK
Continue east on U.S. 360 for 1.8 miles, take the right exit for Va. Highway 156 and go south for 0.6 mile to the Beaver Dam Creek facility on the right.

Beaver Dam Creek
Hanover County, Va.

Beaver Dam (Beaverdam) Creek is a tributary of the Chickahominy River. This site was part of a Union line the Southerners tried unsuccessfully to attack during the Seven Days' Battles.

BEAVER DAM CREEK TO GAINES' MILL
Continue south on Va. 156 for 1.4 miles, turn right (west) on Cold Harbor Road (Va. 156) and go 2.9 miles. Take a right into the Gaines' Mill entrance and go 0.7 mile to the parking lot.

Gaines' Mill
Hanover County, Va.

The Confederates attacked the Union line

here as part of the Seven Days' Battles. There were more than 15,000 casualties. The NPS offers a short, self-guided trail at this tour stop and an interpretive sign.

GAINES' MILL TO COLD HARBOR
Return to Va. 156, turn right and go 0.3 mile to the Cold Harbor entrance on the left. Follow signs for a 1.5-mile loop through the facility.

Cold Harbor
Hanover County, Va.

Along the side of the self-guided motor tour route are trenches used by Confederates, who dug in here in early June 1864 and repulsed a major attack by USA Gen. Ulysses Grant. Entrenchments like the ones at Cold Harbor, military strategists later learned, are nearly impregnable against frontal assaults. Grant lost 7,000 solders in 30 minutes. There is a small NPS visitor center at Cold Harbor that is handicapped-accessible with restrooms and picnic facilities. The center is open daily from 9 AM to 5 PM. A quarter-mile down the road, the old Gathright House (closed to the public) was a hospital.

COLD HARBOR TO FORT GILMER
The road signs are a bit confusing, but stay on Va. 156 south for 4.5 miles to the intersection with Interstate 295. Take I-295 south (follow signs for Norfolk and Rocky Mount) 8.6 miles to exit 22-B (Va. Highway 5). Take Va. 5 west 2.3 miles, turn left (south) onto Battlefield Park Drive and go 0.8 miles to Fort Gilmer on the left.

Confederate Fort System

Fort Gilmer, along with Fort Harrison, Fort Gregg and Fort Hoke, were elements of an elaborate system of Confederate breastworks. After Cold Harbor in June 1864, USA Gen. Ulysses Grant moved his men to this vicinity, crossing the James River to direct his main effort against Petersburg.

You can just
Visit,
or you can'be an
Insider

Insiders' Guide® Books are:

- Updated annually
- Written by local authors
- Perfect for visitors, newcomers and locals
- Logically organized
- Full of pictures and maps
- User-friendly and filled with easy-to-find information

Peninsula Personality: USA Gen. George B. McClellan

USA Gen. George Brinton McClellan was born in Philadelphia in December 1826. His ancestors sailed to New England from Scotland in the early 18th century, and his great-grandfather, Samuel McClellan, served in the American Revolution as a Connecticut officer.

In 1842, George McClellan entered the U.S. Military Academy at West Point and graduated second in his class. For the next two decades, he served in various positions in the U.S. Army. He saw action in the Mexican War then worked in the development of military strategies, training and education. In 1857, he resigned his commission to become an executive with the Illinois Central Railroad, where he met the company's attorney, Abraham Lincoln. By 1860, McClellan became president of the Ohio and Mississippi Railroad. At the outbreak of the Civil War, his military services were sought by both Pennsylvania and New York, but on his way back east he was commissioned into service in Ohio.

Photo: Antietam National Battlefield

McClellan was a superb military organizer and creator of the Army of the Potomac. Known early in the Civil War as "Young Napoleon," he replaced the aging Winfield Scott as general-in-chief of the Union Army in 1861. After 1st Bull Run, McClellan urged President Lincoln to approve a plan by which the Union general would transport troops down the Potomac River and Chesa-

USA Gen. George Brinton McClellan was a military wunderkind who created the Army of the Potomac.

peake Bay to Fort Monroe, then push up the Virginia Peninsula to Richmond. The president reluctantly agreed to the strategy, so long as Washington, D.C., was sufficiently protected.

McClellan instituted his Peninsula Campaign, which ran into delays — first due to the Confederate earthworks at Yorktown and then in heavy spring rains east of Richmond. The general complained to President Lincoln and Secretary of War Stanton about being outnumbered and not getting adequate troop reinforcements. Finally, despite being within 10 miles of the Confederate capital, he was ordered to withdraw, and his troops were attached to USA Gen. John Pope's command.

McClellan got another chance to command the Union Army, but he failed to pursue CSA Gen. Lee following the Battle of Antietam in Maryland. Lincoln then replaced McClellan with USA Gen. Ambrose Everett Burnside, and the "young Napoleon" never again saw action in the field.

In 1864, McClellan was unsuccessful as a presidential candidate against Lincoln. McClellan spent the next three years abroad before taking a position as chief engineer of the New York City Department of Docks. He was governor of New Jersey from 1878 to early 1881. He died in Orange, New Jersey, in October 1885, leaving behind a wife, Ellen, a daughter and a son.

From Fort Gilmer, continue south on Battlefield Park. Drive 0.9 mile to Fort Johnson, then 0.5 mile to Fort Harrison.

Fort Harrison

Grant's men captured Fort Harrison in late September 1864. Fourteen African-American soldiers in the Union Army were awarded Medals of Honor for their bravery in the taking of Fort Harrison. They were among several regiments of African Americans recognized by the Union for their bravery. With the capture, Fort Harrison became a part of the Union defense system around Richmond. There are interpretive facilities here, including an exhibit and audio station. There is a short, self-guided trail as well as picnic facilities, restrooms and a small visitors center that is operated during the tourist season.

From Fort Harrison, continue south on Battlefield Park Drive 1.1 miles to Fort Hoke, then turn left on Hoke-Brady Drive and go 2.8 miles to Fort Brady.

Fort Brady

Fort Brady was built after the Union Army took Fort Harrison. It was designed to neutralize Fort Darling across the James River on Drewry's Bluff and anchor the Federal line from Fort Harrison. There is a great view of the James River from an overlook at Fort Brady. The fort has a short, self-guided trail, and there is a good view of the James River.

FORT BRADY TO MALVERN HILL

Return north on Hoke-Brady Drive 0.9 mile, turn right (east) on Kingsland Road and go 4 miles, then turn right (east) on Va. 5 and go 3 miles to Va. 156 north. Take a left, and follow signs for 1.4 miles to Malvern Hill on right.

Malvern Hill
Henrico County, Va.

Malvern Hill was the last of the Seven Days'

Battles. It was fought on July 1, 1862. USA Gen. George Brinton McClellan's men stood in formation to fire on the attacking Confederates. After this battle, McClellan withdrew to his base at Harrison's Landing, down the James River. The park has interpretive facilities featuring exhibits and an audio station. There are no restrooms at this site, and the difficult terrain makes in unaccessible to the handicapped.

MALVERN HILL TO FRAYSER'S FARM

Continue north on Va. 156 for 1.8 miles to Glendale National Cemetery and Frayser's Farm on the right.

Frayser's Farm
Henrico County, Va.

At the Battle of Frayser's Farm, the day prior to action at Malvern Hill, Confederate troops unsuccessfully tried to assault the Union position, and the circumstances left CSA Gen. Lee thoroughly disappointed. Just to the north is White Oak Swamp, the site of another battle.

FRAYSER'S FARM TO SHIRLEY PLANTATION

Backtrack south on Va. 156 for 3.2 miles, turn left (east) on Va. 5 and go 5.3 miles, turn right on Va. 608 and go 1.7 miles to Shirley Plantation.

Along this section of Va. 5, this tour enters Charles City County, one of the four old boroughs first established in Virginia in the early 17th century. In 1634, the four boroughs were increased to eight "shires," or counties. This original shire was named Charles City to honor England's Prince Charles, later King Charles I.

Beginning in the early part of the 17th century, within years of the 1607 establishment of Jamestown, a number of fine, elegant plantations were built along the stately James River. These estates were situated along both shores of the James, upriver from Jamestown and west as far as Henrico County.

In time, these fine old plantations — including Shirley and Berkeley — were the business and social center of the Virginia colony for most of the 17th and 18th centuries. There is a $25 block ticket available for adults for a one-time visit to each of four plantations — Shirley, Berkeley, Evelynton and Sherwood Forest — during a calendar year. This block also provides a 10 percent discount at two restaurants, Indian Fields Tavern, on Va. 5, and Coach House, at Berkeley Plantation.

Shirley Plantation
501 Shirley Plantation Rd., Charles City, Va. • (804) 829-5121, (800) 232-1613

On the banks of the James River, between Richmond and Williamsburg, the Shirley estate was established only six years after the English settlement at Jamestown. It was the home of two prominent Virginia families, the Hills and the Carters. Construction of the present house began in 1723 by Edward Hill, a Virginia burgess, for his daughter, Elizabeth, who married John Carter, son of King Carter. Ann Hill Carter, CSA Gen. Robert E. Lee's mother, was born at Shirley, and she married

Henry "Light-Horse Harry" Lee at the estate. CSA Gen. Lee received a portion of his schooling at Shirley Plantation. Shirley Plantation is open from 9 AM to 5 PM every day except Christmas. The last tour begins at 4:30 PM. Admission is $7.50 for adults, $6.50 for military members and seniors older than 60, $6 for AAA members, $5 for youths 13 to 21 and $3.75 for children 6 through 12. Kids younger than 6 are admitted free.

SHIRLEY PLANTATION TO BERKELEY PLANTATION
Backtrack on Va. 608 to Va. 5, turn right (east) and go 3.1 miles to the Berkeley Plantation entrance on the right.

Berkelely Plantation
Va. Hwy. 5, Charles City, Va.
• (804) 829-6018

Berkeley, another fine James River plantation, is an attractive three-story brick house that dates to 1726. The building date and the

Berkeley Personality: USA Gen. Daniel Butterfield

USA Gen. Daniel Butterfield was a 30-year-old, college-educated businessman in New York City when the Civil War began. Quickly, he moved up the ranks of the Union Army's 12th New York Regiment.

Butterfield was commissioned a lieutenant colonel in May 1861 during the Peninsular Campaign. At the Battle of Gaines' Mill, despite an injury, he seized the colors of the 3rd Pennsylvania and rallied the regiment at a critical time in the battle. Years later, he was awarded the Medal of Honor for that act of heroism.

Quartered at Harrison's Landing, or Berkeley Plantation, Butterfield, who was made a brigadier general in September 1861, composed "Taps," the familiar military bugle call that is sounded at night as an order for lights out. The slow, soft bugle call is also sounded at military funerals and memorial services.

Following the Peninsular Campaign, Butterfield served at 2nd Bull Run (T-8), Antietam (T-1) and at Marye's Heights in the Battle of Fredericksburg (T-15). He became a major general and served as chief of staff of the Union's Army of the Potomac. He was wounded at Gettysburg (T-6) and then reassigned to the Western Theater. By war's end, he was breveted a brigadier general and stayed in the army after the Civil War, serving as superintendent of the army's recruiting service in New York City.

In 1870, after resigning from the military, Butterfield went to work with the American Express Company. He was in charge of a number of special public ceremonies, including USA Gen. William Tecumseh Sherman's funeral in 1889. Married in 1886 at the age of 55, USA Gen. Butterfield died in 1901. His tomb is the most ornate in the cemetery at West Point.

name of the owners, Benjamin Harrison IV and his wife, Anne, appear in a date stone over a side door. Bricks for the mansion were fired on site.

The nation's first 10 presidents head a list of distinguished guests who visited the Harrison estate. Benjamin Harrison, son of the builder of Berkeley, was a signer of the Declaration of Independence and a three-time governor of Virginia. His third son, William Henry Harrison, was born at Berkeley and later became the nation's ninth president. William Henry Harrison's grandson, Benjamin Harrison, was a Union officer and later the 23rd president.

During the Civil War, USA Gen. George McClellan established his headquarters for a time at "Harrison's Landing," as Berkeley was called. President Lincoln visited the Union general and his 140,000 troops here — the plantation was 3,000 acres in size at the time. "Taps" was composed at Berkeley by USA Gen. Daniel Butterfield while McClellan's troops were camped at the estate.

The grounds at Berkeley Plantation are open 8 AM to 5 PM daily, and the house is open from 9 AM to 5 PM with the last tour beginning at 4:30 PM. Admission is $8.50 for adults, $6.50 for youths 13 to 16 and $4 for children 6 to 12. The estate gives a 10 percent discount on adult admission for AAA members. There is a restaurant, open daily from 11 AM to 4 PM.

Injured near Fair Oaks, CSA Gen. Joseph Johnston was replaced by Gen. Robert E. Lee himself prior to the Seven Days battles.

BERKELEY PLANTATION TO EVELYNTON PLANTATION

Return on Va. 608 to Va. 5, turn right (east) and go 2 miles to Evelynton Plantation on the right.

Evelynton Plantation
Va. Hwy. 5, Charles City, Va.
• (804) 829-5075

Built in the 18th century, Evelynton Plantation was once a part of Westover Plantation and is a fine example of Georgian Revival architecture. It was named for Evelyn, the daughter of William Byrd II of Westover. The house is furnished with family heirlooms, and it has a boxwood garden and grounds that overlook the James River.

Since 1847, Evelynton has been home for the Ruffin family. The family's patriarch, Edmund Ruffin, was born in Prince George County, Virginia, in 1794, attended the College of William and Mary and became known as a writer, agriculturalist and staunch secessionist. He served briefly in the Virginia Senate and published a Petersburg, Virginia, newspaper devoted to agriculture. He was a member of the Palmetto (South Carolina) Guard, and some credit him with firing one of the first shots of the Civil War at Fort Sumter, South Carolina.

In June 1865, Ruffin shot himself to death in Amelia County, Virginia, apparently because of an unwillingness to live under the federal, rather than Confederate, government. Evelynton was the scene of frequent Civil War skirmishes. Confederates who fought on the property were under the command of CSA Gen. Stuart and CSA Gen. James "Pete" Longstreet. Evelynton is open to the public daily from 9 AM to 5 PM. Admission is $7.50 for adults, $6.50 for seniors and active military personnel, $6 for AAA members and $3.50 for children 6 through 12.

EVELYNTON PLANTATION TO WILLCOX WHARF

Return to Va. 5, turn right (east) and go 2.7 miles to Willcox Wharf Road (Va. Highway 618), turn right and go 1 mile to the Lawrence Lewis Jr. Park entrance.

Willcox Wharf

This wharf, sometimes spelled "Wilcox," is at Lawrence Lewis Jr. Park. It was the main Union Army crossing of the James River to Prince George County south of Hopewell, Virginia, used by USA Gen. Grant on his approach to Petersburg in 1864. There are no facilities here, but there is a great view of the James River.

WILLCOX WHARF TO CHARLES CITY COURTHOUSE

Return on Va. 618 (Willcox Wharf Road) to Va. 5, turn right (east) and go 1.8 miles to Charles City Courthouse.

Charles City Courthouse
Charles City County, Va.

The Charles City County seat of government was moved to this place in the 1730s, and the courthouse was built about the same time. During the Civil War, Union soldiers rifled through the building, and many of the records were destroyed. The courthouse is still in use today.

CHARLES CITY COURTHOUSE TO NORTH BEND PLANTATION

From the Charles City Courthouse, continue east on Va. 5 for 1.5 miles to North Bend Plantation on the right.

North Bend Plantation
12200 Weyanoke Rd., Charles City, Va.
• **(804) 829-5176**

North Bend Plantation is a Greek Revival-style home built in the early 1800s. USA Gen. Philip Henry Sheridan occupied the estate in 1864. The desk used by Sheridan at North Bend is now a treasured family heirloom. North Bend's present owner, who is related to secessionist Edmund Ruffin, has restored the home and established a bed and breakfast. (see our Accommodations chapter for more information)

NORTH BEND PLANTATION TO SHERWOOD FOREST PLANTATION

From North Bend Plantation, return to Va. 5, turn right (east) and go 3.5 miles to Sherwood Forest Plantation on right.

Sherwood Forest Plantation
14501 John Tyler Hwy., Charles City, Va.
• **(804) 829-5377**

Sherwood Forest Plantation is the elegantly furnished home of John Tyler, the 10th president of the United States. It is considered, at 301 feet from left to right, the longest frame house in the nation. The home, maintained today by Tyler descendants, has a 68-foot-long ballroom and features an extensive collection of Tyler heirlooms. A national landmark, it is open daily from 9 AM to 5 PM except on Thanksgiving, Christmas and New Year's Day. There are house tours. Admission is $7.50 for adults, $7 for seniors and $4.50 for students (elementary school through college) and children. The 19th century Overseer's House Tavern is available for dining, catered meals, box lunches, receptions and meetings.

SHERWOOD FOREST TO COLONIAL WILLIAMSBURG VISITOR CENTER

Continue east on Va. 5 for 18 miles to the outskirts of Williamsburg and follow the green signs for the Colonial Williamsburg Visitor Center. It is off Colonial Parkway and Va. Highway 132.

Colonial Williamsburg Visitor Center
Va. Hwy. 132-Y, Williamsburg, Va.
• **(757) 229-1000**

There is much to see and do in the Williamsburg area, so this is the best place to begin your visit, particularly if you need help preparing an itinerary. Of course, we also highly recommend that you pick up a copy of our sister publication, *The Insiders' Guide® to Williamsburg*, which thoroughly covers every aspect of interest in this historic village.

Williamsburg was Colonial Virginia's second capital. Established as Middle Plantation in 1633, the seat of government was moved here from Jamestown in 1698. A year later, the community was renamed Williamsburg to honor England's King William III. The town served as Virginia capital until 1780, when the seat of government was moved upland to Richmond.

"The saddest year in Williamsburg's history was 1862," writes historian Parke Rouse Jr., a resident of this historic community. That was when CSA Gen. George McClellan moved

Sherwood Forest Personality: President John Tyler

John Tyler was born a few miles from the Sherwood Forest site at Greenway on March 29, 1790. He attended the College of William and Mary, graduated at 17, studied law under his father and was a practicing attorney by 1809. Two years later, Tyler was elected to the Virginia House of Delegates, where he served on and off for three decades.

Tyler served a two-year term as governor beginning in 1825, then served nine years in the U.S. Senate. In 1840, Tyler was elected vice president on a ticket headed by fellow Virginian William Henry Harrison. This was the one and only time that both members of a presidential ticket were natives of the same state. Harrison, inaugurated in 1841, died after only a month in office, and Tyler became the first vice president to ascend to the presidency.

Tyler's one-term administration was filled with political intrigue and controversy, mainly over his veto of a national bank bill. All but one member of his cabinet resigned. He did attempt a third-party movement in 1844 in an effort to win reelection, but he withdrew after realizing its inevitable failure. The following year he left Washington, D.C., without attending President James Polk's inaugural, and retired to Sherwood Forest.

Tyler was 23 when he married Letitia Christian in 1813 in New Kent County, Virginia. The couple was married 23 years and had eight children before Letitia died in the White House in 1842. Two years later, in the waning years of his presidency, Tyler was observing exercises on the warship *Princeton* and narrowly escaped death when a gun exploded. One of the victims was New York Sen. David Gardiner.

Two months later, the widowed Tyler married the late senator's daughter, Julia Gardiner. She retired to Sherwood Forest with her husband in 1845, and together the couple had seven children. When the first southern states seceded in 1861, Tyler led a compromise movement and was the leading delegate of a peace convention held in Washington, D.C. When that effort failed, he helped created the Confederacy.

Elected to the Confederate House of Representatives, he died in Richmond on January 18, 1862, before he was able to actively serve the Southern cause. Because of his secession activities, his death was not officially recognized in Washington, D.C., and because of his elected position to the Confederate House, it can be said he was the only U.S. president to bear arms against the federal government.

Tyler was buried in Hollywood Cemetery in Richmond (T-17: Richmond). One of Tyler's sons, David Gardiner Tyler, dropped out of Washington and Lee University after his father died and joined the Confederate Army's Rockbridge (County, Virginia) Artillery. Interestingly, John Tyler's immediate family history spans a century and a half. Tyler was born during the administration of George Washington, the nation's first president, and the last of his children, David's sister, Pearl, died during the administration of Harry Truman, the nation's 33rd president.

USA Gen. Daniel Butterfield composed "Taps" while encamped with McClellan's troops at the Berkeley Plantation.

up the Virginia Peninsula, defeated the Confederates at nearby Fort Magruder and put Williamsburg under military guard. The 2,000 residents of the town remained under guard for the duration of the Civil War — a martial-law-type state.

Benjamin Ewell, a West Point graduate and president of the College of William and Mary, became a Confederate engineering officer and helped establish Peninsula defenses against Union attack. Skirmishes were frequent in this quaint little city, which took years to recover after war's end in 1865.

Colonial Williamsburg is a beautiful historic attraction. You can center an entire vacation in the village known as "Little London" in Colonial times. Visit the Colonial Capitol, the Governor's Palace, Carter's Grove and more than 30 homes, craft shops and public buildings in the historic area. Colonial Williamsburg offers a variety of admission packages, including the Patriot's Pass, the Royal Governor's Pass and the basic admission ticket.

The center, operated by Colonial

Photo: Library of Virginia

Williamsburg, is open from 8:30 AM to 8 PM daily from April through October. During the off-season, it is open Sunday through Thursday from 9 AM to 6 PM and from 9 AM to 7 PM on Friday and Saturday. There are restrooms, and the center is handicapped-accessible.

There is much to see and do in Colonial Williamsburg, although the facility is more about Virginia's 17th and 18th century — not the Civil War. We suggest tour travelers park at the center and walk about the Colonial village.

Upper Peninsula Tour Ends

Other Tour Points of Interest

Annual Events

Historic Garden Week in Virginia is held each year in April. **Jamestown Landing Day** is held in May to honor the first permanent English settlement in the New World. The **Virginia Indian Heritage Festival** is held in June at Jamestown. The **Grand Illumination**, the traditional holiday lighting of Williamsburg, takes place on the first weekend in December, and **Jamestown Christmas** is held each year during the last two weeks of the year.

Arts

Colonial Williamsburg offers the **DeWitt Wallace Decorative Arts Gallery**, which has one of the largest collections of 18th century English and American textiles, prints, furniture and other art objects. There is also the **Abby Aldrich Rockefeller Folk Art Center,** across the street from the Williamsburg Lodge in the Colonial village. The **College of William and Mary**, the nation's second oldest institute of higher learning, offers students, townsfolk and visitors a year-long array of performances, concerts and arts programs.

Entertainment

The ultimate entertainment experience on the Peninsula is found at **Busch Gardens**, which offers Old World Europe, shows, concerts, dining and much more. It is located on U.S. 60, 1 mile east of Williamsburg, and is open daily from 10 AM to 10 PM during the June to Labor Day season. Admission is $31.50 for all individuals older than 6. Children 3 through 6 are $24.50. For hours at other times of the year and general information, call (757) 253-3350. The park is handicapped-accessible.

Yes, there's more to do! Kids like **Go-Karts Plus**, which offers two separate race tracks at 6910 Richmond Road (U.S. Highway 60) near Williamsburg Pottery. Also on Richmond Road is the **Old Dominion Opry**, a country music and comedy show for the entire family, is 3 miles west of Williamsburg on U.S. 60. There is one show daily from mid-March through December, and admission is $17 for adults, $15 for seniors, AAA and active military personnel and $10 for youth 13 through 20. Children younger than 13 are free. The Opry is closed in January and has weekend shows only from February to mid-March. For reservations, telephone (757) 564-0200 or (800) 2VA-OPRY.

Water Country USA offers water rides and live entertainment. It is 3 miles west of Williamsburg on U.S. 60. Admission is $23.50 for anyone older than 6; $15.95 for children ages 3 to 6. For information, call (757) 229-9300. Golfers can enjoy no fewer than five major golf course facilities in the Williamsburg area. More information is available at the Colonial Williamsburg Visitor Center.

Historic Sites

Tidewater Touring Inc., in Williamsburg, offers a number of historic and shopping tours in Virginia. Call (757) 872-0897 for information. **Maximum Guided Tours** offers a candle-light tour of "The Ghosts of Williamsburg." This tour includes history stories and interesting trivia about Williamsburg homes and past residents. For information, telephone (757) 565-4821.

Shopping

Williamsburg Pottery, on Richmond Road (U.S. 60) 3 miles west of town, has served visitors and locals for a half-century. This was Virginia's first great outlet mall, a collection of several buildings that sells almost everything. Over the years, Richmond Road has developed into a vast collection of outlets and stores. It's a stretch of highway challenged only by Potomac Mills (see T-14: Northern Virginia, T-15: Fredericksburg) as the ultimate shopping experience in Virginia.

Otherwise, try shopping in the variety of stores and shops in Williamsburg's Merchant's Square, adjoining the historic district. Colonial Williamsburg furniture, crafts and art are available in several stores. Throughout the Williamsburg area are dozens of stores and shops that offer jewelry, antiques and gift items. Several local publishing companies print shopping guides to the Williamsburg area, and these helpful booklets are available at the Colonial Williamsburg Visitor Center and at almost every motel, restaurant and attraction.

Tour 19
Lower Peninsula

TOUR 19
Lower Peninsula

About This Tour

This tour is a natural continuation of T-18: Upper Peninsula, which ended in Williamsburg, Virginia. This route extends east from Williamsburg and incorporates a number of stops in Newport News, Virginia. It ends in Hampton, Virginia, and includes a side trip to Yorktown, Virginia. This tour covers the eastern portion of the Virginia Peninsula, which stretches from Richmond east to Hampton Roads and the Atlantic Ocean. This portion of the peninsula is bordered on the north by the York River and on the south by the James River. This territory is some of the most historic in the nation. Besides Jamestown and Williamsburg (T-18), Yorktown, Newport News and Hampton played significant roles in Virginia — and American — history too. Yorktown was the site of the 1781 British surrender that ended the American Revolution.

At the tip of the peninsula, Fort Monroe sits on a spit of land overlooking Hampton Roads. In May 1861, CSA Gen. John Bankhead Magruder, commander of the Army of the Peninsula, began fortifying the James-York Peninsula against a possible Union attack. Magruder built several lines of defense across the peninsula, stretching from the James River to the vicinity of Yorktown on the York River. One line of defense ran along the Warwick River, in the vicinity of present-day Newport News Park.

In 1862, USA Gen. George Brinton McClellan began his Peninsula Campaign by ferrying a 100,000-man force down the Potomac River from Washington, D.C., into the Chesapeake Bay and on to Hampton, where he began a move upland, west, toward Richmond. Much of the Civil War action in the eastern portion of the peninsula was related to the 1862 Peninsula Campaign and the Con-federate lines of defense against the Union attack in and around Newport News, Hampton and Yorktown.

Travel Tips

Interstate 64 and Newport News streets make up the principal route of this tour. Be on the lookout for heavy, fast-moving traffic in the I-64 vicinity. The city streets are narrow but heavily traveled, so use caution. Various peninsula radio stations report traffic and weather conditions. Citizens band radio users can find traffic information on Channel 19. State police usually monitor Channel 9. Motorists receive a strong mobile telephone signal throughout the peninsula area.

Lower Peninsula Tour Begins . . .

From Williamsburg, travel east on I-64 to exit 250-B (Va. Highway 105, Fort Eustis Boulevard). At end of ramp, continue east on Fort Eustis Boulevard (Va. 105) and go 0.2 mile, turn left (west) onto Jefferson Avenue (Va. Highway 143) and go 0.2 mile, turn right at Constitution Way and then into the parking lot of the Newport News Park visitors center.

Newport News Tourist Information Center
13560 Jefferson Ave., Newport News, Va.
• (757) 886-7777, (888) 493-7386

The city of Newport News operates the information center at Newport News Park. The attractive building is nestled among a grove of trees. Inside, travel counselors are helpful and knowledgeable, with loads of information on area history and attractions as well as suggestions for accommodations and dining. Ask about group and discount tickets to area sites.

Newport News generally is known for its 17th- and 18th-century history and its exceptional maritime heritage, but in recent years the city has bolstered its image as a tourist mecca for Civil War buffs. The upsurge in Civil War promotion can be attributed to the city historian and the director of tourism — two professionals who worked closely together to develop a superb Civil War history program. For example, the city has published a special brochure, "Civil War Sites of Newport News, Virginia," which incorporates information on McClellan's 1862 Peninsula Campaign as well as the famous 1862 battle of the ironclads at Hampton Roads. Ask for the free brochure at the information center.

As of early 1997, the city of Newport News had acquired a number of properties throughout the city as potential Civil War attractions. These sites have been and continue to be in various stages of development. Most of the stops in our tour route are adapted from the city's history program and Civil War brochure. It is best to check at the information center for the very latest news on the development and visitation accessibility of the sites.

The Newport News Tourist Information Center is open daily from 9 AM to 5 PM. It is closed only on Thanksgiving, Christmas and New Year's Day. It has restroom facilities, and it is handicapped-accessible. The 8,000-acre Newport News Park is the largest city park in the nation. It offers countless opportunities for boating, hiking, archery and golf, has picnic shelters and camping areas and rentals for paddle boats, bicycles and canoes. The park includes miles of original Civil War fortifications along a wooded nature trail. The park has one Civil War attraction of particular interest — the site of a battle at Dam Number 1, where there is also an interpretive center.

NEWPORT NEWS TOURIST INFORMATION CENTER TO BATTLE OF DAM NUMBER 1

From the information center, con-

tinue into Newport News Park on Constitution Way, also known as Park Road. Go 0.8 mile to the interpretive center for Dam Number 1, on the right side of the roadway.

Battle of Dam Number 1

The Battle of Dam Number 1 was the only time USA Gen. McClellan attempted to break CSA Gen. Magruder's extensive Warwick River line of defense. The Union force assaulted the Confederate defense line on April 16, 1862.

NEWPORT NEWS TOURIST INFORMATION CENTER TO ENDVIEW PLANTATION

From the information center, exit onto Jefferson Avenue, turn right (west) and stay on Jefferson Avenue for 2.2 miles. Turn right (east) on Yorktown Road (Va. Highway 238) and go 0.3 mile to the Endview Plantation entrance on the right.

Endview Plantation
Yorktown Rd., Newport News, Va.

This historic, white frame house, built prior to 1720, gets its name from the approach to the side entrance to the house. The house, once the home of the Harwood family, saw action in three separate wars on Virginia soil: the Revolutionary War, the War of 1812 and the Civil War. Gen. George Washington and his troops reportedly spent a night on the lawn of Endview just prior to the battle of Yorktown in October 1781. It was the home of CSA Capt. Humphrey Harwood Curtiss, commander of the 32nd Virginia Regiment during the Warwick River Siege of 1862. Endview was used as a field hospital during the war, and more than 100 Confederates are buried in the vicinity. Endview was purchased in 1996 by the city of Newport News, which plans to restore the estate and develop a "living history" museum. It should be open for tours of the grounds and an archaeological site by May 1997; the house will be available for tours sometime in 1998. At present, visitors can view the estate from the Yorktown Road entrance.

ENDVIEW PLANTATION TO LEE HALL

From Endview, return 0.3 mile west on Yorktown Road, cross over Jefferson Avenue, under I-64 and go 0.4 mile to Lee Hall estate on the right.

Lee Hall
Yorktown Rd., Newport News, Va.

Richard Decatur Lee built his two-story, brick Italianate plantation house, Lee Hall, in 1850. He financed the construction, legend has it, with the $10,000 sale of a bumper crop of tobacco. R.D. Lee headed Warwick County's civil defenses at the outbreak of the Civil War, and he advised CSA Gen. John B. Magruder on placing Confederate defenses along the Warwick River. Magruder used the mansion as his headquarters in April and May 1862, during the Warwick River Siege of USA Gen. George McClellan's Peninsula Campaign. A small earthen fort can be seen on the front lawn of the estate, the lone evidence of the its military occupation.

R.D. Lee fell into financial ruin after the Civil War, and that led to his sale of the mansion in 1866. Lee Hall was purchased in 1996 by the city of Newport News, which plans to restore the estate and develop a Civil War museum that is likely to open in 1999. At present, visitors can view the estate from the Yorktown Road entrance.

LEE HALL TO SKIFFES CREEK REDOUBT

From Lee Hall, continue east on Yorktown Road for 0.6 mile to Warwick Boulevard (U.S. Highway 60).

Along the way, this route passes the vicinity of Lee Hall, a rail crossing community that developed in the 1880s. The village took its name from Richard D. Lee's nearby estate.

Continue on Warwick Boulevard for 0.3 mile, turn right (south) at the Oakland Industrial Park on Enterprise Drive and go 0.3 mile to the Army and Air Force Ex-

change Service on the right. Across Enterprise Drive is a wooded area, the site of Skiffes Creek Redoubt.

Skiffes Creek Redoubt
Enterprise Dr., Newport News, Va.

The earthen fortification at Skiffes Creek Redoubt was part of Magruder's second defense line across the James-York Peninsula. The redoubt (another word for earthworks) supported the defense of Lee's Mill, a mile to the east, and blocked McClellan's access to Skiffes Creek, a tributary of the James River that flows west of present-day Warwick Boulevard.

SKIFFES CREEK REDOUBT TO LEE'S MILL BATTLE SITE

Return on Enterprise Drive to Warwick Boulevard (U.S. 60), turn right (east) and go 0.9 mile to Lee's Mill Road, turn right (west) and go one block, turn left on Rivers Ridge Circle and go 0.3 mile to wooded area on left. This forested area is in the midst of a large contemporary subdivision, Lee's Mill.

Lee's Mill Battle Site
Rivers Ridge Circle, Newport News, Va.

In this vicinity was Lee's Mill, on the headwaters of the Warwick River — a tributary of the James River. Lee's Mill was an anchor for one of several lines of defense that were constructed by CSA Gen. Magruder and stretched across the James-York Peninsula. In fact, Magruder's extensive line of defense from Lee's Mill to Yorktown caused USA Gen. McClellan to initiate his month-long Warwick River Siege, which lasted until May 4, 1862. On April 5, 1862, a Union force encountered Confederates at Lee's Mill. The Federals were stopped by heavy rains and the massive earthen fortifications that defended the Warwick River crossing.

LEE'S MILL BATTLE SITE TO WARWICK COUNTY COURTHOUSE
Return to Warwick Boulevard, turn

right (east) and continue on Warwick Boulevard (U.S. 60) for 2.8 miles, turn right on Old Courthouse Way and go 0.3 mile to the Old Warwick County Courthouse.

Old Warwick County Courthouse
Old Courthouse Way, Newport News, Va.

Warwick River County was one of the eight original shires — counties — established in Virginia in 1634. The county name was changed to Warwick in 1642. Warwick County consolidated with the city of Newport News in 1958, and thereafter the county became extinct.

The brick courthouse was constructed in 1810. The building was occupied and looted on April 5, 1862, by units under the command of USA Gen. Erasmus Keyes, who used the courthouse as his headquarters from April to May 1862. Keyes served as a military secretary to USA Gen. Winfield Scott (T-21) in early 1861. Hence, Keyes' troops renamed the Warwick County Courthouse green Camp Winfield Scott.

WARWICK COURTHOUSE TO YOUNG'S MILL

From the Warwick Courthouse, continue east on Old Courthouse Way for 0.7 mile, turn left on Tabbs Lane and go one block, turn right (east) on Warwick Boulevard (U.S.

60) and continue east 1.5 miles to Youngs Mill on the right. Turn into parking area.

Young's Mill
Warwick Blvd., Newport News, Va.

The redoubts at Young's Mill formed the Deep Creek anchor for Magruder's first line of defense across the James-York Peninsula. Young's Mill is at the headwaters of Deep Creek, a tributary of the James River. Confederate troops abandoned Young's Mill on April 5, 1862, in order to make a more resolute stand again Union forces at Lee's Mill, 6 miles to the north.

YOUNG'S MILL TO THE MARINERS' MUSEUM

From Young's Mill, continue east on Warwick Boulevard for 3.4 miles to Museum Drive, turn right on Museum Drive and go 1 mile to the entrance to The Mariners' Museum.

The Mariners' Museum
100 Museum Dr., Newport News, Va.
• (757) 596-2222, (800) 581-SAIL

The Mariners' Museum is one of Virginia's finest attractions and boasts one of the world's largest maritime collections. There are paintings, maps, ship models, watercraft and other maritime memorabilia, including an exhibit on the clash of the Civil War ironsides — the USS

Lee Hall Personality: CSA Gen. John Bankhead Magruder

John B. Magruder was born in Winchester, Virginia, on August 15, 1810. He graduated from the U.S. Military Academy at West Point in 1830 and saw action in the Mexican War. Later, while stationed at Newport, Rhode Island, he was nicknamed "Prince John" for his flamboyant social life and courtly appearance.

After establishing the Confederate Army's lines of defense across the James-York Peninsula and helping delay USA Gen. George McClellan's Peninsula Campaign, Magruder earned high marks from his superior officers. Later, during the Seven Days' Battles on the peninsula, however, he was less impressive. Magruder was sent to the Southwest, and he captured Galveston, Texas, on January 1, 1863.

After the war, Magruder became a major general under Mexican emperor Maximilian, and later returned to the states to lecture on his experiences. Magruder settled in Houston, Texas, where he died February 18, 1871. He is buried in Galveston.

Photo: The Mariners Museum

This wartime deck scene shows the crew aboard the USS *Monitor*.

Monitor and the CSS *Virginia*, formerly the USS *Merrimac*. The Mariners' is the principal museum for the Monitor National Marine Sanctuary, and a video takes visitors on an underwater tour of the *Monitor* graveyard off Cape Hatteras, North Carolina. The museum also has artifacts from both the ironclads — the iron anchor and navigational lantern from the USS *Monitor*, and the steering wheel from the CSS *Virginia*.

Spend a whole day at this one exceptional attraction. The museum is open daily, except Thanksgiving and Christmas, from 10 AM to 5 PM. Admission is $6.50 for adults, $5.50 for seniors, active military personnel and AAA members and $3.25 for students ages 6 through college. It's free for children younger than 5. The museum is in a 550-acre park that features picnic areas, boat and canoe rentals, and a 5-mile walking trail around Lake Maury (see Matthew Fontaine Maury in T-5, T-10 and T-17). There is a gift gallery, a research library and archives open Monday through Saturday from 9 AM to 5 PM. All sections of The Mariners' Museum are handicapped-accessible.

THE MARINERS' MUSEUM TO THE VIRGINIA WAR MUSEUM

From The Mariners' Museum, return north on Museum Drive for 1 mile, turn right (east) and go 3.5 miles on Warwick Boulevard (U.S. 60) to Huntington Park on the right. Turn right onto Hornet Circle and use the parking lot across from the YMCA.

Virginia War Museum
Huntington Park, 9285 Warwick Blvd., Newport News, Va. • (757) 247-8523

Founded in 1923, this museum houses more than 50,000 artifacts related to the nation's war history from the American Revolution to the present. Of particular interest is the Civil War section, which has uniforms, weapons and printed materials. The museum, operated by the city of Newport News, also has a gift shop. It is open Sunday from 1 to 5 PM, and Monday through Saturday from 9 AM to 5 PM and Sunday from 1 to 5 PM every day except Thanksgiving, Christmas, New Year's Day and election day. Admission is $2 for adults and $1 for seniors, military personnel and children ages 6 through 15. The museum is handicapped-accessible.

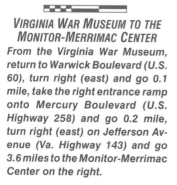

VIRGINIA WAR MUSEUM TO THE MONITOR-MERRIMAC CENTER

From the Virginia War Museum, return to Warwick Boulevard (U.S. 60), turn right (east) and go 0.1 mile, take the right entrance ramp onto Mercury Boulevard (U.S. Highway 258) and go 0.2 mile, turn right (east) on Jefferson Avenue (Va. Highway 143) and go 3.6 miles to the Monitor-Merrimac Center on the right.

Monitor-Merrimac Center
917 Jefferson Ave., Newport News, Va. • (757) 245-1533, (800) 362-3046

The Battle of the Ironclads, the USS *Moni-*

tor and the CSS *Virginia* (formerly the USS *Merrimac*) took place in Hampton Roads on March 9, 1862. The battle was indecisive, but it marked a change in naval warfare from wood and sail to iron and steam.

Today, the Monitor-Merrimac Center houses the largest diorama of the Battle of the Ironclads. The center is open daily from 9 AM to 5 PM, it has restrooms and is handicapped-accessible. Admission to the visitors center is free. The center also serves as the offices for Newport News Harbor Cruises. Jerry Kennett, the main captain of the Harbor Cruises, knows his Civil War history. The cruise goes into Hampton Roads, where the CSS *Virginia* sank the USS *Cumberland* and USS *Congress*, then fought the Battle of the Ironclads with the USS *Monitor*. The cruise also visits Camp Butler, a staging area for Union troops on the James-York Peninsula, and the U.S. Naval Base at Norfolk. The cruise is $14.50 for adults, $13 for seniors and $7.50 for children younger than 12. The cruise leaves the harbor at noon daily.

MONITOR-MERRIMAC CENTER TO FORT MONROE CASEMATE MUSEUM

Return on Jefferson Avenue for two blocks to 14th Street, turn left on 14th Street and go one block, turn left on Terminal Avenue, go a half-block and follow signs for the entrance ramp for Interstate 664 north. Take I-664 for 5.5 miles, then take I-64 eastbound (toward Hampton) and go 4 miles on I-64 to exit 268 (Va. Highway 169). Off the exit ramp, turn left (east) on Mallory Street (Va. 169), go 0.2 mile, turn right on Mellen Street (Va. Highway 143) and go east through the community of Phoebus for 0.5 mile to the main gate at Fort Monroe. Follow signs for one of several bridges over the moat into the enclosed compound. The Casemate Museum is inside the old fortress at Fort Monroe.

Fort Monroe Casemate Museum
Fort Monroe, Va. • (757) 727-3391, (757) 727-3973

Named for President James Monroe, For-

Monitor-Merrimac Center Side Trip: Monitor-Merrimac Overlook Park

From the Monitor-Merrimac Center, return on Jefferson Avenue for two blocks, turn right (east) on 16th Street and go 1.2 miles to the Monitor-Merrimac Overlook Park.

Monitor-Merrimac Overlook Park
Newport News, Va.

From the overlook, view Hampton Roads and the site — about a mile offshore — of the Battle of the Ironclads. The park is open from sunrise to sunset. Parking is free. The park has a pier and an interpretative sign.

tress Monroe is the nation's largest stone fort ever built. It is the only moat-encircled fort still used by the U.S. Army. Fort Monroe is at Old Point Comfort, which traces its history to 1607 when Capt. Christopher Newport's sailing party landed at Cape Henry. The first fort on this site was built in 1609. A new brick fort, named for England's King George II, was built in 1727 after Spain declared war on England. In 1774, during the American Revolution, Virginia built a temporary light on this site to guide ships into Hampton Roads.

In 1800, the federal government completed a permanent light at this site, and during the next two decades the location was witness to considerable history. In 1819, work began on Fortress Monroe — the name later was changed from "fortress" to "fort." Four years later, the fort received its first U.S. Army garrison. A year after that, the Marquis de LaFayette visited during his American tour. In 1828, the garrison included an artilleryman, Sgt. Maj. E.A. Perry, also known as writer Edgar Allan Poe. And in 1831, a young U.S. Army engineer named Robert E. Lee arrived on the scene to supervise the construction of the fort's moat.

During the early days of the Civil War, USA Gen. Benjamin Franklin Butler took command of the fort, which was one of few military facilities in the South that Confederates failed to capture. In 1861, three escaped Virginia slaves made their way to the fort. Rather than return-

ing the trio under the Fugitive Slave Law, Butler declared the slaves "contraband of war" — the first use of the term.

The next year, 1862, was a busy one too. Fort Calhoun, offshore in Hampton Roads, was renamed for USA Gen. John Ellis Wool, who was the commander of the Hampton Roads fortifications. President Lincoln visited Fort Monroe to observe the Union attack on Norfolk. Meanwhile, hundreds lined the fort's ramparts and beaches to see naval history when the ironclad vessels fought in Hampton Roads. USA Gen. McClellan used the fort as the springboard for his Peninsula Campaign in 1862.

CSA President Jefferson Davis, captured after the Civil War, was returned to Virginia and imprisoned at the fort. He was first kept in a casemate — a wall chamber — before being moved to officers' quarters. He was released two years later. The museum has interesting graphic exhibits, including the barren casemate where Davis was imprisoned. The museum is open daily from 10:30 AM to 4:30 PM. It is closed on New Year's Day, Thanksgiving and Christmas. Admission is free. The museum is handicapped-accessible.

The Casemate Museum also serves as the starting point of a walking tour around old Fort Monroe. The walking tour provides a glimpse of the quarters used by U.S. Army Lt. Robert E. Lee while he was stationed at the fort. The building is a private residence and off limits to

Photo: The Mariners Museum

This lithograph shows the USS *Monitor* and CSS *Virginia* (formerly the *Merimac*) in battle.

visitors. Quarters One, also off limits, is the oldest residence on the post. Its list of distinguished guests include President Lincoln and the Marquis de Lafayette. The engineer wharf along the waterfront at Fort Monroe is the place where McClellan began his Peninsula Campaign and where Confederate President Davis came ashore for his imprisonment. The Old Point Comfort lighthouse, in continuous operation since 1802, can be seen but is closed

Fort Monroe Personalities: Harriett Tubman, Nurses

Harriett Tubman was an African American who served as a spy and scout for the Union Army. She was also a nurse, and she cared for a number of individuals who escaped into Union lines at Fort Monroe.

Three months after the war's end, in July 1865, she was honored by an appointment as "...nurse or matron at the Colored Hospital, Fort Monroe, Virginia." Tubman was but one of many nurses that served on the peninsula during the Civil War. The war lured a number of nurses from around the country into military service. For example, Helen Gilson of Massachusetts and Amy Bradley of Maine were just two of many Northern nurses who served during the Peninsula Campaign of 1862.

Fort Monroe Side Trip: Hampton University

Hampton University is at Queen and Tyler streets, and is accessed by exit 267 off I-64.

Hampton University

In 1868, three years after the Civil War ended, USA Gen. Samuel Chapman Armstrong established a school in Hampton to educate freed slaves. Armstrong created a "normal and agricultural institute" with two teachers and 15 students. Later known as Hampton Institute, the school is now Hampton University. Armstrong was school principal until he died in 1893. Booker T. Washington, a Virginia native, was an 1875 Hampton graduate, and he founded Tuskegee Institute with principles he learned from Hampton. Another Hampton graduate, Robert Tussa Moton, a native of Amelia County (T-21), Virginia, served as the institute's administrator from 1890 to 1915, when he succeeded Washington as president of Tuskegee. Moton, an advisor to five U.S. presidents and founder of the Urban League, died in May 1940.

Today, Hampton University has an enrollment of nearly 5,000 students and a faculty of almost 400. Also on campus is Emancipation Oak, where Union soldiers announced to Hampton Roads citizens in 1863 the Emancipation Proclamation that freed slaves. For more information on Hampton University, write the school in Hampton, Virginia 23668, or call (757) 727-5000.

to visitors. The Lincoln Gun, the first 15-inch Rodman made, was cast in 1860, named for the president in 1862 and used to bomb Confederate batteries near Norfolk. The entire fort is listed as both a national and state historic landmark.

Lower Peninsula Tour Ends

Other Tour Points of Interest

For information or reservations, ask for help at the Newport News Tourist Information Center (see listing).

Annual Events

Yearly festivities in the Tidewater area include the *Monitor-Merrimac* battle re-enactment in Newport News in March, *Monitor* Day at The Mariners' Museum in March, **Bay Days** in Hampton in September, the **Newport News Fall Festival** in October, an arts and crafts show and marketplace at the Peninsula Fine Arts Center in November and December and the **Celebration in Lights** in Newport News in December.

Arts

The **Peninsula Fine Arts Center** features collections from other Virginia museums as well as national traveling exhibits. The center develops ongoing educational programs for children and adults. For more information, call (757) 596-8175. The **Virginia Living Museum** has native Virginia animals in their natural habitats. It has an aquarium, aviary, planetarium, observatory and botanical garden. For more information on the museum on J. Clyde Morris Boulevard, call (757) 595-1900. The **Hampton University Museum** has a renowned collection of art and artifacts. For more information, call (757) 727-5308. The **Virginia Air and**

Newport News-Hampton Side Trip: Site of Big Bethel

From I-64, take exit 261 (Hampton Roads Center Parkway) west. At the end of the exit ramp, and beyond Hampton Woods Plaza, turn right (north) and go 3 miles on Big Bethel Road (Va. Highway 600) to the highway markers along the roadway.

Big Bethel Reservoir is a manmade lake that has submerged the site of an 1861 skirmish, the Battle of Big Bethel, considered the first land battle of the Civil War. A group of untrained Union soldiers from Fort Monroe attacked an equally untrained group of Confederates. The Northerners retreated to Fort Monroe after a confusing, two-hour skirmish.

Space Center is a world-class facility with a giant-screen theater. The center, the official visitors center for **NASA Langley Research Center**, offers a unique look at Hampton Roads history. Call (757) 727-0900 for information.

Historic Sites

Historic Hilton Village was the nation's first federally subsidized planned community. The village opened on July 7, 1918, with 500 English village-style houses to accommodate shipyard workers during World War I. Today, Hilton Village is a registered state landmark and has a number of unique shops along the 10000 block of historic Warwick Boulevard (U.S. 60). The **Matthew Jones House**, built in about 1680, includes 90 architectural features. It is on Fort Eustis Army Base. For more information, call (757) 898-5090. The **U.S. Army Transportation Museum** at Fort Eustis has helicopters, landing craft, a flying crane, trains, Jeeps, trucks — anything and everything related to U.S. Army transportation. Call (757) 878-1182 for more information. The **Newsome House**, home of prominent African-American attorney Joseph Thomas Newsome, was built in 1899. For more information on the **Newsome House and Culture Center**, call (757) 247-2380. Hampton Boat Tours has a two-hour cruise that covers much of the Hampton Roads area.

Shopping

The **Historic Hilton Village** area, in the 10000 block of Warwick Boulevard (U.S. 60), has a number of unique specialty shops including clothing boutiques and antique shops. Call (757) 595-1545 for information on Hilton Village. **Patrick Henry Mall**, on Jefferson Avenue off I-64 (exit 255), is the largest indoor mall in Newport News. Open daily, the mall features department stores, movie theaters, a food court and specialty stores.

Photo: The Mariners Museum

John Werden was wartime captain of the USS *Monitor*.

Newport New-Hampton Side Trip: Yorktown

From I-64, take exit 247 (Yorktown Road) and head east on Yorktown Road for 2 miles to the town of Yorktown and the Colonial National Historical Park.

The 9,000-acre Colonial National Historical Park is rich in Revolutionary War history. However, Yorktown also was the scene of Civil War action. CSA Gen. John B. Magruder's defenses bottled up USA Gen. George McClellan for months and delayed his move up the Virginia peninsula toward Richmond. When USA Gen. McClellan finally assaulted Yorktown, the Confederates left behind land mines — a new technique in warfare. For more information on the Colonial National Historical Park, write P.O. Box 210, Yorktown 23690, or telephone (757) 898-3400.

Tour 20
Petersburg

TOUR 20
Petersburg

About This Tour

This tour is a natural continuation of T-17: Richmond, and covers Hopewell and Petersburg, Virginia, both south of the state capital and its environs. This route begins in Richmond, winds through Hopewell and extends to Petersburg, with a side trip to Colonial Heights, Virginia. The main roads of this route are Interstate 95, Va. Highway 10, Va. Highway 36 and U.S. Highway 460, all in the area between Richmond and Petersburg.

Petersburg, like Washington, Fredericksburg and Richmond, sits on the "fall zone" — the natural dividing line that separates the coastal plain to the east and the rolling piedmont to the west. Petersburg, Hopewell and Colonial Heights sit along the banks of the Appomattox River, which joins the James River at Hopewell. Petersburg, a port city on the Appomattox, traces its origins to the mid-1600s, when Abraham Wood established Fort Henry as a trading post in the far "western" reaches of Colonial tidewater Virginia.

In the summer of 1864, Union and Confederate troops clashed at Petersburg. It was the beginning of a long Union siege that lasted until the spring of 1865. CSA Gen. Robert E. Lee began his final retreat from the Petersburg area in early April 1865 and surrendered to USA Gen. Ulysses S. Grant at Appomattox less than two weeks later.

Travel Tips

This tour route begins by leaving Richmond on busy I-95. It is best to avoid this heavily used interstate during morning and evening rush-hour periods. As with other tours along interstate highways, this route uses convenient mile markers as guideposts to mark exits and measure distances. Petersburg is a busy city, and traffic often is congested, particularly in the downtown area. Richmond and Petersburg radio stations report traffic and weather conditions. Citizens band radio users can find traffic information on Channel 19, and state police usually monitor Channel 9. The Richmond-Petersburg corridor is heavily urbanized, and motorists receive a strong mobile telephone signal throughout the vicinity.

This tour ends in Petersburg, where we suggest you plan dining and lodging for the evening. Recommended accommodations are listed in Chapter 22. Dining suggestions are listed in Chapter 23. It is a good idea to review these recommendations before traveling through the region. In addition to our suggestions, there are a number of fast-food eateries, gas stations, convenience markets and shops in Hopewell and Petersburg.

Petersburg Tour Begins . . .

RICHMOND TO DREWRY'S BLUFF
Leave Richmond on I-95 southbound, crossing the James River at mile marker 74. Continue south 7 miles and take exit 67 for Chippenham Parkway. Travel the parkway west 1 mile to U.S. Highway 1-301, and continue south on U.S. 1-301 for 2.4 miles to Va. Highway 656.

Along this portion of the route, the tour enters Chesterfield County, formed in 1748 from Henrico County and named for the Earl

Photo: Library of Virginia

Civil War-era tunnels punctuate the grounds of Petersburg National Park.

of Chesterfield, and Englishman and ardent supporter of the Virginia colony.

Turn left (east) onto Va. 656 (Bellwood Road), and go 0.5 mile, just beyond the I-95 overpass, turn left (north) on Fort Darling Road (Va. Highway 1435) and go another half-mile, parallel to I-95, to the entrance to Drewry's Bluff and Fort Darling, a National Park Service facility.

Drewry's Bluff, Fort Darling
Richmond, Va.

This site, with a 90-foot bluff offering a commanding view of the James River, was named for a local landowner, Capt. Augustus H. Drewry. During the Civil War, the James River was navigable from Hampton Roads at Norfolk to Richmond, and a Union attack on Richmond was a continuous threat during the war. Confederate soldiers built the Drewry's Bluff fortification — known as Fort Darling by the Federals — during the first month of the war, and it remained in existence throughout the war's four years.

Confederate naval vessels fought off Union boats at the base of Drewry's Bluff in May

1862, saving Richmond from a Union assault. Until the spring of 1864, Drewry's Bluff was used for naval training and as a Richmond fortification. USA Gen. Benjamin Franklin Butler advanced within 3 miles of this area in May 1864, but his troops were stopped by a counterattack by CSA Gen. Pierre Gustave Toutant "P.G.T." Beauregard. In early April 1865, soldiers and sailors defending Drewry's Bluff were part of the mass Confederate retreat that ended at Appomattox. That month, President Lincoln passed Drewry's Bluff on his way up the James River from City Point (in present-day Hopewell) to Richmond.

Drewry's Bluff is part of the Richmond National Battlefield Park system and is open from dawn to dusk. There is no admission charge. The facilities at this site include a half-mile walking trail, an observation platform, a Confederate cannon and a few interpretative signs.

DREWRY'S BLUFF TO DUTCH GAP MARKER
From Drewry's Bluff, return to U.S. 1-301, turn left (south) and go south 3.8 miles to Va. Highway 10. Two miles south of Drewry's Bluff is a historical marker for Dutch Gap.

Dutch Gap
Chesterfield County, Va.

Just east of the highway is Dutch Gap on the James River. In August 1864, USA Gen. Butler decided to cut a canal through a 174-yard, horseshoe bend section of the James River, which cut off nearly 5 miles of river travel and allowed Union gunboats easier access to Drewry's Bluff. Union soldiers began digging the canal in August 1864 and essentially completed their first phase of work on New Year's Eve, four months later. Then, after four months additional excavation work, the canal was declared passable in April 1865 — by which time the war was over.

Today, the auxiliary river course still shaves 5 miles off a river cruise. In the vicinity of the historical marker on U.S. 1-301 is Half-Way House, an old inn situated halfway between Petersburg and Richmond along old U.S. 1. The inn served as the headquarters of the Union Army of the James and was a significant location during the Battle of Drewry's Bluff. Today, the inn is operated as a restaurant.

DUTCH GAP TO HOPEWELL VISITORS CENTER
At the intersection of U.S. 1-301 and Va. 10, turn left (east) on Va. 10 and go 8.3 miles, across the Appomattox River and into downtown Hopewell on Randolph Road. The Hopewell Visitors Center is on the left, with parking on the right.

Hopewell Visitors Center
201-D Randolph Sq., Hopewell, Va. • (804) 541-2206, (800) 863-8687

The City of Hopewell operates this quaint visitors center in the downtown area. Travel counselors are knowledgeable and friendly. There is an ample supply of brochures and other travel information. The center has a walking tour brochure of Hopewell, and it features a special driving tour brochure on the Crescent Hills neighborhood and its Sears-Roebuck houses from the early 20th century. The center also features an exhibit of local history and a small gift shop. The center is open daily from 9 AM to 5 PM. It is closed on Thanksgiving, Christ-

mas and New Year's Day. There are restrooms, and the facility is handicapped-accessible.

HOPEWELL VISITORS CENTER TO UNION FORT SITE
From the Hopewell Visitors Center, return west on Randolph Road two blocks, turn right on N. Main Street and go one block, turn right (north) on Appomattox Street and go 0.5 mile to Union Fort on the right.

Union Fort Site
Hopewell, Va.

This historic site, now a public park, was the location of a Union Fort during the Civil War. The small Union Army fort was used to protect the rear flank of USA Gen. Grant during his stay at City Point in Hopewell.

UNION FORT SITE TO CITY POINT UNIT
Continue 0.2 mile on Appomattox Street, turn left on Cedar Lane and go two blocks to City Point Unit, a part of the Petersburg National Battlefield System.

City Point Unit
Cedar Ln., Hopewell, Va. • (804) 458-9504

City Point was established as "Bermuda Cittie" in 1613 by Sir Thomas Dale and has the distinction of being the oldest continuously occupied settlement of English origin in the New World. Incorporated as a town in the 19th century, City Point was annexed by Hopewell in 1923. Today, the City Point Historical District, bordered by the Appomattox River, James River, Cedar Lane and Water Street, is a registered state and national landmark. A walking tour brochure is available at the Hopewell Visitors Center.

For nearly 10 months, beginning in 1864, City Point served as the headquarters for USA Gen. Grant, who moved his Union troops to City Point after battles at the Wilderness (T-16), Spotsylvania Courthouse (T-16) and Cold Harbor (T-18). Grant chose City Point for a reason — this small, river port community was connected to Petersburg by rail, and Hopewell gave him a strategic link with both Hampton Roads to the east and Washington, D.C., to the north.

Grant set up his headquarters at Appomattox Manor, the home of Dr. Richard Eppes. The old homesite was a century old by the time Union soldiers set up their tents on the front lawn. From the manor, the Union general coordinated an operation that included building construction and new wharves as well as a major telegraph system to relay information from Washington to the battlefield and back. Almost overnight, this sleepy community of about 100 residents was turned into a supply center for 100,000 Union soldiers.

Members of a Confederate peace commission visited Grant at his City Point headquarters in January 1865. The meeting was an attempt by Southern leaders to negotiate an end to the 4-year-old war. From City Point, the Confederates were escorted to Hampton Roads for a meeting with President Lincoln, and Lincoln himself visited City Point twice. He joined Grant in June 1864 for a visit to the Petersburg front, and he was back in March 1865 to spend two weeks in meetings with USA Gens. Grant and William Tecumseh Sherman. The three met on the president's ship, the *River Queen*, docked just off shore.

A day after this meeting, Grant moved closer to the Petersburg front and began his final spring offensive against Petersburg. Richmond and Petersburg fell to Grant's troops less than a week later. City Point is open from 8:30 AM to 4:30 PM every day except Christmas and New Year's Day. The facility, operated by the National Park Service, is handicapped-accessible, and there is no admission charge.

CITY POINT TO CITY POINT
NATIONAL CEMETERY
Leaving City Point, return on Cedar Lane and Appomattox Street, cross Randolph Street and go one block to Broadway. Turn right (west) on Broadway and go 0.5 mile, turn right on N. 10th Avenue and go two blocks to the cemetery entrance.

City Point National Cemetery
Hopewell, Va.

There are 6,000 Union soldiers and about 100 Confederate men buried in the City Point National Cemetery. About 4,300 graves can be identified. The national cemetery is open from dawn to dusk with no admission charge.

CITY POINT NATIONAL CEMETERY
TO FORT LEE, U.S. ARMY
QUARTERMASTER MUSEUM
Return on 10th Avenue to Broadway (Va. Highway 36), turn right (west) and go 0.3 mile, turn left (south) on N. 15th Avenue (Va. 36) and go 1 mile, turn left on Arlington Road and go 1 block to Winston Churchill Road. Turn right (west) on Winston Churchill Road (Va. 36) and go 4.2 miles to the entrance to Fort Lee on the left. Note Va. 36 becomes Woodlawn Street before the approach to Fort Lee. At Fort Lee, turn left and enter on Lee Avenue, turn left at the first intersection — A Avenue — and go one block on A Avenue to the Quartermaster Museum on the left. There is parking beside and behind the museum.

U.S. Army Quartermaster Museum
A Ave., Fort Lee, Va. • (804) 734-4203

The U.S. Army Quartermaster Corps was founded in 1775, just two days after the establishment of the U.S. Army itself. Today, Fort Lee is the U.S. Army Quartermaster Center. The museum, a small building within the fort complex, has a number of exhibits on military uniforms, flags, transportation equipment, food services and memorial activities. Among the items featured are Gen. Dwight D. Eisenhower's uniforms and Gen. George Patton's World War II Jeep. There is a gift shop. The Quartermaster Museum is open Tuesday through Friday from 10 AM to 5 PM and Saturday and Sunday from 11 AM to 5 PM. It is closed Mondays and on Thanksgiving, Christmas and New Year's Day. There is no admission, and the facility is handicapped-accessible.

Photo: Library of Virginia

Guns like this one were used during the 10-month clash between CSA Gen. Lee and USA Gen. Grant at Petersburg.

FORT LEE TO PETERSBURG NATIONAL BATTLEFIELD VISITORS CENTER
Exit Fort Lee and return to Va. 36, turn left (west) and go 0.5 mile to the entrance to Petersburg National Battlefield on the right. Enter the battlefield and follow signs to the visitors center.

Petersburg National Battlefield
Va. Hwy. 36, Petersburg, Va.
• (804) 732-3531

In the summer of 1864, Union and Confederate troops clashed at Petersburg. "The key to taking Richmond is Petersburg," said USA Gen. Grant, referring to the four rail lines plus the major overland roadways that converged at Petersburg and provided supplies and equipment to Richmond and the Confederacy. Grant and his counterpart, CSA Gen. Lee dug in at Petersburg and set off a 10-month struggle whereby the Union general slowly forced the Confederate leader to retreat. The Petersburg experience, which lasted until the spring of 1865, has been called the longest siege in American warfare.

The Petersburg National Battlefield contains nearly 2,500 acres just east of downtown Petersburg. The facility, operated by the National Park Service, offers exhibits, a film and a small publications center. There is a 16-mile driving tour that covers all the battlefield's major historical sites. The NPS offers a brochure that includes detailed information on more than 15 separate battlefield sites, including Fort Sedgwick, Poplar Grove Cemetery, Fort Fisher, Fort Gregg and Five Forks. The visitors center is open daily from 8 AM to 5 PM. It is closed only on New Year's Day and Christmas. The battlefield is open from dawn to dusk and requires a $4 admission per vehicle. An annual vehicle pass for the Petersburg battlefield is available for $10. The center is handicapped-accessible and offers a free wheelchair for touring the center and the adjacent, outdoor battery.

PETERSBURG NATIONAL BATTLEFIELD TO BLANDFORD CHURCH

Exit the battlefield and follow signs for Petersburg. The exit ramp leads to Va. 36. Continue west on Va. 36 (Washington Street) 2 miles to S. Crater Road (U.S. Highway 460 and U.S. 301). Turn left (south) on Crater Road and go 0.3 mile to Blandford Church on the left.

Blandford Church Reception Center
111 Rochelle Ln., Petersburg, Va.
• (804) 733-2396

Built in 1735, Blandford Church was abandoned when the old town of Blandford was absorbed by Petersburg. In 1901, the Ladies Memorial Association of Petersburg developed Blandford Church into a Confederate shrine for the 30,000 Southern soldiers buried — graves arranged in order by state —in the church cemetery. That's when Louis Comfort Tiffany was called on to design a series of

Petersburg Battlefield Personalities: Coal Miners and African-American Troops

One Union regiment, the 48th Pennsylvania, included a number of coal miners from the mountains of western Pennsylvania. The regiment was commanded by USA Col. Henry Pleasants, a mining engineer before the war, who devised a unique plan for his miner-troops to dig a mine under a Confederate fort and trenches, fill it with powder and set off an explosion. The 500-foot tunnel was completed after a month's work in the summer of 1864. Then, USA Gen. Ambrose Everett Burnside was assigned the task of attacking the enemy through a gap made by the mine's explosion.

African-American troops were specially trained for the mission but later were withdrawn after Union officers feared political repercussions. Looking for white soldiers to replace the African-American troops, Burnside ordered three division commanders to draw straws to determine who would lead the mine assault. After a faulty fuse failed to set off the 320 kegs — 8,000 pounds — of explosives, two miner-soldiers succeeded in lighting the powder at sunrise on July 30. The destruction left a crater more than 150 long, 60 feet wide and 30 feet deep. More than 250 Confederates were killed or wounded. Fighting ensued, and a Union assault combined with a Southern counterattack left thousands of casualties on both sides. A number of Union officers later were found to be responsible for the "stupendous failure," as USA Gen. Grant described the events at the crater. There is still visible evidence at what the locals simply call The Crater, the last stop on a 4-mile driving tour of the park.

breathtaking stained-glass windows. Each window was donated by a Confederate state in honor of native sons who died in the Civil War. Over the main door is the only Tiffany window in the world that features the Confederate battle flag. Behind the church, along with the Confederate buried, are a number of weathered old tombstones that date to the early 18th century. Confederate Memorial Day, June 9, is observed here each year.

The church has a visitors center and small gift shop but no active congregation. It can be seen daily from 10 AM to 5 PM. Admission is $3 for adults and $2 for people older than 60, younger than 12 or active military. Children younger than 7 are admitted free. Tours run every half-hour ending at 4:30 PM. The church is handicapped accessible.

BLANDFORD CHURCH TO PETERSBURG VISITORS CENTER

Exit the church and return on S. Crater Road for 0.3 mile to E. Washington Street, turn left (west) and go 0.5 mile, turn right (north) on Sycamore Street and go six blocks, turn right (east) on Old Street and go one block to the visitors center parking lot on the right.

Petersburg Visitor's Center
425 Cockade Alley, Petersburg, Va.
• (804) 733-2400, (800) 368-3595

Petersburg, a port city on the Appomattox, traces its origins to the mid-1600s, when Abraham Wood established Fort Henry as a trading post in the then-remote area west Tidewater Virginia. Capt. Peter Jones married Wood's daughter, and he developed the settlement at Fort Henry. In time, it became known as Peter's Point, then Petersburg. In 1781, British Gen. Benedict Arnold raided the community during the American Revolution. Gen. Lafayette, a Frenchman serving the Colonial forces, camped across the Appomattox River at Colonial Heights. A fire in 1815 wiped out much of Petersburg's Old Towne. Once a collection of wooden warehouses and homes, the community rebuilt after the fire, and a number of handsome Federal-style brick buildings survive today.

In time, Petersburg became a major commercial center, serving as a central hub for Southside Virginia farmers who shipped their crops — mainly tobacco — to eastern markets. With the advent of the railroad, Petersburg rivaled Richmond as a major transportation center that linked points throughout Virginia. Petersburg was also a major river port and trade center during the Civil War.

At the beginning of the war, Virginia's African-American population included 490,000 slaves and more than 50,000 free blacks. In Petersburg, there were 18,000 African Americans — 15 percent were free. Thus, Petersburg had more free blacks than any Southern city at the time the war began. This visitors facility is in the attractive McIlwaine House, built in the early 1800s by Petersburg Mayor George Jones. The center is open every day except Thanksgiving, Christmas Eve and

Blandford Church Personality: Mary Logan

U.S. Congressman John Alexander Logan, a former Union general, and his wife, Mary Logan, visited Petersburg in 1867 and were taken by the sight of children placing flowers on Civil War graves at Blandford Church. Returning to Washington, Mrs. Logan urged her husband to establish a national observance in honor of the war dead, and it led to a proclamation issued in early 1868 by the Grand Army of the Republic, a patriotic organization of Civil War Union veterans. Later that year, on May 30, 1868, Decoration Day — later known as Memorial Day — was celebrated for the first time. Two years earlier, the first known memorial day in the U.S. was observed on the second anniversary of the Battle of New Market in Virginia's Shenandoah Valley (see T-3: New Market).

Christmas from 9 AM to 5 PM. There is ample parking (it's free for three hours) in the lot across from the center. Ask travel counselors about block tickets available for various Petersburg sites. Tour guides are available. The center is handicapped-accessible.

PETERSBURG VISITOR'S CENTER TO SIEGE MUSEUM

From the visitors center, walk west along Old Street back to Sycamore Street, go left (south) on Sycamore Street and up the hill one block, turn right (west) on Bank Street and go a half-block to the Siege Museum.

Siege Museum
15 W. Bank St., Petersburg, Va.
• **(804) 733-2404**

The Siege Museum is in the old Exchange Building, which was built in 1839 as a commodities market. It was restored in the mid-1970s. The museum tells how Petersburg residents lived before, during and immediately after the Civil War. There are a number of excellent exhibits, including such subjects as manufacturing, tobacco, cotton, foundry products, transportation, the care of wounded during the war and the role of women during the war. An 18-minute film, *The Echo Still Remains,* is shown each hour on the hour.

An exhibit at the Siege Museum features a letter written in April 1865 by an unidentified Pennsylvania chaplain. It reads: "On April 3, 1865, the guns fell silent. The great feature of the road between here and Petersburg is the debris of two armies. Broken guns, castaway garments, dead horses and mules, broken-down wagons, etc., are strewn all over the ground. Many of the houses are burned. . . . The few inhabitants remaining are old men and women, children, and Negroes. . . . It will take a generation to repair the loss."

The museum is open from 10 AM to 5 PM every day except Thanksgiving, Christmas Eve, Christmas and New Year's Day. Admission is $3 for adults; seniors, active military personnel and children 7 to 12 are admitted for $2. There is a parking lot in the rear of the building, where there is an elevator for handicapped-access.

SIEGE MUSEUM TO CENTRE HILL MANSION

From the Siege Museum, walk back to Sycamore Street, turn right (south) and walk two blocks up the hill to E. Tabb Street, adjacent to the Petersburg Courthouse. Turn left (east) on Tabb Street and walk a block to Adams Street. There are 19 steps leading up the hill to Centre Hill Mansion. For visitors traveling by automobile, there is free parking at the corner of Tabb and Adams streets. Handicapped travelers and others who need special assistance should ask at the Petersburg Visitors Center about automobile access to Centre Hill Mansion.

Centre Hill Mansion
1 Centre Hill Cir., Petersburg, Va.
• **(804) 733-2401, (800) 368-3595**

Richard Bolling, a member of a prominent Petersburg family, built Centre Hill Mansion in 1823. It was constructed in oversize brick in Flemish bond. Later, the 25-room house was remodeled in the Greek Revival design of the 1840s. Downstairs is a view of a tunnel that once connected the mansion with the Appomattox River. The mansion was visited by President Lincoln and USA Gen. Grant.

Recently, an adjacent five-story apartment building was demolished, giving the mansion a panoramic view of downtown Petersburg and across the Appomattox River to Colonial Heights. The mansion is open 10 AM to 5 PM every day except Thanksgiving, Christmas Eve, Christmas and New Year's Day. There is a $3 admission fee for adults, while seniors, active military personnel and children 7 to 12 are admitted for $2. The mansion has a guided tour, a museum and a gift shop.

This concludes the Petersburg tour route. From Violet Bank, return south on U.S. 1-301 to Petersburg for accommodations, dining and shopping. Our next tour, T-21: Appomattox, begins in Petersburg.

Trenches are still carved into the landscapes at Petersburg National Military Park.

Petersburg Side Trip: Violet Bank Museum

Exit Petersburg from N. Second Street (U.S. 1-301), adjacent to the Appomattox River, and go north over the Martin Luther King Jr. Bridge and 0.5 mile into Colonial Heights, where U.S. 1-301 becomes Boulevard. Turn right on Arlington Avenue and go one block to Virginia Avenue and the museum.

Violet Bank Museum
303 Virginia Ave., Colonial Heights, Va.
• (804) 520-9395

This fine old home, once the residence of Thomas Shore, was built in 1815. It was used by CSA Gen. Lee as a headquarters in 1864. Lee was at Violet Bank when he learned of the explosion at the Crater in Petersburg on July 30, 1864. The building is now owned by the City of Colonial Heights, which operates it as a museum. It is open Tuesday through Saturday from 10 AM to 5 PM and Sunday 1 to 5 PM. It is closed on Monday.

Petersburg Tour Ends

Other Tour Points of Interest

Hopewell and Petersburg offers a number of unique attractions and points of interest. For questions or reservations, ask for help at the Hopewell Visitors Center or the Petersburg Visitor's Center (see listings).

Annual Events

The **Appomattox Batteau Day** and the **Battersea Ball** (see Historical Sites, below) are both held each September in Petersburg. **Hooray for Hopewell**, one of Virginia's largest street festivals, is also held in mid-September. Petersburg offers garden and house tours, sports events and a candlelight Christmas tour during the year. Hopewell offers Christmas home tours, a City Point Christmas tour and the **James River Parade of Lights**, all in December each year.

Antiques

Old Towne Petersburg, along Old and River streets, has a number of antique shops. In addition, **South Side Station** on River Street has a flea market that offers crafts, collectibles, maps, memorabilia, Civil War items, gifts and "Made in Virginia" goods.

Arts

The **Petersburg Symphony Orchestra**

Photo: Harpers Ferry National Historical Park

CSA Gen. Robert E. Lee began his final retreat from the Petersburg area in April 1865.

offers a season of classical, modern and popular music. Founded in 1978, the Petersburg Symphony is a full symphonic orchestra with 65 musicians. The **Petersburg Public Forum** offers headline speakers throughout the year. Original art can be purchased in the spring at the **Poplar Lawn Art Festival** and the **Petersburg Art League** opens new art exhibits monthly at its warehouse on Rock Street. Community concerts with free music are held under a tent in the downtown plaza in Hopewell in the spring and fall.

Historic Sites

Battersea is a Palladian-style country house that was built in the 1770s by John Bannister, Petersburg's first mayor. The **First Baptist Church** on Harrison Street in Petersburg is home of the nation's oldest African-American congregation. The **Trapezium House** on Market Street in Petersburg was built in 1817.

In Hopewell, a boat tour of historical sites is available aboard the **Pocahontas II**, which seats 90 and operates from April through October. For more information, write P.O. Box 35140, Richmond, Virginia 23235, or call (804) 541-2616. Hopewell is the gateway to **Virginia's Plantation Country**, and the community offers a link to numerous grand old plantations to the south and east. Combination tickets for the plantation tours are available at the Hopewell Visitors Center.

Shopping

The **Old Towne** and **Courthouse** historic districts in Petersburg have a wide variety of shops and stores. In addition, there is an extensive collection of businesses along Crater Road South (US 301). Take Sycamore Street south from downtown 4 miles to Crater Road.

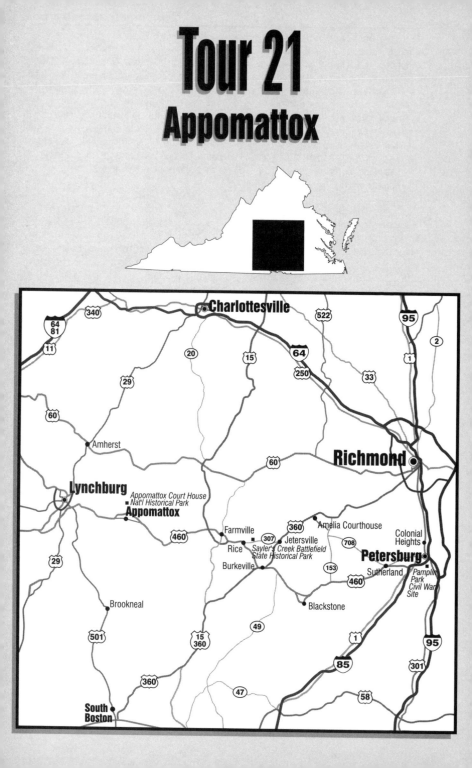

Tour 21
Appomattox

TOUR 21
Appomattox

About This Tour

Our last tour route is a natural continuation of the previous Petersburg tour. It begins in Petersburg, Virginia, and runs west across Virginia's Southside to Appomattox. This route roughly follows CSA Gen. Robert E. Lee's nine-day retreat in 1864 that began west of Petersburg and concluded at Appomattox.

This tour follows U.S. Highway 360 and U.S. Highway 460 as well as a handful of small, rural state routes in the area between Petersburg and Appomattox. Virginia's Southside is a wide geographic band that stretches between the east-flowing Appomattox River and the Virginia-North Carolina border. Native Americans, mainly the Nottoway and Appomattox tribes, lived in this region prior to the 17th century, when Anglos pushed west out of Tidewater Virginia to settle the region. The main river in this area is the Appomattox, named for the Native American tribe. The river originates in Appomattox County and flows east to Hopewell, Virginia. County names reflect the region's Native American heritage and the influence of western-moving Anglo settlers.

In late March 1865 after the fall of Richmond and Petersburg, CSA Gen. Lee and his troops began a western retreat. Just over a week later, on April 9, the retreat ended at the small village of Appomattox, on the rail line from Lynchburg to Petersburg. The series of battles that took place during this period are sometimes known as the Appomattox Campaign, and also "Lee's Retreat."

Travel Tips

Both U.S. 360 and U.S. 460 are divided four-lane highways in this section of southern Virginia. This is tobacco country, with rolling hills west of the "fall zone" at Petersburg all the way to the base of the Blue Ridge Mountains, west of Appomattox. Petersburg and Richmond radio stations report traffic and weather conditions. Farther west, nearer Appomattox, Lynchburg stations provide helpful travel information. Citizens band radio users can find traffic reports on Channel 19. State police usually monitor Channel 9. Motorists receive a strong mobile telephone signal throughout Southside.

An interpretive radio message detailing various stops along the U.S. 460 corridor west of Petersburg can be heard on AM 1610. You can obtain a copy of a "Lee's Retreat" interpretive brochure that coincides with the radio programming. Pick one up at the Petersburg Visitor's Center (see T-20: Petersburg). Also, follow signs along portions of U.S. 460 and U.S. 360 for historic sites associated with the "Lee's Retreat" brochure. This tour ends in Appomattox, where we suggest you plan evening dining and lodging. Recommended accommodations are listed in Chapter 22. Dining suggestions are listed in Chapter 23. It is a good idea to review these recommendations before traveling throughout the region.

Appomattox Tour Begins . . .

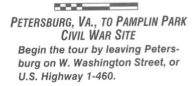

PETERSBURG, VA., TO PAMPLIN PARK CIVIL WAR SITE
Begin the tour by leaving Petersburg on W. Washington Street, or U.S. Highway 1-460.

Outside Petersburg, and beyond the U.S. 1-460 interchange with Interstate 85, this route follows Boydton Plank Road, which leads south to Dinwiddie Courthouse and Five Forks, scene of a major battle on April 1, 1865. Along this route, the tour enters Dinwiddie County, created in 1752 and named for Robert Dinwiddie, who was then lieutenant governor of the Virginia colony.

Just beyond the I-85 interchange, along U.S. 1-460, turn left (east) on Duncan Road (Va. Highway 670) and go 0.5 mile to Pamplin Park.

Pamplin Park Civil War Site
6523 Duncan Rd., Petersburg, Va.
• **(804) 861-2408**

In early 1865, the Confederate army had completed construction of an elaborate string of earthen fortifications around Petersburg. These earthworks stretched as far south as Tudor Hall, a 200-acre Dinwiddie County estate about 4 miles south. CSA Gen. Samuel McGowan converted Tudor Hall into offices and sleeping quarters. On April 2, 1865, a Union force overran McGowan's fortification at Tudor Hall. The assault signaled the end of the Union siege at Petersburg. Less than a mile to the west, that same day, CSA Gen. Ambrose Powell "A.P." Hill was shot and killed by Union troops. That night, CSA Gen. Lee ordered Petersburg and Richmond aban-

doned. It was just a week before the Confederate surrender at Appomattox.

Today, Pamplin Park Civil War Site is a perfect example of how private funds and resources can be utilized to create an interesting, attractive, educational tourist facility. The site includes a 7,000-square-foot interpretive center, complete with a modern museum and store, the restored Tudor Hall estate and a 1.1-mile battlefield interpretive trail. The interpretive center is unique. The concrete cast exterior is shaped to mirror the line of earthworks that run the breadth of the park.

Inside, the center offers an orientation video, a fiberoptic battle map, interactive computer exhibits and a wealth of museum displays. The facility is clean, well-maintained, and remarkably warm in welcoming visitors, particularly youngsters. The trail includes 8-foot earthworks, picket posts, artillery positions and a dam. The interpretive center is open daily from 9 AM to 5 PM and is handicapped-accessible. Special parking spaces are available for handicapped drivers as well as buses and recreational vehicles.

PAMPLIN PARK TO A.P. HILL MONUMENT
Leave Pamplin Park on Duncan Road (Va. 670) and return to U.S. 1-460, turn left (south) and go 0.1 mile, turn right on A.P. Hill Drive

Pamplin Park Personalities:
R.B. Pamplin Sr., R.B. Pamplin Jr.

Two generations after the Civil War, young Robert B. Pamplin left his home in the Tudor Hall neighborhood of Dinwiddie County to attend college at Virginia Tech in Blacksburg. At school, Pamplin roomed with a young Atlanta man, whose family was in the lumber business. Pamplin took a business position with the timber company, Georgia Hardwood Lumber, and before long both the young Virginian and the company grew together until Pamplin became CEO of Georgia-Pacific!

Retired in 1976, Pamplin joined with his son, R.B. Pamplin Jr., to establish a multifaceted corporation with business interests throughout the country. And the father-son team earned a reputation for creative philanthropy. The Pamplins' work included the development of Pamplin Park Civil War Site, which opened in 1994. The energetic, enthusiastic Pamplins have plans to develop the National Museum of the Civil War Soldier, a 21,000-square-foot museum that is scheduled to open adjacent to Pamplin Park on Memorial Day 1999.

and go 0.3 mile — right and about halfway around the circular sub-division road — to a wooded area on the right side of A.P. Hill Drive.

A.P. Hill Monument
Dinwiddie County, Va.

In the trees, about 20 yards off A.P. Hill Drive, is a marker that designates the site where CSA Gen. Hill was shot and killed by Union troops on April 2, 1865 — just days before the Confederate surrender at Appomattox. Today, a local pre-teen, Johnathan Parham, resides at 5937 A.P. Hill Drive and serves as an unofficial neighbor-hood tour guide for the marker site. Catch the 11-year-old after school hours, on weekends and anytime in the summer! Johnathan leads tour bus groups and individual visitors into the wooded underbrush and offers a brief dialogue on the historical significance of the site. His services are free — but he gladly accepts a gratuity!

A.P. HILL SITE TO SUTHERLAND
From the split at U.S. 1 and U.S. 460, just south of the A.P. Hill Site, turn right (west) on U.S. 460 and continue west 6 miles to Sutherland.

Sutherland, Va.

Known as Sutherland Station during the Civil War, this rail community was the scene of an engagement on April 2, 1865, that enabled

A.P. Hill Monument Personality: CSA Gen. A.P. Hill

Affectionately known as "A.P.," CSA Gen. Ambrose Powell Hill was born in Culpeper, Virginia (see T-9: Brandy Station), on November 9, 1825. He graduated from West Point in 1847 at the age of 22, served in the Mexican War and then signed on with the Confederate Army in 1861 as an infantry colonel.

Photo: Library of Virginia

Union troops gunned down CSA Gen. A.P. Hill just a week before the Confederate surrender.

Hill participated in action during the Peninsula Campaign (T-19: Lower Peninsula) in 1862, when his troops became known as "Hill's Light Division" for their marching speed. He achieved distinction at Cedar Mountain (T-9), Antietam (T-1), Chancellorsville (T-16), Gettysburg (T-6) and Cold Harbor (T-18). He rose in rank to lieutenant general, commanding a corps for CSA Gen. Lee. Hill was on sick leave during the Siege of Petersburg (T-20) when he decided to return to the field and rally his men on April 2, 1865. That was a tragic day — the general was shot and killed by Union soldiers just west of the Bowdton Plank Road.

After Hill's death, his troops erected a monument to him in Richmond. The general is buried beneath it. He was survived by his wife, Kitty Grosh Morgan, a sister of prominent CSA Gen. John Hunt Morgan.

A.P. Hill Monument Side Trip: Dinwiddie County

From the A.P. Hill Monument, take U.S. 1-460 south 0.5 mile to the split of U.S. 1 and U.S. 460. Continue south on U.S. 1 for 5 miles to the site of the Battle of Five Forks, named for the junction of five roads in Dinwiddie County.

The Battle of Five Forks was fought on April 1, 1865, and became known as the "Waterloo of the Confederacy." The battle helped break the siege of Petersburg and led to the ultimate fall of Richmond. The next day, Confederates evacuated Richmond and Petersburg; Union troops occupied Richmond a day after that.

USA Gen. Grant's forces to sever the Southside Railroad line, CSA Gen. Lee's last supply link to Petersburg.

SUTHERLAND TO NAMOZINE CHURCH
From Sutherland, take Va. Highway 708 (Claiborne Road) to the right (north) 10.7 miles to Namozine Church.

This stretch of Va. 708, also known as Namozine Road, is a two-lane, rural roadway — the Virginia countryside looks much as it did in Civil War days. The Namozine Church sits on the left at the intersection of Va. 708 and Va. Highway 622. Along this portion of the tour, the route enters Amelia County, created in 1734 and named for Princess Amelia Sophia Eleanora, the daughter of England's King George II.

Namozine Church
Amelia County, Va.
The small, unassuming, box-like Namozine Church was built in 1847. Events at the church reflected the quickly changing luck of the retreating Confederates in April 1865. The church was a Confederate headquarters on the morning of April 3. A rear-guard cavalry skirmish took place around the church as Lee's troops marched toward Amelia Courthouse. By nightfall, the church was a Union stronghold.

NAMOZINE CHURCH TO AMELIA COURTHOUSE, VA.
From Namozine Church, continue

north on Va. 708 (Namozine Road), a small country road, for 10 miles. Turn right (north) on Va. 153 and go 3 miles to Scotts Fort, turn left (west) on Va. 38 and go 6 miles to downtown Amelia Courthouse, the county seat of Amelia County.

Amelia Courthouse, Va.
Confederate forces retreating from both Richmond and Petersburg converged at Amelia Courthouse in April 1865. CSA Gen. Lee spent April 4 and 5 in Amelia, hoping to find cars of badly needed supplies from the Richmond and Danville Railroad. This delay was doubly costly: The supplies never came, and the Confederates lost a full day in their escape from the pursuing Federals. This almost became the site of the Confederate surrender. A statue on the courthouse lawn honors Virginia's Confederate soldiers.

AMELIA COURTHOUSE TO JETERSVILLE, VA.
From Amelia Courthouse, continue 0.5 mile on Va. 38 to U.S. 360. Turn left (west) on U.S. 360 and travel 7 miles west to Jetersville.

Jetersville, Va.
Jetersville, also known as Amelia Springs during the war, was a small rail stop on the Richmond and Danville Railroad line. USA Gen. Philip Henry "Little Phil" Sheridan anticipated that Lee, retreating from Amelia, might shift his force south, toward Danville, Virginia, so

Appomattox Courthouse was an unassuming site for the official end of the Civil War.

Farmville Side Trip:
High Bridge and Cumberland Church

Just north of Farmville, on Va. Highway 45 (the extension of Main Street north) is the site of High Bridge on the Appomattox River. Confederate forces burned four spans of High Bridge, but they failed to destroy the lower wagon bridge. This enabled Union troops to continue their pursuit of Lee's army on April 7, 1865.

Two miles north of the Appomattox River on Va. 45 is Cumberland Church. Union troops successfully crossed the Appomattox River at High Bridge and attacked Lee's army around the white-columned church on April 7, 1865. While at the church, Lee received USA Gen. Grant's first note that sought a Confederate surrender.

Following this side trip, return on Va. 45 to downtown Farmville.

---

he laid in wait at Jetersville on April 5, 1865. The Confederate general countered by shifting north thus avoiding a major confrontation with the Union troops.

JETERSVILLE TO SAYLER'S CREEK BATTLEFIELD HISTORICAL STATE PARK
Continue west on U.S. 360 for 2.5 miles, turn right (north) on Va. 307 (follow signs for Sayler's Creek) and go 6 miles to Va. Highway 617. Along the way, this route crosses over Sayler's Creek, the small stream for which the battle is named. Turn right (north) on Va. 617 and go 6 miles to the Sayler's Creek Battlefield Historical State Park and the Hillsman House on the right.

Along this portion of the tour, the route briefly enters Nottoway County, created in 1788 and named for the Nottoway River, which in turn was named for the Nottoway tribe of Native Americans.

Sayler's Creek Battlefield Historical State Park
Twin Lakes State Park
Va. Hwy. 617, Green Bay, Va. • (804) 392-3435

Even though state and national park ser-

vices spell the battle name "Sailor's Creek," the name should be spelled "Sayler's Creek." That's because the battlefield is the namesake of Sayler's Creek, which was named for the Sayler family settlers in the vicinity. CSA Gen. Lee had pushed west, avoiding a confrontation with Union troops at Jetersville. Spring rains turned area streams into muddy bogs, and Lee's men and their supply wagons got mired at Sayler's Creek. The battle at the creek was fought on April 6, 1865, and it has the dubious distinction of being the last major battle of the Civil War.

Union soldiers fired on Confederates at Hillsman House. In time, CSA Gens. Richard Heron Anderson and Richard Stoddert Ewell surrendered. This cost Lee more than 8,000 men — about half his army — in the largest unstipulated surrender on the continent in history. The Confederate surrender at Appomattox, by that time, was just 72 hours away. The Hillsman House, used as a Civil War hospital at the Sayler's Creek Battlefield, is sometimes opened for living history programs in the summer months.

SAYLER'S CREEK TO RICE, VA.
Return south on Va. 617 to Va. 307. Turn right (west) on Va. 307 and go 7 miles to U.S. 460. Go west on U.S. 460 for 0.5 mile to Rice.

Along this portion of the tour, the route enters Prince Edward County, created in 1753 and named for Prince Edward Augustus, a nephew of England's King George III.

Rice, Va.

Rice, known as Rice Station or Rice's Depot during the Civil War, was the scene of minor skirmishing on April 7, as Confederates entrenched at the rail depot fought with Union troops arriving from the direction of Burkeville, to the southeast. The village of Rice was named for William Rice, who built a church in the area in the mid-18th century.

RICE TO FARMVILLE, VA.

From Rice, take U.S. 460 west 6 miles to Farmville. Follow signs for Farmville's historic district along U.S. 460 (Third Street).

Farmville, Va.

The small tobacco town of 1,500 residents saw both Union and Confederate soldiers on April 7, 1865, as they marched west toward Appomattox. Lee had hoped to issue some rations to his soldiers at Farmville, but he was unsuccessful. Later, Lee crossed to the north side of the Appomattox River into Cumberland County, created in 1749, and named for William Augustus, the Duke of Cumberland and the third son of England's King George II (see T-1: Sharpsburg).

FARMVILLE TO APPOMATTOX VISITOR INFORMATION CENTER

From downtown Farmville, take U.S. 460 (Bus.) west 4 miles and get back on U.S. 460 west, a divided, four-lane highway. Continue 27 miles and follow signs to downtown Appomattox. A mile further west on U.S. 460 (Confederate Boulevard), turn left (south) on Court Street and follow signs for Appomattox Visitor Information Center. Take Court Street for 0.6 mile, turn right on Main Street and go 0.2 mile to the visitors center parking lot on the right.

Appomattox Visitor Information Center

5 Main St., Appomattox, Va.
• **(804) 352-2621**

This visitors center is in the town's old train depot. USA Gen. George Armstrong Custer overtook CSA Gen. Lee's last train of much-needed food and supplies at this old train station on April 8, 1865. The depot burned in 1923 and was rebuilt on the same foundation in 1924.

Today, the renovated depot houses the county's information center and chamber of commerce. This center offers information on various historical sites in the Appomattox area. The visitor information center is open daily from 9 AM to 5 PM, and is handicapped-accessible. It is closed on federal holidays.

Appomattox County was created in and named for the Appomattox River, was named for a Native American tribe area. Appomattox was a rural county the days of the Civil War. Of the ne county residents, more than 54 p African American. Additional fighting in Appomattox on April 9. Follow tion by USA Gens. Philip Sheridan O.C. Ord to block further Confe Lee realized that surrender wa

APPOMATTOX INFORM TO APPOMATTOX C NATIONAL HISTO

Return on Court 460. Turn left (w and go 0.1 mile, on Va. 24 and Appomattox Co Historical Par

Appomattox C Historical Par

Appomattox, V

CSA Gen. Grant here on year Civil Wa soldiers of Le down their ar Lee was on h ready was in W

The park vis

center in the reconstructed courthouse on National Park Service grounds. The center has an information desk downstairs and a museum upstairs. The park facility offers a village of restored and reconstructed buildings, including the McLean House, Meeks Store, the Woodson Law Office, Clover Hill Tavern, the old courthouse, jail, Kelly House, Mariah Wright House, Surrender Triangle, Isbell House and Peers House. Some of these structures, such as the McLean House, are original, but the courthouse is a reconstruction. The national historic park is open daily and charges a $2 admission fee for entrants 17 to 61. During summer months, the hours are 8:30 AM to 5 PM. After October, the hours are 9 AM to 5 PM.

Appomattox Tour Ends

Other Tour Points of Interest

Southside Virginia offers a variety of attractions and points of interest. For questions or reservations, ask for help at the Petersburg Visitor's Center (see T-20: Petersburg) or the Appomattox Visitor Information Center (see listing).

Annual Events

The Tour duPont, America's premier cycling event, sprints through Appomattox each April, the Bateau Festival is held on the James River each June, the **Fall Beef Festival** takes place in September in Appomattox and **Railroad Weekend** is observed in Appomattox each October.

A **Civil War re-enactment** is held each April at Sayler's Creek Battlefield **Oktoberfest** is observed during its namesake month at Longwood College in Farmville. The Farmville Chamber of Commerce sponsors a Christmas show each December.

Arts

Longwood College and **Hampden-Sydney College**, both in Farmville, offer a wide variety of cultural and arts programs during their respective school years. In particular, the **Longwood Center for the Visual Arts**, at the corner of Third and Main streets in downtown Farmville, offers numerous programs that feature local and school artists. For more information, contact the center at (804) 395-2206. To contact the colleges for more detailed information on cultural programs, telephone Longwood College at (804) 395-2020, and Hampden-Sydney College at (804) 223-9933.

Historic Sites

A number of historical sites are located in Lynchburg, 43 miles west of Appomattox (see T-11: Lynchburg for specific listings).

Shopping

Stonewall Vineyards and Winery is in Concord, Virginia, 14 miles west of Appomattox and just off U.S. 460. The vineyard is open

Appomattox Personality: Wilmer McLean

...der the sad story of Wilmer McLean. Prior to the Civil War, McLean owned a ...the Bull Run in Northern Virginia. In 1861, during action at Manassas, an ...ll fell down McLean's chimney and into a stew being prepared for CSA Gen. ...uregard.

...a more tranquil place to live, McLean bought a farmhouse in — of all places ...ttox County. McLean's house was chosen for the surrender meeting ...ant and Lee. The two military leaders met in McLean's parlor, after which ...s stripped the room for souvenirs. The house was dismantled in 1893 for ...m in Washington, D.C. The plan never materialized. The current house at ...park is a reconstruction. As for Wilmer McLean, the Civil War began in the ...first home — and ended in the parlor of his second home.

from March to December and offers a number of special functions including a Mayfest celebration in spring and a Jazz on the Lawn program during the second or third weekend in October. The vineyard planted its first vines in 1978 and produced its first wines in 1982. The vineyard is named not for the general but for Stonewall, an abandoned community in the area. The vineyard plans to begin production of a new semisweet red wine that will be named "Stonewall Brigade" in honor of the Civil War unit led by "Stonewall" Jackson. Stonewall Vineyards offers wine tastings and tours daily from 11 AM to 4 PM, and by appointment. For more information, telephone (804) 993-2185.

After the first day's battle at Gettysburg in June 1863, local resident Sallie Broadhead wrote, "I cannot sleep . . . . We know not what the morrow will bring forth."

Accommodations

In this chapter, we offer a general guide to accommodations available at various stopping points along our 21 individual tour routes. Remember, this is only a sampling of what is out there — places that we have enjoyed and heard good things about — and by no means constitutes a comprehensive listing.

As you will note, many of these destinations are easily accessible off several different tours. For example, accommodations for the Manassas, Northern Virginia and Washington tours are within reasonable driving distances of each other. Likewise, Richmond and Petersburg options are relatively close, as are lodging recommendations for the Brandy Station (listed under Orange, Virginia) and Charlottesville tours. Rates and unique amenities are subject to change. Rate charges for a standard, double-occupancy room are coded as follows:

$	$40 to $60
$$	$61 to $90
$$$	$91 to $120
$$$$	$121 and up

Please note these rates do not include taxes and other add-on charges such as premium movie channels or room service. Unless specified, you can expect all these lodging options to accept your major credit cards. Unless otherwise noted, all accommodations listed offer smoking and non-smoking room options, and many also have handicapped-accessible rooms. Listings also contain information about acceptance of pets. But if you have specific questions, don't hesitate to pick up the phone and put your mind at ease.

Following the city names, listed alphabetically, are the tour routes associated with the location.

Alexandria, Va. (T-7, T-8, T-12, T-13, T-14)

Best Western Old Colony Inn
$$$ • N. Washington and First Sts. • (703) 739-2222

Less glamorous than our other Alexandria choice, the Old Colony Inn is practical, accommodating and convenient. North of historic Old Town on the George Washington Memorial Parkway, this inn is a short trip south to the heart of Alexandria or north to National Airport, the Pentagon and Washington, D.C. The Old Colony has 150 rooms, and it features an outdoor swimming pool. Nonsmoking rooms are available.

Morrison House
$$$$ • 116 S. Alfred St. • (703) 838-8000

A celebrated inn, the Morrison House is an elegant mansion in the heart of Alexandria's Old Town. There are 45 rooms, and each is decorated with Federal-period antiques. Several rooms have fireplaces and four-poster canopy beds. The inn's restaurant and lounge enhance the romantic atmosphere (see our Restaurants chapter), making it the perfect urban getaway for honeymoons or romantic weekends. Nonsmoking rooms are available.

Appomattox, Va. (T-21)

Babcock House Bed and Breakfast
$$-$$$ • 106 Oakleigh Ave. • (804) 352-7532

Three Appomattox women joined forces in 1996, purchased the old Babcock family boarding house and converted it into a charming bed and breakfast. The attractive, white frame house dates to 1884. Debbie Powell, Luella Coleman and Barbara Carr tore out the interior of the structure and decorated the five-room inn with turn-of-the-century decor.

Four of the inn's rooms are on the second level — three have queen beds with private baths; the fourth has a queen bed, a parlor, a private bath and a pull-out queen sofa. A fifth room is on the inn's first floor and is handicapped-accessible. All rooms are nonsmoking, and pets are prohibited. The three owners offer a different breakfast each day. The treats include a sausage-and-egg casserole or French toast, all with fresh fruit, juice and coffee. This inn is a testament to the hard work and ingenuity of the three women owners, who did much of the renovation and decorating work themselves.

From the visitors center in downtown Appomattox, take Main Street a half-block east to Church Street, go left a block to Oakleigh Avenue and go right to the fourth house on the right.

Budget Inn
$$ • Confederate Blvd. (U.S. Hwy. 460 Bus.) • (804) 352-7451

This Budget Inn has 20 rooms, three of which have king beds. The motel accepts small pets, but call first to determine the restrictions. This clean, practical motel is on Confederate Boulevard (U.S. 460 Bus.) in downtown Appomattox.

Super 8
$$ • U.S. 460 W. Bypass • (804) 352-2339

This Super 8 has 46 rooms, with both singles and doubles. Two rooms have king beds, and the motel accepts pets lighter than 20 pounds. From downtown Appomattox, take Court Street north to U.S. 460 (Bus.), continue north two traffic lights to the U.S. 460 bypass, go left on the bypass and a half-mile to the Super 8 on the right.

Baltimore, Md.
(T-7, T-12, T-13)

Admiral Fell Inn
$$$ • 888 S. Broadway • (410) 522-7377

In the historic Fell's Point area, the Admiral Fell is a European-style hotel with the warmth and charm of a traditional inn. The inn is a member of the National Trust for Historic Preservation's prestigious Historic Hotels of America program. The Admiral Fell has 77 rooms and three suites, all custom-styled with Federal-period furnishings. Honeymooners should ask for the two-story suite that has a fireplace and Jacuzzi! Just outside the front door are the Belgian block streets of historic Fell's Point, known for its waterfront docking, tugboats and oodles of restaurants, pubs, shops and galleries. There's free parking, and a courtesy van takes guests to Baltimore's Inner Harbor or Oriole Park at Camden Yards. By the way, historic Fell's Point is named for a Colonial Marylander, William Fell, who was a colonel in the British army! It is a mystery why the inn's founder gave Fell the navy rank of Admiral.

Celie's Waterfront Bed and Breakfast
$$$ • 1714 Thames St. • (410) 522-2323, (800) 432-0184

Born and raised in Baltimore, Celie Ives remembers Baltimore when it was a "big little town." She moved away for three decades, then returned to her native city eight years ago and built a bed and breakfast in the Fell's Point historic area. Celie has just seven rooms, and they're in high demand. She says business travelers have caught on to her homestyle hospitality. Celie's has two rooms that face the harbor and two rooms facing a center courtyard filled with flowers in the summer. There are also two rooms that open onto private balconies with views of the cityscape. A seventh room, the Courtyard, is small but has its own courtyard with table and chairs.

Celie's was cited in 1996 by *Travel & Leisure* magazine as one of the nation's top-50 affordable accommodation spots. The continental breakfast includes fresh fruit, juice, baked bread and cereal. It is served on the roof deck, in the privacy of your room or in the courtyard — it's your call. Celie prohibits smoking everywhere on the premises. She welcomes children older than 10, but pets are not allowed.

Stouffer Harborplace Hotel
$$$$ • 202 E. Pratt St. • (410) 547-1200

The Stouffer in Baltimore is impressive. The

large, steel-and-glass high-rise overlooks the Inner Harbor. In fact, a crosswalk over Pratt Street connects the hotel with the Inner Harbor's pavilions and waterfront attractions. Inside, the Stouffer has more than 600 elegant rooms, plus 40 suites and 18 meeting rooms. It boasts the largest ballroom in Maryland — seating for 2,000 in a theater-style setting — so it's a popular place to host a convention. It also offers a restaurant, two cocktail lounges, a health club with an indoor pool and top-flight concierge service.

Charles City, Va. (T-17, T-18, T-19)

North Bend Plantation
$$$$ • 12200 Weyanoke Rd. • (804) 829-5176

There's plenty of history at North Bend (see listing, T-18). Try staying a day (or longer) in the Magnolia Room, the Sheridan Room, the Rose Room or the Maids Quarters. Children 6 and older are welcome at North Bend; smoking is restricted to designated areas. Proprietors George and Ridgely Copeland think of everything — take a dip in the swimming pool or enjoy a game of billiards, croquet or horseshoes. The Copelands serve a continental breakfast, and they can help with reservations for nearby historic restaurants and taverns. Above all else, ask to see the desk that USA Gen. Philip Henry Sheridan used when his forces occupied North Bend.

Charlottesville, Va. (T-9, T-10, T-11)

Best Western Cavalier Inn
$$ • 105 Emmet St. • (804) 296-8111, (800) 528-1234

If you want to be near the University of Virginia, and you want to pay a moderate price for lodging, then the Best Western Cavalier is the place to stay. The university's mascot is a Cavalier, thus the name of the motel. It's at one of the university's busiest intersections: Emmet Street (U.S. Highway 29) and Ivy Road

(U.S. Highway 250). You can walk to most all of the university's historic attractions. The Cavalier Inn has more than 100 rooms, two suites and three meeting rooms. It's basic, the parking is a little cramped and it can get a little noisy, especially after UVa wins a basketball or football game, but you can't beat the location or the price.

Boar's Head Inn
$$$$ • U.S. Hwy. 250 • (804) 296-2181, (800) 476-1988

The Boar's Head Inn is a resort complex with 175 rooms beside a duck pond on several manicured acres just west of the city. The inn and sports club were the dream of the late John Rogan, a prominent businessman who loved the history of the surrounding countryside of Albemarle County. The Boar's Head caters to every fancy, particularly the expensive ones. There are two restaurants at the property. Ask about special rates and packages. From the University of Virginia area, take U.S. 250 west (Ivy Road) 1 mile to the Boar's Head complex on the left.

Clifton Country Inn
$$$$ • 1296 Clifton Inn Dr. • (804) 971-1800

This fine old Albemarle County inn is east of Charlottesville near Shadwell, Thomas Jefferson's birthplace. The white-columned inn, situated on a 48-acre spread, dates to 1800. *Country Inns* magazine recently named Clifton one of the 12 best inns in the nation. Each room has a private bath and fireplace. Guests can use the kitchen, swim in a lap pool or practice tennis. Youngsters are welcome here, mainly because the extensive rolling hills offer plenty of space to romp and play. From Charlottesville, take U.S. 250 west 10 miles (toward Richmond). Just past Shadwell, turn right (south) on Va. Highway 729 — Clifton Road. The inn entrance is 0.5 mile down Clifton Road across from Stone Robinson Elementary School.

Omni Charlottesville
$$$$ • 235 W. Main St. • (804) 971-5500, (800) 843-6664

Near the downtown Charlottesville mall, the Omni is relatively expensive, but it's convenient to a number of downtown historic attractions and amenities. These include the Albemarle County Courthouse, Jackson Park and Lee Park (see listings, T-10). The Omni has an attractive, multi-story atrium, more than 200 rooms, restaurants, a lounge, a sauna and health club and — a first for downtown Charlottesville — an indoor-outdoor pool.

Fairfax, Va. (T-8, T-13, T-14)

Bailiwick Inn
$$$$ • 4023 Chain Bridge Rd.
• (703) 691-2266, (800) 366-7666
Annette and Robert Bradley have operated this historic inn since September 1994, and it has become one of Fairfax's premiere accommodations. The Bailiwick is a 19th-century brick house just across Chain Bridge Road from the historic Fairfax County Courthouse (see listing, T-14). The inn has 14 rooms, all with feather beds. The rooms offer either a Jacuzzi or a fireplace. The Bailiwick provides an opportunity to stroll along historic Main Street in Fairfax. George Mason University is nearby. It also features a quaint, small dining room: the Belvoir (see our Restaurants chapter).

Frederick, Md. (T-6, T-7)

Hampton Inn-Historic Frederick
$$ • 5311 Buckeystown Pk.
• (301) 698-2500, (800) HAMPTON
In the midst of so many national chain lodging facilities, this sign is a welcome, familiar site. And this particular Hampton Inn gives a special welcome to history lovers: It offers a double room rate of $75 a night for history enthusiasts. This motel is popular with Civil War buffs who want to see the Monocacy battlefield about 1 mile away. This facility has 160 rooms and, like all Hamptons, offers a free continental breakfast. The inn includes an outdoor pool and an exercise room. From downtown Frederick, take Market Street south past Interstate 70 and keep right onto Buckeystown Pike (Md. Highway 85). Continue

on Buckeystown Pike for 1 mile and the motel is just beyond the interchange with Interstate 270.

Tyler Spite House
$$$-$$$$ • 112 W. Church St.
• (301) 831-4455
Dr. John Tyler (see listing, T-7) was a man of prominence and obvious power in old Frederick. He built this house solely to prevent Record Street from being cut across Church Street to W. Patrick Street. He had the house foundation built overnight, and the place became known as Tyler's "Spite" house. Today, Bill and Andrea Myer are the hosts of this nice bed and breakfast. Rooms have 13-foot ceilings, elegant antique furnishings and fine woodwork and moldings. The house has five chandeliers and eight fireplaces, many with imported, carved marble mantles. Plan to tackle a multi-course breakfast and enjoy a 4 PM tea with white linens, fresh flowers and silver service. On weekends (weather permitting), guests get a free carriage ride through historic downtown Frederick.

Fredericksburg, Va. (T-15, T-16)

Econo Lodge South
$ • 5321 Jefferson Davis Hwy. (U.S. Hwy. 1) • (540) 898-5440
This familiar facility offers 175 rooms, continental breakfast served on the premises and an outdoor swimming pool. Two handicapped-accessible rooms are available. Double rooms are sometimes as low as $37. This Econo Lodge is 0.25 mile north of the Spotsylvania County Visitor Center (exit 126 off Interstate 95) on U.S. 1. This motel does allow pets, but only in smoking rooms and only for a one-night stay.

LaVista Plantation Bed and Breakfast
$$$ • 4420 Guinea Station Rd.
• (540) 898-8444
This bed and breakfast is in an 1838 Classical Revival home on historic Guinea Station Road. It offers two choices for a traveler: a

two-bedroom apartment with a private bath or a large formal room/bedroom with a private bath. Each choice offers a fireplace and a television. A fresh egg breakfast is served each morning at this cozy, quaint inn.

Roxbury Mill Bed and Breakfast
$$$ • 6908 Roxbury Mill Rd., Spotsylvania • (540) 582-6611

This house was built as the working mill for Roxbury plantation, which dates to the 1720s. It offers three guest rooms and a fourth room to accommodate children, if needed. The inn has two rooms on the first floor, one with a half-bath and one with a full bath. Upstairs, the inn has a large suite with a kitchen and bath. The children's room is upstairs as well. All the rooms are decorated with antiques, and each has a view of the mill race and nearby dam.

Gettysburg, Pa. (T-6, T-7)

Battlefield Bed and Breakfast Inn
$$$ • 2264 Emmitsburg Rd. • (717) 334-8804

Charlie and Florence Tarbox operate the Battlefield Bed and Breakfast Inn like a 19th-century farm. Florence and her staff take care of the 1809 farmhouse, while "Lieutenant Charlie" and his men tend to the sprawling 46 acres, the horses and the cannon and other military equipment. Cannon you ask? The Tarbox family has turned this inn into a living history experience. Guests are invited to participate in daily Civil War demonstrations that range from cavalry training to artillery target practice!

Charlie was an attorney in California for 21 years before he and Florence took on the eight rooms and suites at the Gettysburg inn. Each room has a theme dedicated to the units that fought on the South Cavalry Battlefield at Gettysburg. The four Union and four Confederate guest quarters have Civil War art, private baths and handmade quilts. Given the farm's size and the educational atmosphere at the inn, the Tarbox crew welcomes children of any age. Sorry, though, no pets. The inn is on Emmitsburg Road just south of town.

Brafferton Inn
$$$-$$$$ • 44 York St. • (717) 337-3423

Jane and Sam Beck purchased this inn in 1993, and they have a gem of a place to visit. It is on the National Registry of Historic Places. During the first day's fighting at Gettysburg, Union troops pushed through the village. Passing an old stone house, site of the present-day inn, the troops opened fire, and a bullet pierced the glass of an upstairs window and lodged in the fireplace mantel. The bullet scar remains for guests to see. Many of the inn's collectibles are Beck family heirlooms, some dating back about 200 years. You have to try the breakfast specialty: Peaches and Cream French Toast. The inn has 10 rooms, all air conditioned and each with an individual bath. Children older than 8 are welcome. From Gettysburg's Lincoln Square, walk a half-block east on York Street to the inn.

Doubleday Inn Bed and Breakfast
$$$$ • 104 Doubleday Ave. • (717) 334-9119

Back in 1994, Charles Wilcox, a busy Chicago business executive, decided to give up his life as a daily commuter. He and his wife, Ruth Anne, escaped the Windy City and purchased the Doubleday Inn in quiet, pastoral Gettysburg. "It's hectic," says Charles of his new lifestyle, "but we love it." That attitude shows in the inn's hospitality. The Wilcox family has completely redecorated the inn, changing the decor from Victorian to Country English. But they still have the various suites named for several of the officers who fought during the first day's battle at Gettysburg in 1863.

The Doubleday Inn is named for USA Gen. Abner Doubleday. It offers a full breakfast that includes blueberry pancakes. From Gettysburg's Lincoln Square, take U.S. 30 west (Chambersburg Street and Buford Avenue) 1 mile past the Gettysburg College stadium area, then right on Reynolds Street for a quarter-mile and over the railroad bridge. Next, turn right and proceed on Wadsworth Street for a quarter-mile to Doubleday Avenue and the inn on the right.

Gettysburg Hotel
$$$ • 1 Lincoln Sq. • (717) 337-2000

The Gettysburg Hotel is a downtown landmark. Established in 1797, it has been remodeled several times — most recently in 1991. Now, this historic landmark is an elegant hotel with 83 spacious guest rooms. Some rooms can be converted to suites, of which 22 have a fireplace. Five additional small suites have a Jacuzzi. Seven of the hotel's rooms have king beds; the remaining rooms offer two double beds. All the rooms are appointed with elegant period furnishings. The hotel has a swimming pool and is in the heart of downtown Gettysburg, on Lincoln Square.

Harrisonburg, Va. (T-3, T-4, T-10)

Comfort Inn
$$ • 1440 E. Market St. • (540) 433-6066, (800) 228-5150

There are 60 rooms at this Comfort Inn, at the intersection of Interstate 81 and U.S. Highway 33. This inn has no restaurant, but it offers a continental breakfast. About 15 of its rooms are nonsmoking, and it offers a heated outdoor pool. A double room rate is $72 in summer.

Joshua Wilton House
$$$ • 412 S. Main St. • (540) 434-4464

The Joshua Wilton House is an elegant Victorian home and one of the finest inns in the Shenandoah Valley. It is on S. Main Street, in the vicinity of James Madison University. Each room is furnished with period antiques, and all five bedrooms have private baths. Expect complimentary wine, beer or sparkling cider, along with cheese, crackers and a fruit basket. The gourmet breakfast includes homemade pastries, fresh fruits and a steaming pot of coffee. A double room is $95 or $105, and you'll need to make your reservations early. A popular place among James Madison University students and their parents, this inn and its restaurant (see our Restaurants chapter) are booked six months in advance for such events as graduation and homecoming.

Sheraton Inn
$$ • 1400 E. Market St. • (540) 433-2521

This Sheraton is at the intersection of I-81

(exit 247) and U.S. 33 (E. Market Street). The inn has 138 rooms and three suites. Also featured are indoor and outdoor pools, a Jacuzzi and a sauna. The Sheraton lounge, Scruples, stays open until 1:30 AM Wednesday through Sunday and 12:30 AM on Monday and Tuesday. They often feature a deejay, comedians and singalongs. The double room weekend rate is $67 nightly when available.

Leesburg, Va. (T-7, T-8)

Best Western Leesburg-Dulles
$$ • 726 E. Market St. (Va. Hwy. 7-U.S. Hwy. 15) • (703) 777-9400

It's an established name, and this Best Western is conveniently located just off Va. Highway 7. The motel has 99 rooms. Pets are prohibited, and all rooms are handicapped-accessible. It also features an outdoor pool for warm weather fun. Room rates range from $63 to $75 year round. This Best Western has a restaurant, Gabrielas, on the premises. The location is a plus for business and vacation travelers who want to be near Dulles International Airport, 9 miles away.

Lansdowne Resort
$$$$ • 44050 Woodridge Pkwy. • (703) 729-8400, (800) 541-4801

Relax in one of Northern Virginia's best resorts, on Va. 7 east of Leesburg in a park-like setting near the banks of the Potomac River. Lansdowne is a popular place for tourists as well as Washingtonians who want a weekend getaway in the country. Just 10 minutes from Dulles International Airport, Lansdowne has a golf course designed by Robert Trent Jones Jr. — a well-known name to golfers. The Lansdowne offers any number of special packages for visitors. For example, a weekend package for about $150 per night includes breakfast in bed and use of the executive fitness center. The inn has a full-service health club, and it even offers a luxury spa weekend package — the price is a bit steep, but you may find the pampering worth it.

Lexington, Va. (T-5, T-11)

Comfort Inn
$$ • U.S. Hwy. 11 S. • (540) 463-7311

This Comfort Inn, just north of town at the intersection of Interstate 64 and U.S. Highway 11, has 80 units that begin as low as $60. The inn offers complimentary continental breakfast and an indoor heated pool.

Llewellyn Lodge
$$$ • 603 S. Main St. • (540) 463-3235, (800) 882-1145

John Roberts is a Lexington native; his wife, Ellen, is a gourmet cook with extensive experience in the travel and hospitality business. Together, they've run this 53-year-old, brick Colonial, six-bedroom inn since 1985. Rooms feature air conditioning and private baths. Well-behaved children older than 10 are welcomed. The hosts serve a full gourmet breakfast from 8 to 9:30 AM. There's no smoking and no pets allowed. John is a trail guide, and he recently developed a printed guide to 20 of his favorite hiking trails. Rooms average about $68 to $98.

Maple Hall
$$$-$$$$ • 3111 N. Lee Hwy.
• (540) 463-6693

Maple Hall is on 56 rolling acres just 6 miles north of Lexington. Maple Hall is a fully restored, 1850 antebellum plantation home. The fine old, three-story brick house features an elegant white-columned front portico. The inn has 21 rooms and features a three-bedroom guest house, three separate dining rooms, a swimming pool, a tennis court, walking trails and a fishing pond. Maple Hall is owned by Historic Country Inns, which operates two other inns in the Lexington area: the Alexander-Withrow House and the McCampbell Inn, both downtown. All three offer decorative antique furnishings and private baths.

Lynchburg, Va. (T-10, T-11, T-21)

Holiday Inn Select
$$$ • 601 Main St. • (804) 528-2500

In the downtown business district, six blocks from the Lynchburg Visitors Center, this Holiday Inn has 243 rooms, of which eight can be converted to suites, each with a Jacuzzi. Children younger than 17 stay free with their parents. The inn features a weight room and an outdoor pool for summertime swimming. From the U.S. 29 bypass, take the Main Street exit and go six block west to Main and Sixth streets.

Lynchburg Mansion Inn Bed and Breakfast
$$$$ • 405 Madison St. • (804) 528-5400, (800) 352-1199

Bob and Mauranna Sherman operate this 9,000-square-foot Spanish Georgian mansion, located on a half-acre in the Garland Hill Historic District. Built in 1914, the house features a 50-foot Grand Hall and cherry and oak woodwork. The Shermans offer five rooms or suites. There is one suite on the first floor, three rooms on the second floor and a suite on the garden level with a separate entrance. Each of the three rooms offer a gas log fireplace, and the inn has a five-person spa on the back porch. There's a lace bag of potpourri tied to the bedposts and satin clothes hangers. Pets are prohibited, but well-behaved children are welcome. Smoking is allowed only on the veranda.

Madison House Bed and Breakfast
$$$$ • 413 Madison St. • (804) 528-1503, (800) 828-6422

This fine old Victorian home is just off Fifth Street, on the route between Lynchburg Museum and City Cemetery (see listings, T-11) in the Garland Hill Historic District. This bed and breakfast offers antique-filled parlors and a library with numerous Civil War books. The Madison House offers the Gold Room, the Blue Room, the Madison Suite, the Rose Room and the Veranda Room. Built by a tobacco baron, the home has original china bathroom fixtures, crystal chandeliers, a stained-glass window and an 1850s English banquet table. The Madison House does not allow smoking. Because of the antiques and fixtures, the home does not allow children or pets.

Manassas, Va. (T-8, T-13, T-14)

Courtyard by Marriott-Manassas
$$-$$$ • 10701 Battleview Pkwy.
• (703) 335-1300

The Courtyard is exceptionally close to the Manassas Battlefield (see T-8). The motel has 149 rooms that range from $69 to $81. A weekly room rate brings the daily price down to $68 to $73. This Courtyard also has an indoor pool. Drive east on Va. Highway 234 (Sudley Road) from the battlefield visitors center toward downtown Manassas. The left turn at Battleview Parkway is just before the Interstate 66 overpass.

Holiday Inn-Manassas Battlefield
$$ • 10800 Vandor Ln. at I-66 and Va. Hwy. 234 • (703) 335-0000, (800) HOLIDAY

This Holiday Inn is a stone's throw off the Manassas Battlefield (see T-8). In fact, the motel's guest jogging path winds its way into the battlefield property. Rooms are available with two double beds or one king bed. At times, a "great rate" is available — it can go as low as $59 to $65. Conference rooms are named Grant, Jackson, Lee and Lincoln. The inn also offers a fitness center and an outdoor swimming pool for the hot summer months. To reach this motel, drive east on Va. 234 (Sudley Road) from the battlefield visitor center toward downtown Manassas. Turn left into the parking area just before the I-66 overpass.

Sunrise Hill Farm Bed and Breakfast
$$ • 5590 Old Farm Ln. • (703) 754-8309

This small, quaint bed and breakfast is in the old Newman House, a pre-Civil War home now in the middle of the 6,000-acre Manassas National Battlefield Park. The Sunrise Hill Farm inn has just two rooms, which run $78 nightly. This house is popular with Civil War buffs, hikers and horse riders. Sunrise Hill boards

horses, and owners Frank and Sue Boberek can recommend a nearby stable if you are looking for a horse to ride. Expect eggs Benedict as a breakfast treat. To reach Sunrise Hill Farm Bed and Breakfast, go west from the battlefield on Va. 234 (Sudley Road) for 1.2 miles, turn right on Poplar Ford Road, then left on Old Farm Lane.

New Market, Va. (T-2, T-3, T-4)

Cross Roads Inn Bed and Breakfast
$$ • 9222 John Sevier Rd. • (540) 740-4157

The Cross Roads is a gem in the midst of abundant Civil War history in the New Market area of the Shenandoah Valley. Mary-Lloyd Freisitzer, a native Virginian, has operated this comfortable, family-style bed and breakfast for four years. She met her husband, Roland, in his native Austria, and he is now in ski management at nearby Bryce Resort. Mary-Lloyd has six rooms at the Cross Roads Inn, each with a private bath. The Cross Roads Inn has a Jacuzzi on the back terrace and a putting green in the back yard.

The inn is on 2 acres near the intersection of U.S. 11 and U.S. Highway 211. From downtown New Market, go north on U.S. 11 and turn right where U.S. 211 turns east — the Cross Roads Inn Bed and Breakfast is just beyond the intersection.

Quality Inn Shenandoah Valley
$$ • U.S. Hwy. 211 • (540) 740-3141

The Quality Inn sign is a recognizable, welcome site along the busy I-81 corridor in the Shenandoah Valley. This Quality Inn is just off the New Market exit. It has 100 rooms, an outdoor swimming pool, a minigolf course, free in-room movies, complimentary coffee in the morning and cider at sunset, a gift shop and a Johnny Appleseed Restaurant. This is a nice, no-frills place to stay along the interstate.

Shenvalee Golf Resort
$$$ • 9660 Fairway Dr. • (540) 740-3181

The Shenvalee (pronounced "Shen-Val-Lee") is as much a historical site as anything in this part of the Shenandoah Valley. Its main attraction is the 27-hole PGA golf course, but the scenic view of the Massanutten Mountains is a great draw too. The Shenvalee has 42 rooms, and each is a basic, functional place to rest after a long day's driving or golfing. Each room has double beds and a refrigerator. The rooms overlook either the fairways or a swimming pool. The Shenvalee has a driving range, a fully equipped pro shop, regulation tennis courts, a fishing pond and a hair salon. Eat in the Shenvalee's dining room, or stop by the Sand Trap Tavern for less formal dining.

Newport News, Va. (T-18, T-19)

Boxwood Inn
$$$ • 10 Elmhurst • (757) 888-8854
Barbara and Bob Lucas purchased this grand old Lee Hall Village house in 1996 and turned it into a bed and breakfast. The house was the home of Simon P. Curtis, "lord" of old Warwick County (now the city of Newport News) back in the 1890s. The building also has been used as a post office, general store and hotel for soldiers during both world wars. It even housed Warwick County records for a time.

Barbara Lucas is the graduate of a French culinary school, and you can expect the very finest hospitality at this inn. We had a chance to visit the Boxwood Inn during its renovation, and Barbara served us a luscious lunch complete with a decadent dessert. The Lucas family offers two bedrooms and two suites, and all four feature private baths. Barbara treats guests to a full breakfast fit for royalty: raspberry French toast, a crockery omelet or banana pancakes. Barbara also has a commercial kitchen under construction, so watch for a new restaurant at the Boxwood Inn by mid-1997 (see our Restaurants chapter).

Omni-Newport News Hotel
$$-$$$ • 1000 Omni Blvd.
• (757) 873-6664, (800) THE-OMNI
The Omni, just off I-64 at exit 258-A, bills itself as being "in the middle of everything." Indeed, the hotel is near most every important location on the Lower Peninsula. The Omni is

20 minutes from Colonial Williamsburg, 15 minutes from Busch Gardens and a little more than 30 minutes to Norfolk Waterside and the oceanfront at Virginia Beach. The Omni has 183 rooms, and four can be converted to suites. All the suites offer a Jacuzzi; one suite has a fireplace. The Omni has an indoor pool and health club, a whirlpool and sauna and a restaurant and club with dancing and entertainment. Three floors of the Omni are smoke free.

Ramada Inn and Conference Center
$$-$$$ • 950 J. Clyde Morris Blvd.
• (757) 599-4460
This Ramada is just off I-64 at exit 258-B. There are 219 rooms, along with an indoor fitness center and a heated indoor pool. Some rooms have refrigerators for long-term guests. And count on the friendly staff at this Ramada to provide complimentary transportation to and from the nearby Newport News/Williamsburg International Airport.

Orange, Va. (T-8, T-9, T-10, T-16)

Holladay House
$$$$ • 155 W. Main St. • (540) 672-4893, (800) 358-4422
Owners Pete and Phebe Holladay have operated the Holladay House since 1989. The six-room inn is an 1830 Federal-style house that has been in Pete's family since 1899. All six rooms have private baths, and there is a four-room luxury suite complete with a sitting room. There is also a "fun bath" that's ideal for a second honeymoon! The inn also offers what Pete says is "the best breakfast in Virginia." It's a three-course special that includes juice, homemade bread, a fruit course and any number of special entrees. Just hope its the fried apples and sausage. The suite is $185 a night; the other single rooms range from $95 to $130 nightly.

Willow Grove Inn
$$$$ • 14079 Plantation Way (U.S. Hwy. 15) • (540) 672-5982, (800) 949-1778
The Willow Grove Inn is recognized as one

of the top accommodations in Virginia. The original portion of the house was built in 1778 for Joseph Clark, a cousin of explorer William Clark. Then, in the 1820s, Thomas Jefferson played a role in designing Willow Grove's addition, a fine example of Classical Revival architecture. The remodeling was done for Joseph Clark's son, another William Clark. Both Union and Confederate soldiers used the grand estate during the Civil War. A cannonball was removed from the roof after the war's end. The house is a registered state landmark.

Today, Angela Mulloy operates Willow Grove Inn with 10 rooms — five in the main house and five in antebellum outbuildings. Willow Grove offers a taste of genteel Virginia plantation living. Room prices range from about $195 to $295 a night, but the price includes both dinner and breakfast (see the Willow Grove Inn Dining Room in our Restaurants chapter). A night in Orange is incomplete without a stay at the Willow Grove, on U.S. 15 north of Orange near Woodberry Forest.

Petersburg, Va. (T-17, T-18, T-20)

Comfort Inn
$$ • 11974 S. Crater Rd. • (804) 732-2900

This 96-room Comfort Inn is pleasant and inviting. Located in a quieter section of Petersburg, away from interstate traffic, the facility offers a continental breakfast and an outdoor pool. This is quality, no-frills lodging. From downtown Petersburg, take S. Crater Road (U.S. Highway 301) 6 miles south.

Ramada Inn
$$ • I-95 at Washington St.
• (804) 733-0730

This Ramada Inn is along the heavily traveled I-95 corridor and just a half-mile north of the interchange of I-95 and I-85. This Ramada has 214 rooms, and a double room is about $52 a night. A full-service convenience store offers snacks, magazines and essentials. From downtown Petersburg, take Wythe Street (one-way east) to Washington Street, and then back track on Washington Street to the Ramada Inn.

Mayfield Inn Bed and Breakfast
$$ • 3348 W. Washington St.
• (804) 733-0866

If you've dreamed of staying in an elegant, historic Southern home, this bed and breakfast offers you the perfect chance. Built in the 1750s, Mayfield is the oldest existing brick house in Dinwiddie County. It's a state and national historic landmark, and it's considered one if the finest mid-18th century residences in the state. Two defense lines were established on Mayfield property during the siege of Petersburg in the Civil War.

Jamie and Dot Caudle have restored and furnished Mayfield with antiques and period reproductions. The owners offer two double bedrooms and two suites, along with 4 acres of attractive grounds, a 40-foot outdoor pool and a full country-style breakfast. The inn also has an exceptionally large herb garden that won a 1996 design award from the National Trust for Historic Preservation. From downtown Petersburg, take Washington Street (U.S. Hwy. 1-460) 3 miles west to the western city limits. The inn is on the left.

Richmond, Va. (T-17, T-18, T-20)

Days Inn
$$ • 1600 Robin Hood Rd. • (804) 353-1287

This Days Inn is conveniently located just off I-95 in the vicinity of the Diamond — home stadium of the Richmond Braves minor league baseball team. The inn has 99 comfortable rooms, but expect few amenities other than a refreshing outdoor swimming pool that is open from Memorial Day to Labor Day. Pets are welcome at this Days Inn, but call in advance regarding restrictions. The inn is convenient to the Metro Richmond Visitor Center (see listing, T-17) at 1710 Robin Hood Road. To reach the motel, take I-95 to exit 78 (Boulevard), go west on Boulevard to the first traffic signal at Robin Hood Road. Turn left (south) on Robin Hood Road, adjacent to the Diamond stadium complex.

Jefferson Hotel

$$$$ • Franklin and Adams Sts.
• (804) 788-8000, (800) 424-8014

The Jefferson Hotel is more than a century old. A large stairway connects the upper lobby to the lower lobby, which features a statue of Thomas Jefferson. The Jefferson Hotel was renovated just over a decade ago and has 274 rooms, meeting space and a top-rated restaurant, Lemaire.

Linden Row Inn

$$$ • 100 E. Franklin St. • (804) 783-7000, (800) 348-7424

Seven antebellum townhouses, three buildings and a carriage house have been restored into this 70-room inn in historic downtown Richmond. Rooms include Empire furnishings. Guests enjoy a continental breakfast. The dining room serves lunch and dinner. Meeting rooms are available.

Marriott Richmond

$$$$ • 500 E. Broad St. • (804) 643-3400

This Marriott, in the heart of downtown Richmond, offers more than 400 rooms, a number of hospitality suites, and three separate restaurants in a 30,000-square-foot complex adjacent to Richmond Centre. There's an indoor pool, weight room, saunas and aerobics instruction. Parking is available free in a 1,000-space lot next door.

Sharpsburg, Md. (T-1, T-2)

Inn at Antietam Bed and Breakfast

$$$ • 220 E. Main St. • (301) 432-6601

This white Victorian farmhouse is on Main Street in Sharpsburg, just south of Antietam National Battlefield. Innkeepers Betty and Cal Fairbourn have turned this bed and breakfast into one of the finest lodging experiences in the region. The inn borders on the national battlefield park, and it has been featured in numerous regional and national magazines. The Fairbourns offer four suites. A double is $95 for a weeknight and $105 on weekends. Well-behaved children older than 6 are welcome. Pets and smoking are prohibited. Con-

tact the inn at least a month in advance for reservations.

Piper House Bed and Breakfast

$$ • Antietam National Battlefield
• (301) 797-1862

This comfortable bed and breakfast is in the middle of the Antietam National Battlefield. The location is hence on hallowed ground, and the site is quiet and serene. Lou and Regina Clark operate the Piper House. They have just three rooms, each with a private bath, and you need to call at least eight weeks in advance during the tourist season to get in. The farmhouse offers period decor, and the Clarks have artifacts from the Antietam battlefield. CSA Gen. James "Pete" Longstreet used the house as a battlefield headquarters during the Battle of Antietam.

Expect a continental breakfast that features fresh-baked muffins and breads along with fresh fruit. Piper House accepts well-behaved children older than 10. All rooms are nonsmoking, and, since they are all on the second floor, they are not handicapped-accessible. The house has no affiliation with the National Park Service, which operates the national battlefield. You'll find the Piper House Bed and Breakfast near the battlefield visitors center entrance.

Shepherdstown, W.Va. (T-1, T-2)

Bavarian Inn and Lodge

$$$-$$$$ • W.Va. Hwy. 45 • (304) 876-2551

This elegant, 11-acre, resort-style facility is a gem sitting on a bluff that overlooks the historic Potomac River. Built in the 1930s, the inn has been owned and managed the past two decades by the Asam family — Carol, an Englishwoman, and her husband, Erwin, a native of Munich, Germany. There are two rooms in the old inn, two suites and 68 chalet rooms, most with a fireplace or a Jacuzzi bath. All rooms have balconies. There is a tennis court and outdoor pool as well as a jogging path along the historic river canal. Package rates are available. The dining experience here is equally divine (see our Restaurants chapter).

Washington, D.C. (T-12, T-13, T-14)

Bed 'N' Breakfast Ltd. of Washington, D.C.

$-$$$$ • P.O. Box 12011, Washington, D.C. 20005 • (202) 328-3510

From budget to luxury offerings, Bed 'N' Breakfast Ltd. of Washington can connect you with an array of private-home lodgings, guests houses and inns. They even know about apartments available for family groups and extended-stay guests. They can also book you into some of Washington's top hotels. The accommodations they offer range in price from $55 to more than $300. Bed 'N' Breakfast Ltd. is a telephone service only; it has no store front.

Mayflower

$$$$ • 1127 Connecticut Ave. NW • (202) 347-3000

This is a popular Connecticut Avenue landmark — a place to see and be seen. The Mayflower lobby takes up an entire block; it has two restaurants and a lounge. This facility, a former Stouffer hotel, has more than 800 units, some with kitchenettes. Many consider this one of the finest hotels in America, based on location and service. Dignitaries often stay here, as the White House is just four blocks away.

Willard Inter-Continental

$$$$ • 1401 Pennsylvania Ave., NW • (202) 965-2300

The Willard is a Washington landmark (see listing, T-13) that almost fell victim to the wrecking ball before it was renovated and reopened in 1986. It is at the intersection of 14th Street and Pennsylvania Avenue, one block from the White House. In fact, the Willard is also a short walk to the Treasury Department, National Theater and the Mall. The Willard has 342 rooms, of which 30 are converted to suites. The Willard also has two lounges a cafe and a formal restaurant -- the Willard Room.

Williamsburg, Va. (T-18, T-19)

Cedars Bed and Breakfast

$$$ • 616 Jamestown Rd. • (757) 229-3591, (800) 296-3591

This charming bed and breakfast is in a residential section near the College of William and Mary. Carol and Jim Malecha have owned and operated the Cedars for nearly four years. The inn is on Jamestown Road (Va. 5), and it has off-street parking in back. Antiques and reproductions decorate the nine rooms and varied suites. The Cedars offers a full breakfast and evening refreshments by the fireplace. The historic area is a brief walk away, but you might decide not to leave. Note that all rooms are nonsmoking.

Colonial Williamsburg

$$$-$$$$ • Williamsburg • (757) 229-1000, (800) HISTORY

Colonial Williamsburg is a popular place and the foundation management knows it, so expect an elitist attitude throughout the Colonial village. Colonial Williamsburg offers a wide variety of accommodations, but many are booked in advance. In addition to the popular Williamsburg Inn and Williamsburg Lodge, there are a number of individual properties available in the historic area. For the latest in lodging information, call Colonial Williamsburg at the numbers listed above.

Motel 6

$$ • 3030 Richmond Rd. • (757) 565-3433

Looking for basic, no frills accommodations? Go no farther than the Motel 6, on Richmond Road just west of Colonial Williamsburg's historic district. The motel offers 169 rooms, all with two double beds. In a sea of expensive motels and lodges, this option offers basic, bargain prices. Each room has a color TV, and the motel offers an outdoor swimming pool for summer. From downtown Williamsburg, take Richmond Road (U.S. 60) west 1 mile beyond the campus of the College of William and Mary.

Winchester, Va.
(T-2, T-3, T-7, T-8)

Best Western Lee-Jackson Motor Inn

$$ • 711 Millwood Ave. • (540) 662-4154

This facility, once called the Lee-Jackson, dates to the 1930s. Owner Donald Vaden remembers when travelers used oil-fired space heaters to keep rooms warm. The Lee-Jackson is much more modern today. Vaden arrived on the scene in the 1960s, and he's been the owner for the past two decades. The motel has 140 rooms, and they are among Winchester's most comfortable. Some rooms have microwaves and refrigerators. From I-81 exit 313, go west on Millwood Avenue (U.S. Hwys. 15, 17 and 522) for 0.2 mile to the Best Western.

Hampton Inn

$$ • 1655 Apple Blossom Dr.
• (540) 667-8011, (800) 426-7866

This is a reliable sign among a host of motels at a busy I-81 interchange. The Hampton Inn offers 103 rooms, and children younger than 18 stay free when accompanied by a parent. The motel has a swimming pool, and a continental breakfast is served in the lobby from 6 to 10 AM daily. From I-81 exit 313, go west 0.25 mile on Millwood Avenue and look for the familiar Hampton Inn sign at the Millwood Avenue intersection with Apple Blossom Drive.

"... all that we have to eat is the cattle killed by the way. No bread or salt in the Regiment, and I am most starved."
— Elisha Rhodes, during the Peninsula campaign, 1862

Restaurants

In this chapter, we offer a general guide to the dining options available at various stopping points along our 21 individual tour routes. As with accommodations, this is only a sampling of what is out there — places where we have had good experiences or that we have heard good things about — and by no means constitutes a comprehensive listing.

Our price coding system is for a dinner meal for two and does not include taxes, gratuity or alcoholic beverages.

$	$20 or less
$$	$21 to $50
$$$	$50 to $75
$$$$	$75 and higher

Cash, traveler's checks and credit cards are the norm for payment. Don't expect an eatery to take an out-of-town personal check. If you are concerned about plastic policies at a given restaurant, call ahead for specifics. Unless otherwise noted, expect all these eateries to offer nonsmoking sections.

Following the city names are the tours from which those cities and restaurants are accessible. As you will note, many of these eateries are easily reachable from several different tours. Manassas restaurants, for example, are within an easy distance of Northern Virginia (Fairfax and Alexandria, Virginia) and Washington. Likewise, Richmond and Petersburg options are relatively near each other as are eating recommendations for the Brandy Station (listed here under Orange, Virginia) and Charlottesville tours.

Alexandria, Va. (T-7, T-8, T-12, T-13, T-14)

Elyssium Morrison House
$$$$ • 116 S. Alfred St. • (703) 838-8000
Here's a new twist: "American-eclectic cuisine" — and the Elyssium has it! The restaurant was chosen one of the top 100 in the Washington area for 1997 by *Washingtonian* magazine. Elyssium is small — it only seats 28 — and it's comfortable and charming. It is a touch classy, and the prices reflect it. But tourists can dine in less fancy attire and still be warmly welcomed. And boy, what a menu! Elyssium features three-, four- and five-course prefix menus that change weekly. Try the quail appetizer and the pumpkin-encrusted pork medallion entree. For dessert, ask for the raspberry mousse and cake with mango sauce and fresh raspberries. There's lots more on the menu, but it all may change before you get there!

The three-course meal is $35 a person; the four-course meal is $45; the five-course meal is $55. These do not include drinks, but the chefs have prepared a recommended wine list to pair with each entree. The Elyssium's wine list has more than 200 bottles and 16 wines are offered by the glass. The restaurant is nonsmoking and it offers complementary valet parking.

Fish Market
$$ • 105 King St. • (703) 836-5676
The First Market is along lower King Street in Old Town — the historic district that stretches along the Potomac River. The restaurant is busy and exciting. Tops on the menu are the oysters, spiced shrimp and a rich, New England clam chowder — especially nice on a snowy evening. During the summer, try a schooner of beer — it helps you forget Alexandria's humidity! The Fish Market is open for lunch and dinner daily, and the bar stays open past midnight every day but Sunday.

Hard Times Cafe
$ • 1404 King St. • (703) 683-5340
Anyone with a hankering for mouth-watering chili should put Hard Times on their list of

must-sees. The exterior appearance is unassuming — the decor is uniquely American West — and the dining area is full of clanging beer bottles and the aroma of beer-battered onion rings in the fryer. Hard Times is known for its chili — Texas-style, Cincinnati-style and vegetarian. Or try the spaghetti with chili on top. Hard Times is a top local eatery in downtown Alexandria, open for lunch and dinner daily.

King Street Blues
$$ • 112 N. St. Asaph St. • (703) 836-8800
    King Street Blues is, interestingly, not on King Street — but on St. Asaph St., a half-block off the main drag of Old Town. As the restaurant claims, "When you're just off King Street, you have the King Street blues." Professionals, tourists and hungry Alexandrians like King Street Blues for its barbecue, burgers, salads and soups. And, yes, it has live blues music performances on Thursday evenings. King Street Blues is open every day for lunch and dinner.

Appomattox, Va. (T-11, T-21)

    Appomattox is a small community (see T-21), that welcomes numerous tourists annually, but there are not many fine dining options in the little town. Still, most all the recognizable fast-food restaurants have opened. These restaurants (all located along U.S. 460 or U.S. 460 bypass) include **Arby's**, (804) 352-0278; **Burger King**, (804) 352-225; **Dairy Queen**, (804) 352-7411; **Little Caesar's Pizza**, (804) 352-0451; **McDonald's**, (804) 352-2878; **Pizza Hut**, (804) 352-5096; **Subway Sandwich Shop**, (804) 352-0930; and **Wendy's**, (804) 352-2122.

Arlington, Va. (T-8, T-13, T-14)

Red, Hot and Blue
$$ • 1600 Wilson Blvd.• (703) 276-7427
    Red, Hot and Blue is on the ground floor of an Arlington high-rise office building, and the interior is glitz, lights and music. But don't

the aesthetics fool you: This is THE place for Memphis-style barbecue ribs, platters and sandwiches. The late Lee Atwater, the Republican political strategist swept into Washington during the Reagan-Bush years, is credited with getting this barbecue place going in the metropolitan area. No question, Atwater knew his barbecue! And get this: You can get a heaping order of barbecue ribs, beans, slaw and bread for $9.49! The restaurant is nonsmoking, but smoking is permitted at a bar near the entrance. The restaurant is every day for lunch and dinner.

Baltimore, Md. (T-7, T-12, T-13)

DiVivo's Pastries and Cafe
$$$ • 801 Eastern Ave. • (410) 837-5500
    DiVivo's is conveniently located at the corner of President Street and Eastern Avenue in the historic "Little Italy" section of Baltimore. DiVivo's is just one of dozens of fine Italian restaurants in this beautiful ethnic section of the city. DiVivo's has a brick oven to bake pizza, and the restaurant also serves countless dishes of traditional and Italian cuisine such as lasagna, spaghetti and seafood over pasta. It also has a widely acclaimed "Dream of Italian Desserts." DiVivo's has a children's menu and is open seven days a week for lunch and dinner.

Obrycki's Crab House and Seafood Restaurant
$$$ • 1727 E. Pratt St. • (410) 732-6399
    A Baltimore restaurant guide would be incomplete without Obrycki's listing. Obrycki's (pronounced — "O-brick-ees") is — you guessed correctly — a crab lover's paradise. This restaurant, which dates to the Civil War, serves the Chesapeake blue crab — the jewel in Maryland's seafood crown. When ordering crabs, ask for Jimmies, which are meatier, male crabs. Obrycki's patrons devour bushels of crabs, steamed to perfection and coated with a spicy, Old Bay-type seasoning. Order up a dozen medium crabs (about $30) and Obrycki's rolls out the brown paper to cover your messy table! If you don't have the time

or patience to crack open the tasty crabs, order Maryland crab cakes or any of a number of other tasty seafood dishes. There is also a non-seafood menu that includes linguine and grilled chicken. The restaurant is nonsmoking, and it offers a children's menu. From the Inner Harbor, take Pratt Street east 18 blocks. The restaurant is open for lunch and dinner seven days a week.

Phillips - Harborplace
$$-$$$ • Inner Harbor • (410) 685-6600
Phillips is a chain seafood restaurant, but it has been in Baltimore for more than four decades. In the Light Street Pavilion at the Inner Harbor, this Phillips is perfect for a family interested in moderately priced dining choices. With its harborfront dining room, Phillips offers endless choices of seafood dishes as well as a sushi and raw bar, a seafood buffet and even carry-out service. There are also steak and chicken entrees for those less interested in seafood. *Baltimore Magazine* rates this Phillips "Baltimore's Best Piano Bar." Phillips has a children's menu and is open for lunch and dinner every day.

Charlottesville, Va. (T-9, T-10, T-11)

Blue Ridge Brewing Co.
$$ • 709 W. Main St. • (804) 977-0017
Blue Ridge Brewing Co. is in an old building on the stretch of Main Street between downtown Charlottesville and the University of Virginia. It bills itself as Virginia's first brew pub. It smells like a brewery — which it is. Beer is made on the premises. Labels include Hawksbill Lager, Piney River Lager, Afton Ale and Humpback Stout. (Piney River is a nearby mountain creek; Afton is a mountain just west of the city). Oh, yes, there's food too. The varied menu caters to university students, townspeople and travelers. The most popular item on the menu is a grilled and marinated Caribbean chicken breast. The restaurant is open for dinner daily and serves lunch every day except Monday and Tuesday. The bar is open daily from 11 AM to 2 AM. This is a choice selection for anyone interested in a late bite or drink.

C&O Restaurant
$$$$ • 515 E. Water St. • (804) 971-7044
One of the best restaurants in the Mid-Atlantic, the C&O gets its name from the old Chesapeake and Ohio train station just across the street. The exterior is unimpressive and deceptive. Inside, the C&O has two places to dine. An upstairs room offers French cuisine with candlelight and white linen tablecloths. Downstairs is a less formal dining area with equally good food. The menu varies, but anything — everything — is first-rate. The upstairs is all nonsmoking. The restaurant has been honored by almost all the food critics, including the reviewers from *Bon Appetit*, *Food & Wine Magazine*, *The New York Times* and *Washington Post*. Make your dinner reservations far, far in advance. A block south of the downtown Mall on Water Street, the C&O serves lunch Monday through Friday and dinner every night, with extended hours on Friday and Saturday. There is also a late-night dinner offering daily from 11 PM to 2 AM. Call now!

The Coffee Exchange
$ • 120 E. Main St. • (804) 295-0975
On the downtown Mall, near 1st and Main streets, The Coffee Exchange is a European-style cafe. With its fresh, bright atmosphere, it is especially nice for lunch. The Coffee Exchange offers fresh-baked breads, homemade soups and fresh salads. The smell of roasted coffee fills the air. It is open for breakfast and lunch seven days a week.

Hardware Store Restaurant
$$ • 316 E. Main St. • (804) 977-1518
When the city converted its old downtown Main Street into a mall, the Hardware Store Restaurant became a popular addition. A local businessman took an ages-old hardware store and turned it into a fun place to eat. Visitors — especially kids — will get a kick out of the decor that includes old hardware store drawers and ladders. The menu is exceptionally varied, with everything from health-conscious salads to hamburgers and fries. One popular dinner entree is pasta with seafood or chicken. Vegetarian items are included. The Hardware Store is on the downtown Mall, near Third and Main streets. The restaurant is open for lunch and dinner every day but Sunday.

Fairfax, Va. (T-8, T-13, T-14)

Belvoir Dining Room
$$$$ • Bailiwick Inn, 4023 Chain Bridge Rd. • (703) 691-2266, (800) 366-7666

The Belvoir Dining Room is a quaint, small attachment to the historic Bailiwick Inn (see our Accommodations chapter). Annette and Robert Bradley, who operate the inn, also take pride in the Belvoir, which seats just 20 in an intimate, candlelight setting. The dining room is all nonsmoking. A popular item on the menu is a roasted rack of lamb with an herb crust and Madeira wine sauce. The Belvoir is open Tuesday to Friday for lunch and every day except Monday and Tuesday for dinner.

Falls Church, Va. (T-8, T-13, T-14)

Peking Gourmet Inn
$$ • 6029-6033 Leesburg Pk. • (703) 671-8088

In a small, obscure strip mall in busy Baileys Crossroads, this Chinese restaurant is the choice of top politicians and locals alike. Former President Bush's motorcade zipped into the parking lot on several occasions (President and Mrs. Bush's photographs adorn the walls inside, along with those of other past and present notables.) The food is divine; the service is attentive. The Peking Duck, carved at your table, is one of the more popular specialties. Locals swarm to the restaurant when leeks and garlic sprouts are in season. The fresh, tasty vegetables are grown by the restaurant owners on a nearby farm, and they add a spicy touch to shrimp, chicken and pork entrees. The restaurant also has a take-out service. The Peking Gourmet is open for lunch and dinner every day, and it is open until midnight on Friday and Saturday.

Frederick, Md. (T-6, T-7)

The Brown Pelican
$$ • 5 E. Church St. • (301) 695-5833

David Sexton is the young, hard-working owner — as well as manager and chef — at The Brown Pelican. He turned this down-the-stairs restaurant into a place talked about as far away as Baltimore and Washington. Folks accustomed to big-city prices will be amazed at what you get here for a few dollars: A grilled salmon entree in herb butter or cucumber dill sauce is $16.95, for example; a walnut bourbon chicken, served with apples, walnuts and cream, is $13.95. And the atmosphere is cozy. The Brown Pelican is open for dinner every day and lunch Monday through Friday. The entire restaurant is nonsmoking, except at the bar adjacent to the dining room.

The Province
$$ • 131 N. Market St. • (301) 663-1441

Back in 1767, when Fredericktowne was just two decades old, a local blacksmith built the first building where the Province Restaurant now stands. In those early days, the community was part of the Province of Maryland — thus the restaurant's name. The Province has been owned and managed for 15 years by Nancy Gleason Floria and her husband, Bill Floria. They constructed a smoke-free, garden dining room in 1980. The room is decorated with handmade quilts and a flower and herb garden. Pick from grilled chicken, roast pork, pasta and — a special treat — Maryland Crab Cake. Lunch is served seven days a week, brunch is served Saturday and Sunday and dinner is offered every night except Monday.

The Province Too!
$ • 12 E. Patrick St. • (301) 663-1441

The owners of The Province Restaurant started this little deli and coffee shop in the downtown historic area. This is where the main restaurant gets its homemade desserts, pies, breads, buns and cookies. Managed by Caroline Murphy, the shop is ideal for early morning coffee and pastries, bagels, and biscuit sandwiches. Try their lunchtime soup-and-half-sandwich with a cookie and drink, all for

$3. Open year-round, The Province Too! is open every day for breakfast and lunch.

Fredericksburg, Va. (T-15, T-16)

Bangkok Cafe
$$ • 825 Caroline St. • (540) 373-0745

Don't be fooled by the small-town, Main Street location — this restaurant offers Thai cuisine you'd expect to find in a metropolitan area like Washington. There are various choices, including chicken, pork, beef — even something to appeal to vegetarians! We had a wonderful lunch with outstanding food, and we particularly liked the rice with coconut milk for dessert. Beware: Bangkok Cafe offers hot, hotter and hottest alternatives, so ask your waiter to explain the fire drill for each! The cafe is open for lunch and dinner every day except Tuesday.

Goolrich's Modern Pharmacy
$ • 901 Caroline St. • (540) 373-3411

In the historic old downtown section of town, on Caroline Street, this is one of the last great drug stores with a lunch counter. It's perfect for a quick lunch: Try a BLT on toast or a cold sandwich, and wash it down with the best milk shake in Virginia! On a hot summer day, relax with a fresh-squeezed lemonade or limeade. Goolrich's is closed on Sunday, but the pharmacy and the lunch counter are open Monday through Saturday from 8:30 AM to 7 PM.

Virginia Deli
$ • 101 William St. • (540) 371-2233

This is a sandwich shop conveniently located in the historic old downtown section, near the Rappahannock River Bridge. This deli offers a wide selection of specialty sandwiches along with soft drinks, waters and juices. The deli also sells many Virginia-made products. Hours are Sunday from 10 AM to 5 PM and Monday through Saturday from 8 AM to 5 PM.

Gettysburg, Pa. (T-6, T-7)

Historic Farnsworth House
$$ • 401 Baltimore St. • (717) 334-8838

Four blocks south of Lincoln Square, at the corner of Baltimore Street, this building was constructed in 1810. During the battle of Gettysburg in 1863, legend tells that a Union Army contingent fired on a Southern sharpshooter in an upstairs window of the Farnsworth House. There are more then 100 bullet holes still visible on the exterior wall of the house from that incident. The house is owned by Loring and Jean Schultz, who have spent a quarter-century developing the Farnsworth House into a "mini complex" with shops, historic programs and a restaurant.

The Schultz children, including son, J.R. Schultz, a daughter, Pattie O'Day, and a daughter-in-law, Cindy Schultz, carry on the family business. According to the Schultzes, the Farnsworth restaurant features Gettysburg's only authentic Civil War dining — that is, game pie, peanut soup, spoon bread and pumpkin fritters. The restaurant also has a children's menu. It is open for lunch and dinner every day except Thanksgiving, Christmas and New Year's Day.

Meanwhile, Pattie tells ghost stories in the basement, while J.R. and Cindy lead visitors on ghost walks in the historic Gettysburg area. A house tour is also available.

Hoss's Steak and Sea House
$$ • 1140 York Rd. • (717) 337-2961

The Hoss's trademark is personalized service. This restaurant is part of a chain, but it's locally owned, and it offers fresh-cut steaks, seafood and chicken meals chosen from the big board at the front door. There's a 100-item salad bar and fresh, locally baked bread. Hoss's has a children's menu, and it offers discounts to seniors. Hoss's serves lunch and dinner every day except Thanksgiving, Christmas and New Year's Day. It is 1.5 miles east of Lincoln Square on York Road, a half-mile before U.S. Highway 15.

Lincoln Diner
$ • 32 Carlisle St. • (717) 334-3900

Across the street from the Gettysburg Information Center (see listing, T-6), this little diner isn't found in the travel brochures and visitor guides. Nick Arahavos has operated his diner for two decades, now with his son, Bob. Locals flock here for the usual diner fare: burgers, chicken and especially the desserts. There's even a no-smoking room. Best of all, the Lincoln Diner is open 24 hours a day.

Lincoln Room Gettysburg Hotel
$$$ • One Lincoln Sq. • (717) 337-2000

This is an elegant dining room off the main lobby of the Gettysburg Hotel. The furnishings of the Lincoln Room are lovely. A nice breakfast buffet is offered for $7.25. For dinner, the restaurant features outstanding beef, veal, and chicken in a white-tablecloth, comfortably formal atmosphere. It is open for breakfast and dinner (no lunch) seven days a week.

Harrisonburg, Va. (T-3, T-4, T-10)

Bar B-Q Ranch Drive Inn
$ • U.S. Hwy. 11 N. • No phone

This old drive-inn restaurant dates to the 1950s — the "Elvis era," as locals say. Four decades later, you can still drive up, check the menu — mainly barbecue as well as hot dogs, hamburgers and french fries — and have a car-hop come take your order. It's truly a time-honored relic and a real treat. Three miles north of Harrisonburg on U.S. 11, the Bar B-Q Ranch is open every day for lunch and dinner. Having gone "upscale" in recent years, the drive inn now offers, in addition to the usual roadside menu, a variety of sauces, mugs and T-shirts.

Blue Stone Inn Restaurant
$$ • U.S. Hwy. 11, Lacey Spring, Va.
• (540) 434-0535

This restaurant has become a landmark on U.S. 11. The restaurant is at historic Lacey Spring (9 miles north of Harrisonburg), where CSA Gen. Thomas Rosser and USA Gen. George Custer fought a small cavalry skirmish during the Civil War. The Blue Stone Inn was started in 1949 by the parents of Karl Olschofka, who ran the restaurant for years

before turning it over to his son and daughter-in-law, Mike and Janet.

The Olschofka family takes advantage of a trout hatchery near the restaurant and offers some of the finest baked and stuffed trout anywhere. A stuffed trout dinner costs $14.95; a regular trout dinner is $13.50. The Blue Stone is also known for its fine steaks. The restaurant is open Tuesday through Saturday for dinner only, and reservations are required for groups of six or more. Smaller groups can take their chances at the door — it's usually a few minutes wait, especially during summer, but it's well worth it.

Joshua Wilton House
$$$$ • 412 S. Main St. • (540) 434-4464

The elegant restaurant at the historic Joshua Wilton House (see our Accommodations chapter) offers one of Harrisonburg's finest dining experiences. Among the many specialties are a fresh, pan-seared mahi mahi served with a sesame-crust top with pickled baikon and served with naki-nori rolls and wasabe soy sauce. Or try the roasted pheasant with a maple glaze and thyme-scented sauce. The restaurant is well-known for its creme brulée dessert. A five-course prix fixe menu is offered for $36 a person; with wine it is $50 a person. The entire restaurant, which seats 26, is nonsmoking. Advance reservations are necessary, and don't forget that fall homecoming and spring graduation at nearby James Madison University fill all local restaurants. The restaurant is open Monday through Saturday for dinner only.

Leesburg, Va. (T-7, T-8)

Potomac Grill, Lansdowne
$$$$ • 44050 Woodridge Pkwy.
• (703) 729-8400, (800) 541-4801

The Lansdowne Resort is a great place to stay (see our Accommodations chapter), but you don't have to be a guest to enjoy the Potomac Grill. This "casual elegant" restaurant, in the lower level of the resort, is open to the public, and you'll see diners in a range of attire — from tuxedos to golf slacks. The Potomac Grill seats 112, overlooks a well-groomed lawn and features New American cuisine. The place might best be described as an upscale steak house. In fact, the beef is all prime, and it's cooked on an open-fire grill with apple and hickory wood. The most popular item on the menu is a certified Angus filet mignon. Tasty? It's fork tender! The restaurant also has fresh seafood shipped in daily. The best-selling seafood dishes include a yellowfin tuna loin and a lobster-shrimp-scallop cake — it's similar to a crab cake, diced with Japanese bread crumbs, pan-seared and oven-baked. For dessert, try the dark chocolate mocha paté or fresh seasonal fruit cobblers. A piano vocalist provides pleasant music on Friday and Saturday. Dinner is served Tuesday through Saturday from 5:30 to 10 PM. The restaurant is closed for dinner on Sunday and Monday, but Potomac Grill serves an upscale lunch seven days a week.

Laurel Brigade Inn and Restaurant
$$ • 20 W. Market St. • (703) 777-1010

Just a half-block from the Loudoun County Courthouse, the Laurel Brigade Inn and Restaurant is a popular historic site in Leesburg. The inn is in a building that dates to 1759, when Leesburg was on the overland trail from Alexandria to Winchester. The restaurant, which seats 150, has been around since 1949. The menu at the Laurel Brigade can be described as traditional American, with a little updating. For years, locals and travelers have become accustomed to the Laurel Brigade's crab cake dinner, the most popular item on the menu. The crab cakes are made using a time-honored, well-guarded secret recipe! Lunch is served seven days a week; dinner is served Tuesday through Saturday (with an "early dinner" Sunday until 7 PM); and there is a Sunday breakfast.

Tuscarora Mill
$$-$$$ • 203 Harrison St., S.E.
• (703) 771-9300

Tuscarora Mill Restaurant and Cafe has three separate restaurants, but the main dining room, in a restored 1899 mill, is the featured place to dine. The main room seats 74, a casual cafe-bar area seats an additional 34 and a garden room and deck seat 63. In the main dining room, try Tuskie's popular sesame-roasted salmon with stir-fried rice.

Another popular entree is the roasted rack of lamb with scalloped potatoes. The menu at Tuscarora changes each season to take advantage of locally grown crops. The restaurant has an extensive wine list, including several Virginia vintages, and it features numerous wines by the glass. Tuscarora also takes advantage of the many micro-breweries in the vicinity and offers 21 beers on tap.

The main dining area and the casual cafe are both places that easily accommodate family diners with children. The restaurants have no kids' menu, but Tuskie's can downscale an entree to a smaller, less expensive portion for youngsters. Lunch and dinner are served daily in the main restaurant, but hours vary — call ahead to ensure they'll be there when you are. For more casual dining, including hamburgers, sandwiches and appetizers, the cafe is open every day for lunch and dinner (later hours on weekends).

Lexington, Va. (T-5, T-11)

Southern Inn
$ • 37 S. Main St. • (540) 463-3612

Locals and alumni from Washington and Lee University and Virginia Military Institute sing the praises of the Southern Inn. Travelers do, too, after they've sampled the southern home cooking. A downtown Lexington fixture since 1932, everyone eventually ends up dining at the Southern Inn. Lunches feature homemade soups and sandwiches. There are full dinners with such staples as chicken and beef, as well as Greek and Italian dishes. Nothing fancy here, just exceptionally good food. The Southern Inn is open seven days a week for lunch and dinner.

Willson-Walker House Restaurant
$$$ • 30 N. Main St. • (540) 463-3020

In historic downtown Lexington, this 1820 Classic Revival home was built for William Willson, one-time postmaster, merchant and Washington College treasurer. In 1911, Harry Walker converted the fine home into a meat and grocery store. Now a registered Virginia landmark, the Willson-Walker House has been featured in *Travel and Leisure* magazine as one of the outstanding places to dine in Virginia. The menu offers American cuisine. It features its Famous $5 Lunch Special, which includes an entree, soup or salad, bread and a beverage — all for just $5. A three-course dinner of local trout with a Rockbridge County chardonnay wine is $50 a couple. Reservations are recommended. Lunch and dinner are served Tuesday through Saturday, but the restaurant does not serve Saturday lunch during the off-season, January to March.

Lynchburg, Va. (T-10, T-11, T-21)

Jefferson's Restaurant
$$$ • Holiday Inn Select, 601 Main St.
• (804) 528-2500

Jefferson's Restaurant offers American cuisine as well as shrimp Italian style, boneless Chicken Coleone and beef steaks. French Silk Pie is the most popular dessert. Jefferson's Restaurant is conveniently located in the Holiday Inn Select in downtown Lynchburg. It is open daily for breakfast, lunch and dinner.

Morrison's Family Dining
$$ • 3405 Candlers Mountain Rd.
• (804) 237-6549

There's nothing more convenient than fine food served cafeteria style. Morrison's is in the River Ridge Mall, off U.S. Highway 460 south of town, and it is part of the chain that offers a wide selection of economically priced meals. Local checks are accepted here. The restaurant is open every day for lunch and dinner.

Shakers
$$ • 3401 Candlers Mountain Rd.
• (804) 847-7425

Shakers is at the entrance to River Ridge Mall, and it is a popular spot for locals. An all-American menu is offered: steaks, chicken, fish, salads, sandwiches and pasta. The decor has lots of ficus trees and plants. Shakers has a lunch buffet and offers take-out service. There is a children's menu. Shakers is open daily for lunch and dinner.

Manassas, Va. (T-8, T-13, T-14)

Applegates Restaurant
$$ • Holiday Inn-Manassas Battlefield, 10800 Vandor Ln. at I-66 and Va. Hwy. 234
• (703) 335-0000

This restaurant is convenient to Civil War touring in Manassas. It is in the Holiday Inn adjacent to the Manassas National Battlefield Park. Applegates begins serving hotel guests complementary coffee at 6 AM, and it remains open for breakfast until 11 AM. The restaurant also offers dinner seven nights a week. The menu offers standard American fare. There is live music performed in the lounge after 9 PM Tuesday through Saturday.

Brady's Restaurant and Pub
$$ • 8971 Center St. • (703) 369-1469

This is a fun spot in downtown Manassas. Dennis Brady opened the restaurant in 1975. Jim Grafas bought it in 1990, but he still uses Brady's name. Brady's Irish Burger is served with corned beef and topped with cabbage, and it costs $6.75. The menu offers other strange but delightful fare: a chicken teriyaki club sandwich, a variety of pasta dishes, fish entrees and even a choice of Mexican dinners. This is a local hangout, and the dining area is pleasant and enjoyable. The dining room has an adjacent bar. The restaurant opens every day for lunch and dinner, and the bar stays open late on Friday and Saturday nights. In downtown Manassas, take Center Street one way west, and go three blocks beyond the Main Street intersection to Brady's.

Courtyard by Marriott-Manassas
$$ • 10701 Battleview Pkwy.
• (703) 335-1300

The cafe in the Marriott (see our Accommodations chapter) is a convenient place for Civil War travelers. The Marriott is near the Manassas National Battlefield Park. The cafe serves a buffet-style breakfast every day.

New Market, Va.
(T-2, T-3, T-4)

Southern Kitchen
$-$$ • U.S. Hwy. 11 • (540) 740-3514

The Southern Kitchen is a New Market attraction. Locals and visitors have flocked to this great old Southern restaurant since 1955. The restaurant has a main dining area, all nonsmoking, that seats 100. It also has a 40-seat fountain room, with booths and counter seats, where smoking is permitted. The food at the Southern Kitchen is, simply put, sublime. Fried chicken, hot roast beef and steaks are staples. There's a great peanut soap on the menu too. And let's not forget the homemade desserts — our favorites are the blueberry pie and the peanut butter pie. Southern Kitchen is open for breakfast, lunch and dinner seven days a week. It is on U.S. 11, five blocks south of the main New Market intersection of U.S. 11 and U.S. 211.

Shenvalee
$$ • 9660 Fairway Dr., off U.S. Hwy. 11 • (540) 740-3181

This three-room restaurant is at the Shenvalee Golf Resort (see our Accommodations chapter), and it is open for three meals a day, seven days a week. Try the catfish filet, broiled chicken breast or a wide selection of beef — from steaks to filet mignon. Also in the restaurant is the Sand Trap Tavern for less formal dining. The restaurant seats 140 and is on U.S. 11, 1 mile south of the main New Market intersection of U.S. 11 and U.S. 211.

Johnny Appleseed
$$ • U.S. Hwy. 211 at I-81 • (540) 740-3141

At the Quality Inn Shenandoah Valley (see our Accommodations chapter) in downtown New Market, the Johnny Appleseed is a popular spot for family dining. Catfish is a specialty that is served every Friday night, and crowds clamor to New Market to dine on the delicacy. The restaurant also serves basic fare: hamburgers, soups, salads and even vegetable plates. For dessert, the Johnny Appleseed is known for its apple fritters. With seating for 120, the restaurant serves three meals every day. There is a children's menu.

Newport News, Va.
(T-18, T-19)

Boxwood Inn Restaurant
$$$ • 10 Elmhurst • (757) 888-8854

Barbara and Bob Lucas purchased this grand old Lee Hall Village house in 1996 and turned it into a bed and breakfast (see our Accommodations chapter) and restaurant. We had a chance to visit the Boxwood Inn during its renovation, and Barbara served us a delicious lunch complete with a wonderful chocolate dessert. Barbara's new restaurant (scheduled to open in mid-1997) uses antique furniture to seat 55 for both lunch and dinner. It offers fireside dining in the winter and candlelight dining in the summer. Dinner is served only on Friday and Saturday evenings; lunch is served every day.

The Lucas family offers a package plan that combines a stay in the inn and meals in the restaurant. Barbara Lucas' trademark cuisine is also featured at her first restaurant, The Briar Patch Tea Room, at 475-I Wythe Creek Road in Poquoson, Virginia. Now six years old, The Briar Patch seats 85 and serves lunch only. The most requested item on her menu is a sampler plate for $6.95 — the price will never change, Barbara says — that includes samples of all her finger sandwiches, a fruit or garden salad, soup of the day and dessert.

Orange, Va.
(T-8, T-9, T-10, T-16)

Firehouse Cafe
$$ • 137 W. Main St. • (540) 672-9001

This attractive restaurant is near the Orange County Courthouse on Main Street in Orange. Formerly the Main Street firehouse, the building was converted to a restaurant in 1990. It offers a varied menu of mainly American cuisine and homemade items. The Firehouse Cafe offers homemade soup, quiche and salad for both breakfast and lunch. For dinner, on the more fancy Saturday night, try filet mignon or salmon. The Firehouse Cafe is open for breakfast Monday through Saturday, brunch on Sunday from 11 AM to 3 PM and dinner on Friday and Saturday only.

Willow Grove Inn Dining Room
$$$$ • 14079 Plantation Way (U.S. Hwy. 15) • (540) 672-5982, (800) 949-1778

Eating in the dining room at Willow Grove is as fine an experience as staying overnight in the inn (see our Accommodations chapter). The dining room offers "Virginia regional cuisine," and that means such entrees as house-smoked chicken Napoleon, bourbon molasses-glazed quail, and Rag Mountain Smoked Trout Cake. The top dessert: Bourbon Walnut Chocolate Pie. There's musical entertainment on Friday and Saturday nights. The dining room offers Sunday brunch, and dinner Sunday, Thursday, Friday and Saturday. The Willow Grove Inn also has a tavern with casual dining. It is open every day but Monday, from 5 PM to midnight.

Richmond, Va. (T-17, T-18, T-20)

Extra Billy's Steak and Bar-b-que
$ • 5205 W. Broad St. • (804) 282-3949

This restaurant has a Civil War history connection. It is named for William "Extra Billy" Smith, who was Virginia's governor in Richmond (see T-17) during the war. Near the Willow Lawn Shopping Center on West Broad Street, Extra Billy's is a barbecue lover's heaven. This is a large, busy restaurant that's ideal for families with children. It has a non-smoking section. Extra Billy's is open every day but Sunday for lunch and dinner, with later hours on Friday and Saturday.

The Tobacco Company
$$ • 1201 E. Cary St. • (804) 782-9431

In an old tobacco warehouse in Richmond's historic Shockoe Slip, The Tobacco Company is open daily for lunch and dinner, and it offers cocktails, dinner and dancing too. The restaurant features a three-story atrium and antique furnishings. The most popular item on the dinner menu is prime rib — a complete dinner for two is $42, not including beverages. Equally known for its en-

tertainment, The Tobacco Company is a magnet for young adults interested in tasting Richmond's night life. It has a dance floor upstairs and a club downstairs. The club has a $3 cover charge, but it waives the charge if you have dinner at the restaurant.

Petersburg, Va. (T-17, T-18, T-20)

Alexander's
$$ • 101 W. Bank St. • (804) 733-7134

Alexander's is a local hangout, and the food is exceptional. The dining room is cramped, but patrons flock to Alexander's for breakfast, lunch and dinner. Family-style dinners include leg of lamb, lasagna, chicken parmesan and a variety of salads and desserts. Alexander's offers take-out orders and catering. The restaurant is open Monday and Tuesday for breakfast and lunch, and Wednesday through Saturday for breakfast, lunch and dinner. Alexander's is two doors down from the Siege Museum (see listing, T-20).

Annabelle's Restaurant and Pub
$$ • 2733 Park Ave. • (804) 732-0997

This restaurant was built within the walls of an old, stone dairy barn. There are a number of old collectables — including a used gas streetlamp — to make the visit intriguing and interesting. The American-style menu offers a variety of choices, from beef and chicken to seafood and pasta. Annabelle's is part of a Southern chain and is open for lunch and dinner every day. There are extended hours on Friday and Saturday. A children's menu is available. Take Sycamore Street south from downtown to S. Crater Road. Turn right (south) on Crater Road, go past the Norfolk & Western railroad overpass and take the third right on Park Avenue. Annabelle's sits behind a row of fast-food restaurants. It has ample parking.

Nanny's Family Restaurant
$ • 11900 S. Crater Rd. • (804)733-6619

Excellent food, family atmosphere, friendly service and inexpensive dinners: This is a real gem. Linda Stewart, her husband, Ronnie, and their sons, Tim and Jeff, serve some of the finest barbecue and chicken in Southside Virginia. Ronnie offers rib specials each Friday and Saturday. A rib dinner comes with baked beans, fries, slaw and hushpuppies. A half-rack rib dinner is $6.95; a full rack is $11.75. Remember, this is Brunswick Stew area, and Nanny's has a great recipe. *The New York Times* even mentioned Nanny's Brunswick Stew in a 1993 article.

With seating for more than 100, this is a very popular local hangout. Nanny's also has banquet facilities and a catering service. You don't need reservations because there's plenty of room. Closed on Tuesday, Nanny's is open the other six days for lunch and dinner. Take S. Crater Road (U.S. 301) out of downtown, and go 2 miles to Nanny's on the right.

Sharpsburg, Md. (T-1, T-2)

Red Byrd Restaurant
$ • Md. Hwy. 34 • (301) 791-5915

The Red Byrd is on Md. Highway 34, north of Antietam Battlefield toward Boonsboro just beyond Antietam Creek. This restaurant — like the adjacent Red Byrd Motel — is right out of the 1950s or '60s. In fact, the restaurant was opened nearly four decades years ago, and the food and service is strictly family-style. Nothing fancy — just really good! Dinner platters, for example, range from country ham and rib steaks to grilled liver and Maryland crab cakes. Each dinner meal is in the $7 to $9 range, and the restaurant frequently offers all-you-can-eat specials. This is a welcome site for families with lots of mouths to feed. It is open seven days a week from 8 AM to 8 PM.

Shepherdstown, W.Va. (T-1, T-2)

Bavarian Inn and Lodge
$$-$$$ • W.Va. Hwy. 45 • (304) 876-2551

Like the inn and lodge (see our Accommodations chapter), the restaurants here are superb. Owner Erwin Asam is a native of Munich, Germany, so you might expect to find some of the finest German dining this side of that town. The Bavarian Inn's cuisine is known throughout the region — travelers from as far away as Washington and Baltimore make the trek to Shepherdstown to sample Asam's award-winning menu.

Two musts: Bavarian Sauerbraten ($15.75, complete with potato dumpling, red cabbage and a house salad), and Wiener Schnitzel ($16.50, and served with two vegetables and a house salad). And there's more — everything from venison and daily-baked bread to a "game festival" each fall that features rabbit, roast venison, pheasant and roast wild boar. Fireplaces provide a romantic European atmosphere, and the Rathskeller downstairs is a place for casual and weekend dining. The restaurants here are worth the visit to Shepherdstown. Breakfast, lunch and dinner are served daily.

Tony's Pizza Den and Subs and Stuff
$ • 126 E. German St. • (304) 876-2720

This is just what it's name implies — a restaurant for pizza, subs and other stuff like burgers, chicken wings and nuggets and salads. This is just the place for locals, Shepherd College students and travelers. And it's a great place for a fast snack that's reasonably priced. The den also has a bar, and the entire restaurant allows smoking. It is open from 11 AM to 2 AM daily.

Washington, D.C. (T-12, T-13, T-14)

Blackie's House of Beef
$$$ • 1217 22nd St., NW • (202) 333-1100

This Washington landmark dates to 1946. It is just off M Street, between Georgetown and downtown. Blackie's features antiques, paintings and cozy rooms with fireplaces. As its name suggests, this restaurant features beef and beef — from thick steaks to succulent roast beef. Blackie's is open for lunch and dinner seven days a week.

Clyde's of Georgetown
$$ • 3236 M St., NW • (202) 333-9180

Another Washington institution, Clyde's is a street-front restaurant on busy M Street in Georgetown. Owners Stuart Davidson and John Laytham started Clyde's in 1963. Now, three decades later, these two restaurateurs have nine quality dining spots in the Washington area. The Clyde's in Georgetown is the first — still in its original location. It is a fun, dependable place with broad appeal. Patrons will likely include grad students, young professionals and old-line establishment types. Have drinks at either of two bars, and enjoy fresh pasta and seafood in the back dining area. Clyde's also has steaks, sandwiches and its own brand of award-winning chili. Everything on the menu comes in huge proportions! The owners only recently refurbished the interior, including the kitchen. Clyde's is open for breakfast, lunch and dinner every day, with varied opening times in the morning. The bars keep the fun flowing until 2 AM Sunday through Friday and 3 AM on Saturday.

The Monocle
$$ • 107 D St., NE • (202) 546-4488

This traditional, stately restaurant is a half-block from the U.S. Senate office buildings on Capitol Hill. It is the place to see a number of Hill notables, particularly when Congress is in session. Catch your favorite legislator or lofty lobbyist having a quick respite at the bar or dinner with friends and colleagues. The food doesn't offer a lot of surprises, but everything tastes terrific. Owner-manager John Valanos and his friendly associate, Nick Selimos, greet each guest at the door as if they're a future president — and some guests are! The Monocle is open Monday through Friday for lunch and dinner.

Williamsburg, Va. (T-18, T-19)

Bassett's Restaurant
$-$$ • 207 Bypass Rd. • (757) 229-3614

Families with children will particularly enjoy Bassett's with its informal atmosphere and multiple television screens. Bassett's offers a variety of entrees, sandwiches and burgers, and it includes a children's menu. Young adults migrate to the bar adjacent to the dining area. Bassett's is open every day except Thanksgiving and Christmas Day. It serves lunch and dinner year round, and breakfast as well during the tourist season. During the slow months, breakfast is only served on Saturday. It also serves a Sunday brunch from 9 AM to 2 PM year round.

Shields Tavern
$$ • Duke of Gloucester St.
• (757) 229-2141

If time is a test of a restaurant's value, then Shields Tavern would win any contest. This restaurant dates to the 1740s, when James Shields had a — yes — tavern. Today, the interior is decorated as it was during Shields' day. The menu features the top meal choices of yesterday: spit-roasted chicken, baked rockfish, roast pork chops and seafood items. The Shields Sampler, a super choice, includes authentic 18th-century food. Reservations are absolutely necessary, especially in the summer season, but visit in casual attire. The entire restaurant is nonsmoking. The restaurant is open every day for breakfast, lunch and dinner except for some Wednesdays, particularly in the months of May, September, November and December. Contact the restaurant or the Colonial Williamsburg Visitor Center (see listing, T-18) for hours and reservation assistance. The tavern is at the capitol side of Duke of Gloucester Street.

Trellis Restaurant and Grill
$$$-$$$$ • Duke of Gloucester St.
• (757) 229-8610

The Trellis has a national reputation, so telephone well in advance for a reservation. The Trellis also has an outdoor cafe on Duke of Gloucester Street, and it offers seating on a first-come, first-served basis. Fresh entrees include seafood, beef, poultry and sausage, with excellent soup, salad, dessert and wine choices. This is the ultimate dining experience. *The New York Times* once wrote that the Trellis is the "best restaurant in this part of Virginia." The review is worth editing to say "anywhere in Virginia." The Trellis is open seven days a week, serving lunch and dinner.

Weather permitting, you can eat at the outdoor cafe.

Winchester, Va.
(T-2, T-3, T-7, T-8)

Cork Street Tavern
$$ • 8 W. Cork St. • (540) 667-3777

In historic Old Town Winchester, the Cork Street Tavern repeatedly wins the community award for "best ribs in the Shenandoah Valley." Besides ribs, the tavern offers chicken, steaks and hamburgers in a casual atmosphere. This is the place for a hearty appetite, open seven days a week for lunch and dinner.

T. Jefrey's
$$ • 168 N. Loudoun St. • (540) 667-0429

T. Jefrey's has a unique dining arrangement that suits both the casual and the more serious diner. Deli sandwiches are available for drop-in traffic. For those with more time, T. Jefrey's has a nice menu that includes steak, lamb, soups and salads. On the downtown mall, T. Jefrey's is open for lunch and dinner with later hours on Friday and Saturday.

The Old Post Office Restaurant
$$ • 200 N. Braddock St. • (540) 722-9881

The Old Post Office Restaurant is one of the fancier places in Winchester. Yes, it is located in the community's elegant, old post office building. The menu here is "uptown" — elegant items include fresh veal, pasta and seafood, along with beef and chicken. This restaurant offers banquet rooms for special occasions, and the restaurant will cater special functions. The Old Post Office is open for lunch Monday through Friday and dinner Monday through Saturday.

Advertisers Index

Index

Kelly House 270
Kelly's Ford 110
Kemp Hall 81
Kemper, James Lawson 114
Kenmore 196
Kennedy, Mrs. Howard 7
Kenton, Simon 106
Kernstown, Va. 32
Key, Francis Scott 85, 146, 148
Keyes, USA Gen. Erasmus 242
Kilpatrick, USA Gen. Hugh Judson
        "Kill Cavalry" 75, 106
King Street Blues 288
Kings Dominion 225
Kurtz Cultural Center 26, 27

L

Lacey Spring, Va. 44
Ladysmith, Va. 210
Lafayette Square 168
Lake Anna State Park 207
Lake Anna Winery 207
Lansdowne Resort 278
Laurel Brigade Inn and Restaurant 293
LaVista Plantation Bed and Breakfast 276
Le Tort, James 3
Lee and Jackson Statue 146
Lee, Ann Carter 177
Lee Chapel 60
Lee, CSA Gen. Fitzhugh "Fitz" 7
Lee, CSA Gen. Robert E.
        xvi, 3, 8, 15, 18, 23, 55, 56, 70, 81,
        87, 96, 105, 111, 112,116, 146, 176, 199, 203,
        204, 210, 214, 218, 227, 230, 231,
        245, 251, 256, 260, 263, 266, 269
Lee, CSA Gen. William Henry Fitzhugh
        "Rooney" 98
Lee, Francis Lightfoot "Frank" 89, 199
Lee, George Washington Custis 175
Lee Hall, Newport News 241
Lee, Henry "Light-Horse Harry" 177
Lee House 60
Lee Park 126
Lee, Richard Decatur 241
Lee, Richard Henry 199
"Lee vs. Grant: The 1864 Campaign" 202
Lee-Jackson Day 56
Lee-Jackson House 60
Lee's Mill 241
Lee's Mill Battle Site 241
"Lee's Retreat" 263
Leesburg, Va. 89
Leesburg, Va., Accommodations 278
Leesburg, Va., Restaurants 292
LeMoyne, Francis 68
LeMoyne, Pa. 67
Letcher, John 56
Lewis, Meriwether 119
Lexington Carriage Company 64
Lexington Coffee Roasting Co. 65
Lexington Historical Shop 65
Lexington Market 150
Lexington Presbyterian Church 59
Lexington, Va. 56

Lexington, Va., Accommodations 279
Lexington, Va., Restaurants 293
Lexington Visitor Center 58
Libby Hill Park 218
Library of Congress 156
Library of Virginia 217
Lime Kiln Theater 64
Lincoln Diner 291
Lincoln, Franklin 44
Lincoln Gun 247
Lincoln Memorial 164
Lincoln, Nancy Hanks 44
Lincoln Park 157
Lincoln, President Abraham xii, xxv,
        9, 34, 84, 144, 254
Lincoln Room, Gettysburg Hotel 292
Lincoln Statue 159
Lincoln, Thomas 44
Lincoln, "Virginia John" 44
Linden Row Inn 283
Little Giant xxv
Little River Turnpike 94
Little Sorrel 63
Llewellyn Lodge 279
Locust Dale, Va. 113
Logan, John Alexander 257
Logan, Mary 257
Lomax, CSA Gen. Lunsford Lindsay 37
Longstreet, CSA Gen. James
        "Pete" 7, 70, 94, 233
Longwood Center for the Visual Arts 270
Longwood College 270
Lora Robins Gallery 225
Loudoun County Courthouse 90
Loudoun Heights 18
Loudoun Museum 89
Loudoun Rangers 89
Loudoun Visitors Center 89
Lower Peninsula xvi, 239
Lyceum 180
Lynchburg Fine Arts Center 139
Lynchburg Mansion Inn Bed and Breakfast 279
Lynchburg Museum at the Old Courthouse 136
Lynchburg Symphony Orchestra 139
Lynchburg, Va. 133, 134
Lynchburg, Va., Accommodations 279
Lynchburg, Va., Restaurants 294
Lynchburg Visitors Information Center 135

M

Madison House Bed and Breakfast 279
Madison, James 103, 123
Madison, Nelly Conway 34
Maggie Walker National Historic Site 225
Magruder, CSA Gen. John
        Bankhead 239, 240, 241, 242
Malvern Hill 231
Manassas, Va. 93
Manassas Battlefield 95
Manassas Cemetery 100
Manassas Fall Jubilee 100
Manassas Museum 98
Manassas National Battlefield Park 104

Y

Going Somewhere?

Insiders' Publishing Inc. presents 40 current and upcoming titles to popular destinations all over the country (including the titles below) — and we're planning on adding many more. To order a title, go to your local bookstore or call (800) 765-2665 ext. 238 and we'll direct you to one.

Atlanta, GA

Boca Raton and the Palm Beaches, FL

Boulder, CO, and Rocky Mountain National Park

Bradenton/Sarasota, FL

Branson, MO, and the Ozark Mountains

Cape Cod, Martha's Vineyard and Nantucket, MA

Charleston, SC

Cincinnati, OH

Civil War Sites in the Eastern Theater

Denver, CO

Florida Keys and Key West

Florida's Great Northwest

Golf in the Carolinas

Indianapolis, IN

The Lake Superior Region

Lexington, KY

Louisville, KY

Maine's Mid-Coast

Minneapolis/St. Paul, MN

Mississippi

Myrtle Beach, SC

North Carolina's Central Coast and New Bern

North Carolina's Mountains

Outer Banks of North Carolina

The Pocono Mountains

Relocation

Richmond, VA

Southwestern Utah

Tampa/St. Petersburg, FL

Virginia's Blue Ridge

Virginia's Chesapeake Bay

Washington, D.C.

Wichita, KS

Williamsburg, VA

Wilmington, NC

Insiders' Publishing Inc. • P.O. Box 2057 • Manteo, NC 27954
Phone (919) 473-6100 • Fax (919) 473-5869 • INTERNET address: http://www.insiders.com